Countering the Culture

The Novels of
Christiane Rochefort

Countering the Culture

The Novels of
Christiane Rochefort

by

Margaret-Anne Hutton

UNIVERSITY
of
EXETER
PRESS

First published in 1998 by
University of Exeter Press
Reed Hall, Streatham Drive
Exeter EX4 4QR
UK

British Library Cataloguing in Publication Data
A catalogue record for this book is available
from the British Library

Paperback ISBN 085989 586 6
Hardback ISBN 085989 585 8

Typeset in Plantin Light by Exe Valley Dataset, Exeter

Printed and bound in Great Britain by
Short Run Press Ltd, Exeter

For Renate Hutton, with love

Contents

Acknowledgements

I would like to thank Durham University for a generous publication grant and for giving me research leave. Thanks to my colleagues in the Department of French, who put up with my corridor-pacing, to our secretary, Heather Fenwick, for her patience and good humour in the face of my frequent interruptions and hijackings of her hardware, and to Janet Starkey for compiling the index. Thanks also to CPEDERF, who proved invaluable in extracting sales figures from recalcitrant publishers. My colleague, Jennifer Britnell, who read the entire manuscript at various stages, was both tactful and insightful in her criticism, and always ready to answer a stream of inane questions on a range of topics. More crucially, she gave me encouragement throughout the period of writing, and for this I am extremely grateful. Finally, thanks to Carol Adlam for her lucidity, enthusiasm and support throughout the various stages of this project.

Some of the material in chapters 1 and 9 originally appeared in *Forum for Modern Language Studies* and *The Modern Language Review* respectively and I am grateful for the editors of these journals for their permission to reprint here.

Introduction

Je crois que la seule relation vraie à la littérature est d'en faire et d'en
lire, deux façons équivalentes de faire l'amour avec, et tout le reste est,
excusez-moi je dois aller au bout de mon analogie, masturbation,
d'ailleurs c'est on ne peut plus exact (voire un peu optimiste).
(Rochefort, *C'est bizarre l'écriture*)

[*I think that the only real relationship you can have with literature is to
produce it and read it, two equivalent ways of making love with it, and all the
rest is, forgive me but I have to follow my analogy through, masturbation, besides that's as exact an analogy as there could be (if a
touch optimistic).*]

Rochefort: woman and writer

If, as the epigraph suggests, writing is tantamount to making love, then
Christiane Rochefort was involved in a passionate affair which lasted over
forty years, from her first short story, 'Le Démon des pinceaux' (1953),
to her final works, *Adieu Andromède* and *Conversations sans paroles*,
published just one year before her death on the 24 April 1998.

Judging by the sales figures, the love affair attained orgiastic
proportions: Rochefort's *Les Petits Enfants du siècle* (1961) has sold in
excess of one and a half million copies; *Le Repos du guerrier* (1958) and
Les Stances à Sophie (1963) each total sales of well over half a million;
overall sales for the author's nine novels exceed four million copies in
Grasset and Livre de Poche editions (see Appendix). Although, as this
introduction will suggest, literary credentials cannot be gauged by
popularity alone, Rochefort's career was an immensely successful one by
any standards: her work, which is acknowledged in all contemporary
dictionaries and anthologies of French literature, has received consistent
and widespread coverage across a broad spectrum of the French press, as
well as British and American journals; she was the 1988 laureate of the
'Prix Médicis' (for *La Porte du fond*), having already received the less
mainstream 'Prix de la nouvelle vague' for *Le Repos du guerrier*, and 'Prix
du roman populiste' for *Les Petits Enfants*, which was also short-listed for

1

the prestigious Goncourt; her novels appear on both school and university programmes in France, Britain and the US.

Rochefort's writing career took off when the publishing house Grasset accepted *Le Repos du guerrier* in 1958, and much to her irritation, this was the work with which many people associated her most closely. As Jacques Chancel pointed out in a radio interview of 1976,[1] provoking a weary acknowledgement from Rochefort, 'Vous êtes pour tout le monde l'auteur du *Repos du guerrier*' ['everyone thinks of you as the author of *Le Repos du guerrier*'[2]]. Prior to *Le Repos* Rochefort had published two short stories, 'Le Démon des pinceaux' (1953), and a sequel, 'Le Fauve et le rouge-gorge' (1955), both representing the struggles of aspiring abstract painters, both critiques of the art world. Of the two works it is 'Le Démon des pinceaux', with its representation of lost inspiration and a destructive sexual relationship (between the artist Jean-Paul Salvat and his socialite wife Marie-Laure), which has the closest affinity with Rochefort's later work, specifically, with Renaud and Geneviève, central characters of *Le Repos du guerrier*.

According to popular belief, and indeed most dictionaries and anthologies of French literature (with the notable exception of the 1994 *Dictionnaire Bordas de littérature française*), these two short works were succeeded by *Le Repos du guerrier*, claimed to be Rochefort's first novel.[3] In fact, as both the card-index and printed catalogue of the Bibliothèque nationale in Paris indicate, there exists another novel, entitled *Cendres et or*, also written by one Christiane Rochefort, and published by Editions de Paris in 1956, two years before *Le Repos du guerrier*. There is no doubt that this novel, which traces a period in the life of its central protagonist, Juliette Mallet (from secretary, to wife of social high-flier Etienne Forgeat, to disillusionment and a new beginning), and which shares many elements with the later *Les Stances à Sophie*, was Rochefort's first published novel, as extracts cited below in Chapter 3 should confirm. There is, to my knowledge, no publicly available copy of *Cendres et or* outside the Bibliothèque nationale, and for this reason I have chosen to exclude it from this study.

If little is known of *Cendres et or*, the same can be said of Rochefort's work as a translator. Over some two decades she translated (from Hebrew to French) four novels (*A la Gare*, 1964; *Le Cheval fini*, 1966; *Holocauste II*, 1976; and *La Route d'Ein Harod*, 1984) and one collection of short stories (*Les Tireurs de langue*, 1962) written by Israeli pro-peace militant Amos Kenan. Working with Rachel Mizrahi she also translated Beatle John Lennon's *In His Own Write* (1964) as *En flagrant délire* (1965). Irreverent, anti-establishment, written with a strong dose of black humour, Lennon's work was a natural choice for Rochefort, whose translation on this occasion called as much upon her verbal skills as upon her fluency in the English language. With its punning and intricate word-play, *En flagrant délire* is reminiscent of Rochefort's own *Une Rose pour Morrison*, which was written the following year.

As its title indicates, this study concentrates on the author's fiction alone. I have therefore excluded the recent collection of poems, *Adieu Andromède* (1997), as well as the autobiographical *Ma Vie revue et corrigée par l'auteur* (1978), an eclectic collection of anecdotes, recollections, epigraphs, proverbs, fables, letters, and discussions by the author on the process of writing, based on a series of taped conversations with editor Maurice Chevardès. Readers with a desire to learn more about Rochefort's life, or indeed about the manner in which the genre of the autobiography can be subverted, may wish to consult this highly self-conscious and typically humorous work. *Conversations sans paroles* (1997), a very brief first-person narrative which touches upon mother-hood, mortality, and the natural world and its destruction at the hands of mankind, but which focuses primarily upon the eponymous 'conversa-tions without words', or extra-linguistic forms of communication, is also an autobiographical work which has consequently been omitted.[4] Also excluded is *Le Monde est comme deux chevaux* (1984). Published as part of a series aptly entitled 'La Part Obscure', this is a bizarre, though curiously readable, hybrid text which is both a fable, an analysis of current affairs (newspaper headlines are cited and reworked to parodic effect), and a rather hermetic commentary on diverse subjects (war, religion, ecology, consumerism, so-called progress). Although Rochefort's two works of non-fiction, *C'est bizarre l'écriture* (1970), which is primarily an account of her writing of *Printemps au parking*, and *Les Enfants d'abord* (1976), an essay on children's rights, are not singled out for detailed discussion, aspects are incorporated in Chapters 4 and 7 respectively.

Rochefort was in many ways something of an elusive figure. Reluctant to grant interviews, especially later in her career, she frequently expressed a strong distrust of any 'establishment' figure, university lecturers included. Consequently, her biographical details are slight. As Herz notes, she was born in Paris on 17 July 1917, spent part of her childhood in the Limousin, before returning to, and remaining in, Paris (taking frequent trips to the US and Canada). After a brief and disillusioning spell at the Sorbonne—one psychology lecture proved to be one too many, although she did gain some knowledge of ethnology and psychiatry—she subsequently turned her hand to sculpting and painting, and also worked as a press attaché for the Cannes Film Festival for many years.[5]

Rochefort was at the forefront of political protest throughout her career. She was a signatory of what came to be known as the *Manifeste des 121*, a text drawn up in September 1960 calling for the rights of French soldiers to absent themselves without leave rather than take part in the Algerian War. On the 26 August 1970 (fiftieth anniversary of female suffrage in the US) she participated in one of the resurgent French feminist movement's most well-documented protest actions, the famous wreath-laying at the Arc de Triomphe, on which occasion women carried banners bearing the slogans 'un homme sur deux est une femme' ['one man in two is a woman'] and 'il y a plus inconnu encore que le soldat: sa femme' ['there is someone more unknown than the unknown soldier: his wife']. The following year (5 April 1971) she featured among the signatories of the pro-choice 'Manifeste des 343', a front-page feature in the *Nouvel observateur* declaring that all those women who had signed (including Beauvoir, Catherine Deneuve, Marguerite Duras, Violette Leduc amongst others) had had illegal abortions.[6] On 26 January 1977, alongside well-known public figures such as Aragon, Barthes, Beauvoir, Bory, Deleuze, Jack Lang, Sartre and others, she signed a petition in *Le Monde* protesting against the imprisonment of three men jailed for engaging in sexual acts with consenting minors (see below, Chapter 4).

Often politically high-profile, yet by no means recognized as a public figure; readily identified as a writer, yet for many known only as the author of one or two novels, Rochefort was something of a conundrum. In *La Porte du fond* the first-person narrator proclaims with considerable satisfaction 'Je suis une paradoxe!' ['I'm a paradox!'] (47), and the same can be said of the author and her work. In the following sections it will be suggested that the paradox extends into several domains, a paradox which is played out in the breaking down of accepted binaries, be they related to gender (female/male), sexuality (gay/straight), language (formal/informal; written/spoken), or, as the following discussion will suggest, literary categorization ('popular'/'high').

Literary labelling: 'popular'/'high' literature

In a recent text on French cultural studies it is suggested that when Rochefort's early novels first appeared, 'critics were uncomfortably divided between assigning them a place within contemporary realist literature and airily dismissing them as pulp fiction'.[7] Perhaps part of the problem lay with the popularity of Rochefort's work: could public approval be reconciled with 'great works'? The question remains today. Is Rochefort's work part of the canon of mainstream 'high' French literature, or should we rather pigeon-hole her in the somewhat indeterminate category 'popular writer'? And what do we understand by these apparently mutually exclusive labels?

Adapting one of Raymond Williams's definitions as a starting point, we might first suggest that 'popular literature' is literature which is 'well-liked by many people'.[8] The sales figures quoted at the beginning of this introduction certainly place her firmly in this category. Several print-runs of her novels in the Livre de Poche format further attest to Rochefort's popular success. Given the pressures of commercialization, any attempt at literary classification must take market-forces into account. The very existence of this cheap paperback series, launched just five years before Rochefort's first big commercial success, *Le Repos du guerrier* (1958), led to the partial undermining of fixed boundaries separating so-called 'high' and 'popular' culture: 'It was the first of many cheap paperback collections in which the classics of French literature jostled with contemporary popular fiction for a place on railway station bookstalls.'[9] It may be of passing interest to note that Rochefort's last works were readily available on the shelves of a Calais supermarket only weeks after their publication.

Of course, any definition of 'popular' literature must extend beyond the idea of a well-liked and much-read corpus of texts. Developments in the field of cultural studies have opened the debate on issues of literary categorization and the politics of canon-formation. The need to collapse the perceived dichotomy between 'popular' and 'high' culture is well-rehearsed and this is not the place to reiterate it. Two points can, however, usefully be made at this stage. First, it must be acknowledged there are many definitions of the 'popular', including those which paradoxically erase the very term as a viable discrete category. Texts such as Dominic Strinati's *An Introduction to Theories of Popular Culture* reveal that any theory inevitably creates its own object of study: a 'popular' text may be defined by feminist, Marxist, neo-Marxist, structuralist, or postmodernist theories, to name just some.[10] It follows that Rochefort's work will inevitably be different things to different people. What is striking is that the very issues played out at the level of theoretical debate can be identified within Rochefort's texts. Furthermore, these texts—and herein lies the first paradox—reveal aspects which are associated with approaches to *both* 'popular' and so-called 'high' literature.

At one end of what might be identified as a spectrum of theories of popular culture we find the so-called 'dominant ideology thesis'. At the risk of gross simplification, we might say that those who subscribe to this line would state that popular cultural products work to secure the socio-political status quo. A popular text would thus be perceived, for example, to represent women or other oppressed groups in such a manner as to reinforce and naturalize that oppression; such a text might be little more than a standardized, formulaic commodity on the market; it would function to secure the on-going economic, political and ideological domination of capital; it would reinforce hegemony, that is, 'a cultural and ideological means whereby the dominant groups in society [. . .] maintain their dominance by securing the "spontaneous consent" of subordinate groups [. . .] through the negotiated construction of a political and

5

ideological consensus which incorporates both dominant and dominated groups.'[11]

Rochefort's work would appear to stand in diametric opposition to such an approach. When asked if she has any ultimate goal in life, the first-person narrator of *La Porte du fond* hesitates for a fraction of a second before formulating a reply which one can easily envisage coming from Rochefort herself: 'Si j'en ai un tiens. Emmerder le monde' ['Actually yes, I do have one: to be a pain in the arse to as many people as possible'] (116). As the main body of this study will reveal, Rochefort's work is contestatory, anti-establishment, anarchic, counter-cultural. The very tenets of the 'dominant ideology thesis' are played out *within* her works, as her characters rail against the capitalist system (the 'Force Aveugle' or 'Machine' as she calls it), its regulatory institutions (the school system, psychiatry, the nuclear family), its complicit foot-soldiers or unthinking 'cogs in the machine' (the bourgeois young executive, parents). Rather than reinforcing an oppressive status quo, Rochefort's texts function precisely to de-naturalize or 'translate' the circumscribing discourses which emanate from those in power. Her works share a common call for individuals to show 'conscience', that is, to be aware of, and resist, the mechanisms of oppression. This is a far cry from the passive, readily-indoctrinated reader constructed by the 'dominant ideology thesis' theorists.

Furthermore, Rochefort's texts *represent* (what the author perceived as) forms of popular culture, thematizing the very thesis we have been discussing. Thus as early as *Le Repos du guerrier* the popular romance genre is undermined as Rochefort sets up, then subverts, the traditional 'happy ending'. *Les Petits Enfants du siècle* takes this a step further by inviting us to read the text's disastrous unhappy ending against the backdrop of the saccharine romances read by the narrator's mother. The narrator of *Les Stances à Sophie* is set against glossy women's magazines and marketing hype. Christophe, narrator of *Printemps au parking*, is explicitly described as 'un cas de non-conditionnement spontané aux masses-média' ['a case of spontaneous non-conditioning by the mass-media'] (126). The dystopic *Une Rose pour Morrison* reveals the potential for cultural indoctrination run riot as citizens living in the atomized society so deplored by mass-culture theorists fall prey to the 'cybernéma' and state-controlled 'mégavision'. Finally, *Quand tu vas chez les femmes* dramatizes the Gramscian notion of hegemony as those involved in minority sexual practices struggle against the forces of socio-cultural recuperation.

It follows that from one theoretical standpoint at least, Rochefort's work cannot be readily identified as 'popular'. If we now go to the opposite end of the theoretical spectrum and consider a populist approach such as

Fiske's, we find at least some congruence between definitions of the 'popular' and Rochefort's work, if, as Fiske argues, the popular can be equated with the offensive and the scandalous, for, to a greater or lesser extent, all of the author's texts deal with subjects which have been, or still are, deemed to be risqué or taboo.[12] With *Le Repos du guerrier* Rochefort dared to broach the subject of female sexuality; *Les Petits Enfants* not only attacks government policies (pro-natalism and council housing) but also presents its readers with a sexually active young child; *Les Stances à Sophie* adopts a feminist line well before the regeneration of the French feminist movement and seeks to undermine the comfortable, and apparently mindless, middle classes; *Une Rose pour Morrison* (1966) prefigures the civic unrest of 1968; *Printemps au parking* (1969) pleads the case for gay rights at a time when French legislation remained firmly homophobic; *Archaos*, which best encapsulates its author's views, represents (in both senses of the word) incest, child sexuality, anarchism, and a damning opposition to orthodox Christianity; *Encore heureux qu'on va vers l'été* (1975) condemns the state education system and promotes children's rights almost a decade before these became a public issue; *Quand tu vas chez les femmes* (1982), pushing ever further into the realms of the taboo, explores the world of s-m sex.

This view of Rochefort's 'popular-because-scandalous' status in turn opens up questions about her reception in the academic world, traditionally the enclave of 'high' literature and protector of the canon. If we accept Powrie's statement that 'literary hierarchies seem, like rats, to show great resistance to the weapons deployed against them', then, given Rochefort's anti-establishment approach and willingness to engage with taboo areas, it would hardly come as a surprise if the (conservative?) academic establishment neglected her work.[13] Given her views, we might ask if Rochefort would even have wanted to be a part of the literary establishment. Her response upon being asked about her presence in the canon suggests an answer in the negative: 'I'm not part of any consensus, so to the extent that the words canon and consensus can be confused [. . .] my work doesn't stand much chance of being included. [. . .] To tell you the truth, I couldn't care less.'[14] And as a woman Rochefort faced another hurdle: not only have women writers been neglected by academic critics for decades (indeed centuries), they have been, as Rochefort notes in *New French Feminisms*, expected to conform with the norms of 'littérature féminine': 'you are supposed [. . .] to write about certain things: house, children, love'. As Rochefort adds, *Le Repos du guerrier* was read 'below the belt' because she was a woman, whilst *Les Stances à Sophie* won her the contempt of male critics.[15] An article in *Le Monde* written on the occasion of the 1988 'Prix Médicis' award suggests that Rochefort's work may quite simply have been too extreme, too

7

forward (or forward-looking) for the taste of the French literary establishment:

> Peut-être avait-elle l'ironie un peu trop violente, l'humour un peu trop noir et décapant, et le verbe un peu trop haut. Ce sont des choses que les hommes—majoritaires dans les jurys des prix littéraires—tolèrent mal de la part des femmes, quoi qu'ils en disent.[16]

> [*Maybe her irony was a little too savage, her humour too black, too caustic, and her voice a little too loud. These are things which men—who are in the majority on the juries for literary prizes—have difficulty accepting from women, whatever they may say to the contrary.*]

It is hardly coincidental that wider recognition in the form of the Médicis award came only when Rochefort fell into step with mainstream policy and concerns by writing a work on child sexual abuse in the late 1980s (*La Porte du fond*).

The next question must then be: has Rochefort's offensive, scandalous 'popularity' indeed served to exclude her from the academic literary mainstream? Here, too, paradox is present. Although Rochefort's status is acknowledged via her presence in anthologies, the press, and academic journals, and although she received literary prizes, what is lacking is the all-important back-up of critical material, and as anyone involved in the teaching of literature knows, the inclusion of texts in student courses relies at least in part on the availability of secondary material. Returning to the love-making analogy, evidence of the solitary pleasure of the literary critic is sadly lacking. As Herz points out in the recent *French Women Writers: A Bio-Bibliographical Source Book*, no major study providing an overview of Rochefort's work has (until now) been written.[17] To date, only two substantial pieces have been produced, both written in French, and each dealing primarily with a single novel: Nilsson's *Le Mot chien n'aboie pas* (1990), an analysis of *Quand tu vas chez les femmes* (1982), and Constant's *Les Mots étincelants de Christiane Rochefort* (1996), which focuses on *Archaos, ou le jardin étincelant* (1972). Beyond these texts there exist only some two dozen articles. Critics, it would seem, remain curiously unwilling to engage with this body of work.

Rochefort does, however, find a niche in the academy, and it is principally in those areas which have split off from the mainstream, those areas which, eschewing the vagaries of ill-defined and ill-defended aesthetic determinants of taste and value, have adopted a politicized approach to literary studies. One such area in which critical material on Rochefort's work is grouped can loosely be described as 'women writers', or 'women's studies'. We thus find Ophir's analysis of *Les Stances à Sophie* in *Regards féminins* (1976); Bartowski's comparative study of *Archaos* in

Feminist Utopias (1989); Becker's 'Rebellion, alternative life-styles and visions of utopia: Christiane Rochefort, Violette Leduc, Monique Wittig, and Hélène Cixous', in *Twentieth Century Women Writers* (1989); Holmes's 'Realism, fantasy and feminist meaning: the fiction of Christiane Rochefort', in *Contemporary French Fiction by Women: Feminist Perspectives* (1990); and Loffredo's *A Portrait of the Sexes: The Masculine and the Feminine in the Novels of Simone de Beauvoir, Marguerite Duras and Christiane Rochefort* (1979). A number of interviews predominantly dating from the late 1970s (Arsène, Crochet, Courtivron, Hirsch, Green and Higgins, and an hour-long radio interview with Jacques Chancel) focus largely on Rochefort's status as a woman writer. Rochefort has also made a limited appearance in the field of gay studies, featuring in Robinson's *Scandal in the Ink* (1995), Marks and Stamboulian's *Homosexualities in French Literature* (1979), with a walk-on part in Martel's *Le Rose et le noir* (1996). It seems more than likely that the representation of lesbian and gay sexuality in Rochefort's work has impacted upon the production of critical material: there is perhaps a certain reluctance amongst the 'straight' community to engage with non-straight material.

The reason for Rochefort's inclusion in these academic areas is obvious enough (indeed one of the objectives of this study has been to focus upon the representation of gender and sexuality) but what should we think of these categorizations? Powrie and Atack note that texts may be taken up to serve a wider agenda; women writers are adopted because 'they have written texts which, it is considered, can service cultural studies or area studies courses'.[18] Certain problems certainly arise from this situation, the first being that a work's categorization as that of a 'woman writer' amounts to a ghettoization signalling a failure to consider those works as having equal status to those produced by a male author. Rochefort herself objects strongly to the classification 'woman writer': 'A man's book is a book. A woman's book is a woman's book'; noting, in addition, that it is plainly ridiculous to suggest that a homogeneous category 'women writers' is sustainable.[19] Certainly she rejects any notion of 'écriture féminine' or a biological specificity to women's writing (see Chapter 3 below). And the classification of Rochefort as a 'woman writer' or indeed 'gay writer' leads to further potential pitfalls: the recuperation of a contestatory body of work; the reinforcement of the very hegemony her texts seek to undermine. As Quinn notes in *Gay and Lesbian Studies*, although courses and categories which politicize literature may themselves be regarded as threats to the establishment—'The charge of modishness has too often been used by establishment critics to stigmatize disruptive ways of reading'—the danger of assimilation and recuperation is always present: 'there is the threat that we will be assimilated into a system that views our work solely in terms of its marketability'.[20]

One final area of the academy in which Rochefort's work appears remains for consideration, and that is courses which focus upon the socio-politics of contemporary France. Again, it is easy to see why she should 'service' such courses: as the following chapters will reveal, Rochefort's work has a great deal to teach us about life in France from the late 1950s to the late 1980s, whether it be in the form of life on housing estates, life as gay man, the civil unrest of the late 1960s, or the education system. But, again, there are limitations to this pigeon-holing act, and the first of these has to do with relevance, another key word not only for populists such as Fiske ('popular art is valued to the extent that it is "of interest", that is, interested in everyday life and not distant from it') but also for those like Easthope who seek to identify criteria of literary value which cross the 'popular'/'high' divide.[21] A text should have relevance which extends beyond the time and place of its production:

> A text of literary value can be distinguished from one with merely historical interest by the degree to which its signifiers have actively engaged with new contexts, contexts different ideologically but also different in the protocols of literary reading in which the text is construed.[22]

Rochefort's work may be taken up by writers such as Ross, whose *Fast Cars, Clean Bodies* uses *Les Petits Enfants du siècle* and *Les Stances à Sophie* as examples of the work of writers who 'historicized their era [. . .] and [who] gave full voice to the debates and controversies surrounding modernization', but such appropriations must not be at the expense of re-contextualized readings. As Fiske notes, relevance, unlike opaque aesthetic judgements, is time- and place-bound.[23] Rochefort's work does have a place in studies of contemporary France, but it can, and should, be read both in the light of its continuing relevance to society today, and from the perspective of recent theoretical developments. The final section in this introduction will suggest just one possible avenue for further work (queer studies), but there are many more which extend far beyond the scope of this book.

One final issue remains. The classification of Rochefort's work as that of a 'woman writer', 'gay writer' or writer about contemporary France all too often leads to a failure to engage with the very *writing* of the texts; narrative, structure, language, reflexivity are shunned in favour of a purely thematic approach. If we return briefly to a lay definition of a 'popular' novel, it might be suggested that such a work is structurally simple, perhaps formulaic; its narrative is uncomplicated; it falls into an easily-identifiable generic category ('realist'; 'science-fiction'); it is not reflexive. Certainly Rochefort's work can be differentiated from one particular form of 'high' literature which emerged when she was at the height of her career: the 'nouveau roman' or New Novel. Indeed, Rochefort decries the all-consuming influence of such works: 'On est complètement terrorisé, surtout en France [. . .] on est terrorisé par une certaine idée de l'écriture' ['people are completely terrorized, especially in France [. . .] terrorized by a certain concept of writing'].[24] In her eyes, such formalist texts, far from engaging their reader in an active pact or intimacy, lead to a sterile intellectual oppression:

> There is also [as well as snobbery] a terrorist dimension. I can conceive of it as a communication with the reader in order to take power over him. For psychological reasons. One needs to compensate for something, one needs power. I have often seen that kind of literature connected to people in power. It seeks to establish a power it doesn't admit. I think it's an erotic literature in the sense of dominant/dominated.[25]

Yet although Rochefort may apparently disdain the more reflexive games of the nouveau roman, one of the primary aims of this study will be to redirect attention to those aspects of her work which are, again paradoxically, most often associated with 'high' literature. This study will thus include the discussion of the following areas: the reliability of the first-person narrator and the reader's role (*Le Repos du guerrier*, *Les Petits Enfants*, *Quand tu vas chez les femmes*, *La Porte du fond*); the complexities of narrative voice (*Les Petits Enfants*, *Les Stances à Sophie*, *Printemps au parking*, *Encore heureux qu'on va vers l'été*); the presence and function of 'mises en abyme' (*Le Repos du guerrier*, *Printemps au parking*, *Archaos*); structural complexities; and the presence and function of intertextual material drawn from both 'popular' and 'high' texts.

Contestatory language

In many respects language and the manipulation of language is the single most important aspect of Rochefort's work. Its ideological status emerges as a constant, if modulated, concern, from *Le Repos du guerrier*, in which the two protagonists require a metaphorical dictionary to translate the language of love, to *La Porte du fond* with its undermining of medicalized (psychiatric) discourse. But if language, as Rochefort puts it, is a weapon wielded by the powerful, it is also the key to resistance. The subversive linguistic tactics employed by Rochefort, which include parody, reframing, irony, shifts in register, puns, neologisms, hybrid narrative constructions and, of course, humour, are discussed in each of the following chapters. The conclusion to this study will focus upon one particular area of language in Rochefort's work, that is its function in the construction and deconstruction of identity, but for now a brief discussion of the role and status of language in France may help to contextualize Rochefort's writing practices.

The fact that language is much more than a medium of communication is nothing new; language is political, and one manifestation of this politicization lies in the links between language and national identity, more specifically in this context, the centralized regulation of the French language. Rigby, for example, indicates that 'notions of "la culture française" are inseparable from notions of "la patrie". One still comes across writers who have a virtually mystical view of the special and transcendent qualities embodied in the French language.'[26] From the founding of the Académie française in 1634, language in France has been subject to state control, as the centre sought to police regional variation and popular speech-forms. As Kelly notes:

> The following characterization of the Academy's aims by one of its seventeenth-century members is revealing of the élitism which, then as now, inspired the purist enterprise: 'nettoyer la langue des ordures qu'elle avait contractées, ou dans la bouche du peuple, ou dans la foule de Paris' ['to cleanse the language of the filth it had acquired, either in the mouths of the people, or among the Paris crowd'].[27]

In a similar vein Ager suggests that the triumph of the Academy-imposed Ile de France dialect represented the triumph of 'centralising, élitist, military, diplomatic and ecclesiastical power over feudal fragmentation and over the lower orders of society'.[28]

It is in the light of such politicized linguistic protectionism that Rochefort's own subversive use of the French language must be considered. In spite of the centre's attempts to regulate language in France, to impose 'the official, highly regimented variety of speech and (more especially) writing', colloquial or popular language could not be eradicated: an official/unofficial dichotomy remained and still remains.[29] As Chapter 2 of this study indicates, Rochefort's very individual style, which first emerged in *Les Petits Enfants du siècle*, a style which she dubs the 'écrit-parlé' ['written-spoken mode'], breaks down these binaries—formal/informal; spoken/written—as informal language characterized by incorrect grammar, slang and vulgarity co-exists with standard or even hyper-standard French.

Uncertainty over the status of Rochefort's work as 'popular' may owe much to the orality of her writing, traditionally demeaned in opposition to so-called 'high' cultural forms. Once more, Rochefort's writing conforms with Fiske's views: 'popular culture is often attacked for its (mis)use of language'; it is offensive, in both senses of the word, it reveals and undercuts the rules.[30] Indeed, although Rochefort's hybrid style is particular to her, it shares its irreverence and overt vulgarity with other popular genres: the repertoire of figures such as singer-songwriter Georges Brassens, whose sexual, anti-establishment lyrics led to radio bans in the 1950s; the BD ('bande dessinée' or comic strip) which flourished in the 1960s and 1970s, cultivating an adult market with its 'anarchic sense of wilful transgression'. The year 1960 saw the launch of the popular BD *HaraKiri* and in November 1970 its weekly spin-off, *Hebdo-Hara-Kiri*, was banned for lampooning the death of De Gaulle— two years after Rochefort's *Une Rose pour Morrison* had done precisely the same thing (see below, Chapter 5).[31]

The deregulation of language characterized by the 'écrit-parlé', and further manifested in the range of subversive linguistic enterprises discussed below, is best summed up by Rochefort's own neologizing pun: 'dépolisser' (to 'unpolish'—in fact the correct verb form is 'polir') means 'dépolicer' (in the sense of 'de-police'—'policer' is in fact an archaic version of 'to civilize' or 'to govern'). We might add that 'dépolisser' amounts to 'politiser' (to politicize).

In the chapters which follow I have attempted to represent Rochefort as a contestatory writer whose complex works deserve a great deal more attention than they have so far been granted. As befits an introductory study, a chronological approach has been adopted in order to allow for a contextualization of each text. I have also, however, sought to adopt as comprehensive an approach as possible within the limited scope of a single study, and have consequently focused upon the following key areas: a critical analysis of narrative and structure; a critical analysis of the representation of so-called minority groups (children, women, gay men and women); a discussion of intertextual material; an examination of the development of the author's use of, and thematization of, language as a political tool. My own love affair with Rochefort's writing has lasted some four years. I can only hope that this study will stimulate the desire of others, and that further, more specialized works may be generated in the future.

CHAPTER ONE

Le Repos du guerrier

> Let man fear woman when she loves.
> Then she bears every sacrifice and every other thing she accounts valueless.
> (Nietzsche, *Thus Spoke Zarathustra*)

'Le roman qui met le lit dans le livre et les ébats dans le débat' ['the novel which puts the sex in the text and the passion in the polemic'].[1] Drawn from an early review, this rather lame but nonetheless revealing quip serves to remind us that *Le Repos du guerrier* was something of a 'succès de scandale' when it was first published in 1958. Rochefort, who had considered adopting a male pseudonym, pointed out some years later that had the book been written by a man, the critics might have commented on its style; they might even have had the magnanimity to praise the book as a worthy first novel.[2] As things turned out, it was the sexual dimension of *Le Repos* which became the primary focus of attention. Here was a text written by a woman, narrated in the first person by a nice bourgeois girl, which dealt openly with female sexual desire. As Rochefort observed with a certain wry detachment almost two decades after the text's publication: 'une femme ne doit pas parler de "ça", et ne doit pas parler comme ça' ['a woman should not speak about "that" and should not speak in "that" way'].[3] Sex and scandal are powerful marketing forces: *Le Repos du guerrier* was to become one of Rochefort's greatest commercial successes. Four years after its publication it was adapted for the cinema under the direction of Roger Vadim, with Robert Hossein and Brigitte Bardot in the lead roles. In spite of some hostile critics (notably François Mauriac) who dubbed it pornographic, establishment recognition was conferred on the novel in the form of the Prix de la nouvelle vague.[4] Of course times and expectations change, and the sexual dimension of the text would be unlikely to raise any eyebrows, far less pulses, today. Of greater interest are the difficulties readers evidently face in attempting to establish where the text stands on the subjects of love and sexuality.

The novel charts the relationship between the two principal characters, Geneviève Le Theil and Renaud Sarti, from its abrupt inception to its

14

conclusion. Representing two different sectors of society, the protagonists hold radically opposed views of love: Geneviève, 'jeune fille bourgeoise', is set against Renaud, alcoholic drop-out, disillusioned communist and ex-writer caught up in the political despair of the post-Hiroshima, Cold War era. Any comprehensive view of love and sexual desire emerges from the interaction of these two figures, and from two sets of secondary figures: the bourgeois representatives in Part I, Geneviève's mother, her fiancé Pierre and friend Claude Amyot; the bohemian artist Katov and, more importantly, his partner Rafaele, in Part II. The retrospective first-person narrative adds to the ambiguities of a text which provides no easy answers for its readers, no clear authorial stance. Geneviève may tell all, but she is not a reliable narrator, something which many critics have failed to perceive. Adding to the reader's difficulties is a conclusion which proves to be rather inconclusive, providing no straightforward vindication of either Renaud's or Geneviève's beliefs. The following discussion will suggest that although certain changes occur in Geneviève, she holds fast to a view of redemptive love (love conquers all; the power of love) which casts her in the role of victim or even martyr to her cause, whilst Renaud's cynical denial of love in the name of a nihilist political agenda is ultimately revealed to be as idealistic as Geneviève's.

At the start of the text, Geneviève sees the world through the eyes of the middle-class, well-brought-up 'jeune fille'. She is the Parisian 'little Miss', disdainfully mocking what she perceives as the tawdriness of the provincial town in which she arrives in order to settle an inheritance from a wealthy aunt. Geneviève's life is admirably mapped out: she will complete her psychology degree, marry her fiancé, and, with her new riches, bring to fruition a long-standing project to set up a children's home with her friend Claude Amyot. When she accidentally opens the wrong hotel room with her own key and discovers the inert body of the suicidal Renaud, her life is dramatically altered. Although she had planned to stay only one day, she finds herself collecting Renaud from the hospital the following morning, and immediately begins to spend her money on his meals, cigarettes, alcohol and a train ticket to Paris. Ultimately her entire legacy, clearly symbolic of her class status, will be dissipated in her attempts to keep Renaud happy. From the very beginning, the contrast between the two characters is clear: Renaud has no money, no identity papers, and no plans.

The reader should be alert from an early stage in the text to Geneviève's attempts to rationalize her behaviour. Although she clearly experiences a disturbing sexual desire from the outset (leaving the hospital where she visits Renaud she feels uncomfortably flushed), she seeks to frame her decision to stay in terms of a 'bonne action' in keeping with her status as ex-'scoute' [former girl-guide] once dubbed 'Abeille

Laborieuse' ['Busy Bee'] by her peers (64). Soon, however, she is confronted more forcibly with her sexual feelings: 'mon cœur battait, ma gorge était nouée'; 'le sang me vint au visage. Ces mains, je voulais qu'elles me touchent' ['my heart was pounding, I had a lump in my throat'; 'blood rushed to my face. I wanted those hands to touch me'] (43). At this stage, such desire does not enter into her value-system or her lexicon, and she is consequently left with two alternative possible means of situating her sexuality within her existing frame of reference. The first of these is to equate desire with madness: 'Je suis folle' ['I'm mad'] (43).[5] This move, however, is rapidly succeeded by a further tactic, and Geneviève translates her sexual feelings into a more acceptable code: 'J'aime cet homme. Et depuis le début' ['I love this man. I've loved him from the very beginning'] (43). By the close of the second chapter she has had sex in—of all places, as she acknowledges in passing—the aunt's bed in her newly acquired property, thereby ironically actualizing the hotel owner's earlier suspicion that she and Renaud had arranged a tryst, a suggestion which provoked her outrage at the time. The apologetic explanation of the hôtelier that in his job 'on a l'habitude de bâtir des romans' ['you get into the habit of making up stories'] (23) is retrospectively apposite: Geneviève's concept of love would not be out of place in a popular sentimental novel.

Renaud's installation in her Paris apartment and Geneviève's open acknowledgement of her sexual inexperience—'je ne connais pas le plaisir' ['I've never experienced pleasure'] (48)—lead to further developments in terms both of the character's values and of narrative focalization. The third chapter is marked by a sustained use of the historic present tense which throws focalization firmly into the past, underscoring the force of a desire which seems to break down all categories of time and space. The bed around which Geneviève's life revolves becomes 'ce monde sans temps, où aucun ordre, aucun repère, aucun point d'appui n'apparaissent' ['this timeless world, devoid of any order, any landmark, any stable centre'] (63). Readers may be reminded of a famous scene in the film *Et Dieu créa la femme* (1956), in which the young couple Michel and Juliette (also played by Bardot) make love for the first time, their sexuality expressing open revolt against the bourgeois society of the time.[6]

Whereas in earlier chapters Geneviève's perspective was restricted to that of her class, and thereby to a value-system in which a woman's sexual desire could not be articulated, there now takes place a splitting process which allows the character to objectify and judge her previous self. The 'old' Geneviève remains, lamenting her loss of moral sense, and fearing that her education at Renaud's school of sexuality signifies a sinful fall: 'où sont mes valeurs? [. . .] Je ne sais plus si je déchois ou si je me forme'

16

['what's happened to my values? [. . .] Am I demeaning myself or just maturing? I don't know any more'] (62). From the perspective of this Geneviève she is 'une obsédée sexuelle' ['a sex maniac'], a slave to her sexuality ('une esclave', p. 62). However, for the first time she can also admit that her prior views were limited and limiting: 'Est-il possible qu'il y ait tant de nons dans le corps d'une femme? Comme j'en avais une image bornée!' ['Can a woman's body possibly say no in so many ways? What a blinkered view I had of it before!'] (60). That part of Geneviève which has split from her previous perspective is able to integrate sexual desire into a conception of womanhood: perhaps she is becoming 'une vraie femme' ['a real woman'] (90). It is this Geneviève who rejects those secondary characters who represent bourgeois society: her mother, whom Geneviève scathingly notes stands for 'la Loi [. . .] Mon Bien [. . .] l'Ordre' ['the Law [. . .] Everything that is Good for me [. . .] Order'] (88), and whose dismissal is described by Geneviève herself as her true loss of virginity; the fiancé Pierre, and with him 'les bonnes manières du sentiment' ['emotional niceties'] (67); Claude Amyot, now perceived as just another individual living in a pitiable 'lethargie du sens' ['lethargy of the senses'] (61).

The split in Geneviève's perspective seems to indicate a move away from her previous stance, and to suggest a more positive view of womanhood which would embrace sexuality, but the position is, in fact, rather more complex. The splitting process is described in the following terms: 'Il y aura donc deux Geneviève: Mlle Le Theil; un fossé creusé au bulldozer; et puis la maîtresse de Sarti' ['So now there will be two Genevièves: Miss Le Theil, a great gulf carved out by a bulldozer, and on the other side, Sarti's mistress'] (90). At this stage, there is clearly no integration of the two parts, no indication of how the 'fossé' is to be bridged. The two aspects seem to be defined each from the point of view of the other: to Renaud she is the prim and proper Mlle Le Theil; from the bourgeois perspective, she assumes the illicit position of mistress.

It is striking that in both cases Geneviève can define herself only in relation to a male other: she either assumes her family (father's) name, or the role of mistress to Sarti. On at least two occasions in the text, strong links are established between Geneviève's father and Renaud, suggesting that in some sense the latter merely substitutes for the former. The night following her rescue of Renaud, Geneviève has a nightmare: she is in a public place, inadequately dressed, and surrounded by men who mock her. Significantly, this dream, banal in itself, had haunted her childhood years, vanished, then briefly reappeared after her father's death. When Geneviève comments on the disturbing recurrence of the nightmare sequence, syntactic ambiguity is such that the reader may hesitate: is she referring to her father or to Renaud?: 'J'espérais qu'il [le rêve] avait perdu ma trace. Mais non. Le voici. Je pensai que cet homme d'hier était mort, finalement' ['I had hoped that I had shaken the dream off. But no. It's back. I thought at long last that yesterday's man was dead'] (25). The parallel between the two male figures is reinforced later in the text when Renaud comments on the large dimensions of the bed he and Geneviève are to occupy, and is informed that it had been made for another very tall man: Geneviève's father (58).

It seems that in spite of the split perspective, Geneviève has not achieved a sense of selfhood centred on an autonomous point of view. She can see herself as a sexual being, but only by defining herself from a male (Renaud's) perspective. Indeed, when she launches into a criticism of Claude, her hostility and the savagery of her language remind us strongly of Renaud's own terminology: 'pauvre Claude! si vierge, si fermée; ses lèvres sont serrées et ses jambes doivent l'être autant; elle sèche sur pied' ['poor Claude! such a little virgin, so reserved; I'm sure her legs are clamped together as tightly as her lips; she's shrivelling up on the spot'] (90). If statements such as these represent a move away from the bourgeois code, they do little to promote female solidarity. Furthermore, although she acknowledges her sexual pleasure, Geneviève continues to frame her relationship in terms of true love, and in so doing remains firmly opposed to Renaud's point of view. *Le Repos* is structured in such a way that the reader is constantly prompted to assess Geneviève's stance in a distanced, critical manner; her values are repeatedly thrown into relief by Renaud's opposing position. For him, love remains an empty and futile concept which, in the face of atomic atrocities, can no longer bind together or help individuals. Indeed, individual concerns become anathema: 'Ce tapage et cette pagaille des douleurs, aimer fait là-dedans l'effet d'une aile de papillon, frrr, frrr. . . Vous me faites chier avec vos petites histoires personnelles' ['Set against all the clamour, the chaos of pain, love is nothing more than the thrum of a butterfly wing, whirr whirr. . . You make me bloody sick with your little personal anecdotes'] (132). Renaud will insistently refute Geneviève's protestations of love, and attempt to force her to see the relationship for what he believes it to be: sex, and nothing more.

Although Geneviève may come to see sexual desire in more positive terms, she and Renaud remain on different wavelengths; we might say that they speak a different language. Geneviève herself acknowledges the gap when she states that 'pour comprendre cet homme il suffit en somme d'un dictionnaire' ['when it comes down to it you need a dictionary to understand this man'] (42). For Rochefort, the question of language is a crucial one, for as she frequently pointed out in interviews, and as will become clear in the following chapters, language is inextricably linked to class and power:

18

> The dominating class has appropriated the language, has given words their connotations according to its own purposes. Language is not simply a way to express oneself, as is commonly believed: it is a weapon in the hands of the ruling class.[7]

When Renaud laughs at Geneviève's response to her first orgasm ('la première de Madame. [. . .] Elle pleure. Mais moi, je trouve ça plutôt gai, mon minet! Depuis le temps que je m'y emploie' ['Madam's first ever. [. . .] She's crying. Me, I find the whole thing rather jolly, my little kitten! Given how long I've been working at it'], p. 83), he points out that his ridicule is directed not at her person, but at the terminology she employs, a choice of words which remain bound up with her class: 'je me suis pas moqué de toi, je me suis moqué de ton vocabulaire. Amour, tu appelles ça' ['I wasn't mocking you, I was mocking your vocabulary. You call that love'] (83). Renaud seeks to undermine Geneviève's attempts to classify her sexual desire under the label 'love', and in this he directly echoes Rochefort, who denounced the devaluation and misappropriation of the term: 'take the word "love", the most miserable of all, formerly so beautiful, now almost impossible to write without washing one's hands afterwards.'[8]

In *Le Repos* the weapon that is language changes hands. For Renaud, sex may be a weapon—as he puts it, 'un homme en colère, mon minet, choisit sa meilleure arme' ['an angry man, my little kitten, selects his best weapon'] (169)—but so is speech. As Rochefort observed, it was not merely the subject of *Le Repos* which raised objections ('une femme ne doit pas parler de "ça"' ['a woman should not speak about "that"']), but the manner in which it was spoken of ('et ne doit pas parler comme ça' ['and should not speak in "that" way']). For Rochefort, Renaud was primarily the key to a new style of writing which allowed her to break out of the conventional mode of written French: 'Ce qui m'a intéressé, c'est que j'avais un alcoolique, et que cet alcoolique s'est révélé être un véhicule d'écriture. Renaud débouchait sur une forme d'écriture'. ['What I found interesting was that I had an alcoholic on my hands, and that alcoholic turned out to be a vehicle for writing. Renaud opened up a form of writing'].[9] Throughout the text Renaud's speech is opposed to Geneviève's usually restrained, rather correct French. Especially in his lengthy, baroque speeches, Renaud's style is distinctive: heavily metaphorical, punctuated by rhetorical questions, irreverent, often brutally sexual, accumulating phrases and literary allusions in a breathless show of virtuosity. For Rochefort, not just language but grammar itself is tied to class, and it was with considerable irritation that she noted that the manuscript of *Le Repos* had been tampered with:

> I saw that the editors had added a lot of commas and exclamation
> points. It is very significant that these commas had been imposed on
> the text of the non-conformist character. I myself had used them in
> the discourse of the conformist character. I suddenly understood that
> punctuation is Order. Grammar and syntax are instruments of power,
> so we have to change them.[10]

So alien to Geneviève is Renaud's language that the first time he
speaks she assumes that he is under the influence of some mind-altering
substance: 'était-ce l'effet ordinaire du poison? Lui avait-on donné une
drogue? J'étais hébétée' ['was this the effect poison usually had? Had he
been drugged? I was stupefied'] (29). In spite of the apparent changes in
her view of sexuality, her inability to admit Renaud's point of view is
reflected in her continued dismissal of his words: 'c'est toujours lorsqu'il
est très malheureux et perdu qu'il se met à délirer. Comme si le désespoir
le droguait' ['it's always when he's very unhappy and lost that he begins to
rant and rave. As if despair acted like some sort of drug'] (78).

As the first half of the text unfolds, a pattern emerges whereby
Geneviève is pushed into ever greater humiliation by Renaud, who strives
to break down, and force Geneviève to see, what he regards as her
hypocritical morality and sentiment. Both characters have a specific
agenda which subtends the relationship. Geneviève, who discovers that
Renaud is an alcoholic, decides to rescue him from his demons in what
the reader can perceive as yet another manifestation of the 'bonne action'
['good deed']: 'je commençai de nourrir l'envie de le sauver. [. . .] Je
retrouvai ma vocation ancienne' ['I began to nurture the desire to save
him. [. . .] I rediscovered my former vocation'] (98). From this point on,
she will endure all that Renaud can throw at her—and do so in the name
of love. For his part, Renaud will continue to humiliate in the name of
class warfare:

> Hypocrite! Ce que tu cachais sous tes cols blancs et tes cheveux tirés!
> Toi entre des millions bien sûr, ce n'était pas à toi que j'en avais, tu
> n'es pas une exception, tu es le cas général. Or ça, je hais. Et quand
> ç'a été fini, je me suis dit, j'en ai eu un! (160)
>
> [*Hypocrite! Just look at what you were hiding behind your starched collars
> and scraped back hair! You and millions of others, needless to say, it wasn't
> you I had it in for, you're not the exception, you're the norm. And that's
> something I just can't stand. And when it was over, I said to myself, got
> one!*]

The relationship, however, has more to it than a clash of social values,
although the power-games which Renaud and Geneviève engage in are

played out in the social arena. The relationship mapped out in the first part of *Le Repos* typifies the type of master/slave dynamic to be found in another text which had proved to be a 'succès de scandale' some three years before: Pauline Réage's (Dominique Aury's) *Histoire d'O*.[11] Whilst sado-masochism may conjure up images of damp dungeons, whips and chains in the public imagination (all of which are readily available in Réage's text), the master/slave dynamic can manifest itself in less colourful and visible forms. New light can be cast upon *Le Repos* by psychoanalyst Jessica Benjamin's *The Bonds of Love*, which explores the aetiology and dynamics of relationships based on domination and submission.[12]

Using a feminist object-relations theory, Benjamin examines the impact of early relations upon the infant's psychic life, drawing on the work of both W. D. Winnicott and Margaret Mahler, and an intersubjective model. Her approach thus represents a shift away from the classical intrapsychic model most commonly associated with Freud (who sought to explain masochistic and sadistic tendencies in terms of drives and defences). For Benjamin, the roots of patterns of domination and submission can be traced back to early social relationships, more specifically, to the relationship between the infant and her/his mother. Benjamin argues that from early childhood (the mother/infant bond) individuals have to reconcile two forces, which we might term self-assertion or independence, and recognition or dependence. A successful relationship with another individual requires a balancing of these forces, a maintaining of tension:

> In mutual recognition the subject accepts the premise that others are
> separate but nonetheless share like feelings and intentions. The subject
> is compensated for his loss of sovereignty by the pleasure of sharing,
> the communion with another subject.[13]

The subject must sustain a paradox: to recognize his/her own agency, he/she must necessarily recognize the agency of the other. In existential terms, the subject requires the other (*autrui*) to validate his/her own sense of self. When, however, the tension between independence and dependence cannot be maintained, the paradox is given up in favour of a polarization, and mutuality gives way to opposition: doer and done-to, master and slave, sadist and masochist. When this happens, 'the assertion of one individual (the master) is transformed into domination; the other's (the slave's) recognition becomes submission. Thus the basic tension of forces *within* the individual becomes a dynamic *between* individuals.'[14] Furthermore, the dominant party splits off dependence and projects it upon the submissive party, whilst conversely, the submissive party splits

21

off assertion and projects it upon the dominant party. In simple terms, the master recognizes dependence only in the slave, whilst the slave recognizes assertion only in the master.

Offering a psychological reading of *Le Repos* places the would-be exegete in a difficult situation. To impose such a framework is, if we are to believe Renaud, another bourgeois attempt at reductive recuperation. As he says to Geneviève: 'Jouir incite les femmes à l'apostolat psychologique' ['A good orgasm converts women to psychology'] (84)! Be that as it may, *The Bonds of Love* provides us with a useful interpretive grid. Drawing specifically on *Histoire d'O*, Benjamin indicates the central paradox which lies at the heart of the master/slave dynamic, namely that the master-figure requires active resistance on the part of the submissive party in order to maintain an imposition of will, to assert his power:

> The story is driven forward by the dialectic of control. Since a slave who is completely dominated loses the quality of being able to give recognition, the struggle to possess her must be prolonged. O must be enslaved piece by piece; new levels of resistance must be found, so that she can be vanquished anew—She must acquiesce in ever deeper humiliation, pain, and bondage, she must will her submission ever anew, each time her master asks her, 'O, do you consent?' The narrative moves through these ever deeper levels of humiliation, tracing the impact of each fresh negation of her will, each new defeat of her resistance.[15]

A similar dynamic characterizes the first half of Rochefort's text. From the earliest moments of the relationship, Geneviève identifies Renaud as a master-figure and positions herself as victim or slave—'Le monde entier s'ordonne autour de ce nouveau venu, *il est déjà le maître*' ['The whole world revolves around this newcomer, *he is already the master*'] (47, my emphasis)—whilst she is the 'victime continûment dévorée et consentante' ['endlessly willing and endlessly devoured victim'] (60).

The pattern of submission and domination is played out in the sexual arena, for it is here that Geneviève's moral qualms and modesty provide Renaud with the resistance he requires to assert his dominance: 'ce jeu l'amuse, de m'obliger à me compromettre, à montrer mes désirs et mes sentiments' ['he enjoys this game; forcing me to compromise myself, to reveal my desires and feelings amuses him'] (53). Each time Geneviève holds back, Renaud further asserts his will, in a spiralling process of ever deeper humiliation: 'Rien qui l'éperonne mieux qu'un "non" tremblant: un "non", ce n'est rien d'autre que ce qu'il faut changer en oui' ['Nothing spurs him on more than a tremulous "no": a "no" is just something which must be changed into a yes'] (60). The humiliation is not restricted to sexual acts; each time Geneviève talks of love, Renaud will seek to force her to translate her terminology into that of desire:

—Je te fais jouir?
—Oui.
—Tu aimes ça?
—Oui.
—Dis-le.
—J'aime ça. (75)

['*Do I make you come?*'
'*Yes.*'
'*Do you like it?*'
'*Yes.*'
'*Say it.*'
'*I like it.*']

In her exploration of the aetiology of the masochistic personality, Benjamin emphasizes the importance of the early mother/child bond. Masochism, she states, 'reflects the inability to express one's desire and agency', and finds its origin in a primary relationship in which the child who seeks to separate by asserting his/her will is punished by retaliation or withdrawal. Fearing loss or abandonment, the child adapts by surrendering to the will of the all-powerful mother.[16] In the adult master/slave relationship the submissive and dominant parties are acting out this early situation: 'Like the sadist's aggression, the masochists's submission is ambiguous, conflating the repetition of an old frustration and the wish for something new.'[17] Bearing this in mind we can see that Geneviève's mother is more than a representative of the bourgeois order; she is also the archetypal powerful mother spoken of by Benjamin. Indeed, her tendency to dominate her daughter carries over into the latter's adult relationships. When Geneviève fails to contact her mother upon her return from the provinces, she immediately manifests intrusive behaviour, responding to Geneviève's excuses with a typically punitive reaction of withdrawal: 'Écoute, quand tu auras retrouvé tes esprits, tu m'appelleras, puisque apparemment tu n'as pas envie de me voir aujourd'hui. Tâche de ne pas attendre une semaine tout de même [. . .]. Si tu me le permets!' ['Listen, when you've come to your senses, call me, since you apparently don't want to see me today. Try not to leave it for a week though [. . .] if you don't mind'] (56).[18]

The master/slave dynamic is such that for the masochistic party, the greatest fear consists in an abandonment which repeats the earliest withdrawal of the mother. Here again, clear parallels between *Le Repos* and *Histoire d'O* can be identified. When O's lover René leaves the Chateau de Roissy where she has been imprisoned, the threat of abandonment precipitates a terrified response: 'Dire que O, dès la seconde où son amant l'eut quittée, commença à attendre, est peu dire: elle ne fut plus qu'attente et que nuit' ['To say that O started to wait the second that her lover had left her was an understatement: she was anticipation and darkness personified'] (92). Similarly, each time Renaud threatens to walk out, Geneviève responds with a disproportionate degree of horror. When left alone overnight for the first time, she suffers an acute anxiety attack, entering a state of almost paralytic anticipation: 'j'entrais dans la pure attente' ['I entered a state of pure anticipation'] (104).

Once the dynamic is at work, the master can tighten the metaphoric bonds by a show of indifference which elicits in the submissive party a fear of loss or abandonment. For O, René's offer of freedom, indicative of an apparent lack of need, is horrifying: 'c'est que René la laissait libre, et qu'elle détestait sa liberté. Sa liberté était pire que n'importe quelle chaîne' ['the fact was that René gave her her freedom, and she loathed that freedom. Her freedom was worse than any chains'] (175). Sir Stephen, the master-figure who succeeds René, wields the same powerful weapon: 'tu es toujours libre, tu le sais, de refuser d'être à moi' ['you know you're always free to refuse to be mine'] (271). In Geneviève's case, Renaud's offers of freedom merely underline her state of metaphorical imprisonment: 'L'œil rusé me rappellait que [. . .] j'étais libre. Libre de m'intéresser, ou pas. [. . .] Hélas! Je n'étais plus libre' ['His sly look reminded me that [. . .] I was free. Free to show an interest or not. [. . .] Alas! I was no longer free'] (42–3). There may be no physical torture in the relationship, but the lack of need manifested by Renaud becomes a bludgeon which forces Geneviève into a no-win situation: 'Renaud n'a rien demandé; ce que je fais, je veux bien le faire; si je ne le faisais pas, il s'en passerait; Renaud n'a rien à perdre' ['Renaud has asked for nothing; what I do, I do of my own free will; if I didn't do it, he would do without; Renaud has nothing to lose'] (70). Just as an offer of freedom was worse to O than any chain, so Renaud's 'indifférence méprisante' ['contemptuous indifference'] is more painful than 'ses plus douloureuses entreprises' ['his most painful actions'] (61).

The fourth chapter of the text marks a shift in the balance of power. When Geneviève finds Renaud (drinking heavily) in the Black-Out bar, and, as has become her routine, attempts to take him home, Renaud seeks to impose the ritual humiliation by unbuttoning her blouse in order to display her breasts to his fellow-drinkers. At first, Geneviève resists ('au deuxième bouton, je bronchai' ['at the second button, I flinched']), but when she capitulates, her submission is described in strikingly different terms: 'Soudain ma résistance s'effrondra. Quelque chose s'ouvrit,

24

la sérénité déferla. Il est vrai: tout cela m'était complètement égal'
['Suddenly my resistance fell away. Something opened up inside me, and
a sense of peace washed over me. It's true: it was all a matter of complete
indifference to me'] (117). Geneviève's passivity, her lack of open
resistance, immediately deflates Renaud, who returns home with her,
curiously subdued. To Geneviève, this is clearly a victory of sorts: 'Sa voix
avait perdu de sa conviction. Je venais de marquer un point mystérieux
quelque part' ['His voice had lost something of its conviction. Somehow,
in some way, I'd just scored a point'] (118).

How is this episode to be interpreted? The incident has been read as a
liberating moment for Geneviève and a move towards a more positive
representation of female sexuality: Geneviève finally opens herself to an
expansive sexuality.[19] But is this the whole story? Certainly the master/
slave dynamic is broken. By adopting a conscious strategy of non-
resistance, Geneviève effectively prevents Renaud from asserting his will:
with nothing left to oppose, he can no longer dominate. As Geneviève
herself points out: 'Renaud [. . .] combattait avec fureur l'adversaire
silencieux et docile, trop docile, né sous sa férule' ['Renaud [. . .] was
struggling furiously against this silent and all too compliant adversary, an
adversary born of his own uncompromising domination'] (119). And yet,
although Geneviève may have overcome the sexual prudishness which
Renaud strove to undermine, the split which we saw earlier remains. That
side of Geneviève which believes in redemptive love, the bourgeois Mlle
Le Theil, persists in the belief that she can change Renaud, and bring
about a happy ending. She may have rid herself of the role of nobly
resisting victim, but she continues to suffer at the hands of Renaud. The
shift in her position seems merely to have cast her into another traditional
female role: that of the martyr who is willing to suffer in silence for her
cause, which remains that of redemptive love. Indeed, such is the
continued strain experienced by Geneviève that she is hospitalized. To the
outsider, the doctor Alex, she is quite simply mad: 'Vous êtes folle, mon
petit, et je vous traite comme telle. [. . .] Je vous fais un certificat
d'internement s'il le faut, et je vous mets la camisole' ['You're mad, my
dear girl, and I'm treating you accordingly. [. . .] If necessary I'll have you
committed and put you in a strait-jacket'] (140). Certainly, if she is sick,
then she is sick with (what she believes to be) love, for her treatment for
TB only begins to take effect when Renaud returns from the prolonged
absence which had prostrated her.

The hospitalization of Geneviève provokes important changes in
Renaud, who for the first time experiences need or dependence. Whilst
this might be regarded as a normal part of human interaction, from
Renaud's point of view it represents a weakness which should be resisted:
'j'avais attrapé une dépendance, je m'étais affaibli' ['I'd caught a bad case

25

of dependence, I'd weakened'] (156). Now that Geneviève no longer represents the dependent party (at least visibly), the twin forces of assertion and dependence which had been polarized, held in tension *between* Renaud and Geneviève, are now resited *within* Renaud himself. Benjamin notes that the admission of dependence is often accompanied by a fierce struggle:

> His need for the other [. . .] seems to place him in the other's power, as if dependency were the equivalent of surrender. When the subject abandons the project of absolute independence or control, he does so unwillingly, with a persistent, if unconscious, wish to fulfil the old omnipotence fantasy.[20]

Each admission of need on Renaud's part is accompanied by a violent internal struggle: 'Il me fit une grande crise [. . .] il se mit à me haïr; je crus qu'il m'arracherait tous les cheveux [. . .]. Mais je lisais dans l'excès même de sa cruauté qu'il se battait contre son propre cœur' ['He threw a major tantrum, he began to hate me; I thought he'd tear all my hair out [. . .]. But the very excesses of his cruelty showed me that he was fighting against his own feelings'] (212). As Renaud himself states: 'Il y a un Renaud qui t'aime, dit-il, et un qui te déteste. La vérité est que je déteste celui qui t'aime' ['There's a Renaud who loves you, he said, and one who detests you. The truth of the matter is that I detest the one who loves you'] (248). Although by the close of Part I the sexual schooling of Geneviève is over, the battle continues.

In what amounts to a repetition and intensification of a process which was only apparently completed in Part I, Geneviève once again, and this time definitively, rejects her bourgeois acquaintances at the start of the second part of the text. Turned away from the hospital and kept in the dark about Geneviève's whereabouts, the mother is not mentioned again in the text. Hopeful fiancé Pierre, seeking a bedside reconciliation, is dismissed. Most arresting of all is Geneviève's attack on Claude. Plans for the joint venture in a children's home are rejected in no uncertain terms: 'que les enfants malheureux se débrouillent [. . .] j'avais compris que mieux valait pour ces petits d'être couverts de bleus qu'aux mains d'une femme qui ne jouit pas' ['let the unfortunate children fend for themselves [. . .] I'd come to see that those children were better off covered in bruises than looked after by a frigid woman'] (164). And when Renaud informs her that he had arranged for Claude to be raped, Geneviève remains coolly indifferent.

The introduction of a new set of characters drawn from a bohemian artistic milieu does not indicate a shift in the relationship between the two principal characters—as Geneviève notes, 'le cauchemar avait changé de milieu' ['the nightmare had relocated'] (182)—but it does provide the reader with new insights into Renaud. In an exchange with the artist Katov and his partner Rafaele, Renaud reveals the political despair which had led to his change of status from writer to nihilist alcoholic. Claiming that artists no longer have a political agenda and are by this token 'tous officiellement bourgeois' ['all officially middle class'], he expresses the despair shared by many communists in France: 'la vertu, c'était la révolte. Et maintenant la révolte est sans espoir' ['virtue lay in rebellion. And now that rebellion is hopeless'] (199). The 1950s were difficult times for the PCF (Parti Communiste Français). Signs that all was not well in the USSR had already begun to emerge in the 1940s as rumours of the existence of Soviet labour camps spread. By the late 1940s the Cold War escalation was well under way. In February 1956, only two years before the publication of *Le Repos*, Khrushchev denounced Stalin's crimes in his report to the 20th Congress, the proceedings of which were published in *Le Monde* on 6 March. November of that same year was marked by the crushing of the Budapest uprising by Soviet troops. Responding to the news, thousands of Parisians took part in violent demonstrations outside the Communist Party headquarters. The offices of the communist newspaper *l'Humanité* were ransacked. Many party memberships were not renewed in 1957.

Rochefort went through a number of narrative permutations in her draft versions of *Le Repos*, and her observations on this subject reveal something of her own standpoint vis-à-vis her characters: 'Je voulais écrire ça de mon point de vue à moi: celui qui est devenu dans le livre Rafaele' ['I wanted to write it from my own point of view; the point of view that became Rafaele's in the book'].[21] Rafaele, whose very name, that of an archangel, is suggestive of a mediation between the human and the divine, represents an alternative middle-ground between Geneviève's and Renaud's extreme views. Renaud's political nihilism, linked throughout the text to an idealist, absolutist concept of love, is countered by Rafaele's more pragmatic stance: 'l'espoir ou pas l'espoir [. . .] qu'est-ce que ça change à ce qu'on a à faire' ['hope or no hope [. . .] what's that got to do with what has to be done'] (199). With her cropped hair, wearing trousers and a man's shirt, sitting with one ankle balanced on her thigh 'à la façon dégagée d'un garçon' ['casually, like a boy'] (196), Rafaele is an androgynous figure whose attitude to love is clearly differentiated from Geneviève's as well as Renaud's. To Geneviève, whose persistent belief in redemptive love emerges clearly at this point, Rafaele's unwillingness to surrender all in the name of love means that she is quite simply not 'a real woman': 'elle était à cent lieues du sacrifice. Pas faite pour acquitter le prix fort pour un homme. Pas femelle' ['there was no way she would ever sacrifice herself. She was simply not made to pay the ultimate price for a man. She was not female'] (271). Where Geneviève's relationship with Renaud is, as we have seen, marked by oppressive power-plays, the alternation of slave and master roles, Rafaele becomes sister, twin, and perhaps most importantly, muse to Renaud. The creative energy released in the ludic interaction between the two characters stands in stark opposition to the debilitating battles which rage between Renaud and Geneviève. More significantly, Renaud's and his Muse's imaginative creations can be read as 'mises en abyme', reflexive commentaries on the action, which represent an important counter-balance to the first-person narrative point of view.

The couple's first creative venture is inspired by a conversation about Renaud's past (largely fictitious): 'Renaud eut neuf suicides, dont fut faite une chanson sur l'air de *Malborough*, à couplets' ['Renaud had nine suicide attempts, and from these they composed a song in verse to the tune of *Malborough*'], featuring Geneviève in the tenth verse, 'avec une clef, d'or bien sûr, qui ouvrait ma propre porte et celle du Royaume des Morts' ['with a key, made of gold of course, which opened my own door and that to the Kingdom of the Dead'] (219). The reference to the gold key alludes back to a psychological parlour game of the familiar sort 'if you had a key, what sort of key would it be?' played earlier in the text. Geneviève's reply had one again reinforced her faith in the power of love: 'si j'en ai une en tout cas elle n'ouvre qu'une porte. Mais elle est en or' ['if I have one it only opens one door, that's for sure. But it's made of gold'] (206). The key, evidently, is to Renaud's heart. Renaud's sarcastic rejoinder, 'j'en étais sûr' ['what a surprise'], had already signalled his distaste, which is further emphasized by the mocking reiteration of the song: from Renaud's perspective, far from giving Geneviève access to his heart, the gold key opens Geneviève's own door ('qui ouvrait ma propre porte')—that is, we might assume, her sexuality—and the gateway to the kingdom of the dead. But what are to understand by this: does Geneviève free Renaud from death, or condemn him to it? Is love victorious or damning? The answer is revealed in the second of Renaud's and Rafaele's musical creations: the reworking of the myth of Orpheus and Eurydice.

In the original version of the myth, Orpheus, poet and musician, is granted permission to enter the Underworld in order to bring Eurydice back from the dead, on one condition: that he does not turn around and look at her as they re-enter the realm of the living. Unable to resist the temptation, Orpheus looks back and thereby loses his lover a second time. The tragedy does not end here, for Orpheus thereafter renounces love, and is consequently torn apart by the neglected Thracean women, or, according to a variant of the myth, by Bacchantian followers of Dionysus, angered by the poet's cult of Apollo (Orpheus's patron, and in some versions his father, who taught him to play the lyre).

The version conjured up by Renaud and Rafaele, to be entitled *Eurydice*, is both a sequel and a rewriting of the original tale. More specifically, it is to be based on an existing version: 'un oratorio, dit Rafaele, qui voulait qu'on ouvrît sur les dernières mesures de l'*Orpheo* de Monteverdi' ['an oratorio, said Rafaele, who wanted it to begin with the closing bars of Monteverdi's *Orpheo*'] (220). Though nothing more is said on the subject, the selection of Monteverdi's opera (first performed in Mantua in 1607) is a significant one, for it allows for a choice to be made between two alternative endings. The librettist Alessandro Striggio hesitated in using the tragic Greek ending, which did not seem in keeping with the pastoral tradition with which Monteverdi's opera was embued. This was, however, to be his final choice, and his libretto closes with the Bacchantes engaged in dyonisiac celebrations prior to the violent death of Orpheus, which was left to the audience's imagination. But 'there are discrepancies between the libretto and the score'. Monteverdi's score omits the Bacchantes dénouement, 'replacing it with the appearance *deus ex machina* of Apollo, who, after a dialogue with Orpheus, ascends with him to heaven while a chorus sing the happy outcome'.[22] Significantly, Renaud and Rafaele choose the tragic ending as the start of their tale: Orpheus, representing Renaud, is dismembered, 'en punition d'avoir, dit Renaud, préféré l'amour humain à l'amour divin' ['as a punishment, said Renaud, for having preferred human to divine love'] (219), an allusion to the fourth act of the opera which takes place in the Underworld: 'ciò che vieta Pluton comanda Amore' sings Orpheus ['that which Pluto forbids, Love commands'].

The choice of Striggio's ending and the subsequent reworking of the Orpheus myth gives the reader an insight into Renaud's view of events which differs radically from that of Geneviève, the first-person narrator, and projects an unhappy ending to *Le Repos*: Renaud's relationship with Geneviève is a weakness which will result in his metaphorical death. Geneviève's point of view is further undermined as Rafaele and Renaud go on to outline the plot-line of their new opera, in which Geneviève-Eurydice sets out on a determined, and highly comical, quest to reassemble the dismembered Renaud-Orpheus. Perhaps influenced by Cocteau's reworking of the myth of Orpheus in his play *Orphée* (1926) and film of the same name (1950), Rochefort includes elements drawn from the popular genres of the thriller and detective story in Rafaele's and Renaud's projected opera.[23] Geneviève is aided in her task of re-assemblage by police sniffer-dogs and a detective; her attempt to secrete chunks of Renaud-Orpheus in a bank-vault are foiled by a dastardly bank-raid organized by a Puckish figure representing Rafaele. In the ensuing battle with the police, the bodily fragments are torn into ever smaller pieces. Bawdy humour challenges Geneviève's sentimental concept of love: 'J'avais, dit Renaud-Orphée, déjà mis la main sur plusieurs morceaux, dont un fort important, sur la nature duquel il m'ôta toute espèce de doute en m'obligeant à constater sa vivante présence' ['I had already, said Renaud-Orpheus, laid my hands on various bodily parts, including one very important one, about whose nature he left me in no doubt by forcing me to acknowledge its very real presence'] (219).

In the original version of the myth, Orpheus's lyre charms Charon, keeper of the Underworld, into permitting him to cross the river Styx. In Renaud's version of events, Geneviève-Euridyce carries not a lyre but her own bleeding heart (with all the English connotations): 'pour lyre, j'avais mon propre coeur [. . .] dont je tirais des accords à fendre celui des démons qui détenaient les morceaux d'Orphée' ['as a lyre I carried my own heart [. . .] on which I played chords which could melt the hearts of the demons who held the fragments of Orpheus'] (219). The Rafaele-Renaud version of the myth ends in a second tragedy: Geneviève-Eurydice succeeds in reconstructing Orpheus, but the musician is robbed of his magical musicianship: 'c'était hideusement faux, hélas! il ne savait plus' ['alas! it was horribly off-key; he could no longer play'] (220).

To read *Eurydice* as a 'mise en abyme' of *Le Repos*, is to gain an insight into how to interpret the text's conclusion: Geneviève's unremitting love will prove to be fatal, rather than redemptive; Renaud will be robbed of his voice, and will suffer a metaphorical death at the hands of Geneviève. This reading is at odds with the interpretations of many critics, who insist on reading *Le Repos* as a love-story with the classic happy ending: 'la rencontre amoureuse enfin vraie'; 'l'idée généreuse du salut et de la rédemption par l'amour'; 'à force d'amour, l'héroïne du *Repos du guerrier* fera du piètre héro un homme, car rien ne résiste à l'amour' ['the story of true love'; 'the noble idea of salvation and redemption won through love'; 'the heroine of *Le Repos du guerrier* will make a man of its wretched hero by sheer dint of love, because nothing can resist love'].[24] The traditional elements of the love-story—Geneviève's pregnancy and Renaud's subsequent proposal of marriage—seem to blind readers to the realities of what is in effect a disastrous outcome, though critics may be aware of apparent inconsistencies. McMahon describes the text as 'a fretfully powerful novel which diminishes into a long and exasperating whine under the burden of a Legion of Decency ending', adding: 'where is the sense [. . .] which would allow the reader to believe that some invulnerable logic is at work behind this, some logic that would make us believe that redemption is possible for these people?'[25] The answer to the question is quite simple: there is no sense, no logic, because there is no

'Legion of Decency' ending, as an attentive reading of the text should reveal.

When Renaud learns of Geneviève's pregnancy, he apparently surrenders to her point of view: ' "L'amour vainqueur. Eh bien oui, dit-il. Il l'est" ' [' "Love conquers all. And so it does", he said'] (282). Adopting her way of seeing things, of seeing love, means renouncing his own stance, the idealist nature of which emerges clearly. Love is a divine quest, and Renaud, alluding to another myth, the search for the Holy Grail, states that he is not fit to occupy the 'Siège Périlleux', a seat left vacant at the Round Table for the chaste knight who would accomplish the Grail Quest (283). This position is now apparently surrendered: 'Je rends mon tablier d'idéaliste à vide' ['I quit my position as ineffectual idealist'] (283). Earlier in the text Renaud had pointed to the grim alternative left open to the individual who has lost faith:

> Si je ne croyais à rien, mon chou, peux-tu m'expliquer pourquoi je ne gagnerais pas mon pain dans un office? [. . .] Dans une fabrique de roulements à billes, une école de placiers en machines à laver ou une œuvre pour enfants malheureux? (78)

> [*If I believed in nothing, my sweet, can you explain to me why I shouldn't earn a living in an office? [. . .] In a ball-bearing factory, a training-school for washing-machine salesmen, or a charitable organization for under-privileged children?*]

It is this bourgeois path which Renaud is apparently going to follow. But is this a genuine choice, a willing shift to Geneviève's value-system? Renaud speaks not from conviction but from desperation, as his bitter mimicry reveals: 'je veux dire Bonjour Comment allez-vous Très bien merci et vous, je veux aller moi aussi dans la grande Machine à Laver' ['I want to say Hello How are you Very well Thank-you and you, I want to go to the land of the great big Washing Machine'] (285). His language, taking up the master/slave imagery which had characterized the first part of the text, speaks of defeat, enforced capitulation: 'Epingle-moi. Je t'en prie. J'en ai assez. Je cale. Je cède' ['Pin me down. I beg you. I've had enough. I can't go on. I give up'] (282); 'enchaîne-moi. Je veux des chaînes, le plus de chaînes possibles, et lourdes, que je ne puisse bouger' ['cover me in chains. I want chains, as many chains as possible, heavy ones, so I can't move'] (283); 'passe-moi les menottes' ['pass me the handcuffs'] (284). When he was still fighting, Renaud had identified himself as a warrior:

> L'amour toi tu ne sais pas ce que c'est [. . .]. C'est l'impossible. Je suis très fatigué. Repose-toi. Toi tu es le repos du guerrier, du guerrier

31

lâche, de l'embusqué; Notre-Dame des Déserteurs, aie pitié de moi. Je veux dormir-mourir, et pour ça une femme c'est le meilleur système. L'amour c'est une euthanasie. (234)

[*You don't know what love is* [. . .]. *It's the impossible. I'm very tired. Rest. You, you're the warrior's rest, the cowardly warrior, the ambushed warrior, Our Lady of Deserters, have pity on me. I want to sleep to die, and a woman's the best recipe for that. Love is euthanasia.*]

'Man should be trained for war and woman for the recreation of the warrior. All else is folly.'[26] Zarathustra's pronouncement, which gives Rochefort's text its title, is turned on its head: war becomes the preserve not of man but woman. Geneviève's own words on love are couched in the militaristic vocabulary of winner and loser: 'Mon amour est plus fort que toi, Renaud [. . .] tu consentiras enfin au bonheur, bientôt toi et moi nous trouverons la paix, nous nous reposerons. Nous nous reposerons' ['My love is stronger than you Renaud [. . .] eventually you'll consent to happiness, soon you and I will find peace, we will rest. We will rest'] (212). Woman may indeed represent rest, but it is rest of a definitive kind: that brought by death. Geneviève's words echo the closing lines of another text, Chekhov's *Uncle Vania*, in which Sonia's speech to Vania Voinitskii suggests that rest will be found only in another life:

We shall rest! We shall hear angels, we shall see all the heavens covered with stars like diamonds, we shall see all earthly evil, all our sufferings swept away by the grace which will fill the whole world, and our life will become peaceful, gentle, and sweet as a caress. [. . .] You've had no joy in your life, but wait, Uncle Vania, wait . . . We shall rest [. . .] We shall rest! We shall rest![27]

By now it should be abundantly clear that the ending of the text is certainly not a happy one for Renaud, but what of his partner? Geneviève had claimed that her struggle in the name of love could have only one of two possible outcomes: 'un jour tout serait fini, ou parce que je serais morte ou parce que j'aurais gagné; j'aurais la paix, celle du tombeau ou celle du triomphe' ['one day it will all be over, either because I'll be dead, or because I'll have won; I'll have peace, that of the tomb or that of victory'] (241). Neither of these sentimental endings is granted her. She will be neither the martyr dying for the cause of redemptive love, nor the victor. The final page of the text expresses not the joys of love conquering all, but the acute guilt and attempted abnegation of responsibility born of her realization that Rafaele's and Renaud's Orpheus tragedy has come true: 'C'est lui qui fait tout, pas moi. Moi je ne fais rien, je n'ai rien fait, ce n'est pas moi, ce n'est pas moi, je le jure' ['He's the one who's doing it all, not me. I'm not doing anything, I haven't done anything, it's not me, it's not me, I swear'] (286). The closing words of the text uttered by the doctor, Alex, forecast Renaud's metaphorical death: 'Ce n'est tout de même pas la chaise électrique' ['It's not the electric chair after all'].

It is important to note that the story does not end here, but circles back to the opening page, which in effect comprises the end-point of the diegesis (Geneviève after Renaud has gone), before beginning in earnest in classic narrative style ('une affaire de succession m'amenait dans cette ville, où rien n'indiquait que ma vie s'allait jouer' ['I went to this town to settle an inheritance. Nothing hinted that my very life would be at stake here'], p. 10). This prologuic opening page once more reveals the imagery of war: 'le terrain est déblayé. Nu. Complètement nu. Et m'appartient' ['the ground is clear. Stripped bare. Completely stripped bare. And it belongs to me'] (9). Geneviève now acknowledges responsibility and the triumph of her will: 'c'est fait. J'ai ce que j'ai voulu' ['it's done; I've got what I wanted'], but the 'victoire si totale' ['comprehensive victory'] which she has won is accompanied by uncertainty.[28] Earlier in the tale she had taken up the gauntlet thrown down by Renaud: 'Tu m'as lancé un défi, tu as lancé un défi à l'amour même; je le relève. On verra si l'amour est une brèche ou un pont' ['You challenged me, you challenged love itself, and I'm taking up your challenge. We'll see if love is a gulf or a bridge'] (107). Now the image of the bridge is repeated, but rather than vindicate her point of view by indicating the triumph of love, it suggests an insecure future: 'les ponts sont coupés derrière moi il faut avancer. J'ai fait le vide sous mes pas, où marcherai-je?' ['the bridges are burned behind me, I have to advance. I've left myself with nothing to stand on, where shall I go now?'] (9).

Although she has broken out of her submissive role, her employment, as retrospective narrator, of the vocabulary of war (the opening pages of the text, as we have seen, are shot through with such imagery) is symptomatic of Geneviève's continuing entrapment within a power-based dynamic. The same critic who underlined the sex in the text ('le lit dans le livre'. . .) identified Rochefort as the herald of a 'règne des femmes heureuses' ['an era of contentment for women'], a prophet articulating a new voice for women.[29] Yet *Le Repos du guerrier* presents a rather bleak outlook for female desire. Geneviève may have discovered sexual pleasure, but she ends up alone, aware that she must leave Renaud and face single parenthood.

CHAPTER TWO

Les Petits Enfants du siècle

Quant à Emma, elle ne s'interrogea point pour savoir si elle l'aimait. L'amour, croyait-elle, devait arriver tout à coup, avec de grands éclats et des fulgurations, – ouragan des cieux qui tombe sur la vie, la bouleverse, arrache les volontés comme des feuilles et emporte à l'abîme le cœur entier.

(Flaubert, *Madame Bovary*)

Les Petits Enfants du siècle (1961) won its author more recognition than any other of her works. Short-listed for the prestigious Prix Goncourt, it has featured regularly on school syllabuses in both France and Britain; indeed the majority of the critical material relates to its usefulness as a pedagogic tool.[1] Sales figures currently stand in excess of one and a half million copies. Rochefort seems to have come a long way from the oppressive atmosphere of *Le Repos du guerrier*, with its claustrophobic and ultimately destructive relationship set against the stifling backdrop of Cold War disillusionment. And yet, although *Les Petits Enfants* certainly brings a change of tone, with a witty and colloquial narrative style which was to become Rochefort's trademark, the work, like its predecessor, tells a tale of oppression and loss of individual liberty. Josyane, the feisty first-person narrator, ultimately falls prey to her life-sapping environment; more specifically, to the twin state policies of public-housing programmes and pro-natalism. As was the case with *Le Repos*, the reader of *Les Petits Enfants* must remain alert to the ambiguities of the narrative voice. Although Josyane is in many respects a more reliable narrator than Geneviève, the apparent simplicity of the retrospective narrative can be misleading. Equally problematic is the text's treatment of sexuality. It is somewhat ironic that whereas the representation of an adult woman's sexual desire in *Le Repos* came in for damning criticism and charges of obscenity, only three years later the depiction of Josyane's under-age sexual liaisons with both her peers and older men (one married) seemed barely to impinge on the public consciousness. Today's readers, living in a climate of acute awareness of child abuse and exploitation, may respond rather differently.

After completing *Le Repos du guerrier* Rochefort worked on a second draft of a novel undertaken some years before; the work which was to become *Archaos* (see below, Chapter 6). During this period she attempted to secure accommodation on the Boulevard Saint-Jacques, only to be informed by the Parisian housing authorities that the area was designated for demolition. Instead, she was offered a place on the Bagnolet 'grand ensemble' (home to the Rouvier family in *Les Petits Enfants*), where she remained only until such time as the royalties from *Le Repos* allowed her to move; long enough, however, for her to have felt the full horror of her temporary environment: 'Moi j'ai ressenti avec violence, cette architecture qui impose un mode de vie, un mode de pensée'; 'je comprenais ce que c'était, à quoi ça allait servir: A VIDER LES GENS PAR L'INTÉRIEUR. C'était, cette pensée architecturale, une machine diabolique, machine de mort mentale' ['I had a violent reaction to that kind of architecture, an architecture which imposes a way of life, a way of thinking'; 'I understood what it was, what function it was going to serve: TO EMPTY PEOPLE OUT FROM THE INSIDE. This architectural design was a diabolical machine, a machine bringing mental death'].[2] Inspired (if that is quite the right word) by her experience of the 'grands ensembles', Rochefort wrote *Les Petits Enfants* 'd'une seule traite. Sur l'horreur. Un tout petit bouquin court, ciselé par l'horreur' ['straight off. Out of horror. Just a short little book carved out of horror'].[3]

The 'grands ensembles', represented in Rochefort's text by Bagnolet and Sarcelles, triggered the writing of *Les Petits Enfants*, but just what are these constructions, and why were they built? During the post-war years France's population saw a dramatic increase, with a net rise of 6.6 million between 1946 and 1962. Indeed, in less than forty years after the Second World War, the population increased by over 14 million, compared to a rise of only 12 million over the preceding century and a half.[4] This nation-wide boom in births, coupled with an accelerating process of urbanization (between 1954 and 1968 the urban population grew by some 10 million), forced the government to adopt a radical housing policy in the form of the construction of large apartment blocks of public housing, the 'grands ensembles', usually, but not exclusively, on vacant land on city peripheries. In the course of the 1950s and 1960s these buildings were to provide accommodation for over 10 per cent of the population in France.[5] Often low-cost and of prefabricated design, the 'grands ensembles' were far from ideal:

> The Parisian *grands ensembles*, built from 1956 onwards, suffered from many initial problems and failings as a result of the scale of their construction. They epitomized the problem of suburban living; people

isolated while living among great numbers of others, in cramped apartments, without facilities for shopping or child-care, with 'dead' indefensible space between the blocks. The *grand ensemble* at Sarcelles in the northern suburbs [. . .] gave its name to an illness based on depression caused by these very difficult living conditions.[6]

As the narrator of *Les Petits Enfants* points out, housing policy dictated that large families were often allocated places on the 'grands ensembles': 'dans cette Cité les familles nombreuses étaient prioritaires' ['large families had priority on this housing estate'] (11). With ten siblings, Josyane is represented as a victim not only of what might be termed an inadequate housing policy (quite apart from the generally sterile environment, the Rouvier family is forced to engage in ergonomic feats with the birth of each new child due to the cramped conditions in their apartment), but of another key governmental policy operating in the post-war years, that of pro-natalism, a policy viewed with unequivocal distaste by Rochefort: 'Établir un statut d'objecteur de conscience à la politique nataliste de cette contrée arriérée n'est pas totalement impossible, il y faut seulement consacrer des années de sa vie' ['becoming a conscientious objector to the pro-natalist policy of this backward country isn't totally impossible; you just have to dedicate years of your life to it'].[7]

The demographic trend in France in the nineteenth and early twentieth century was characterized by stagnation, especially if compared to other European countries. Two world wars resulted in further demographic depletion, with a total population deficit estimated at 3 million as a result of the First World War, and almost one million as a result of the Second.[8] Alarm over decreasing population figures had already lead, in the 1920s, to measures prohibiting abortion and the sale of contraceptives. (These were reversed by the Loi Neuwirth, 28 December 1967, allowing the sale of contraceptives, and the Loi Veil abortion legislation, promulgated on the 17 January 1975.) Further steps were to be taken in the 1930s. *Les Petits Enfants* opens with the celebrated line: 'Je suis née des Allocations et d'un jour férié' ['I was born of welfare benefits and a bank holiday'] (7), a reference to the family allowance system, codified in 1939, which was to provide families with a strong financial incentive to have children. Winchester notes that: 'By 1949, allowances, tax incentives and family incentives took an astonishing 22 per cent of Gross Domestic Product, showing the importance attached to population in the reconstruction of the war-torn economy.' Citing Thody's introduction to *Les Petits Enfants*, she adds that in the late 1950s allowances and tax relief could constitute between one third and one half of the take-home pay of a manual worker (such as Josyane's father).[9]

Les Petits Enfants was written in order to reveal the alienation which results when individuals are raised in a soulless concrete environment, in economic circumstances which dictate the worth of a human life in terms of hard cash and consumer durables. In many respects the storyline speaks for itself. Josyane, an intelligent and vivacious child, is obliged to play mother to an ever-increasing horde of siblings. The accelerated pace of the narrative—six births in the space of fourteen pages—coupled with the narrator's casual reference to the appearance of each new child, serves to underline, indeed to parody, the alarming growth of the Rouvier clan. Although capable in her school-work, Josyane is discouraged from pursuing her education by her parents' indifference and her careers advisor's lack of imagination. Josyane's mother remains trapped in a vicious circle of exhaustion, ill-health, a need to go on working and a desire to secure the latest Moulinex food mixer, whilst her father and eldest brother, Patrick, adopt the stereotypical line that men's work should remain in the public sphere. Josyane, as we shall see, is doomed to repeat her mother's life, whilst at least two of her siblings fall foul of the system: Catherine is dispatched to an asylum; Patrick ends up in trouble with the law.

The textual events make the point clearly enough, but it is the language of the work, the compelling and engaging nature of the narratorial voice, which plays a key role. As Rochefort said: 'sans le style, ça ne tient pas' ['without the style it doesn't hang together']; the text is held together by 'le ton monocorde, et grammaticalement très étudié, de la petite fille' ['the unvarying and very grammatically studied tone of the little girl'].[10] Readers of *Les Petits Enfants* may be surprised by the phrase 'grammaticalement très étudié'. A cursory reading of the text gives the impression of casual speech, a simple transcription of the speaking voice. Rochefort's style is in fact rather more complex, combining elements of formal and informal language, of both written and spoken French. In the autobiographical *Ma Vie revue et corrigée par l'auteur* Rochefort comments on the problems she faced when transcribing tapes of her conversations with her interviewer, Maurice Chavardès, noting that she writes naturally 'en langage parlé' ['in spoken language'], but that a strict line must be drawn between what she calls 'l'écrit-parlé' ['the written-spoken mode'] and 'le parlé-parlé' ['the spoken-spoken mode']. The latter would be a simple transcription of speech; the former, which characterizes *Les Petits Enfants* and indeed Rochefort's subsequent work, far from comprising a spontaneous and unworked outpouring, is, in the author's words, 'le fruit de longues recherches, sans lesquelles ne saurait émerger ce qu'on appelle, en italique pour plus de sûreté l'*écriture*' ['the product of a lot of work, without which what is called—in italics to be on the safe side— *writing* could not emerge'] (11); 'l'écrit-parlé est tout ce qu'il y a de

37

sophistiqué, en fait d'*écriture*' ['the written-spoken mode is an extremely sophisticated form of *writing*'].[11]

Although a full analysis is beyond the scope of this study, some of the linguistic features of the text can be briefly examined. *Les Petits Enfants* combines registers drawn from both a formal, written medium, and an informal, spoken mode usually associated with conversation. In his *Varieties of Contemporary French*, Malcolm Offord proposes a simple categorization of register which corresponds to three major varieties of French: R3, or hyper-standard French, is a literary form, grammatically very correct, and most often to be found in the written medium; R2, standard French; R1, or substandard French, is the most informal register, and tends to occur in the spoken medium. It can be described as:

> Language which is casual, familiar and colloquial; this means that the language is marked by incorrectness in terms of grammar and is liable to be characterised both by redundant and elliptical expressions; the lexis associated with the R1 division includes slang and vulgar expressions.[12]

The R1 category can be further subdivided to include R1*, that is, a register which is not appropriate in polite usage and which might cause offence.

Les Petits Enfants is written in the past historic tense usually associated with formal, written French. In accordance with the use of the past historic, the literary past anterior is also employed, but the situations in which it is to be found are often humorously subversive. Thus we find the past anterior in the context of Josyane's sexual liaison with a young boy: 'dès qu'on fut couché sous les arbres dans un coin tranquille il releva mon pull-over' ['As soon as we'd lain down under the trees in a quiet spot he pulled my jumper up'] (107). Or referring to having sex with Philippe (her husband-to-be) for the first time: 'Dès qu'il m'eut prise je fus heureuse' ['As soon as he had taken me I was happy'] (153). One can only imagine the consequences of using these examples in a first-year language class. Figures of speech such as zeugma, again associated with the written medium, are also employed in humorously deflatory contexts, combining in the following example with colloquial expressions usually associated with speech: 'La mère, ne sachant pas si c'était du lard ou du cochon, me regarda en coin pour se faire une opinion, mais *j'avais pris un air con et une autre assiette*, et elle ne put pas se la faire' ['Mother, who wasn't sure if I was for real, watched me out of the corner of her eye to try and work it out, but I'd picked an idiotic expression and another plate'] (83, my italics).

Throughout the text the formal past historic is used in conjunction with elements from Offord's R1 register category: 'elle était déjà patraque

[R1] quand je la connus' ['she was already kind of washed-out when I knew her'] (8); 'papa lui en fila une bonne [R1]' ['dad gave him a good clout'] (9); 'Patrick eut les jetons [R1] et fila [R1] juste assez droit pour ne pas se faire virer [R1]' ['Patrick got the wind up and stayed more or less on the straight and narrow, enough to avoid getting kicked out'] (26); 'quand Patrick en attaquait un il avait l'autre sur le poil [R1] et il était obligé de caner [R1], comme le jour où, l'ayant mis au sol, ils lui cognèrent dessus avec des pierres' ['when Patrick attacked one of them he had the other one breathing down his neck and he had to chicken out, like the day when they'd got him on the ground and were hitting him with stones'] (27). Language marked out by the Collins-Robert dictionary as unsuitable for polite usage (Offord's R1*) is common, for example: 'J'étais enragée. Je les aurais tués. Y compris le sale con [R1*] de l'émission [. . .] qui restait comme une andouille [R1] à se faire foutre [R1*] de sa poire [R1] par dix million d'autres cons [R1*]' ['I was furious. I could have killed them. Including that stupid git on the TV who just sat there like a lemon getting the piss taken out of him by ten million other stupid gits'] (47). Or again: 'Catherine prit le fou rire, comme chaque fois que Patrick ouvrait le bec [R1], que ce soit pour dire la pire des conneries [R1*]' ['Catherine got a fit of the giggles like she did every time Patrick opened his gob even if it was only to come out with something bloody moronic'] (47).

In *Ma Vie* Rochefort points out that the language she terms 'parlé-parlé', that is transcribed spoken French, is almost impossible to follow: 'c'est pas lisible avec les euh ben alors voyons enfin tu vois bon je veux dire euh les répétitions phrases pas finies une vraie panade, on comprend rien' ['you can't read it with the ums, ers, you knows, yes well let's sees, I means, ums, the repetitions, the unfinished sentences, it's a complete mess, it's incomprehensible'] (11). Although *Les Petits Enfants* avoids incomplete sentences and repetitions, as well as most of the phatics noted by Rochefort, it does nonetheless include many of the linguistic features which Offord recognizes as typical of the mode 'spontaneous conversation'.[13] Thus we find fillers such as 'bref', and 'c'est-à-dire', as well as other phrases associated with the conversing mode (my italics): 'j'hésitai quelques secondes, je n'avais pas tellement d'opinion et le temps que j'en cherche une il était pratiquement trop tard *et puis zut*' ['I hesitated for a few seconds, I didn't really have an opinion and by the time I tried to form one it was more or less too late and oh what the hell']; 'je vis que Pascale était sur celle de Didi, il s'était débrouillé *en somme*' ['I saw that Pascale was on Didi's [bike], in other words he'd got it sorted'] (109).

Spontaneous conversation is also marked by the use of vague words and the abbreviated 'ça', both of which are extremely common in the text: 'je leur donnais à manger rien que des trucs qu'ils n'aimaient pas' ['I only served up stuff to eat that they didn't like'] (87); 'c'est ça le grand truc des motos' ['that's the big thing with motorbikes'] (124); 'C'était raisonnable et je me tus. D'ailleurs ça ne faisait pas si mal que ça' ['It was reasonable and I kept quiet. In any case, it wasn't as painful as all that'] (107). The negative particle 'ne' is frequently omitted, and as Thody notes, further examples of (almost untranslatable) grammatical incorrectness specific to French can also be found: 'papa et moi on se regarda' ['dad and I looked at each other'] (146); 'nous on mettait de la moutarde dans tout' ['we put mustard on everything'] (10); 'la machine n'était même pas finie de payer' ['the machine wasn't even paid up yet'] (9); 'avec cinq tous petits enfants à s'occuper' ['with five young kids to look after'] (9).[14]

'Car des fautes ça j'en faisais' ['because as far as mistakes go, I sure made them'] (24), Josyane points out, recalling her teacher's criticisms. Rochefort's use of language in the text, however, should not be regarded merely in terms of an attempt to represent a young girl's linguistic short-comings. The deliberate co-mingling of formal and informal language is far removed from any concerns with strict realism; the question 'would a young girl speak like this?' is largely redundant. What is significant is that the education system as it is portrayed in *Les Petits Enfants* clearly fails to meet Josyane's needs. Classes take the form of the strict application of grammatical rules. Paradoxically, parsing sentences is an activity which Josyane relishes precisely because it appears to serve little purpose beyond constituting a welcome break from household chores: 'Même je crois que plus ça ne servait à rien plus ça me plaisait. J'aurais bien passé ma vie à faire rien que des choses qui ne servaient à rien' ['In fact, I think that the more useless it was, the more I liked it. I would happily have spent the rest of my life doing nothing but utterly useless things'] (24).

In her later works, *Encore heureux qu'on va vers l'été* (1975), and *Les Enfants d'abord* (1976), Rochefort singles out the education system as a typical example of a state-controlled institution which seeks to perpetuate the values of the dominant ideology and mould the young into desirable citizens (see Chapter 7). In the previous chapter we noted Rochefort's irritation over the fact that her manuscript of *Le Repos* had been altered; the speech of the non-conformist Renaud was re-punctuated by the publishers. *Les Petits Enfants* represents the same politically-motivated desire to subvert standard language which is regarded by Rochefort as a tool and perpetuator of the dominant ideology. The juxtapositioning of standard, substandard, and hyper-standard language constitutes a break with the system, establishing the presence of a non-conformist voice. Rochefort creates her own language. Given this, talk of grammatical 'errors' itself becomes problematic: the hybrid 'écrit-parlé' is governed by its own rules. It is interesting to note that some sixteen years after the publication of *Les Petits Enfants*, the language of the text was causing some concern in certain circles. An article in a left-wing publication discussing the neutrality or otherwise of the state education sector cites a letter written by a secondary-school headmistress to one of her colleagues, in which she objects to the inclusion of *Les Petits Enfants* on the syllabus:

> Je crois de mon devoir de vous indiquer le danger qu'il y a, pour de jeunes esprits—en l'occurence les classes de 5eF—de leur proposer la lecture de Christiane de Rochefort [sic]. Le style et le vocabulaire ne sont pas de nature à enrichir et à améliorer ceux de ces jeunes enfants.[15]

> [*I believe it is my duty to point out to you to the potential danger to young minds—in this case the classes of 5eF—given Christiane de Rochefort [sic] to read. Neither the style nor the vocabulary is of a kind which is likely to enrich and improve the style or the vocabulary of these young children.*]

The headmistress may have had reservations about the text's edifying qualities, but there is little doubt that this is a work which appeals—in the sense of addressing itself—to a certain audience. As one commentator puts it: 'L'efficacité du message est "garantie" par l'héroïne-témoin, qui parle à la première personne et semble s'adresser, dans un ton familier et direct, à celles et à ceux qui, par leur âge et leur condition, sont proches d'elle' ['The effectiveness of the message is "guaranteed" by the heroine-witness who speaks in the first person and seems to address, in a direct and familiar tone, those of both sexes who are close to her in age and social status'].[16] Irrespective of their actual age and socio-political situation, readers are tacitly invited to take the place of a youthful and rebellious addressee akin to Josyane. Evidently some readers will be more compliant than others. If Josyane is selected as narrator, it is because she stands outside the system; as elected mouthpiece for the author, she is set up as the critical outsider and cynical observer of her environment. The narrator's attitude to multiple motherhood, fruit of the pro-natalist policy, is unambiguous; she consistently employs the pejorative term 'bonnes femmes' when referring to the women around her, and launches bitter and explicit attacks: 'Bon Dieu ce que j'aimais pas les bonnes femmes!' ['God how I disliked housewives!'] (120). Her disassociation from the female species, as she witnesses it, is clear. She is the knowing subject; the women are the objects of her critical distancing: 'je ne connais rien de plus inutile sur la terre que les bonnes femmes. Si. Ça pond' ['I don't know anything on earth more useless than housewives. No wait. They produce the odd kid'] (121).

No-one is spared from the global tirade: Josyane's mother is just one bloody fool among many: 'C'est comme Catherine, expliqua ma mère aux autres conasses' ['Just like Catherine, explained my mother to the other stupid cows'] (71). The narrator's attitude is set in opposition to that of the adults around her. Whilst her parents welcome the news of a new pregnancy ('les vieux étaient contents' ['the olds were happy'], p. 84), Josyane's awareness of the dehumanizing repercussions of the system of 'allocations' is expressed either directly—'cette Cité c'est pas de l'habitat c'est de l'élevage' ['this estate isn't a place to live in, it's a battery farm'] (85)—or via the sustained use of irony. If her parents are happy, it is because they will be able, thanks to the benefit system, to continue payments on a new car, thereby keeping up with the Jones's (or in this case the Mauvin family) who, after all, are already the proud possessors of 'un mixeur et un tapis en poil animal' ['a blender and an animal-skin rug'] (84). When a neighbour produces another son in a long line of male children, Josyane indicates the state's controlling role with typical savagery:

Elle fournirait au moins un peloton d'exécution à la patrie pour son compte; il est vrai que la patrie l'avait payé d'avance, elle y avait le droit. [. . .] Je pensais au jour où on dirait à tous les fils Mauvin En Avant! et pan, les voilà tous couchés sur le champ de bataille, et au-dessus on met une croix: ici tombèrent Mauvin Télé, Mauvin Bagnole, Mauvin Frigidaire, Mauvin Mixeur, Mauvin Machine à Laver, Mauvin Tapis, Mauvin Cocotte Minute, et avec la pension ils pourraient encore se payer un aspirateur et un caveau de famille. (86)

[It [the family] would at least provide the fatherland with its own platoon; true enough the fatherland had paid for it up front, it had every right to it. I thought of the day when the order would be given to all the Mauvin sons: Forward! and bang, there they all are lying on the battlefield, with a cross placed over each body: here fell Telly Mauvin, Motor Mauvin, Fridge Mauvin, Blender Mauvin, Washing-machine Mauvin, Carpet Mauvin, Pressure-cooker Mauvin, and with the war pension they'd still be able to buy themselves a vacuum-cleaner and a family vault.]

If Josyane has insight into the inhuman consequences of the 'allocations familiales', she is equally critical of the soulless 'grands ensembles'. Here, too, the narrator is represented as a lone voice crying not so much in the wilderness (which has been bulldozed) but in the concrete jungle. Apparently alone amongst her peers, Josyane is saddened by the irresistible encroachment of construction-work upon green zones: 'Il y avait un lilas dans les deniers jardinets que la Cité n'avait pas encore bouffés. Quand je revenais de l'école je le voyais, mais je ne disais rien, les autres filles se seraient payé de ma tête' ['There was a lilac tree in the last of the small gardens which the estate hadn't gobbled up yet. I saw it on my way back from school, but I didn't say anything because the other girls would have taken the mickey'] (36).

Rochefort uses humour—*Les Petits Enfants*, like the majority of the author's works, has the rare capacity to elicit genuine laughter from its readers—to reinforce her spokeswoman's point of view. Josyane ponders the wisdom of fencing off trees when the local louts merely make a game of destroying both enclosure and tree: 'ce que je me demande c'est pourquoi on ne fout pas plutôt les mômes dans les grillages et les arbres en liberté autour' ['what I want to know is why they don't shove the bloody kids in the enclosures and leave the trees outside in the open'] (80). Humour and irony are powerful tools. To get the joke, to detect the irony, is to understand, perhaps a first step towards agreement with the point of view put forward. Irony, however, has its drawbacks. An indirect condemnation can be read 'straight'. In the following description of the Bagnolet 'grand ensemble' the single word 'cauchemar' provides the only unambiguous signal that Josyane's depiction of happy families is indeed ironic:

Le soir les fenêtres s'allumaient et derrière il n'y avait que des familles heureuses, des familles heureuses, des familles heureuses, des familles heureuses. En passant on pouvait voir [. . .] les bonheurs à la file, tous pareils comme des jumeaux, ou un cauchemar. Les bonheurs de la façade ouest pouvaient voir de chez eux les bonheurs de la façade est. (81)

[*In the evenings the lights would come on in the windows and inside were nothing but happy families, happy families, happy families, happy families. When you went by you could see [. . .] row upon row of happy people, all identical, like twins or a nightmare. From where they sat the happy people on the west side could see the happy people on the east side.*]

Any doubt as to the irony of the description is dispelled later in the text when Josyane's attitude is expressed more directly by members of the communist Lefranc family:

—Si le bonheur consiste à accumuler des appareils ménagers et à se foutre pas mal du reste, ils sont heureux, oui! éclata Frédéric. Et pendant ce temps-là les fabricants filent leur camelote à grands coups de publicité et de crédit, et tout va pour le mieux dans le meilleur des mondes . . .
—Capitalistes, dit le père. (135)

[*'If happiness consists of accumulating household gadgets and not giving a damn about anything else, then yes, they're happy,' Frédéric shouted. 'Meanwhile the manufacturers churn out their tat with lots of publicity and credit and everything is for the best in the best of all possible . . .' 'Capitalist worlds,' finished the father.*]

Both of these passages foreground the issue of alienation. It is suggested that Josyane's parents, representative of the typical working-class family, lack insight into their condition, fail to see that they are the hapless victims of the system. We might justifiably ask whether Rochefort's work singles out the most appropriate targets: Josyane's condemnations and ironic onslaughts fall almost exclusively upon individuals, with little direct focus upon the state system itself. Equally, we might question the rights of a middle-class author to dictate the nature of true happiness to others. *Les Petits Enfants* won the Prix du roman populiste, but it also, as Thody points out, provoked some adverse comments from the Left, who criticized Rochefort for replicating stereotypes of the working-class.[17] Although Rochefort acknowledges that her position was a contentious one, she perhaps brushes off criticism a little too casually:

Une fois je suis allée débattre à Sarcelles sur Les Petits Enfants du Siècle. Les rencontres à ce propos en Grands Ensembles étaient souvent un peu chaudes. 'Quoi, vous venez nous balancer que nous ne sommes pas heureux? C'est bien vous les intellectuels tiens! Eh bien figurez-vous, à part quelques affaires de chasse d'eau nous sommes bien contents et de quoi vous mêlez-vous?' Allez donc répondre à ça. L'aliénation ne se connaît pas comme telle tra la la.'[18]

[*Once I went to take part in a discussion on Les Petits Enfants du siècle at Sarcelles. Meetings on this subject in the housing estates were always a bit heated. 'What, you come here to tell us just like that that we're not happy? Typical intellectuals! Well it just so happens that apart from the odd problem with the plumbing we're perfectly happy and what business is it of yours anyway?' Go on, answer that. People are never aware of their own alienation, blah blah blah.*]

In addition to the question of the rights or wrongs of the author's adopted stance, the representation of alienation in *Les Petits Enfants* raises certain problems with respect to textual inconsistency, or at least ambiguity. Although Josyane's function in the text is to serve as a clear-sighted critic of her elders and peers, there are occasions when the narrator's status is ambiguous. Rothenberg cites a particular passage, taken from Josyane's description of Sarcelles, which reveals the difficulty readers may face in attempting to identify the intentional source of irony in the text: 'Les boutiques étaient toutes mises ensemble, au milieu de chaque rectangle de maisons, de façon que chaque bonne femme ait le même nombre de pas à faire pour aller prendre les nouilles; il y avait même de la justice' ['The shops were all grouped together in the middle of each rectangle of houses, so that each housewife had to walk the same number of steps to get her pasta; there was even justice in the system'] (125). Stating that 'Rochefort's own view is quite clear' (the passage highlights the inhuman scale of Sarcelles), Rothenberg adds: 'this is one of a number of occasions where the author creates an ironical distance between herself and her character'.[19] Is Josyane represented as blind to the reality of the situation, a victim of the system, or does the pejorative 'bonne femme' signal her own critical distance? Josyane comments on the facilities available in the new housing development: 'un autre [chalet] en bois imitant la campagne était marqué: "Maison des Jeunes et de la Culture"; les Jeunes étaient dedans, garçons et filles, on pouvait les voir rire et s'amuser au grand jour' ['another mock-rural wooden chalet had a sign on it saying "Youth and Culture Centre", and there the Youth was inside, boys and girls laughing and having fun in broad daylight'] (125). Irony or praise on the part of the narrator? On this occasion the capitalization seems to signal Josyane's distance, as it does throughout the text. Thus we see her commenting on her father and brother Patrick idly watching television while she organizes a meal: '"Y va pas les avoir, dit le père à son Fils Aîné. /—Il a l'air d'une cloche," approuva Celui-Ci' ['"He's not going to beat them," said father to his Son and Heir / "He looks like a real twerp," agreed said Son and Heir'] (47); Josyane on the subject of her father's driving skills, 'papa conduisait comme un cochon [. . .] c'était une vieille traction ce qu'on avait, il disait que ça devait doubler tout, à cause de la Tenue de Route; la Tenue de Route ça devait être vrai, sinon avec papa elle n'y serait pas restée longtemps' ['daddy was a bloody awful driver [. . .] we had an old front-wheel drive and he said that it ought to be able to overtake anything because of its good Road Holding power; he must have been right about the Road Holding because otherwise with him driving, the car wouldn't have seen much of the Road'] (52).

If these examples seem to indicate that Josyane is to be regarded as the voice of irony, further instances of her appraisal of Sarcelles are more problematic: 'Ça c'est de l'architecture. Et que c'était beau!' ['That's what I call architecture. And it was so beautiful!'] (126). Attempts to analyse the apparently fluctuating narrative point of view—Josyane as spokeswoman for the author; Josyane as foil to the author's own irony—are further complicated by the fact that the focalization of the narrative shifts to embrace changes in Josyane's attitudes: descriptions and comments, in other words, may represent views which are subsequently superseded, a point underlined by repeated references to Josyane's growing up: 'ce qu'on peut être bête quand on est gosse' ['you can be really stupid when you're a kid'] (100); 'quand j'étais môme' ['when I was a kid'] (140). Josyane may initially be awe-struck by the scale of the 'grands ensembles', but awe later gives way to depression and distaste. As she states: 'les blocs d'en face ne me faisaient plus peur' ['the blocks of houses opposite didn't scare me any more'] (140). In an early description of Sarcelles, repetition alone signals opposition to the housing development:

> Sur des kilomètres et des kilomètres et des kilomètres, des maisons des maisons des maisons. Pareilles. Alignées. Blanches. Encore des maisons. Maisons, maisons, maisons, maisons, maisons, maisons, maisons, maisons, maisons, maisons, maisons, maisons, maisons. Maisons. Maisons. (124–5)

> [*Kilometre upon kilometre upon kilometre of nothing but houses houses houses. All the same. In a row. White. More houses. Houses, houses, houses, houses, houses, houses, houses, houses, houses, houses, houses, houses, houses, houses. Houses. Houses.*]

At this stage, the force of the repetition is ambiguous: it might indicate little more than amazement, or fear, on the narrator's part. Later in the text, however, Josyane's own position is clarified: 'je mourrais, seule au milieu des grandes maisons. Maisons, maisons, maisons, maisons. Comment vivre dans un monde de maisons?' ['I was dying all alone in the middle of huge houses. Houses, houses, houses, houses. How can you live in a world of houses?'] (141).

The narrative style of *Les Petits Enfants* is not as straightforward as it might at first appear. Readers not only have to distinguish between the narrator as subject or object of ironic pronouncements, they must also be alert to the author's innovative manipulation of complex forms of direct and indirect speech. In some cases, direct speech is used in a fairly straightforward manner. Rochefort, for instance, allows characters to condemn themselves out of their own mouths. In the third chapter of the text, which is given over to the Rouvier family holiday, the sheer length of the assembled fathers' endless exchanges on the subject of cars (the direct speech runs on with minimal narratorial intervention for several pages) combines with their mouthing of consumer clichés ('l'économie c'est bien mais la sécurité d'abord, dit papa' [' "economy's all very well but safety's what really counts", said daddy'] p. 65) to satirical effect. Josyane's distance from the others is clearly signalled in this instance by a simple framing device; the lengthy passage of direct speech is preceded by an ironic observation which effectively guides the reading: 'd'ailleurs les autres bonhommes étaient également des puits de science, ils étaient intarissables sur n'importe quoi' ['and besides, the other blokes were also founts of knowledge, they could talk endlessly about any subject'] (63).

On other occasions Rochefort combines direct and indirect speech, and does so in a rather less conventional manner:

> Je sais pas comment tu t'arranges disait le père, je sais vraiment pas comment tu t'arranges, et la mère disait que s'il n'y avait pas le PMU elle s'arrangerait sûrement mieux. Le père disait que le PMU coûtait rien l'un dans l'autre avec les gains et les pertes qui s'équilibraient et d'ailleurs il jouait seulement de temps en temps et s'il n'avait pas ce petit plaisir alors qu'est-ce qu'il aurait, la vie n'est déjà pas si drôle. Et moi qu'est-ce que j'ai disait la mère [. . .] (14)
>
> [*I really don't know how you do it, said father, I really don't know how you do it, and mother said that if it wasn't for the betting she would doubtless do it a lot better. Father said that the betting cost nothing in the long run what with his wins and losses which balanced out and anyway he only played from time to time and if he couldn't have that little pleasure in life what could he have and anyway life is no joke. And what about me, what have I got, said mother.*]

Various linguistic elements combine to subvert the speech (and attitudes) of Josyane's parents. A sense of endless bickering is conveyed by the incantatory repetition of the phrases 'disait le père'; 'le père disait'; 'disait la mère'; 'la mère disait'. The suppression of punctuation within the indirect speech ('que le PMU [. . .]') seems to mimic an endless litany of woes. The deliberate employment of the formal 'père' and 'mère', as opposed to the familiar 'papa', 'maman', emphasizes Josyane's distance from her parents. Rochefort breaks 'the rules' by removing quotation marks to introduce direct speech at the start of the text ('je sais pas comment tu t'arranges'), and by combining elements of direct speech ('d'ailleurs'; 'alors'; 'la vie n'est déjà pas si drôle') within the passage of indirect speech. The latter is itself unusually long, and lacks the expected markers of indirect speech, for example: 'et *que* d'ailleurs il jouait'. The narrator's distance is further emphasized by a framing remark which follows the extract: 'j'ai horreur des scènes' ['I hate scenes'] (15).

In the above passage the question of voice—who speaks?—remains unambiguous, but this is not always the case, as the following account of further holiday conversations reveals:

> La conversation se mit sur le boulot, chacun racontait le sien, on comparait les avantages et les inconvénients; ça s'animait. *Dommage que ce soit fini on commençait vraiment à s'y mettre hélas! les meilleures*

choses n'ont qu'un temps. D'ailleurs dans le fond on aime bien retrouver son petit chez-soi. On est content de partir mais on est content aussi de revenir. Les nouveaux débarquèrent pendant qu'on chargeait les paquets. (76, my italics)

[*The conversation turned to jobs, everyone talked about their own, they compared the advantages and the disadvantages; the conversation became animated. It's a shame it's over we were really beginning to enjoy it, ah well the best things in life never last. Besides at the end of the day it's nice to get back to your own little house. It's good to get away but it's good to go home as well. The latest arrivals disembarked while the luggage was loaded into the car.*]

The passage of what appears to be direct speech (marked out in italics), which again appears without the conventional quotation marks, comprises another series of clichés, uttered by the anonymous, because interchangeable, adults who surround Josyane. Although the framing of the direct speech and the sequence of tenses signal the narrator's distance, it is just possible to include Josyane in the impersonal 'on' ('on commençait vraiment à s'y mettre'), and thereby attribute the words to her, although her jaded attitude to holidays discourages such an interpretation. Similarly, with the following extract, which describes Mme Rouvier's ill-health and eventual decision to stop work, the reader must decide whether Josyane stands as part of the group ('on n'avait plus avantage' [. . .]), or comments upon it as an outsider:

Après la naissance de Chantal elle s'arrêta complètement, *d'ailleurs on n'avait plus avantage, avec le salaire unique, et surtout pour ce qu'elle gagnait, sans parler des complications avec la Sécurité à chaque Arrêt de Travail, et ce qu'elle allait avoir sur le dos à la maison avec cinq tout petits enfants à s'occuper,* ils calculèrent qu'*en fin de compte ça ne valait pas la peine, du moins si le bébé vivait.* (8–9, my italics)

[*After Chantal was born she stopped altogether, anyhow there wasn't any point any more, what with only one salary, and especially given the pittance she earned, not to mention the hassles with social security every time she stopped work and everything she was going to have on her plate at home with five small children to look after, they worked out that at the end of the day it wasn't worth it at least not if the baby lived.*]

Written in conventional free indirect speech, the italicized passage once again creates a powerful effect of mimicry. The reader is left to work out that the rather callous throwaway remark about the potential death of a child represents the point of view of Josyane's parents, and not the narrator herself.

Two further examples typify Rochefort's subtle manipulation of voice, and exemplify what Bakhtin labels a 'hybrid construction':

> What we are calling a hybrid construction is an utterance that belongs, by its grammatical (syntactic) and compositional markers, to a single speaker, but that actually contains mixed within it two utterances, two speech manners, two styles, two 'languages', two semantic and axiological belief systems.[20]

In both cases, statements made could, syntactically, be attributed either to the narrator or to her parents. Both examples typify the black humour of the work; both reflect a feckless inhumanity. In the first example Josyane comments on her brother's early delinquency: 'Il n'avait pas trois ans quand il mit un chaton dans la machine à laver; cette fois-là tout de même papa lui en fila une bonne: *la machine n'était même pas payée*' ['He wasn't even three years old when he put a kitten in the washing-machine; that time daddy gave him a good clout though: *the machine hadn't even been paid for*'] (20, my italics). On this occasion the familiar 'papa' is employed quite deliberately; Josyane is distanced from her father's callous stance (never mind the cat, what about the machine). This example typifies what Bakhtin refers to as 'pseudo-objective motivation': formal markers, in this case the presence of the colon, suggest that the logic of the sentence is the narrator's (Josyane's father clouts Patrick because he may have ruined the washing-machine), but in fact signal the belief system of another character.[21] The second example follows a similar pattern. Josyane comments on her twin brothers, whom the Rouvier parents believe are not in fact theirs (due to a hospital oversight!): 'Je savais que toute la question était de retrouver les vrais avant de lâcher ceux-là, pour conserver le chiffre, et *si les autres étaient morts c'était embêtant*' ['I knew that it was all a matter of finding the real ones before getting rid of the other ones, to keep the numbers right, and *it would be a real hassle if the other ones were dead*'] (93, my italics). Again, the casual inhumanity of the italicized passage might, syntactically, be attributed to either Josyane or her parents, although we assume that she does not in fact condone this attitude herself.

From what we have seen so far it can be suggested that with the exception of certain ambiguities surrounding irony, Josyane is a reliable narrator who takes a stand against the dehumanizing environment in which she lives. Readers of *Les Petits Enfants* are faced with a more intractable problem when it comes to the narrator's sexual relationships. Josyane has sex with Guido, a number of her peers, René, a married man, and finally Philippe. In at least some of these cases readers may find themselves reading 'against the grain', parting company with the narrator's standpoint (and with that of the author, implied or otherwise). Although the sexual scene which takes place between Josyane and the construction-worker Guido is by no means explicit, the physical situation, with Josyane standing against a tree and Guido on his knees, and the reference to the narrator's evident sexual pleasure—'à la fin il y eut une limite, je fus obligée de gémir' ['in the end there was a limit and I had to moan'](44)—seems to suggest that the couple are engaging in oral sex. There is no doubt that Josyane views her sexual experience with Guido in an unequivocally favourable light. This is, at least at face value, a fully consensual relationship: 'il levait les yeux vers moi et me posait une question, si je voulais bien [. . .]. je n'avais pas envie de l'empêcher, pas du tout et de moins en moins, à mesure que ses lèvres m'approchaient [. . .] alors pour un empire je ne l'aurais arrêté' ['he looked up at me and asked me if I really wanted to [. . .]. I didn't want to stop him, not at all and less and less as his lips came closer [. . .] I wouldn't have stopped him, not for all the world'] (44).

Guido, unlike Josyane's parents, treats her as a subject in her own right: 'il me parlait comme à une personne' ['he spoke to me as if I was a real person'] (38). Their brief relationship is characterized by mutual understanding. Josyane describes Guido to her young brother Nicolas as an alien being hailing from a distant land: 'Chez lui, tout le monde avait une âme, tout le monde se comprenait. Ici personne ne parlait à personne, les gens étaient enfermés dans leur peau et ne regardaient rien' ['Where he comes from everyone has a soul and everyone understands each other. Here no-one speaks to anyone, people are locked away inside themselves and never look at anything'] (40). In later chapters we shall see that Rochefort suggests that sexual experiences can lead to a raising of consciousness, an insight into the workings of oppression. Josyane's liaison with Guido is certainly portrayed as having a liberating effect. Returning to the Rouvier home after the scene with Guido, the narrator shows signs of rebellion against her role as household skivvy, refusing her mother's request that she help out in the kitchen: 'Finalement je lui dit merde. Elle était tellement peu habituée de ma part à ce genre de reparties, généralement réservées à Patrick, qu'elle en resta penaude' ['In the end I told her to stuff it. She was so unused to this sort of answering back from me—usually it was Patrick—that she just stood there sheepishly'] (47). Sex leads to a powerful 'prise de conscience'; for the first time Josyane realizes that there is more to life: 'Et penser que j'aurais pu vivre cent ans sans qu'un seul me fasse soupçonner qu'il y avait autre chose dans la vie que leur sacré râpé, le vermicelle et la Sécurité! Ah les vaches' ['And to think that I might have lived for a hundred years without a single person letting me see that there was more to life than bloody macaroni cheese and Social Security! God, the bastards!'] (48).

Everything in the text, in other words, seems to indicate that Josyane's sexual relationship should be interpreted in a positive light, a reading which is consistent with the author's extra-textual comments. As we shall see in subsequent chapters, Rochefort advocates consenting sexual relationships involving children. Responding to an interviewer's question asking whether she saw any link between a writer's own sexuality and her work, Rochefort refered approvingly to the sexual scene in *Les Petits Enfants*:

> Yes. I can say that lots of my fantasies appear in my books. The fantasy of relations between a little girl and a grown man who talks to her in *Les Petits Enfants du siècle*, for example. The kind of sexuality that doesn't go any further, doesn't go as far as what we usually call 'making love', but is expressed in caresses, caresses that are not mutual, where the man is on his knees. That is a fantasy: that particular caress and a little girl, outside, in the woods.[22]

And yet, in spite of textual signals, and the narrator's own stance, there can be little doubt that this incident will promote a sense of deep unease in readers. The last chapter of this study is given over to an analysis of Rochefort's *La Porte du fond* (1988), an exploration of the difficult subject of child abuse, and we shall see that there are close parallels between the two texts. Guido (whose role can be compared to that of the character Paul in *La Porte du fond*) is the only individual in *Les Petits Enfants* (with the possible exception of Josyane's young brother Nicolas) to show Josyane affection: 'Il me prit par la main. [. . .]. Personne ne m'avait jamais pris la main, et j'eus envie de pleurer' ['he held my hand [. . .]. No-one had ever held my hand before and I felt like crying'] (40). Guido's affection marks him out as a positive character, but studies of sexual abuse emphasize the fact that children often trade off sex for affection. And what are we to make of the narrator's age? Guido is, by Josyane's reckoning, about thirty years old. Although we have no explicit indication of her age, we do know that Josyane lies when she tells Guido that she is eleven (39), and we might safely assume that she raises rather than lowers her true age. Josyane agrees to sex, but is an eleven-year-old in a position to consent? The legal position is clear. According to the old Penal Code in operation at the time of the text's publication, Guido's advances would be condemned under section 331, 'attentats à la pudeur' ['indecent assault']. Engaging in a sexual act committed 'sans violence ni contrainte ni surprise sur la personne d'un mineur de quinze ans' ['committed with no

element of violence, coercion or surprise against a minor of fifteen years']
would incur a penalty of three to five years' imprisonment and a fine of
6,000F to 60,000F, or both.

Although readers may find themselves reading against the grain of the
text when it comes to Josyane's relations with Guido, their response to the
narrator's sexual liaisons with her peers are perhaps less problematic. Sex
in this instance takes place when Josyane is somewhat older (approximately fourteen), and with boys who are more or less her own age. Some
reservations may, however, remain. Readers may balk at the off-hand
descriptions of Josyane's sexual experiences, even though (or perhaps
because) these are often represented with some humour. For the most
part Josyane narrates events in a brisk, matter-of-fact tone. Although her
relationships culminate with her having sex with four boys when no other
girls turn up to a pre-arranged rendezvous, the narrator makes the point
that she has no regrets: 'c'était une belle nuit de juin. Chaude. Je ne la
regretterais jamais' ['it was a beautiful night in June. Warm. I would never
regret it'] (122). There are two dissenting voices in the text: that of the
young Nicolas ('Si j'étais grand, tu n'irais pas avec les garçons' ['If I was
grown up you wouldn't go with boys'] p. 110), and that of Ethel Lefranc
('pourquoi tu ne viens pas avec nous le dimanche, au lieu de traîner avec
ces types?' ['why don't you come with us on Sundays instead of hanging
around with that lot?'] p. 114), but for the most part Josyane's sexual
experiences remain free of any value-judgements.[23] Paradoxically, whereas readers may find themselves reading against the narrator's positive
portrayal of her relationship with Guido, it is the lack of response, the
very neutrality of the representation of Josyane's sexual relations with her
peers, which may provoke a response, as Thody's comments reveal:

> One would also have liked a book inspired, as it is, by the essentially
> moral idea that children are to be treated as people and not as a
> means of acquiring money, to do more than hint that there are other
> disadvantages to indiscriminate sexuality apart from being made
> pregnant by the nicest boy you know.[24]

For Josyane, sex represents both a way to while away time after she has
left school and, initially at least, a means of procuring transport in order
to seek out Guido (sex is exchanged for motorbike lessons). The narrator
strives, and fails, to repeat the (apparently) genuine feelings of
understanding and pleasure she had found with Guido (her attempts to
improve Didi's sexual technique clarify—should clarification be
required—the precise nature of the act carried out with Guido). The
potentially empowering symbol of the motorbike ('même une fille là-
dessus, ça se sent un homme' ['even a girl feels like a man when she's

riding one'] p. 124), which gives her literal and symbolic mobility, merely propels her to Sarcelles. The role-reversing quest fails; Josyane on her mechanical steed fails to find Guido.

If Guido is represented in a positive light, René, father of one of Josyane's classmates, provides a marked contrast: where the first relationship is characterized by reciprocity and trust, the latter is marred by hypocrisy and double standards. Josyane's narration of events is far removed from the neutrality which marked her assessment of her trysts with Didi and Joël. René suffers from a guilty conscience, but as Josyane points out with cool irony, his lust overcomes his scruples:

> Il était installé de tout son poids et arrimé à fond. 'Quand je pense que j'ai une fille de ton âge, quand je pense que j'ai une fille de ton âge, répétait-il, quand je pense que j'ai une fille de ton âge', et il n'y mettait pas moins de cœur. (116)

> [*He had all his weight on me, he was right inside me. 'When I think that I've got a daughter your age, when I think that I've got a daughter your age,' he repeated, 'when I think that I've got a daughter your age', and he went at it with no less enthusiasm.*]

Repetition on this occasion creates a powerful effect: René has sex with a minor to the rhythmic beat of his own hypocrisy. This is a man who bears all the hallmarks of bad faith, and, indeed, of the abuser who seeks to abnegate responsibility. Josyane, he suggests, coming out with the age-old cliché, was asking for it: 'tu ne devrais pas regarder les hommes comme tu fais, qu'est-ce que tu veux c'est ta faute aussi! Ils sont faibles les hommes, ils ne peuvent pas résister quand une fille les regarde comme tu fais. . .' ['you shouldn't look at men like that, what do you expect, it's your fault as well! Men are weak, they can't resist when a girl looks at them the way you do'] (117). A similar attitude is adopted by the abusive father in *La Porte du fond*. Josyane notes in passing that men prove to be more pleasurable than boys (apparently weight, not size, is what counts), but she ultimately knows where to draw the line, and throws René's double standards back in his face: 'je ne couche plus avec des pères de famille' ['I don't sleep with family men any more'] (119). In some respects the narrator appears to have the controlling role in her relations with René. Having sex with a married man is interpreted by her as an act of rebellion against the 'bonnes femmes', who label her a tart: 'je n'étais plus une bonne petite maman' ['I wasn't a real little mum any more'] (120). And yet, although the primary target of the narrative is René, the reader sees more than Josyane, whose options are limited indeed: young mum or tart, whore or Madonna, the traditional stereotypic alternatives remain in force.

Towards the end of the text Josyane records her discovery of True Love: 'Philippe. Mon amour. C'est peu à peu qu'on se mit à s'aimer' ['Philippe. My love. We fell in love little by litttle'] (147). Whilst the conclusion of *Les Petits Enfants* has all the ingredients of the traditional happy ending, complete with baby and marriage, Rochefort claimed that to read it in this manner was to misinterpret: 'On m'a reproché d'avoir fait une fin optimiste. Ha ha ha. C'est un roman d'épouvante si vous voulez savoir' ['People have rebuked me for giving it a happy ending. What a joke. It's a horror story if you really want to know']; 'Je me souviens quand j'ai commencé *Les Petits Enfants du siècle* [. . .] ce que j'étais optimiste: je croyais que Josyane allait finir rue Blondel' ['I remember when I started writing *Les Petits Enfants du siècle* [. . .] I was so optimistic: I thought Josyane would end up in the rue Blondel'].[25] The rue Blondel was (and is) a renowned red-light district in Paris. In *Les Stances à Sophie* (1963) Rochefort was to suggest that marriage is little more than an institutionalized form of (unpaid) prostitution: Josyane, it is implied, would be as well to make an honest living. Thody's expressed hope that the reference to the rue Blondel is no more than a throwaway remark is misguided: Rochefort's remark is serious, if deliberately provocative.[26] The famous final line of the text, 'je lui indiquai Sarcelles' ['I pointed to Sarcelles'], indicates that for all her horror of the 'grands ensembles', Josyane will be condemned to play out a repetition of her mother's life. Pregnant with her first child, the narrator is seen to echo her parents' concerns about missing the deadline for the 'allocations': 'à quinze jours on loupe la prime' ['we've only got a fortnight to get the bonus'] (7).

Further parallels signal the tragedy of repetition. As a young child, the narrator studies a photograph of her newly married mother on a motorbike, and marvels at the metamorphosis which has taken place: 'même en me forçant, je ne pouvais pas croire que c'était la même fille, sur le vélomoteur' ['even if I tried really hard I couldn't believe it was the same girl on the scooter'] (30). The reader is left to imagine a future generation gazing with the same wonderment at a photograph of Josyane as the inexorable cycle of generations is repeated.

If these pointers are not sufficient to undermine a 'happy ending' interpretation, then the parodic style which marks the narration of the great love affair certainly should be. Josyane's account might be drawn from any popular romance or women's magazine: 'Pourquoi, avec Philippe, rien que de marcher l'un près de l'autre, les doigts emmêlés, c'était quelque chose de merveilleux? Pourquoi lui? Et lui se demandait Pourquoi elle?' ['Why was it so wonderful with Philippe, even if we were just walking next to each other, our fingers entwined? Why him? And he wondered, Why her?'] (150). Or:

> C'était notre soleil. Notre aubépine en fleur, et il y eut notre violette, notre pousse de muguet, encore rien qu'une pointe verte à peine visible mais on la vit, c'était la première; la nôtre. La première du monde. A nous pour toujours. Ah! (152)
>
> [*It was our sun. Our hawthorn in full blossom, and there was our violet, our sprig of lily of the valley, still little more than a tiny green shoot, but we saw it, it was the very first, ours. The first in the world. Ours forever and ever. Ah!*]

And finally: 'Tous les trois pas on s'arrêtait pour se regarder. / "Jo . . . / — Philippe . . ."' ['We stopped every three steps to look at one another. / "Jo . . ." / "Philippe . . ."'] (152–3). The last of these examples may remind readers of another tale of misplaced love which has a far from happy ending: Flaubert's *Madame Bovary*. As their relationship heads towards consummation Emma and Rodolphe utter similar sentimentalities (a calculated ruse on the part of Rodolphe), and similar interjections: 'Emma! Emma! / —Oh! Rodolphe'.[27] In fact, a parallel between Emma and Josyane can be established earlier in the text. After the thrill of the Vaubyessard ball, Emma plunges into depression. Sitting by the window, a motif which is repeated throughout *Madame Bovary*, overcome by tedium vitae, she awaits an event—any event—which might stir her from her lethargy, as she numbly watches the villagers leaving the church.[28] Josyane, deserted by Guido, is left in a similar position. Mourning her lost childhood, when she, like her brother Nicolas, scribbled promises of rebellious future deeds on pieces of paper, Josyane can do no more than sit and wait: 'quand j'étais môme j'écrivais des trucs sur des bouts de papier. Plus maintenant. Je restais des heures devant la fenêtre en faisant semblant de coudre, à regarder tomber l'eau, et les gens entrer et sortir à la grille' ['when I was a kid I wrote stuff on bits of paper. Not any more. Now I sat at the window for hours pretending to sew, watching the rain fall, and people going in and out of the gate'] (140). Emma Bovary's ennui is emphasized in the passage alluded to above by the accelerated passage of time: a reference to spring—'le printemps reparut' ['spring reappeared']—is followed in the next sentence by the onset of summer: 'Dès le commencement de juillet' ['from the very start of July'].[29] A similar device is used in *Les Petits Enfants*: 'Le printemps arriva. L'été. Puis l'hiver' ['Spring arrived. Summer. Then winter'] (94); 'L'hiver passa. Le printemps revint' ['Winter passed. Spring returned'] (97). Time for Josyane, as for Emma, passes both painfully slowly and with all the rapidity which characterizes an inexorable process.

As we know, Emma Bovary was, during her convent years, a covert reader of romantic novels. At the age of fifteen, a 'vieille fille' provided her with unsuitable works: 'ce n'étaient qu'amours, amants, amantes [. . .] troubles de cœur, serments, sanglots, larmes et baisers' ['it was full of love and lovers [. . .] emotional turmoil, pledges of love, sobbing, tears and kisses'].[30] Commenting on the parodic style of the closing pages of *Les Petits Enfants*, Rothenberg suggests that Josyane too has been overly influenced by her reading-matter:

> It is not surprising that she is ready to abandon all her critical intelligence when her first real love affair presents an apparent escape, and she describes her relationship with Philippe in the sort of romantic novelette style which she might have picked up from her holiday reading.[31]

According to this reading, the narrator is no longer a reliable voice by the close of the text; she is to be regarded as an alienated victim of the system, with no critical distance on events. Whilst there is no doubting the validity of this reading, the text is in fact rather more ambiguous than Rothenberg's interpretation suggests. Josyane's apparent leap from ironic distance to passive lack of insight is perhaps a little hard to swallow. Are we invited to accept the fact that the narrator has effectively forgotten her mocking response to her 'holiday reading', which is sent up earlier in the text: 'L'héritière épousa le duc-fils, qui du coup n'était plus son frère, et ils eurent beaucoup de petits ducs' ['The heiress married the duke's son who was suddenly no longer her brother, and they had lots of little dukes'] (76)? Or that she has blanked out her ironic reflections on the trashy magazine love-stories Catherine read aloud to their ailing mother:

> Quand j'entrais dans la chambre avec le plateau à dîner j'entendais 'Mon amour ne me quitte pas je ne peux pas vivre sans toi!' ou 'Va-t'en femme perfide tu as gâché ma vie!' Le reste c'était pour moi, les basses besognes, durant que ces dames se livraient aux pures joies de l'esprit [. . .]. (144)

> [*When I went into her bedroom with the supper-tray I would hear: 'My beloved, don't leave me, I can't live without you!', or 'Quit my sight treacherous woman, you have destroyed my life!' The rest was left to me, the dirty jobs that is, while these ladies of the manor surrendered themselves to the pure pleasures of the mind.*]

Is Josyane deliberately mocking her own naive appraisal of her relationship with Philippe by employing the cloying vocabulary of the Mills and

Boon novel, or is she the brunt of Rochefort's irony? There are no simple answers to these or other similar questions. How are we to interpret the ironic interjection 'heureux' in the following passage, given that the word has, earlier in the text, been associated with Josyane's ironic stance?:

—Ma cherie. Tu es à moi?
—Oui.
—Pour toujours?
—Philippe mon amour.
—Jo ma cherie. Comme on va être heureux!"

'Heureux?'

'Et comment qu'on va être heureux' (156).

[*'Darling. Are you mine?'*
'Yes.'
'Forever?'
'Philip my darling.'
'Jo my sweet. How happy we shall be.'

'Happy?'

'You bet we're going to be happy.']

On this occasion the irony surely reads as the narrator's, as indeed it does when capital letters are employed: 'ce qui nous manquait à chacun, c'était l'Autre' ['what each of us lacked was the Other'] (151); 'Rien que nos Noms, ça contenait Tout' ['our Names alone said it All'] (153).[32] It is difficult to square an interpretation of Josyane as alienated object of the author's irony with ironic remarks which read as the narrator's own. Josyane continues to display a robust sense of humour, as her reported impatience to have sex with Philippe reveals: 'Depuis le temps aussi, qu'il m'avait planté sur mon seuil, en feu. Quatre jours. Une femme ne peut pas attendre' ['He left me standing on my doorstep burning with lust for ages. Four whole days. A woman can't wait'] (153). Is Josyane really duped by love or, rather, is she all too aware of her beloved's shortcomings? It is, after all, she who comments perhaps a little bitterly on Philippe's desire to father a child: 'Il me dit que chaque fois qu'il m'avait fait l'amour il y avait pensé. [. . .] ça le faisait jouir de me faire un enfant. Eh bien, il était fait, il n'avait pas joui pour rien' ['He told me that each time he'd made love to me he'd thought about it. [. . .] the thought of making me pregnant made him come. Well the deed was done all right, he hadn't come for nothing'] (158). Philippe, like Rodolphe, clearly has seduction in mind from an early stage, but whose irony is expressed in the following passage?: 'on s'étaient enroulés dans la couverture qu'il avait prise dans la voiture *à tout hasard je suppose*' ['we'd wrapped ourselves in the blanket he'd found in the car, *by chance I guess*'] (154, my italics). Josyane's husband-to-be, who wants a frilly cot, blue for a boy and pink for a girl, has all the traits of the conventional traditionalist, but is the ironic reference to his broad-mindedness to be read as the author's or the narrator's?: 'ce n'était pas pour le principe il s'en fichait il avait les idées larges, mais il voulait que je sois encore toute fine quand il sortirait de la Mairie, avec lui à mon bras' ['it wasn't a matter of principle he didn't give a damn about principle he was broad-minded, but he wanted me still to be slim when he came out of the town hall with me on his arm'] (158).

The ending of *Les Petits Enfants du siècle* is marked, some might say marred, by ambiguity. If we are to adhere to Rochefort's own interpretation, then we must accept that the concluding pages of the work were intended to represent a dramatic change in the text's narrator from ironic commentator to blind victim, duped by love: 'Non, finalement, "L'amour" (faux, illusoire) aura sa peau. Moi je constate avec tristesse la puissance de l'oppression par l'urbanisme. On nous confond souvent avec nos personnages' ['No, in the end "love" (false, illusory love) will get her. As for me, I just register with some sadness how powerful the oppression born of town planning can be. We're often confused with the characters we create'].[33] The implication is clear: Josyane's account of her love for Philippe should be read as a representation of the narrator's delusions; the irony and satire are Rochefort's.

As we have just seen, however, the text lends itself to another interpretation, one which establishes Josyane as the ironic subject who mocks her own infatuation. In fact, neither reading makes sense if we attempt to assess the text in terms of realism. We can decide to read the irony and satire as Josyane's. In this case, given that we are (apparently) dealing with a retrospective narrative, we are left in the absurd situation of having to project beyond the scope of the text, assuming that the speaking voice is located in some fictive future time and place, and that Josyane, although she married Philippe, somehow escaped alienation, found her voice, and told her ironic tale. Alternatively, we accept Rochefort's argument, in which case we are faced with the unrealistic proposition that Josyane suddenly loses all her critical acumen. And even if we are to accept that Josyane becomes a victim of oppression, the question of the location of the speaking voice remains. The answer, of course, is that the text simply cannot be judged in terms of realism. Josyane is not a 'realistic' character. She is, as the author herself pointed out (although she did not follow through with the literary implications), an amalgam: 'La petite Josyane, je suis liée à elle, par la compassion si vous voulez. Et je suis aussi derrière elle, en train d'essayer (?) les possibilités qu'elle a d'être sauvée' ['I'm linked to little Josyane, via compassion if you like. And I'm also behind her, trying out the various possibilities she might have of being saved']; 'In *Les Petits Enfants du siècle* the little girl who is the narrator (and myself at the same time) [. . .]'.[34] Rochefort might echo Flaubert's famous pronouncement: 'Josyane Rouvier, c'est moi' ['I am Josyane Rouvier']. Disillusionment with married life was to set in fast for Flaubert's heroine. In Rochefort's next work, *Les Stances à Sophie*, Céline, another first-person narrator, finds herself asking the same question as Emma Bovary: 'Pourquoi, mon Dieu, me suis-je mariée?' ['Why, dear God, did I ever marry?'] [35]

CHAPTER THREE

Les Stances à Sophie

> Dans une société où les maris sont la nuit si occupés par le vin et les danseuses, les femmes devaient fatalement se rapprocher et trouver entre elles la consolation de leur solitude. De là vint qu'elles s'attendrirent à ces amours délicates, auxquelles l'antiquité donnait déjà leur nom, et qui entretiennent, quoi qu'en pensent les hommes, plus de passion vraie que de vicieuse recherche.
>
> (Pierre Louÿs, *Les Chansons de Bilitis*)

Although *Les Stances à Sophie* (1963) takes its title from a bawdy, and extremely sexist, medical-school ditty about prostitutes, it also alludes to the wisdom gained by its protagonist, Céline.[1] By this stage we can detect a clear pattern of thematic concerns in Rochefort's work, and a marked development in narrative technique and style. Like *Le Repos du guerrier*, this is a text which explores the dynamics of an oppressive relationship. Once again, a bourgeois representative is set in opposition to a non-conformist, although this time it is a woman, the first-person narrator Céline, who takes the rebellious role. As was the case with *Les Petits Enfants du siècle*, the oppression of the individual is explored within a specific social framework, although Céline, unlike Josyane, is far from being a helpless victim of the system. Whereas *Les Petits Enfants* (according to one interpretation) ends with the projected marriage and apparent integration of the initially rebellious Josyane, *Les Stances à Sophie* charts the breakdown of a marriage, and represents an open critique of both the institution, and the capitalist, consumer society in which it functions. Céline, armed with an insight into the mechanisms of oppression, articulates all that her younger counterpart Josyane could merely fall prey to.

Les Stances proved to be another commercial success for Rochefort, selling in excess of 600,000 copies. In 1971 the novel was adapted for cinema under the direction of Moshe Mizrahi, with Bernadette Lafont and Bulle Ogier as Céline Rodes and Julia Bignon respectively; Michel Duchaussoy and Serge Marquand taking the male parts of Philippe

Aignan and Jean-Pierre Bignon. Rochefort acknowledged that this was the most autobiographical of her novels, and in this respect the work falls very much into a category of texts written by women in which 'the personal is political' stands as a central premise; texts in which those aspects of women's experience which had long been unwritten are given voice.[2] It also represents an early example of a feminist work which seeks to reveal and demystify the power of language, and in this, Rochefort, writing in advance of the 1968 watershed for French feminism, was ahead of her time.

As we saw in the previous chapter, the unhappy ending of *Les Petits Enfants* is sealed by pregnancy and marriage. It is also marked by the effacement of Josyane's point of view: in the closing pages of the text the narrator does little more than report Philippe's words. Although *Les Stances* brings a change of social milieu, from council housing estates (HLMs) and TV fitter (Philippe's job in *Les Petits Enfants*) to the 'jeune cadre' ['young executive'] (Céline's husband, also Philippe) and bourgeois 'intérieur', the novel could be said to begin where the earlier text left off. No sooner are marriage plans first aired than the 'love' between Céline and Philippe deteriorates into a battleground. In *Le Repos du guerrier* sexuality served as a site where socio-political battles were fought: to force Geneviève to submit, was, at least in Renaud's eyes, to score a point against the bourgeoisie. In *Les Stances* Philippe's primary aim is to effect a metamorphosis: the non-conformist Céline, who, like her counterpart Renaud, has no job and no family ties (and unlike Geneviève, has a history of sexual encounters), must become the perfect bourgeois wife, Mme Aignan. As Philippe reveals with typical pragmatism: 'si j'ai une femme c'est pour sortir avec' ['I have a wife so that I can be seen with her'] (89). This battle, however, will be sited in the world of words: to speak or to remain silent; to be silenced. Marriage for Céline is rapidly dubbed 'Carmel', a silent religious order in which Philippe assumes the role of deity: words of wisdom issue from his mouth ('Sa bouche'); crossing him (Him) is to elicit the wrath of God: 'son regard se détourne de moi; le soleil se voile, la terre s'obscurcit' ['he turns his gaze away from me; the sun is eclipsed, darkness falls upon the face of the earth'] (19).

Love, as we know, is blind, but once Céline marries it must also be dumb. As she points out early on: 'le malheur c'est que du fait qu'on dispose de la parole on est constamment tenté de la prendre; alors que ce serait tellement plus malin de se taire' ['the problem is that because we can speak, we are constantly tempted to do so, when it would be so much smarter to keep quiet'] (26). The reader must remain alert to the double voice which characterizes the narrative throughout the text. Céline's statement can and must be read on several levels. From Philippe's point of view, though he might not be ready (or able) to admit it, the claim is to be taken at face value: Céline should either agree with him and all that he represents, or keep quiet. For the Céline who thinks she is in love, and who values Philippe's presence above her own autonomy and freedom of expression—the Céline who starts out as naive as Josyane and who has yet to perceive the oppressive workings of society—the necessity for silence must also be read 'straight'. But from the point of view of the retrospective narrator Céline, the statement can only be ironic: as will become clear, speaking out becomes the only viable alternative to a complete loss of identity.

In the sado-masochistic world of *Le Repos du guerrier* physical violence is secondary to emotional power-plays, although it remains a permanent threat and exists as a muted presence throughout. In *Les Stances* we witness an escalation of the physical force exerted by Philippe as an occasional alternative to verbal coercion, an assertion of his will brought to bear whenever Céline distances herself from the role of ideal wife. Showing all the characteristics of the bully, Philippe browbeats Céline until she acts in such a way as to allow him to adopt a stereotypic male protective role; 'feminine' tears are his reward, just as Geneviève's sexual submission was Renaud's prize. As Céline comes to realize: 'il a puisé de nouvelles forces dans le constat de ma faiblesse' ['he's drawn new strength from his awareness of my weakness'] (23). A show of 'unladylike' drunkenness at the wedding reception triggers the first of many acts of physical violence as Philippe wrenches Céline from the scene—'il doit confondre un peu de vent dans les voiles avec la polio; il me fait mal' ['he must be confusing a little tipsiness with polio; he's hurting me'] (55)— and shoves her into the car 'avec une brutalité qui appelait, de la part d'une moins lâche que moi, la paire de gifles' ['with a brutality which was asking for a slap in the face from someone less cowardly than me'] (60). Seven years before *Les Stances* was published, the link between marriage and the pressures to conform brought to bear on women had already been articulated by Rochefort in *Cendres et or*. When Jacques proposes marriage to the protagonist Juliette, she is quick to refuse the enslavement and potential reprisals such a bond would represent: 'Tant qu'on joue vôtre jeu, c'est le paradis. Mais si l'esclave se révolte, vous devenez méchant' ['As long as we follow your rules it's paradise. But if the slave revolts, you turn nasty'] (CO, 68).[3]

Any assertion of autonomy on Céline's part is punished. When she develops an interest in tapestry-work, and later in painting, Philippe's objections clearly extend far beyond his concern for monetary outlay. At first sight such a reaction may seem incongruous: do needlework and amateur canvases not constitute stereotypic feminine pastimes? Significantly, Rochefort comments on her own rehabilitation as a creative artist within her marriage: 'I stopped writing when I was married. I couldn't even talk, really, for weeks. Finally I began to paint, and I painted a portrait of myself in oil.'[4] This initial step was to be superseded by writing itself—and divorce. Rochefort suggests that only when free from pressures to conform to a socially-imposed female role can true self-expression take place: 'I think there is a connection between the refusal of one's role as a woman and writing.'[5] A strikingly similar sentiment is expressed by another writer who was to come to prominence several years later. In *Autrement dit*, a work co-authored by Annie Leclerc and Marie Cardinal, the latter states: 'Si je veux entrer dans le jeu de la féminité il faut que je compose un personnage, il faut que je m'abandonne pour trouver la femme. Donc je ne suis plus libre, donc je ne peux plus écrire' ['If I want to play along with the idea of femininity I have to construct a character, I have to abandon myself in order to find the woman. So I'm no longer free, so I can no longer write'].[6]

For Céline, both tapestry and painting, undertaken with 'une passion ravageuse' ['an all-consuming passion'], represent a first move towards self-expression and an attempt to break with the Mme Aignan role, the 'jeu' or indeed 'je' of 'féminité': it is no coincidence that her first tapestry depicts not a decorative rosebush, as her mother-in-law recommends, but the temptation scene from the Garden of Eden (a scene which was to take on a key role in *Archaos*; see below, Chapter 6). Renaud sought to humiliate Geneviève by displaying her breasts to his fellow-drinkers; Philippe achieves a similar effect when he shows Céline's amateur paintings to an art dealer, and does so with his customary violence, seizing the canvas from her hands 'd'un mouvement brutal' ['brutally'], showing 'une détermination violente' ['a violent determination'] (186). By the close of the text, Céline can stand clear of the destructive dynamic and articulate it in a parting letter to Philippe: 'Je ne vois pas que tu aies à souffrir de la perte d'une personne dont tu n'aimais rien, sauf la défaite' ['I don't see how the loss of someone you loved only inasmuch as you could defeat her can cause you suffering'] (246).

For Rochefort, class-conflict pivots around a commandeering of language; the ultimate aim of the dominant class is the silencing of potentially subversive parties: 'tous leurs mots, tous les mots employés par l'oppresseur, n'ont qu'un unique et seul sens; c'est: "Vous, tenez-vous tranquille", "ne venez pas nous déranger", "vous avez des caprices, vous avez des envies d'originalité, vous êtes folles, hystériques"' ['everything they say, every word uttered by the oppressor, has a single solitary meaning: "You there, keep quiet", "don't come bothering us", "you have tantrums, you want to be different, you're crazy, you're hysterical"'].[7] Representing the dominant ideology, Philippe exemplifies just such a strategy, although there is nothing subtle about his approach. Céline's attempts to discuss his and his colleague Jean-Pierre's respective government posts 'à la Décentralisation' and 'au Regroupement' (a typical snipe at bureaucracy on Rochefort's part), are foreclosed by a blank denial of the validity of her position: 'n'y faites pas attention c'est une maniaque' ['just ignore her, she's crazy'] (88). A discussion with the Aignan clan on the market economy is similarly curtailed—'tu dis un peu n'importe quoi ma chérie' ['you're talking nonsense, my dear'] (74)— whilst Céline's interests are disregarded: 'toi et tes westerns c'est une vraie manie' ['you and your westerns, you're really obsessed'] (151); 'tu sais Céline je crois que tu es vraiment folle' ['you know, Céline, I think you're quite mad'] (159). A desire to take the wheel in Philippe's new car (to get in the driving seat) is met with apparent incredulity: 'qu'est-ce que tu as Céline en ce moment? Jamais je ne t'ai vue capricieuse comme ça!' ['what's got into you Céline? I've never seen you perverse like this'] (140). Any signs of life are written off as symptoms of potential mental disturbance: '—Qu'est-ce que tu as Céline ces temps-ci? / Moi? Je vais très bien. / —Tu es nerveuse, agitée' ['"What's got into you Céline?" / "Me, I'm perfectly all right" / "You're nervous, jumpy"'] (150). If Céline is not dismissed as half-crazed, then her point of view is subjugated to her physical condition: excessive argument during the wedding lunch can be explained by over-excitement: 'tu es déjà suffisamment énervée' ['you're quite over-excited enough'] (53); an outspoken attack on consumerism is conveniently put down to exhaustion: 'ce doit être la fatigue' ['she must be tired'] (71).

Philippe's discursive interaction with Céline, like the dynamic of sado-masochism, is marked by opposition with no possibility of a third term, no opportunity for compromise or dialogue. We might say that Philippe's ultimate aim, translated into verbal terms, is the monologue. His initial success in this is emphasized in the opening pages of the text by a paratactic run-on technique which accumulates imperatives and stresses Céline's non-participation:

> Tiens ta fourchette dans l'autre main, ne ris pas comme ça c'est vulgaire, ne fais pas des boulettes c'est sale, tiens-toi droite, tu fumes trop tu te noircis les dents, ne bois pas tant ce n'est pas bien pour une femme, tu n'as pas bonne mine tu devrais voir un docteur, Pourquoi ne cherches-tu pas un vrai travail au lieu de faire trente-six choses qui ne te mènent à rien, ton insouciance me navre, où te conduira-t-elle, tu te ruinera la santé avec tous ces cafés-crème, Promets-moi que demain tu te coucheras à minuit, pour me faire plaisir, disait Philippe, si tu le fais pas pour toi fais-le au moins pour moi, je me demande ce que tu fabriques au milieu de cette bande de ratés, qu'est-ce que tu leur trouves? (11–12)

[*Hold your fork in the other hand, don't laugh like that it's vulgar, don't play with the bread it's dirty, sit up straight, you smoke too much your teeth are turning black, don't drink so much it's not nice for a woman, you don't look well you should see a doctor, Why don't you look for a real job instead of doing a hundred and one things which get you nowhere, your casual attitude is breaking my heart, where will it lead you, you'll ruin your health drinking all that coffee, Promise me that you'll go to bed at midnight tomorrow, just to please me, said Philippe, if you won't do it for yourself at least do it for me, I really wonder what you're playing at with that bunch of losers, what do you see in them?*]

The desire for a single voice or monologue also manifests itself in an emphasis on logic, where the logical is equated once again with Philippe's point of view. Céline's objections to having to attend confession prior to the wedding ceremony on the grounds that she does not believe in a Christian God are met with the statement:

Mais ma chère amie voyons sois un peu logique: ou tu n'accordes aucune importance à ces choses-là comme tu le prétends et par conséquent il t'est indifférent de mettre les pieds comme tu dis dans une église, ou bien, si cela ne t'es pas indifférent, c'est que tu accordes de l'importance et en ce cas cesse de jouer les esprits forts. (40)

[*But my dear girl, come now, try and be logical: either you think these things are totally unimportant, as you claim, in which case going to church means nothing to you one way or another, or else, if you're not indifferent, then I have to assume you think it is important, in which case stop claiming to be rational.*]

Céline's ethical stance is deformed by Philippe, who translates her perfectly logical proposition into an apparent contradiction. The original statement becomes a binary opposition supported by rhetorical appeals— 'comme tu le pretends'—which effectively put words into her mouth. A similar pattern emerges later in the text when Céline decides, 'histoire de rire un peu' ['for a laugh'], that she requires a piano. On this occasion Philippe is blind (deaf) to the irony of Céline's reasoning. Deliberately drawing on consumer clichés culled from magazines such as *France-Femme* (which Philippe is only too happy to see her read), Céline first argues her claim on aesthetic grounds—'un appartement sans piano ce n'est pas complet. Ce living appelle un piano' ['a flat without a piano is just not complete. This living-room is crying out for a piano']—before insisting that if a piano is to be bought at all, it may as well be a good (expensive) one so that she can play it. Philippe, typically, can only resort to a lame reiteration of his monologic position: 'enfin Céline tu n'as aucune logique' ['really Céline, you're completely illogical'] (158).

Céline's analysis of the speech patterns which surround her draws attention to the fact that Philippe's inability to engage in dialogue is typical of his social group:

> L'un mettons dit Blanc (peu importe le sujet, un film, les Russes, la question n'est pas là); l'autre dit Noir. Blanc parle, Noir attend; pas la conclusion: un creux, alors il s'y précipite en boulant sa phrase. Blanc n'écoute pas: il surveille Noir pour ne pas louper le moment où il fera un creux [. . .] afin de s'y ruer à son tour et se mettre à parler. (123–4)

> [*Let's say one of them says White (the subject isn't important—it could be a film, the Russians—that's not the issue); the other one says Black. White talks, Black waits; not for the conclusion, for a gap, then he rushes in tripping over his words. White doesn't listen: he watches Black so that he doesn't miss the moment when White leaves a gap [. . .] so he can rush in in turn and begin to speak.*]

Not only do Céline's observations point to the egocentrism which accompanies the monologic stance—she notes that individual utterances typically open with an incantatory 'moi je'—they also reveal the ambiguous status of individuals within society: the 'moi je' assertion of subjectivity is commonly succeeded by a stream of consumer clichés: 'Car ce qu'il y a de remarquable c'est qu'une fois placé le Moi Je ils répètent mot pour mot ce qu'ils ont piqué à l'extérieur, contenu, syntaxe et vocabulaire' ['Because the amazing thing is that once they've come out with the Me I they repeat verbatim something they've picked up elsewhere, content, syntax, and vocabulary included']. Those so eager to speak are spoken through by the dictates of society; their speech may be little more than an act of ventriloquism. As Céline points out at the close of the text, Philippe is 'à la fois un rouage inconscient, et un exécuteur' ['both an unthinking cog and an agent'] of 'la Machine' (246).

The oppression operating at the microcosmic level of the couple is seen as symptomatic of a capitalist consumer society in which market forces command, and in which all aspects of social interaction fall prey to economic considerations. The importance of language is stressed throughout, and perhaps best exemplified by one of several set-pieces in the text, an episode which opens with a typically humorous gnomic pronouncement: 'Qui n'a jamais de sa vie choisi des doubles rideaux ne peut pas savoir. On n'y resiste pas. On se croit fort, mais les doubles rideaux sont encore plus forts' ['Anyone who has never chosen lined curtains simply has no idea. You can't win. You think you're strong, but the curtains are even stronger'] (67).[8] Céline expands on her abortive shopping trip, developing her account into an open critique of the mechanisms of a society which dictates needs to its consumers. Language becomes once more a mediator and a tool: Philippe's mother-in-law and an eager shop-assistant 'ont la même syntaxe' ['share the same syntax'], and Céline notes that she herself is all too susceptible to consumer-talk: 'la couleur; le tissu; la tombée du tissu (on se met à employer de ces mots!)' ['the colour, the fabric, the way the fabric hangs (you begin to use these kinds of words!)']. Her desperate search for plain curtain fabric is thwarted by a mind-set enslaved to the restrictive spell cast by names and labels: 'Ils [les gens] ne savent plus ce que c'est qu'une chose, ils savent seulement ce que c'est qu'un nom' ['People don't know what things are any more, they only know what names are'] (69). Her decision to use 'doublure' (lining) instead is met with horror. The word defines and delimits the function of the object: lining is for lining. Céline feels that she is trapped in 'la prison du verbe' ['the prison-house of language'], silenced by society just as she is by Philippe. As she notes, 'c'est de la dictature' ['it's tyranny'] (68).

Just as Mme Aignan speaks the language of consumerism, so her son's discourse reveals his own economic preoccupations. Céline is urged to go through with the prenuptial confession for the sake of logic, but also because, as Philippe points out, 'c'est même payé' ['it's even been paid for'] (40). Money infiltrates his speech, whether he is encouraging Céline to change her appearance—'cela ne devrait pas te coûter' ['it shouldn't put you out/cost you anything'] (10)—or suggesting that the so-called sexual liberation of women may be exploited by certain unscrupulous men: 'pour eux c'est bien pratique et quelle économie' ['it's very convenient for them, and what a saving'] (11). As the text progresses, marriage is increasingly revealed to be based on economic foundations. Céline is quick to see that if Philippe is prepared to spend vast sums of money for her extravagant dinner parties it is because 'ça rapporte. Ce n'est pas de la dépense c'est du placement' ['it's profitable. It's not an expenditure, it's an investment'] (123). The good service of an obedient wife has its own exchange value: compliance can be purchased with a mink coat or string of pearls. Céline, in ironic mode, considers patenting a 'Noce de Fourrures' ['Fur Coat Anniversay'] or 'Noce de Perles' ['String of Pearls Anniversary'] (130). Physical violence can be bought off, a piano for a slap in the face. In exchange for services rendered in the advancement of Philippe's political career, Céline procures herself a car: after all, as she states with a healthy dose of irony, 'tout se paye' ['everything has its price'] (232).

Once again we can find echoes of *Les Stances* in Rochefort's *Cendres et or*. Juliette's wealthy husband Etienne may buy her a mink coat, but by the close of the text she has learned the high price which must be paid. Leaving Etienne a parting letter just as Céline does before walking out on Philippe, Juliette conveys the lesson which she has learned: material comfort, 'ce que vous m'offrez de sécurité, de confort, de luxe' ['what you give me in the way of security, comfort, and luxury'], is the market-price for a pretty wife ('mon apparence pour vous flatteuse, je crois' ['my looks, which are good for your image']). Marriage, seen in these terms, is little more than prostitution: 'Le nom que "cela" porte, je l'ai compris ce soir' ['This evening I've realized what "it" is called'] (CO, 182). Earlier in the same text a similar sentiment emerges in a conversation between Juliette and a previous partner, Alain:

> —Pourquoi faut-il, au fait, épouser? poursuivit Juliette, se parlant à elle-même.
> —Tu as raison, dit Alain. [. . .] A quoi servons-nous dans la vie des femmes, si elles ne veulent pas être des prostituées? Il faudrait que nous soyons des hommes, au moins. . . et nous sommes devenus des machines à gagner de l'argent. (CO,173–4)[9]

> [*'Why do people have to get married,' continued Juliette, talking to herself. 'You're right,' said Alain. [. . .] 'If women don't want to be prostitutes, what purpose do we serve in their lives? We should be real men at least . . . and we've become money-making machines.'*]

Three years after the publication of *Les Stances*, Godard's *Une ou deux choses que je sais d'elle* (the 'elle' refers to 'la région parisienne') showed married women from the 'grands ensembles' prostituting themselves whilst their husbands worked. Women, like consumer goods, have their own exchange value. Underlining the connection, the film ends on a close-up of various brightly packaged household products.[10] The apparent love which initially exists between Céline and Philippe is ultimately likened to an institutionalized form of prostitution. Marriage, in Céline's dictionary of terminology (more of which later), becomes: 'A: pour une femme; consécration totale à la vie domestique, avec service de nuit. B: pour un homme; être content avec ça' ['A: for a woman, devotion of one's whole life to domesticity, with night-service included. B: for a man; being happy with that situation'] (221). Almost a century earlier, Engels had pointed to the connection between monogamous marriage and the emergence of capitalism. According to *The Origins of the Family, Private Property and the State*, men and women in marriage stand as bourgeois and proletariat. Within a system of capitalist production, marriage is an economic unit with nothing to do with 'individual sex love'; a unit which:

> turns often enough into the crassest prostitution—sometimes of both partners, but far more commonly of the woman, who differs from the ordinary courtesan in that she does not let out her body on piece-work as a wage worker, but sells it once and for all into slavery.[11]

Céline's world-weary exposition of marriage to Stéphanie expresses a similar sentiment:

> Je conclus enfin, compte tenu des inconvénients, au moins égaux à celui aux pièces, du travail à forfait, qu'en fait de putasserie, la plus sûre, la moins fatiguante, à condition de l'aborder avec un bon esprit, c'est-à-dire strictement pratique, c'est encore le ma- (196–7)

> [*In the end I came to the conclusion that given the disadvantages, which are at least as great as those involved in doing piecework, or flat-rate work, that as far as whoring around goes, the safest, the least tiring option, as long as you approach it with the right attitude, that is strictly pragmatic, is still ma-*]

The equation of marriage with prostitution is taken to its logical conclusion when Philippe, seeking to secure a post as a right-wing MP, gives Céline unlimited funds in order that she might dress to impress. When she returns triumphant, having organised several private rendez-vous with the very people Philippe sought to win over, he is somewhat aggrieved. Having one's own logic brought into the open is clearly an uncomfortable experience: 'on envoie sa femme putasser avec quatre cent milles balles sur le cul et puis après on voudrait [. . .] que ça s'appelle autrement. Maintenant il l'a dans le baba' ['you send your wife out whoring with four hundred thousand bloody francs' worth of clothes on her back then you want to call it something else. So now he's pissed off'] (240).

Clearly love and marriage do not go together in *Les Stances*, but does Rochefort offer any affirmative images of relationships to counter the bleak battle of the sexes and classes represented by Céline and Philippe? The answer is yes, and the two principal relationships in question, one sexual, the other not, are formed between women: Céline and Julia, Jean-Pierre's wife; and Céline and Stéphanie, Philippe's younger sister. Drawing on a rather eclectic series of ideas, Céline expresses a number of different philosophies concerning love and sexuality, the first of which emerges in a conversation with Julia, in which Céline sketches out an almost pantheistic, mystical view of sexuality. 'Jouir' ['experiencing sexual pleasure'], she states, requires inspiration, and this inspiration is to be drawn from the context in which sexual relations takes place. Human relationships are described by Céline in terms of fragments ('morceaux') which can only contribute to a higher, transcendent perfection—'faire un tout' ['make a whole'] (116)—when other factors are brought into play: 'Je mélange avec d'autres trucs, le paysage, le temps qu'il fait, une chanson qu'on joue au même moment. Ça arrive à faire un tout. C'est mystérieux tout ça. Une fois j'ai fait l'amour avec la lune' ['I mix it up with other things, the countryside, the weather, a song being played at the same time. And it makes a whole. These things are mysterious. Once I made love with the moon'] (116). This view is later reiterated in an exchange with Stéphanie:

> La perfection est au ciel et sur la terre il n'y a que des petites lueurs dispersées et c'est ça l'amour des hommes mais c'est la chose la plus merveilleuse du monde surtout si en même temps il fait beau et si le vin est bon et il faut faire l'amour avec la lune par lueur interposée. (197)

> [*Perfection is in the heavens and on earth there are only little scattered glimmers of light and that's human love but it's the most wonderful thing in the world especially if the weather's fine and the wine's good and you have to use the light to make love with the moon.*]

A similar sentiment, in which human relations are closely linked to surrounding natural phenomena, had already been introduced in *Les Petits Enfants du siècle*: Josyane's sexual relations with Guido take place out of doors, amidst trees and birdsong; the narrator later reflects on the importance of the natural setting in her relationship with Philippe:

> Il nous fallait la Nature, en définitive. Je me demande même si au fond ce n'était pas la Nature qui faisait tout, c'est difficile à dire, je ne peux pas aller jusqu'à prétendre que je me faisais baiser par les étoiles mais il y a de ça. (149)

> [*In fact we needed Nature. I even wonder if when it comes down to it it wasn't Nature that did everything, it's hard to say, I can't go so far as to claim that I was screwed by the stars, but there's something of that in it.*]

Céline's comments on love may be somewhat abstruse, but what is clear is a marked difference in attitude from that expressed by Philippe, who

70

labels and condemns her previous sexual relationships as mere promiscuity. On two occasions he asks Céline what these relationships have left her with. The first time, eager not to displease, she states quite simply 'rien' (28). But later, when she recalls Philippe's question, the original statement is revised, though significantly the new version is not communicated to Philippe:

'Et peux-tu me dire ce qu'il t'en reste?' Eh bien il m'en reste les villes; des musiques du vin des odeurs des couleurs des sons des lumières; il nous en reste la vie même. Ce qu'on est. Plus autre chose, qu'on avait pas avant, et qu'on entrevoit que si on s'est fait suffisamment culbuter dans l'âge propice. Quelque chose à propos de l'amour même, et qui l'élargit quelque peu. (64)

[*'And what have you got to show for it?' Well I've got the cities; music wine smells colours sounds lights life itself. What we are. And something else as well, something we didn't have before, and that we only glimpse if we've been screwed enough at the right age. Something to do with love itself, something which expands love a little.*]

Although this remains somewhat opaque, the concept of an opening out to experience, and the emphasis on a form of transcendent communion with the world, is reminiscent of concepts of female sexuality, 'jouissance', articulated by Cixous and popularized in Annie Leclerc's *Parole de femme* (1974).[12] In many respects, Philippe typifies Leclerc's vision of a male mind-set centred on linearity, the project, conquest and possession: 'ça te mène à quoi?' ['where is it getting you'] is, after all, one of his favoured questions. We might also note that Leclerc's tendency to link male values with death and female values with life (a simplistic binary opposition which serves a largely rhetorical purpose in her text) is echoed in *Les Stances* in Céline's condemnation of a capitalist system perceived to be run by, and for, men: 'la Machine [. . .] qui est, pour nous qui respirons encore, un instrument de mort' ['the Machine which for those of us still breathing is an instrument of death'] (246).

Céline's views can also be linked to the work of the philosopher Marcuse, whose critiques of capitalist society gained an almost cult following in the counter-culture of the 1970s. In *One-Dimensional Man*, Marcuse suggests that the onset of mechanization has effectively altered modes of sexuality, reducing the scope of libido, barring it from previous means of realization. Pre-technical society had a 'landscape', a medium of libidinal experience, which has vanished from contemporary society:

With its disappearance (itself a historical prerequisite of progress), a whole dimension of human activity and passivity has been de-eroticized. The environment from which the individual could obtain pleasure—which he could cathect as gratifying almost as an extended zone of the body—has been rigidly reduced. Consequently the 'universe' of libidinous cathexis is likewise reduced. The effect is a localization and contraction of libido, the reduction of the erotic to sexual experience and satisfaction. For example, compare love-making in a meadow and in an automobile [. . .]. In the former case[s], the environment partakes of and invites libidinal cathexis and tends to be eroticized. Libido transcends beyond the immediate erotogenic zones [. . .]. In contrast, a mechanized environment seems to block such self-transcendence of libido. Impelled in the striving to extend the field of erotic gratification, libido becomes less 'polymorphous', less capable of eroticism beyond localized sexuality [. . .].[13]

Sexuality, in other words, can and should extend beyond the limited zone of genital activity. As Céline and Josyane put it (see above), in rather lyrical terms, 'il faut faire l'amour avec la lune'; 'je ne peux pas aller jusqu'à prétendre que je me faisais baiser par les étoiles mais il y a de ça'. Some two decades after the publication of *Les Stances*, Rochefort expressed a very similar view:

La sexualité n'est pas la génitalité, on confond souvent. Le sexe est partout. Quand je suis au milieu d'un vol de martinets par exemple, j'éprouve une sensation physique et sensuelle: pas génitale, mais sensuelle.[14]

[*Sexuality isn't genital sex; the two are often confused. Sex is everywhere. For example when I'm in the midst of a flight of swifts I experience a physical and sensual feeling: it's not genital, but sensual.*]

Céline's first observations on love and sexuality are subsequently expanded upon in her exchanges with Stéphanie, and on this occasion she employs explicitly platonic terminology: 'le Dieu mon cher Phèdre est dans celui qui aime' ['the God, my dear Phaedrus, is in the one who loves']. The lover perceives the divine 'à travers son incarnation' ['via its incarnation'] thereby gaining access to a higher realm: 'la passion est le Chemin de la Connaissance' ['passion is the route to knowledge'] (199). The *Phaedrus* perhaps more than any other of Plato's dialogues points to passion as a gateway to a transcendent reality. Via the sensory apprehension of beauty, reminiscent of the Forms known to the soul before its fall and incarnation, lovers may regrow their wings and ascend towards the realm of Forms, the only true reality.[15] Clearly Céline's reading of Plato is a rather idiosyncratic one; certainly the *Phaedrus* does not suggest that 'se faire culbuter' could lead to an enlightenment

72

experience! As Céline herself says at one point of her interpretation: 'C'est Platon, modifié Rodes 1963, Paris' ['It's Plato, revised by Rodes: Paris, 1963'] (200).

Whilst in some respects her relationship with Stéphanie does have what might loosely be termed platonic elements, for example the mentor/pupil relationship, the knowledge gained by Stéphanie is rather more pragmatic in nature than the absolute suggested by the capitalized 'Connaissance'. We should also note that although Stéphanie clearly invites a sexual relationship, and it is suggested that Céline is tempted, no physical elements develop. Although the reasons for this are never spelled out, the relationship can be viewed in the light of Céline's suggestion that the act of loving another whilst expecting nothing in return constitutes the highest form of love, a definition noted by Stéphanie: 'Amour: acceptation et contemplation d'un Autre que soi-même, pris comme il est, et sans attente de retour' ['Love: the acceptance and contemplation of an Other, taken as s/he is, with nothing expected in return'] (221).[16] The contrast with Philippe, who sets out to change every aspect of Céline, could not be more marked.

Turning to Céline's relationship with Julia, the first point to note is that it does include a sexual dimension, although the sexual aspect is effectively written out of the text. Céline states: 'on a eu envie de se faire plaisir. On l'a fait. Comme ça, simplement. Juste pour le plaisir' ['we felt like giving each other pleasure. So we did. Just like that. Just for the pleasure'] (135). This ellipsis can be assessed in two ways. First, we might note that it represents a deliberate stance on the part of the author who states: 'Ce que je préfère dans *Les Stances à Sophie*, c'est les coupes' ['It's the omissions I like best in *Les Stances à Sophie*'].[17] Rochefort's aim was to preclude the sort of voyeuristic response which *Le Repos du guerrier* elicited, and we might note that her action seems to presuppose a particular readership: 'ce public des classes moyennes qui s'intéressaient à des sujets "sexys", qui cherchaient de quoi s'exciter [. . .] je supprime tout ce qui pourrait lui plaire, tout prétexte qu'il trouverait à son excitation' ['those middle-class readers who were interested in "sexy" subjects, who were looking for a cheap thrill [. . .] I removed anything that could please them, any pretext they might find to titillate themselves']. We should also note, however, that although (because?) the lesbian relationship represents a potentially powerful challenge to patriarchal norms and the nuclear family—the suggestion that close friendships between women may easily develop into sexual relations, the 'enemy within'[18]—it nonetheless remains quite literally behind closed doors, though in the spare room rather than the closet.

Attempting critically to assess Rochefort's representation of lesbianism is not an easy task, not least because the sexual orientation of the reader is bound to effect any judgement (a truism relating to any critical act, of course, but one which is brought into sharp relief by this text). In some respects, Rochefort's portrayal seems quite positive. The emphasis on pleasure ('juste pour le plaisir') breaks with a common representation of sexual relations between women as little more than emotional or consolatory. The almost passing reference to the sexual nature of the relationship might also be seen as a means of avoiding making an issue of something which the author wishes to represent as normal, a point on a continuum of sexual relations. Certainly Céline challenges heterosexist views in her discussions with Julia: 'Ma pauvre Julia mais t'es juste normale! T'es seulement con d'écouter la rumeur' ['My poor Julia you're just normal! You're just a bloody fool for listening to what people say'] (166). Hostile to any entrapping labels, Céline questions the very use of the word 'lesbian': 'c'est pas parce qu'on fait un extra qu'on doit se mettre en catalogue' ['just because we have a little treat it doesn't mean we have to label ourselves'] (164). Céline's views are aligned with those of Rochefort: 'to stick labels like lesbian, hetero on someone—I hate that. [. . .] the horror of being stigmatized for sexual morals, or other things for that matter, the horror of someone labelling and imprisoning you is very real to me.'[19]

Having said this, the refusal of the term 'lesbian' can be interpreted differently: it may typify a bisexual stance, or even, in some cases, signal a degree of homophobia. If we look to Rochefort's later comments on the text, a further explanation presents itself. Rochefort states quite clearly that she believes lesbians are made and not born. Sexual relations between women, she suggests, often result from a refusal on the part of women to tolerate the oppression which goes with so many heterosexual relationships. It is precisely on these grounds that she justifies the refusal of the term 'lesbian': 'In fact, that has been the case with many women who are called lesbians. It's just that they can no longer tolerate oppression.'[20] Frédéric Martel makes a similar point in his *Le Rose et le noir: les homosexuels en France depuis 1968*:

> De l'homosexualité à l'hétérosexualité, toutes les nuances sont possibles: les féministes semblent recouvrir l'ensemble du panel. Certaines bien sûr sont ouvertement 'homosexuelles'. Pour d'autres, le lesbianisme est une attitude choisie *en situation*, selon le mot de Beauvoir: il est un moment ponctuel de subversion contre le pouvoir mâle, une cure de désintoxication au moins provisoire.[21]
>
> [*There are all sorts of gradations between homosexuality and heterosexuality, and feminists seem to run the whole gamut. Of course some are openly 'homosexual'. For others, lesbianism is an attitude chosen in a specific situation, to use Beauvoir's term: it's a temporally-circumscribed subversive act challenging male power, a temporary detox cure.*]

74

What of course remains unclear is whether naming a homosexual relationship as 'un extra', and considering it as a temporary escape from heterosexual relations, continues to underwrite a heterosexual norm by suggesting that homosexuality remains something of a *pis-aller*. If it is oppression which engenders desire, then it might be argued that women are not responsible for their own desire, whose source leads back into the laps of men. Other aspects of the portrayal of the relationship between Céline and Julia might also be questioned. When the characters, eyeing up a woman in the street, try and decide how a possible encounter might be smuggled into the household accounts, they eventually settle upon a heading 'Produit de Beauté' ['beauty product']: a sideswipe aimed at the role of the feminine woman and her cosmetics, and perhaps a further, displaced, vision of woman as object. Furthermore, it is clear that heterosexual relations remain primary for the characters concerned: Céline not only refers to 'faire un extra', she also notes that 'dans les harems c'est courant. C'est un luxe, quoi' ['it's common practice in harems. It's a luxury'] (164), reiterating the idea of a supplementary leisure-time activity, secondary to the heterosexual norm. The claim by both women that 'je n'aime pas les femmes' ['I don't like women'] seems to be something of an exercise in bad faith. Finally, we should note that when Julia dies a violent death in a car-crash caused by her husband's reckless driving (in a race against Philippe), she suffers a fate common to all too many homosexual characters in film or text, who are regularly crushed by lorries, shot by madmen, or turn into vampires.

Looking back on *Les Stances*, perhaps significantly after 1968, Rochefort made the point that the word 'luxe' ('c'est un luxe, quoi') might better be replaced by 'privilege', stating on this occasion that homosexual relationships are linked to a greater comprehension and openness: 'The exclusion of homosexuality prohibits moving on to communication through sex and so prohibits real sexuality. To limit oneself to heterosexuality is to not really comprehend, not be able to comprehend.'[22] This statement points to a crucial aspect of the relationship between Céline and Julia which sets it in opposition to that of Céline and Philippe, and that is comprehension and communication. If the bond between Céline and Philippe breaks down, it is, Céline suggests, because it was built upon inadequate foundations. What she had initially perceived as love is revealed to have been little more (or less) than Philippe's sexual adroitness: 'cette faculté de m'émouvoir au bon endroit' ['his ability to arouse me in all the right places'] (17).

Like Geneviève in *Le Repos du guerrier*, and to some extent Josyane with Philippe in *Les Petits Enfants du Siècle*, Céline mistakes 'la bonne manière' ['sexual proficiency'] for love; the 'surprise' of good sex is falsely interpreted as a 'Coup de Foudre' (63). The physical, sexual aspect of the relationship cannot, however, shore up a basic lack of common ground. Whereas, as we have seen, Céline and Philippe cannot engage in dialogue, conversations between the two women are characterized by quick-fire repartee during which one party will often continue a sentence begun by the other, in which terms, irony and jokes do not need to be explained because they are already understood. As Céline says: 'Dans la vie pour se comprendre il n'y a qu'un moyen: se comprendre' ['There's only one way to understand one another in life: you have to understand one another'] (59). Philippe's complete lack of comprehension is epitomized on the wedding night when he is transformed, Hyde-like, into the husband demanding his conjugal rights, prompting Céline to a despairing repetition: 'Tu ne pouvais pas comprendre? Tu ne pouvais pas comprendre? Tu ne pouvais pas comprendre? Tu ne pouvais pas comprendre?' ['Couldn't you understand?'] (60). In sharp contrast, Julia and Céline are on the same wavelength from the outset. The women's ability to communicate, and the singular failure of communication between man and woman, is typified by a lengthy passage of counterpoint narrative during which Céline and Julia's happy exchanges concerning their holiday plans intersect with Philippe and Jean-Pierre's discussion of cars (171).

The relationship between the two women, however, extends beyond one of simple mutual understanding: it promotes an awareness of the nature of oppression. Rochefort stated that her own homosexual encounters towards the end of her marriage led to such a process of consciousness-raising:

> C'étaient vraiment des rencontres d'opprimées où le type 'on se raconte nos malheurs' était tout de même transcendé en 'Mon Dieu, mais qu'est-ce qui se passe, qu'est-ce que c'est que ça, de quoi s'est fait? Comment ça se fait que ça marche si mal? Quelle est la façon dont les hommes abordent la sexualité et qui ne va pas?' Même si on est contente, il y quelque chose qui ne va pas là-dedans. Et c'était finalement des espèces d'embryons de groupes de conscience, à deux.[23]

> [*They were actually meetings of the oppressed, but they went way beyond the 'let's tell each other our problems' thing to 'My God, what's going on, what the hell is this, what's it all about? Why is it that it all goes so badly wrong? What is it about the way men approach sexuality that just doesn't work?' Even if you're happy, there's something not quite right there. In the end they became sort of rudimentary consciousness-raising groups for two.*]

Commenting specifically on *Les Stances*, the author described the relationship between Céline and Julia as 'a meeting of the oppressed and a sudden consciousness of their condition. It's the first socialization. [. . .] It's a love based on sisterhood, a "sisterhood is powerful" where sexuality is an extension of communication.'[24] Although this is never explicitly articulated in the text, the importance of the relationship between Céline and Julia is quite clear. At a certain point in the text, the splitting process which takes place in Céline reaches a peak, as the compliant Mme Aignan, the *Femme vertueuse*, takes over. The suppression of the rebellious Céline Rodes is tantamount to a stifling of all life-forces: books become 'que des caractères imprimés' ['just print'] (127), music 'que des sons' ['just sounds'] (128); sexual desire vanishes, 'rien ne bouge là-dedans' ['there's nothing moving in there'] (131). It is at this stage that the relationship with Julia begins, and the return to life which this bond occasions—'avec Julia, je revis un peu. Un jour, j'ai même ressuscité' ['with Julia, I felt a little reinvigorated. One day I even came back to life'] (135)—is accompanied by a refusal of the Mme Aignan role:

> Je me suis regardée dans la glace. Je me suis reconnue immédiate-ment. C'est moi, celle-là. Moi! Moi! Où j'étais donc passée? Où j'étais disparue? Qui est cette autre qui erre dans les corridors de l'appartement là-bas rue de la Pompe? C'est Madame Philippe Aignan. (136)

> [*I looked at myself in the mirror. I recognized myself at once. That woman there, that's me. Me! Me! Where had I been? Where had I vanished to? Who is this other woman who roams the corridors of the apartment in the rue de la Pompe? It's Madame Philippe Aignan.*]

A similar 'mirror' scene takes place in *Cendres et or*, although, in this case, Juliette's (Mme Forgeat's) coming to awareness is accomplished alone:

> Dans le grand miroir à trois faces, Juliette pouvait voir Mme Etienne Forgeat dans toute sa splendeur. Splendeur glacée, à des millions de kilomètres d'elle, figurine étrangère, moulée avec précision dans un personnage donné et accepté tel, selon les lois de l'Apparence. (CO, 154)

> [*In the big three-sided mirror Juliette could see Mme Etienne Forgeat in all her splendour. An icy splendour a million kilometres away, an unfamiliar figurine, moulded with precision into a character offered up and accepted as she was, in accordance with the laws of Appearance.*]

Consciousness, the ability to perceive oppression in all its forms, and thereby act against it, is central to Rochefort's work. 'Writing as a woman', for Rochefort, has nothing to do with biology and everything to do with women's situation in society. A distinction must be made between a literature of the dominant, and of the dominated: 'I consider women's literature as a specific category not because of biology, but because it is, in a sense, a literature of the colonized.'[25] Those who belong to the dominated class may, or may not, escape the mechanisms of oppression; may, or may not, gain a critical insight into their situation. Juliette is the first of Rochefort's characters to have such a critical, distancing capacity, though she lacks the ability to articulate her position clearly. Renaud's vision is clouded by political idealism and alcohol; he cannot square his private and public politics, whilst Josyane is ultimately sucked into the system. *Les Stances* is marked by, and indeed is a product of, what Rochefort refers to as 'the privilege of consciousness', a politicized state of awareness which is closely linked to language:

> But there is a difference between what I'd call the style of the oppressed and the style of the oppressor. The oppressed sometimes imitate the style of the oppressor, but the oppressed have the privilege of consciousness. The oppressed know it, the oppressors don't.

Writing as a bisexual woman, Rochefort must employ 'the language of the oppressor', but must seek to distance herself from that language, to subvert it by any available means:

> It is difficult not to distort one's thinking in using the language of the oppressor. One must almost write as if twice removed, frame everything in irony and derision, or find other forms, another syntax, break down the whole thing.[26]

Although Rochefort had yet to break free of conventional language and form in the writing of *Cendres et or*, at a thematic level we can already detect in Juliette an awareness of the ventriloquism involved when one is forced to speak the 'language of the oppressor':

> La voix qui sortait de ses lèvres, Juliette l'entendait comme celle d'un autre. Elle n'était pas plus réelle que son reflet dans la glace. Chaque phrase prenait sa place dans un cadre fixé d'avance, qu'on remplissait. Les mots étaient vides de toute substance, les gestes n'avaient pas de poids—théâtre d'ombres—et elle jouait son propre rôle. Ainsi à la trois centième, les acteurs ne se donnent plus; ils débitent mécaniquement le texte auquel ils ne parviennent plus à croire. (CO, 155–6)

> [*Juliette heard the voice which issued from her lips as if it belonged to someone else. It was no more real than her reflection in the mirror. Each*

sentence took its place in a pre-existing frame that was then filled. Her words were devoid of all substance, her gestures had no weight—a shadow-puppet—and she was playing her own part. Just like the three hundredth performance when actors don't try any more, they mechanically recite a part they can no longer believe in.]

We have already seen that Renaud's speech in *Le Repos du guerrier*, and the narrative style of *Les Petits Enfants du siècle*, marked the author's break with conventional language. In *Les Stances*, the 'privilege of consciousness', signalled by a reappropriation of language, is played out at every level of the text. At the level of the diegesis we can perceive Céline's gradual shift from compliant silence and splitting (outwardly she plays the Mme Aignan role, but her thoughts remain those of the non-conformist), to the voicing of rebellion. The narrative level, however, bears the stamp of the consciousness of the retrospective narrator from the very outset. The first words of the text exemplify the ironic appropriation of the oppressor's terminology: 'Ce qu'il y a avec nous autres pauvres filles, c'est qu'on n'est pas instruites' ['The problem with us poor girls is that we're just not educated'] (9). 'Pauvre fille' is, of course, a term employed by both Philippe and his mother on many occasions. This hijacking of language is used throughout Céline's account, for instance in her ironic assessment of the female role: 'nous avons des blocages, nous autres femmes, touchant à l'esthétique, des décisions délirantes peuvent être prises sur du chiffon' ['we women have mental blocks when it comes to aesthetic matters, we can make quite staggering decisions about the least bit of cloth'] (34).

The text not only opens on an ironic tone which typifies the distanced position of the speaker; it is also framed at the close. As was the case with Rochefort herself, Céline's conscious grasp and articulation of 'conscience', expressed in a parting letter to Philippe and signed, significantly, under her maiden name, coincides with the termination of her marriage: 'Pour moi je pars sans regrets: ce n'était pas du temps perdu; grâce à toi, par les hasards de l'amour, j'ai pu approcher la Machine' ['As for me, I'm leaving with no regrets: it wasn't wasted time; thanks to you, thanks to the vagaries of love, I was able to approach the Machine'] (246). We saw in the previous chapter that some difficulties arose with regard to the narrating voice: Josyane's detached articulacy seemed to be at odds with the suggestion that she had been assimilated and silenced by the system. *Les Stances* resolves such ambiguities. Rochefort stated that her own marriage stifled the possibilities of self-expression: 'You know *A Room of One's Own*? I had this problem.'[27] The closing words of *Les Stances*— 'enfin seule' ['alone at last']—point to a new beginning for Céline: in her room, alone, the narrator is now free to cast her mind back over her marriage.[28] The text, in other words, circles back upon itself; it is the product of Céline's distanced stance.

Various narrative techniques are mobilized to emphasize the retrospective, objective stance of the narrator. Readers should be alert to the layering of tenses which conveys Céline's dual perspective throughout the text. Present or perfect tenses, combining with deictics, give us access to the Céline who has yet to emerge to tell her cautionary tale: 'maintenant je ne conteste plus' ['now I'm not arguing any more'] (119); 'hier il m'a demandé' ['yesterday he asked me'] (33); 'à deux heures du matin Philippe, hier' ['Philippe yesterday, at two in the morning'] (205). Each time, however, the focalization is dramatically altered by a past historic tense which serves to remind us that this is all very much in the past; that the Céline who speaks is a different person, distanced from, and thereby distancing us, from events. Entire sections narrated in the present tense, for example the account of the wedding night (59–65), are framed by a preterite—'on partit à l'aube' ['we left at dawn']—or pluperfect tense: 'il l'avait eue sa Nuit de Noces' ['he had had his wedding night'] (65). Following a similar pattern, Céline's verbal onslaught directed at both Jean-Pierre and Philippe, expressed in sustained dialogue, is cast firmly into the past in the concluding lines of the chapter: 'Jean-Pierre Bigeon ne mourut pas [. . .] Et il conduisit d'autres voitures' ['Jean-Pierre Bigeon did not die and he drove again'] (182). The shifting tenses, emphasizing the gap between past and present, silent compliance and the speaking out which is the very act of narration, may be juxtaposed: 'il est là. Il parle. Et moi je l'écoutais' ['he's there. He's speaking. And I listened to him'] (13).

The empowering of the narrating voice is also stressed by a hybrid form of indirect speech which punctuates the text. The following example comes at a point in the tale when Philippe berates Céline for her promiscuity and suggests that she might dedicate herself more conscientiously to him. As with free indirect speech, the indicator of indirect speech, 'il disait que', is omitted, but we also see a transposition of the second person to the first, and a subversive use of both a parenthesized aside and an ironic capitalization. The combination serves once again to focus attention on the speaker. Céline speaks, and assumes for herself, Philippe's words:

> Ah mais non. Pas comme j'ai fait. Comme j'ai fait ce n'était pas vraiment aimer. Ça porte au reste un autre nom (j'avais oublié, avec les autres, on couche) et puis je ferais aussi bien de ne pas le rappeler, il n'y a pas tellement de quoi se vanter, outre que ce n'est rien d'agréable à entendre pour Celui qui est là à présent et qui constamment, par courtoisie pour moi, s'efforce de l'oublier. Et, puis-je dire ce qui m'en reste?—Rien.—Alors tu vois. Ça t'a avancé à quoi? (27–8)

[But no. Not how I did it. What I did isn't really love. It's called something else (I'd forgotten, with other people you have sex) and I'd do well to forget it, it's not much to boast about, not to mention that it's not very nice for Him who is there now to have to hear about it, He who constantly and out of courtesy to me, is trying to forget it. And can I say what I have to show for it? 'Nothing.' 'So, you see. Where did it get you?']

A similar mechanism is employed later in the text when Philippe's pompous style (further ridiculed by the presence of the unfamiliar first-person imperfect subjunctive form) is parodically replicated and reported. Here, too, the subversive process is heightened by parenthetical interjections:

Un grand dîner (merde) très important dit Philippe, et à ce propos il fallait donc que je connusse (c'est le moment c'est l'instant) les Grands Projets fameux et jusque-là secrets, dont il serait peut-être parlé à table parce que maintenant c'était fait c'était Officiel (qu'est-ce qu'il se rengorgeait), et que je fusse en mesure de réagir, en fonction desdits, dans le sens de nos Intérêts Communs, respirez. (235)

[A very big dinner (shit) very important said Philippe, and while we're on the subject it would be as well that I be appraised of (here it comes) the famous Momentous Plans kept secret until now, which there might well be talk of at table because now it was done it was Official (he was so full of it) and I would do well to be in a position to react appropriately with respect to the above-mentioned Plans, in such a way as to promote our Common Interest, pause for breath.]

The technique of the aside in itself serves to relativize and subvert Philippe's speech throughout the text. On these occasions the syntactic marker 'pensais-je' (or 'pensai-je') is omitted as Céline's thoughts are communicated to the reader. Such thoughts may be unexpressed, but they do indicate the sustained presence of the rebellious Céline, and create a degree of complicity between the narrator and the reader, who has privileged access to her thought processes. In each case, we see a discrepancy between thought and word (my italics): 'Voilà, tu raisonnes. / *Je raisonne.* / Et toi qu'est-ce que tu fais?' ['You see, you're picking an argument. / *I'm picking an argument* / And what are you doing?'] (28); 'Tu n'as pas envie parfois d'avoir une vie normale? disait Philippe. / *Normale. Qu'est-ce que ça veut dire?*' ['Don't you want to lead a normal life? / *Normal. What does that mean?*'] (13). This technique is often sustained over a number of pages, for example the account of Céline's dread of early morning starts:

—Oui oui ce n'est pas une réponse.

—Comme tu veux mon chéri, susurre tendrement le robot gardien de ma tranquillité.

—Mais non pas comme je veux! dit le mari d'une voix perforeuse, je dois savoir, et toi tu dois prendre des dispositions.

Dispositions. Brrr. Attention mot méchant, le robot tire le signal d'alarme.

—Attends un tout petit peu. (94, my italics)

['*Yes yes isn't an answer.*'

'*If you say so darling,*' whisper the honeyed tones of the robot protecting my peace and quiet.

'*No, not if I say so!*' says husband in a piercing tone, '*I have to know, and you have to make arrangements*'.

Arrangements. Brrr. Beware, dangerous word, the robot pulls the alarm cord.

'*Wait just a second.*']

A similar distancing effect is created by the use of stage directions. Here, too, the emphasis is on the narrator's ability to stand back and view the action dispassionately (my italics throughout): '—Et moi je commence à me décourager . . . A me demander si je ne perds pas mon temps. Alors que. *Soupir.* Vois-tu Céline, j'en suis arrivé à un moment crucial dans la vie d'un homme' ['I'm beginning to lose heart . . . I'm beginning to wonder if I'm wasting my time. Whilst. *Sigh.* You see Céline, as a man I've reached a crossroads in my life'] (20); 'J'essaye seulement de mettre un peu d'ordre dans cette petite tête. *Il caresse ladite.* C'est plein de fausses idées' ['I'm just trying to put a bit of order in that little head of yours. *He pats aforementioned head.* It's full of wrong ideas'] (23). Or, in a sustained passage of typical humour:

. . . et moi, vois-tu, *il avale une huître,* je ne veux pas que tu te fasses mal; *il avale une huître.* Inutilement. *Il avale.* J'ai envie que tu sois heureuse. *Il avale.* Même malgré toi. *Il avale une huître.* Et toi, tu pleures! Allez, mange, elles sont délicieuses. (23)

[*..as for me, the thing is, he swallows an oyster, I don't want you to hurt yourself, he swallows an oyster. Needlessly. He swallows. I want you to be happy. He swallows. Even in spite of yourself. He swallows an oyster. And you, you're crying! Go on, try some, they're delicious.*]

The speaking voice may also be brought into sharp relief via the use of register. Céline's narration is marked by the type of language deplored by Philippe. There is a strong discrepancy between the role-playing

Mme Aignan (junior) who listens in silence and plays the game, and the straight-shooting Céline Rodes who tells her tale. Céline may restrain herself in consumer hell, but her feistiness comes across clearly to the reader: '"Mais Madame nous en vendons beaucoup", voilà l'argument clé. Eh, qu'est-ce que j'en ai à foutre de ce que les autres aiment?' ['"But Madam we sell lots of them", there's the crucial argument. So what the fuck do I care what other people like?'] (68). She may appear to submit to the tyranny of medicalization, but as she tells us in no uncertain terms: 'à tout hasard j'ai foutu les petites pilules dans les chiottes' ['I flushed the sodding pills down the bog just in case'] (80). This perfect housewife knows how to call a spade a bloody shovel: 'le papier est renouvelé dans les chiottes à mesure' ['the bog-roll is replaced as required'] (119); 'je fais repasser les plats trois fois, toujours bien pleins (ce qu'on peut foutre en l'air comme boustifaille dans cette baraque c'est un scandale)' ['I hand the dishes round three times, always nicely full (it's bloody scandalous the amount of food thrown down the bloody toilet in this dump)'] (121).

Whilst the narrative throughout reveals the rebellious voice of Céline, at the level of the diegesis we can detect a gradual shift from silence to outspoken combativeness. As Céline suggests in the opening pages, consciousness of oppression takes time, and 'en attendant, il faut se le faire' ['in the meantime, you have to put up with it'] (9). For a short period she follows Julia's lead and plays the game, avoiding conflict by assuming the role of woman mapped out by Philippe and those of like mind. The two women play the part of idiot housewife to perfection:

On leur passe des vrais festivals de connerie feminine telle qu'ils l'attendent, pourquoi les contrarier puisque rien les convaincra? Deux vraies conasses. On récite France-Femme [. . .] Comme ça ils sentent qu'ils ont des femmes. Chiantes, mais tout est à sa place et eux sont en paix. (151)

[*We put on some real festivals of feminine stupidity of the kind they expect, why go against them since nothing will convince them? Two real bloody idiots. We recite chunks of France-Femme [. . .] That way they feel like they've got wives. Bloody irritating, but everything's as it should be and they're happy.*]

Julia's death at the hands of Jean-Pierre marks the end-point of this tactic. Thereafter, Céline is prepared to do battle, and her shift in attitude is reflected in her ever-increasing focus on language itself. Like Renaud in *Le Repos du guerrier,* she is all too aware of the semantic barrier which separates her from Philippe: 'il manque le dictionnaire qui nous permettrait de nous parler, toi et moi' ['the dictionary which would allow us to speak to one another is missing'] (203), and she begins with an unspoken 'translation' of his words:

> —Ce n'est peut-être pas nécessaire de te forger des obsessions.
> Obsession: conscience d'une chose réelle. (Note pour le dictionnaire Célino–Philippien). Fonction du mot: faire passer la chose réelle, qui gène, pour une imaginaire de façon à la faire avaler et que la fête continue. [. . .] En fait Célino–Philippien est un titre trop restrictif pour un ouvrage de cette importance. Il mérite la généralisation. Il est d'intérêt public. Je l'appellerai Dictionnaire Sémantique Neo-Bourgeois. (217)

> [*'And is it really necessary to cultivate these obsessions?'*
> *Obsession: awareness of a real phenomenon. (Note for the Céline–Philippe dictionary). Function of the word: to make the real phenomenon which is an irritation seem imaginary so that it is acccepted and let the fun continue. [. . .] In fact Céline–Philippien is far too limited a title for such an important work. It deserves something more wide-ranging. It is of general interest. I'll call it the Neo-Bourgeois Semantic Dictionary.*]

In time the silence is broken, and after several unspoken examples drawn from her dictionary ('Hypersensible: susceptible de ressentir des impressions' ['Hypersensitive: able to experience sensations'] p. 219; 'Enseignement: Comment ça pense l'homme' ['Education: what men think'], p. 220), Céline confronts Philippe and effectively deconstructs and demystifies his discourse:

> .   —Top! Deuxième exemple. Semer le doute.
> —Evidemment si tu t'arrêtes à tous les mots! ça devient de la paranoïa.
> —Top.
> —Mais, tu es folle!
> —Top.
> —Oh, ça va! (222–3)

> [*'Beep. Example number two: sowing doubt.'*
> *'Well obviously if you stop at every word! This is developing into paranoia!'*
> *'Beep.'*
> *'But you're completely crazy!'*
> *'Beep.'*
> *'Oh alright alright.'*]

Confronted by his own oppressive linguistic ploys, Philippe is finally reduced to stammering uncertainty and. . . silence. The battle of words is won.

After defeating Philippe at his own verbal game, Céline will no longer seek to try and communicate, choosing rather to walk away. Links have been forged with like-minded parties—not only Julia and Stéphanie, but those men who stand outside the patriarchal 'Machine', like Thomas and Nicolas. For Rochefort, communication with those who are excluded from the system is the key to revolutionary action:

> Ce qui est subversif, c'est de communiquer avec des autres êtres. Ce que je peux dire, c'est que ce qui défend la vie, là où on défend sa vie, où on essaie de rester vivant, c'est subversif; là où on essaie de communiquer horizontalement entre nous, et non pas verticalement avec un pouvoir, c'est subversif.[29]

> [*It's communicating with other people which is subversive. What I can say is that whatever fights for life, situations in which we fight for our lives, in which we try to stay alive, that's subversive. Subversive is when we try to communicate horizontally amongst ourselves, and not vertically with someone or something in a position of power.*]

Such communication, of course, extends beyond the intratextual dimension. Rochefort suggests that oppression is the bridge between author and reader; texts, too, may serve to raise consciousness. *Les Stances à Sophie*, Rochefort pointed out with amused satisfaction, may have alienated her from most male readers, but 'as for the women, they spoke of oppression. I got piles of letters from women who said, "So I'm not crazy after all, that happened to me, too." '[30]

CHAPTER FOUR

Printemps au parking

Nous voici quelques-uns épris du plaisir d'aimer sans réserve, assez passionnément pour offrir à l'amour le lit somptueux d'une révolution.
(Raoul Vaneigem, *Traité de savoir-vivre à l'usage des jeunes générations*)

If this book followed the chronology of publication of Rochefort's novels, then this fourth chapter would by rights turn to *Une Rose pour Morrison*, published in 1966. As it is, there are good reasons for breaking the pattern, since it can be argued that *Printemps au parking*, published in 1969, predates *Une Rose* both thematically and in terms of its writing. In 1970 Rochefort published *C'est bizarre l'écriture*, a short essay based on notes taken during her writing of a second draft of *Printemps*, a version which she had begun in November 1968.[1] In this essay, which is primarily 'le journal du livre' ['the journal of the book'] which was to become *Printemps*, we learn that a first version of the novel was actually undertaken in 1964. Unhappy with her manuscript, Rochefort put it aside and wrote *Une Rose*, subsequently returning to and reworking the first draft of *Printemps*. Rochefort indicates that in many respects her new version adhered to the earlier draft and was, in any case, written 'as if' it predated 1968: 'j'écrivais "dans le passé"' ['I was writing "in the past"'] (CB, 63). To rewrite from the perspective of the new society which emerged from the 1968 events was absolutely impractical: 'Ça pas question d'y toucher, car en 68 le monde change [. . .] et j'aurais dû *tout* modifier, depuis et y compris la première phrase, car le langage ne saurait être le même' ['No way could I do that, because in 1968 the world changed [. . .] and I would have had to alter *everything*, from and including the first sentence, because the language couldn't have been the same'] (CB, 62).

Printemps tells the tale of the young Christophe who runs away from home, enters a new world, and returns to the family unit a changed man. His socio-political journey leads him from inarticulacy—'ils me font chier' ['they piss me off'] (7), is the closest he can initially come to a formulation of his motivation for escape—to the all-important clear-

86

sighted 'conscience' which has been seen to lie at the centre of the author's work. Such inarticulacy was, Rochefort suggests, unthinkable at the time of the rewriting in 1968/9: 'à présent les Christophe ont des mots' ['now the Christophers of this world have the words to express themselves'] (CB, 62). She adds: 'j'avais fait un livre d'"attente" d'événements, et le ton d'attente n'est pas le ton du constat. Il devait donc rester où il était' ['I'd written a book which anticipitated events, and a tone of anticipation is not a factual tone. So it had to stay as it was'] (CB, 63). Paradoxically then, *Printemps*, written in final form *after* the 1968 events, harks back to a time which preceded the social upheaval, whilst *Une Rose*, which *predates* 1968, is uncannily prophetic in its representation of mass unrest and, finally, revolutionary action.

'Conscience', which in Rochefort's terminology, as we saw in the previous chapter, means an awareness of, and ability to articulate, the causes of oppression at work in society, once again forms the core of this novel. Like Céline in *Les Stances à Sophie*, the young narrator Christophe breaks with his past and faces a radically altered future by the close of the text. What has changed is the time-span involved. In the previous text we saw Céline start out as a rebellious figure, fall into a pattern of complicit role-play in the stifling bourgeois environment into which she was transplanted, before re-emerging all the stronger for having grasped the workings of the social mechanisms which had threatened to submerge her. Christophe, too, changes milieu, from the working-class HLMs to the intellectual student milieu of the Parisian left bank, but his passionate relationship with Thomas and, perhaps, his youth, are such that his metamorphosis is completed in a mere three days. Christophe was a one-man rebellion waiting to happen. As he himself points out when he likens his situation to that of a crystal precipitating into a chemical solution, he had reached saturation point, sickened by inane TV game-shows and a school system which was totally inadequate to his needs or interests.

Whilst *Printemps au parking* shares some stylistic features with *Les Stances*, it also introduces a number of new elements. Both novels are written in the first person, and both are retrospective narratives. Although the preterite and perfect tenses remain in *Printemps*, etching out a clear chronological line of narrative progression, the text favours the historic present tense. As with *Les Stances*, the narrator's past thoughts tend to be represented in a present tense with the syntactic markers of reportage ('j'ai pensé', 'je pensai', etc.) omitted. This technique, coupled with a substantial increase in the use of dialogue, which often stretches over several pages with minimal narratorial intervention, lends the text considerable dramatic force. *Printemps* differs from *Les Stances* in two key areas. Firstly, whereas *Les Stances* was marked by a play of shifting points of view—the rebellious and the conforming narrator, 'then' and 'now',

Céline Rodes and Mme Aignan—Christophe's narrative keeps pace with the unfolding events of the diegesis: the narrator does not flaunt his retrospective status; there is no split perspective. As we shall see, this has important repercussions when we come to consider the reader's stance vis-à-vis the unfolding relationship formed between Christophe and Thomas. Secondly, a strong reflexive element is introduced into the text. The act of narrating, of telling stories, is constantly brought to the attention of the reader, who is prompted to reflect upon the power of narrative, the role of context and of the addressee, the effects of 'histoires' upon both teller and audience.

Printemps au parking might be described as Christophe's narration of his narrations, the story of his story-telling, in every sense of the expression. Throughout the text stories are told several times over, first (in terms of the time of reading) in the outer frame of the narration, where Christophe stands as narrator with no intratextual narratee, and subsequently to various intratextual addressees. We, as readers, consequently view Christophe both as a narrator addressing 'us', and as a character addressing other characters. This pattern is maintained through much of the text, and two examples will suffice here to examine the mechanisms at work. At the start of the text Christophe explains that he was prompted to leave home when his father insisted that he shift from in front of the TV screen—which was blank. The episode is narrated simply, with a short account of events, a few lines of dialogue between father and son, and a final comment: 'Non, c'était trop bête, non?' ['It was really too idiotic, wasn't it?'] (8). On this occasion, because there is no intratextual addressee, and because of the force of the first-person mode (the 'je' inevitably invoking a 'tu' or 'vous'), the reader tends to assume the role of addressee. Indeed, this response is elicited by the employment of a second-person plural pronoun: 'tout ce que j'ai envie si vous voulez savoir c'est de tourner le dos et m'en aller' ['all I really wanted to do, if you'd like to know, was to turn my back and go'] (7). The story of the TV screen and Christophe's departure from home is subsequently repeated a further three times: to Bambi, a girl living on the same estate whom he visits on the first evening, to Thomas, and finally to Thomas and two of his friends.

Christophe's first account, which is addressed to Bambi, reveals both the importance and benefits of a receptive audience, and its potential pitfalls. Initially Christophe is unable to articulate his reasons for leaving home. Only in a dialogic context, when he is pressed by his interlocutor, does he begin to verbalize what had previously eluded verbal expression. As he points out, 'c'est bon de parler à quelqu'un' ['it's good to talk to someone'] (15). As he begins his story, verbalization and realization fuse. The very act of telling 'realizes' in the sense of making real and, more crucially, gives Christophe insights into his experiences: 'Je lui filai l'histoire, qu'une seconde avant j'aurais cru impossible à raconter, et en sortant elle prenait un aspect superbe, elle tenait sur quatre phrases, pas de doute elle avait eu lieu' ['I came out with my story, a story which a second earlier I'd have thought just couldn't be told, and as it came out it became quite wonderful, it all hung on four sentences, there was no doubt about it; it had happened'] (15).

There is, however, a more negative aspect at work, for as he warms to his task, Christophe begins to project himself as a film hero: 'je me sentis redevenu adulte et contemporain et même en train de jouer dans un film' ['I felt that I'd become an adult again, here and now, I even felt like someone starring in a film'] (16). Slipping away from authenticity, he defines himself and his life in terms of the mass-media culture which he professes to despise, no longer telling his tale, but told by it; written by the pre-scripted scenario. To tell a tale is, of course, to be in a position of power and control. Bambi sees a new Christophe; she did not think he had it (the story?) in him. As befits a Departing Hero, he earns a night of sex. What he does not realize is that once he has projected himself in this role, he must face the repercussions. Taken in by the 'hard man' image, Bambi goes on to involve Christophe in shady deals with local petty criminal Jeff. Christophe learns the hard way that a role may take over reality, learning also that a story-teller has to gauge his audience carefully. When Jeff asks him why he ran away, he realizes that discretion may be the better option; that not all audiences are as receptive as Bambi: 'Mon histoire n'allait pas passer. Pas intéresser. Inutile. Bavardage' ['My story wouldn't go down well. It wouldn't interest anyone. Pointless. Idle chit-chat']. Jeff is presented with a reduced and simplified version of events: 'j'en ai eu marre de la vie de famille' ['I got sick of family life'] (95).

A new interlocutor not only conditions the telling of the tale, he or she also provides a new reading of the tale. When the TV screen episode is later repeated to the student Thomas, he offers Christophe a Freudian interpretation of events: 'c'est un Œdipe splendide' ['it's a splendid example of the Oedipus complex'] (74). The point is implicitly made that a repetition is never a repetition; each new telling brings into play a new context and new addressees. The narrative has a potential which far exceeds the intentions of the teller, a fact which we will see has considerable implications for both authors and readers. The third and final version involves a repetition of both story and commentary, when Christophe and Thomas retell the tale to two of Thomas's friends. This latest version involves a new interpretation, as Christophe is identified as 'un cas de non-conditionnement spontané aux mass-média' ['a case of spontaneous non-conditioning by the mass media'] (126). This is, of course, rather ironic. Although Thomas and his friends are impressed, like Bambi, by Christophe's tale ('je dois dire ça a fait monter immédiatement ma cote' ['I must say that it immediately raised me in the popularity stakes'] p.126), they fail to see that Christophe still conceptualizes himself and his life in terms of those very 'mass-média': 'je leur racontais mon film: La Fugue Tragique du Mineur' ['I told them my cinematic story: The Tragic Flight of the Minor'] (127). It seems that he is unable to escape from those deeper powers of conditioning which force experience into pre-moulded schemata.

The second example of the dramatization of story-telling centres around Christophe's pursuit of a girl he first sees in the Jardins de Luxembourg. Once again telling himself stories, the narrator imagines himself in her bed, and when she agrees to an early-morning rendezvous, glories in his apparent power to turn an imagined script into reality: 'Matérialisé. Comme si je l'avais embarquée dedans au passage; dans mon cinéma' ['Materialized. As if I'd taken her on board into my cinema as I went along'] (54). The tale of the easy pick-up is retold to Thomas, who builds on Christophe's assumption that the girl was attracted to his youthful naivety, joking: 'elle veut peut-être te donner le sein. Avec les croissants' ['maybe she wants to breast-feed you. And feed you croissants'] (85). Christophe's designated role, constructed from his exchanges with Thomas, is thereby formulated: when he returns for his breakfast meeting he will play the part of the Puceau Maladroit ['Inept Virgin'] and sensitive, attentive son. The power of the teller is evident once more, and telling stories becomes synonymous with lying as Christophe regales his conquest with tales of an ailing mother reliant on her generous child: 'je m'inventai une mère alanguie et je me métamorphosai en fils attentionné' ['I invented a sickly mother and took on the persona of the attentive son'] (111). Taken in by the narrative line, the girl is as impressed as Bambi. Once more Christophe's skills as yarn-spinner are rewarded with sex.

It again becomes clear, however, that role-play is not without its hazards. Christophe's belief that he had successfully dragged the girl into his lustful dreams proves to be wide of the mark: it turns out that she, and not he, had been in control. Innocent virgins may be taken advantage of. Matters become yet more complex when he recounts his story to an attentive audience of Thomas and his friends. Christophe revels in being the centre of attention: 'c'est triste à dire mais qu'on me donne un auditoire attentif et je ne peux pas me tenir' ['sad to say that once I've got a captive audience there's no holding me back'] (128). Gauging that the reality of the situation and the Innocent Virgin version is beyond him ('ce n'est pas des histoires faciles à raconter' ['these aren't easy stories to tell'] p.130), he changes script to that of the Insatiable Vampire, placing undue emphasis on the girl's prominent teeth (which had earlier caused the

Innocent Virgin some concern during an act of fellatio!). Such is the power of his tale that the young men prepare to visit this 'Vampire du Quartier' en masse. Alarmed by his own powers, Christophe is forced to backtrack, admitting 'je suis un menteur' ['I'm a liar'] (132), who had lengthened the girl's teeth 'pour la beauté de l'histoire' ['to make a good story'] (132). Stories, it would seem, can prompt actions beyond the control of the teller.

As we have seen, Christophe's narrating powers can be abused; 'raconter des histoires' ['telling tales'] can amount to downright lying. Not only does Christophe embroider or exaggerate, he can, when the situation suits, create a fictive self and past. To the mother of Fabrice (elder brother of Boubou, one of Thomas's friends), he is the studious son of a factory worker ('employé, ça fait mesquin' ['office worker sounds too petty'], p. 169), struggling to pass exams. The reader, of course, is in a privileged position and can see through Christophe's tales. What emerges in *Printemps* is that stories, as ready-made or prescripted (and prescriptive) accounts of reality, may hide important truths. 'C'est une longue histoire' ['It's a long story'], a phrase repeated many times in the text, can be a tantalizing lure ('go on, tell me more!), but more often it is a means of silencing those one does not wish to explain matters to (when Fabrice enquires into the outcome of Christophe's meeting with Thomas, he is fobbed off with a dismissive 'oh c'est une longue histoire', p. 238).

What the text does not spell out, but what the reader can perceive, is that stories are linked to society's desire to label and control the individual. Christophe himself falls victim not only to his created roles and tales, but to those of others. Early in the text he alludes briefly and rather enigmatically to 'l'histoire de ma sœur' ['my sister's story'] (21). Only after his relationship with Thomas has opened his eyes does he realize that this 'histoire' had been accepted unquestioningly by him. The pre-packaged inviolable 'histoire' won his silent complicity; as his father had said: 'Ça c'est des choses dont on ne parle pas. Fini, nettoyé' ['We don't talk about that kind of thing. End of story'] (240). The sister had been given the role of madwoman in a story of insanity, and packed off accordingly to an asylum: 'J'avais cru—cru quoi, une fois de plus? cru eux; cru un mot. Folle, alors folle. J'avais cru l'étiquette, comme un con' ['I'd believed it—believed what though? Believed them; believed a word. Mad, okay, she was mad. Like a bloody fool I'd believed in the label'] (241). In just the same manner Christophe initially disavows his sexual desire for Thomas, thereby becoming a complicit addressee of society's tales of perversion. After the two men have sex, Christophe can only wonder at his acceptance of such prescriptive narratives: 'déjà on se demandait: Pourquoi avoir fait une pareille histoire?' ['we were already asking ourselves why we'd made such a big deal of it'] (208).

Christophe's role as story-teller, as we have seen, is a complex one: he spins tales to others, yet is himself a victim (at least initially) of society's more pervasive master-narratives. But what of the reader, who assumes the position of addressee with regard to the central story of the text, that of the relationship between Christophe and Thomas? It has already been stated that Christophe's account, although dramatized throughout via the use of the historic present and dialogued sections, is retrospective. In other words, we might expect that Christophe tells his tale in full knowledge of its outcome; he knows that his relationship with Thomas ultimately develops into a sexual one, but does he signal this early on, or, as a consummate story-teller who knows that timing is everything, does he keep his 'punch line' under wraps? If we turn now to the reader's developing perception of the central relationship in the text we will see that *Printemps* once again raises important questions concerning intentionality and the nature of narrative.

There is little doubt as to Christophe's sexual orientation in the opening stages of the text. After spending a night with Bambi, his first interaction with Thomas, centring on the loan of a student-card, firmly inscribes both men as heterosexual. Then, as he waits for his rendezvous with Thomas in the Minus-Bar, Christophe states: 'j'étais fantastiquement attiré par Merdier Occidental' ['I was incredibly attracted to Western Balls-up'] (the nick-name he has given Thomas, gleaned from snippets of conversation) (56). Is Christophe attracted by Thomas's difference as intellectual student? By a certain paternal or big brotherly image? On a first reading of the text the remark is unlikely to have any significant resonance. The idea of homosexuality is first raised in the Minus-Bar where Christophe encounters Thomas's friends. The topic, however, is treated as a joke, a mimicry of homosexuality, as remarks—'il nous avait caché ça', 'félicitations [. . .] il est ravissant' ['he'd kept that hidden', 'congratulations [. . .] he's stunning']—are exchanged 'sur un ton tantouzard' ['in a camp manner'] (62–3). In this camped-up role-play, Boubou assigns Thomas the part of Socrates to Christophe's Phaedrus: 'Si la présence de Phaidros n'obscurcit point trop les esprits de Socrate, dit Deux' ['If Phaedrus's presence isn't troubling Socrates too much, said Two'] (63). Limp wrists and wiggling bottoms complete the parody.

Paradoxically, the role-play tends to reinstate Christophe's heterosexuality: play cannot be real; acting presupposes a hidden reality. Christophe's uncertainty as to whether they are 'for real' and his (disingenuous?) use of the present tense, removes him further from the 'homosexual' tag: 'Ils n'en avaient pas l'air à les voir, *mais je ne suis pas un expert'* ['they didn't seem to be as far as I could see, *but I'm no expert'*] (64, my emphasis). Once the others have left, Thomas reassures Christophe as to his heterosexual credentials: his friends left not 'par discrétion' ['to be tactful'], as they pretended, but for a prearranged outing to the cinema. Thomas jokes that he had begun to feel like a 'pucelle effarouchée' ['timid virgin'] (71), and over dinner praises the existence of women: 'Bénies soient les femmes, dit Thomas, heureusement pour nous il y a les filles, moi aussi j'ai eu mes fenêtres ouvertes dans mon temps' ['Thank God for women, said Thomas, lucky for us girls exist, I've had my share of open windows too in my time'] (88).

At this point, there is little doubt that the reader will be reading 'straight', although the theme of homosexuality has been raised. By the following morning in his continuing adventures, Christophe is dreaming of his half-clad future conquest, and Thomas. The syntax is such that both, whether intentionally or not, are presented in a sexual context:

> La vérité c'est que tout ce que j'arrivais à voir [. . .] c'était ce lit—un lit! [Christophe has spent a bad night in a park]—avec cette fille dans sa chemise de nuit—et la gueule maigre, hirsute, rêveuse, et tellement sympathique, de Merdier Occidental. (109)

> [*The truth is that all I could see [. . .] was that bed—a bed!—with that girl in her nightgown—and Western Balls-up's thin, stubbly, dreamy, and incredibly attractive face.*]

Matters remain complicated, however. Christophe loses his virginity for a second (and third, and fourth!) time with his 'fille-Vampire', but then feels he has betrayed Thomas by missing their library rendezvous. And is the fact that he runs to the belated meeting significant: 'Six heures! Je courais' ['Six o'clock! I ran'] (118)? In the Minus-Bar the camp game continues when Thomas puts his arm around Christophe's shoulders (in a matey way?), prompting a jokey response: 'Voyons, essaye de te contenir dit Miguel' ['Come on now, try and control yourself!, said Miguel']. Thomas's response is certainly open to interpretation: 'je ne peux pas dit Thomas c'est plus fort que moi il me plaît ce gosse. Je ne plaisante pas, ajouta-t-il d'un air sauvage' ['I can't, said Thomas, it's stronger than I am, I like the kid. I'm not joking, he added ferociously'] (127). And what of the lingering handshake which seals the evening of the same day? The possibility of a generalized camaraderie keeps the reader guessing:

> On avait pas envie de se quitter, on restait là tous les trois souriant bêtement. J'étais complètement heureux. Je pensais en majuscules. Ça restera, le coin de la rue Thénard, Un Moment Exceptionnel dans ma Vie. (143)

[*We didn't want to part, the three of us stayed put smiling inanely. I was perfectly happy. I was thinking in capital letters. The corner of Thénard street will always be an Exceptional Moment in my Life.*]

When Christophe and Boubou arrive at the latter's family home and meet the openly gay Fabrice, Christophe balks at the offer of clothes which threaten his heterosexuality: 'C'est rudement beau, mais est-ce que ça ne fera pas un peu pédé' ['It's really nice, but won't it look a little poofy?'] (147). In his dream that night he sits on a runaway bulldozer which threatens to mow down Thomas, and tries desperately to regain control: 'j'avais cessé de regarder la route pour essayer de retrouver les pédales' ['I'd stopped looking at the road to try and find the pedals again'] (157). He himself acknowledges the word-play—'pédale' is slang for 'poofter'— but offers no interpretation. Only when Fabrice leaves him at the Minus-Bar with the words 'je sais que tu en aimes un autre' ['I know you love someone else'] (182), does the nature of the relationship between Christophe and Thomas finally begin to become clear.

How are we to assess this shifting play of homo- and heterosexual markers? One possibility would be to read in terms of clues and bluffs, indeed double-bluffs in the case of the camp role-play which takes place. Commenting on Thomas's skills as a poker-player, Christophe points to his ability to keep his fellow-players guessing: 'en fait il était arrivé à les confondre tellement qu'ils ne pouvaient plus savoir du tout s'il bluffait ou pas et il faisait à peu près ce qu'il voulait' ['in fact he'd managed to confuse them so much that they had no idea if he was bluffing or not, and he could more or less do what he wanted'] (121). Is the poker-game, then, a suitable metaphor for the writing/reading process? Is Christophe as retrospective narrator, and, of course, Rochefort herself, doing a similar thing: keeping their cards close to their chest, not revealing their hand, staying 'poker-faced'? To adopt this reading requires us to infer intentionality, but if we turn to *C'est bizarre l'écriture*, we will see that the matter is rather more complex. Rochefort states that her first version of *Printemps*, written in 1964, represented no more than 'une amitié très convenable' ['a very respectable friendship'] (CB, 66). Only when she reread her draft in 1968 did she come to see that Christophe and Thomas were in love, indeed experienced an intense passion. The first 'clue' which alerted her to this state of affairs was Christophe's running to his meeting with Thomas after his night of passion with the fille-Vampire: 'Il court. Et alors, court-on comme ça pour rien?' ['He's running. Well come on, do people run that like for no reason?'] (CB, 66). Once this new reading presented itself, further indicators came to light: Thomas's 'il me plaît' ['I like him'] was only a game, says Rochefort ('on jouait, je sais' ['it was a game, I know']), but his angry 'je ne plaisante pas' ['I'm not joking'] surely pointed to something which extended beyond a joke, beyond friendship. Rereading indicated to her that the camped-up role-play was equally revealing. Making the point that one cannot write explicitly—'à découvert' —she suggests that the game-play constituted a 'voile' or mask hiding a deeper level of truth:

> On aurait vraiment dit que c'était exprès: apparu dès la première seconde, il donnait la parodie d'une réalité ignorée, de moi inclus, et ainsi, lui coupant l'herbe sous les pieds, la tournant d'avance en dérision et lui ôtant toutes ses chances, protégeait nos innocences à tous. (CB, 85)
>
> [*It really did look as if it was done deliberately: the mask appeared from the outset, and it was a parody of a truth which wasn't yet revealed to anyone, me included, and it cut the ground out from under the truth, it made a mockery of it, destroyed any chance it might have, and that way it protected everyone's innocence.*]

Clearly what is important here is that the author herself claims to have been duped; it had not been her intention to write a text about homosexual love, though her subsequent reading showed her that such love was written all over the text: 'Quoi, ces gens-là s'aiment depuis le début, c'est écrit noir sur blanc, par moi, et plusieurs fois [. . .] et moi je passe là innocente, les yeux bandés' ['What, these guys have loved each other from the outset, it's written in black and white, by me, and several times at that [. . .] and I wander by all innocent, blindfolded'] (CB, 80). Rochefort's comments prompt the question why she did not 'see' what was, apparently, there to be seen (why, as she puts it in typically forceful manner, she had 'la merde dans les yeux' ['shit in her eyes'], CB, p.80). Her favoured response to the question was that she had set out to write 'l'histoire d'une quête' ['a quest story'], and that once this rigid framework was in place, it effectively precluded any elements which did not 'fit in'. She too, like Christophe, fell prey to a prescripted story: 'Là je fais une bêtise: je mets une étiquette; je me programme; je me retire ma liberté: en fait, je n'ai pas à savoir une histoire de quoi c'est, d'avance' ['At that point I did something stupid: I labelled it, I programmed myself, I took away my own freedom: in fact I've got no business knowing what a story's about beforehand'] (CB, 88). Rochefort's second explanation for her failure to see, is that she quite simply did not want, at some level, to write about male homosexuality: 'j'aurais eu un refus latent d'aborder des rapports passionnels entre garçons pour des motifs dissimulés dans mes replis' ['I had a latent resistance to depicting passionate feelings between boys for reasons hidden away deep inside me'] (CB, 87). This

95

explanation, too, leads back to the pernicious effects of society's prescripted and prescriptive labelling.

The notion that there is no such thing as a repetition is one we have already explored in relation to Christophe's story-telling. It is also pertinent to Rochefort's reappraisal of her draft of *Printemps*. Rereading the text in 1968 meant rereading in a radically altered context, more specifically, at a time when the author might have been less reluctant (however consciously or unconsciously) to portray a gay relationship. The early 1960s were marked by homophobic legislature. On the 18 July 1960 Paul Mirguet, a Gaullist MP, put forward an amendment to the penal code which recommended that homosexuality be classed as a 'social plague' ('fléau social') alongside tuberculosis, alcoholism, and prostitution. The proposal became law on the 30 July, and resulted in the addition of a paragraph to article 330 of the penal code, dealing with 'affronts to public decency' ('outrage public à la pudeur'), allowing far greater penalties to be meted out if the acts in question were of a homosexual nature.[2] Repressive social attitudes are alluded to in *Printemps* when Boubou, watching two policemen pass by, comments: 'en ce moment c'est le grand safari-pédale' ['open-season on queers'] (70). Attitudes were to change dramatically in the 1970s and 1980s. On the night of 27 June 1969—the year *Printemps* was published—a police raid on the gay café The Stonewall Inn in Greenwich Village, New York, triggered the Stonewall riots which were to open a new chapter in the fight for gay rights. Although Rochefort decided upon the name 'Christophe' towards the end of November 1968, thus before the Stonewall riots took place, her narrator's name, perhaps coincidentally, turned out to be highly significant: the Stonewall Inn was located at number 53, Christopher Street.[3]

As well as highlighting the importance of the context of reception, Rochefort's comments, like Christophe's experiences of story-telling, reveal that a narrative's potential inevitably exceeds its author's intentions. Rereading her text, the author steps aside from a privileged position, becomes a critical reader like any other. The information provided in *C'est bizarre l'écriture* also raises important questions concerning teleology. Rochefort may have seen Christophe's running to his meeting as a 'clue', but of course a clue is only a clue when, and if, the end-point of the story (the sexual relationship) is envisaged. The first version of the text, dealing with friendship, could strictly speaking have no clues (or bluffs); only when the author *amended* the original ending of the text which otherwise remained more or less unchanged up to the point where Christophe returns to the Minus-Bar with Fabrice, could elements of that first version be reinterpreted. We should also note that once she had decided on her new conclusion, Rochefort added short descriptors— 'titres' as she calls them—at the head of each chapter. The chapter in which the 'jeu du minet' takes place includes the epigraphical phrase 'les masques sont une vérité qui s'ignorent' ['masks are a truth hidden even to themselves'] (61), a clear authorial pointer to the true nature of the relationship between Thomas and Christophe, though one which, Rochefort states, readers appear to pass by: 'Bref, j'ai mis mes têtes de chapitres; après ça il est arrivé une chose curieuse: personne ne les a vues' ['In short I added my chapter headings and afterwards something odd happened: no-one saw them'] (CB, 118).

In view of the above comments on the teleology of writing and (re)reading, another metaphor or 'mise en abyme' of the reading act presents itself, and one which may be more appropriate than the poker-game analogy already discussed. Early in the text Christophe watches two children playing with toy boats in the 'bassin' of the Luxembourg gardens:

Des gosses jouaient au bateau sur le bassin. Il y en avait un avec un bateau très compliqué, à moteur, et un avec un bateau à voile. Le bateau à moteur traversait le bassin tout droit d'une rive à l'autre tout le temps et son môme cavalait en demi-cercle pour le renvoyer. Le bateau à voile se prélassait. Son môme zigzaguait, essayant de prophétiser son arrivé. (35–6)

[*Some kids were playing with boats on the lake. There was one who had a very complicated boat with an engine, and one with a sail-boat. The motorboat crossed the lake in a completely straight line from one bank to the other, and the kid rushed round in a semi-circle to send it back across again. The sail boat idled along. The kid who owned it zigzagged about, trying to predict where it would end up.*]

In terms of the act of reading (and indeed writing), the motorized boat can be taken to represent the teleological reading, a reading during which the outcome of the plot is known. The sail-boat, zigzagging erratically and unpredictably across the pond, forms a pattern which echoes the 'naive' reader's (that is, the reader who reads the text for the first time) apprehension of plot perceived now in terms of heterosexuality, now homosexuality, in which the outcome or final destination cannot be predicted. But this metaphor extends beyond the reading act, for it can be linked to the representation or articulation of sexuality itself.[4] The teleological or 'straight' reading presupposes an essentialist definition of sexuality based on the outcome of the relationship between the two boys, an outcome which is seen to define and fix their sexuality once and for all. To read comments such as 'il me plaît' as clues, or, equally, to read references to desire for women as 'bluffs', presupposes that Christophe and Thomas *are*, essentially, gay, that their identity or nature is fixed by their sexual acts. Ironically, the straight (motorboat) reading defines the boys as 'bent'. The sail-boat reading, that is the non-teleological reading, going now one way then the other, by contrast allows for a shifting pattern of desire. Sexuality is redefined in terms of an ongoing process. The text, in other words, breaks down the strict either/or binary which would categorize individuals as hetero- or homosexual, and, unlike *Les Stances à Sophie*, which by defining lesbianism as a 'luxe' or 'extra' risks reinforcing a hierarchical conception, places their respective desires on an equal footing. The reader who insists on reading in terms of bluff and clue (the very word 'clue' has unpleasant connotations of crime) is inevitably also engaging in a process of static categorization or labelling, putting the characters in tidy boxes just as society labelled Christophe's sister crazy and put her in a place for crazy people.

Christophe, towards the end of the text, is quick to dissociate himself from such a process. Addressing the incredulous Nicolas, whom he has just told about Thomas, he states: 'Non. Je ne suis pas pédé, j'aime quelqu'un; qui est un homme' ['No I'm not a poof; I love someone, who's a man'] (261), adding in same breath that he also has his eye on Nicolas's young twin sisters (aged twelve. . .).[5] Rochefort herself makes a similar point about her own sexuality: 'I've loved people, and sometimes it's been women, sometimes men, and that's all there is to it.'[6] When Christophe cries in the street and is comforted by Thomas, the latter points out that society cannot cope with un-labelled or un-categorized desire: 'l'homosexualité est interdite sauf aux homosexuels' ['homosexuality is forbidden to everyone but homosexuals'] (225). To name is to control: once placed in a special category, a subset defined in relation to 'the norm' and hence reinforcing that norm, homosexual desire is safely recuperated by the system:

> Faut être dans les schémas. Tu vois, si on était des, des pervers mettons des homosexuels, mais institutionnalisés, avec les conduites du groupe et notre étiquette sur le front et une fois pour toutes ils ne feraient pas attention, ça ils connaissent, c'est digéré. [. . .] Cependant il paraît qu'il y a une chose qu'ils n'arrivent pas à récupérer c'est ce qui est vrai. (197)

> [*You've got to fit in the pigeon-holes. You see, if we were, let's say perverts, homosexuals, but institutionalized ones, with the appropriate group behaviour and our label stuck on our foreheads once and for all, then they wouldn't pay any attention to us, they're used to that sort of thing, it's been digested. [. . .] But it seems that there's one thing they can't recuperate, and that's what's real/true.*]

The previous chapter discussed briefly Marcuse's claim that sexuality in modern industrial society is reduced and channelled into genital activity. Although a detailed account of Marcuse's work is beyond the scope of this study, a simplified account of some key ideas should serve to reveal the influence of his work in *Printemps*. In *Eros and Civilisation* Marcuse states that contemporary society has effectively institutionalized sexual permissiveness; the apparent liberalization of sexual mores is, in fact, a means whereby potentially subversive sexual desire can be controlled and regulated. Marcuse coins the term 'repressive desublimation' to indicate this process.[7] Sublimation can be described as the diversion of the sexual drive to non-sexual aims whose objects are usually socially valued, for example, in the form of artistic production. Desublimation might thus be regarded as a freeing of the sexual drive, a lifting of repression or diversion. 'Repressive desublimation', however, indicates the release of sexuality in modes and forms which not only reduce and weaken erotic energy (for example, the reduction to genital activity discussed in the previous chapter), but are actually dictated and contained by the system. Writing on the emerging counter-culture of the 1970s, Theodore Roszak notes that such apparently liberalized sexuality: 'creates no binding loyalties, no personal attachments, no distractions from one's primary responsibilities—which are to the company, to one's career and social position, and to the system generally.'[8] Roszak points out that capitalist technological society (what he calls the 'technocracy') is increasingly 'capable of anabolizing every form of discontent'.[9] Thomas employs a similar vocabulary: 'ça ils connaissent, c'est digéré'. For Thomas and Christophe 'ce qui est vrai' represents that aspect of their relationship which escapes or stands outside the system. Roszak suggests that any hope of change lies with the young. In the following chapter we will see that Rochefort's *Une Rose pour Morrison* represents just this hope for the future.

With Thomas, Christophe breaks away from his tendency to conceptualize himself in terms of pre-scripted plots and stories. If their relationship is repeatedly described as 'vraie', it is precisely because it does not follow an already existing storyline or plot, and because neither he nor Thomas can be fitted into familiar roles. Of course, this is only the case with respect to Christophe's and Thomas's point of view, and that of the reader who rejects the teleological, essentialist, reading. To outsiders, who see only two men together, the picture may tell a different story. Towards the close of the text Christophe briefly toys with the idea of jumping from the roof of the HLM to which he has returned. Imagining a scenario in which Thomas's student-card is found in his possession, he tells himself another story: 'l'affaire se corse. Quand avez-vous vu l'enfant pour la dernière fois? Thomas se trouble, il rougit, il begaye [. . .] Il est inculpé de détournement de mineur' ['Things start to hot up. When did you last see this child? Thomas is embarrassed, he blushes, he stammers [. . .]. He's charged with corrupting a minor'] (250). (Christophe is sixteen years old and Thomas ten years his senior. Their sexual relationship at the time, if we assume the story unfolds in 1969, was thus illegal according to paragraph 2 of article 331 of the old penal code. The age of consent for homosexual relations was set at eighteen years of age; the heterosexual age of consent was fifteen. Parity was finally achieved, after a long campaign, on 27 July 1982. We might note that in 1977 *Le Monde* published an appeal against the imprisonment of three men convicted 'pour attentat à la pudeur sans violence sur mineurs de 15 ans consentants'. Rochefort's name figured amongst the signatories.)[10] To society, homosexuality is a tale of crime and punishment, a version of events which we, as readers, see as a travesty of the truth. Christophe's story on this occasion smacks of the parodic, and parody, as we know, is the mark of consciousness.

Rochefort's text seeks to break with restrictive views of sexuality, but how does she handle the representation of the sexual scene itself?[11] The chapter in which the two characters finally accept, and act upon, their desire, is followed by a commentary on events, and it is to that commentary which we shall first turn. Seeking to answer Christophe's question 'why?'—why the reluctance, why the repression?—Thomas begins his analysis with the refrain: 'là alors c'est une longue longue longue histoire' ['that's a long long long story'] (211). He will not, however, shelter behind prefabricated stories, setting out instead to demystify the very narratives and categorizations to which he had himself fallen victim. Picking up on a critique of society's hijacking of language initiated in *Les Stances à Sophie*, Rochefort, via Thomas, shows again how words can entrap even the most liberal of individuals. Assessing his own behaviour, Thomas (whose name itself reflects his own doubting, his failure to follow his feelings) admits that he had hidden behind a prescripted moral code: the ready-made phrases 'Protection de l'Enfance' ['Child Protection'] and 'Maîtrise de Soi' ['Self-Control'] prevented him from acting (213).

A clear parallel can be drawn between the author herself and Thomas. Rochefort notes in *C'est bizarre* that she had hesitated for some time from representing the sexual relationship between her characters, finding various excuses in alternative versions (they had no place to go, no opportunity, etc.) before finally facing up to the real question: 'Nous avions une passion c'est sûr—mais, que se passe-t-il dans le pantalon?' ['there's passion here, that's for sure—but what's going on in their pants?'] (CB, 97). Using the identical expression, Thomas realizes that he had hidden his physical desire. The so-called liberal intellectual ('some of my best friends are gay') was liberal only in theory, open to anything, 'sauf ce qui se passe dans le pantalon' ['except what's going on in the pants'] (212). In the final resort, and in the absence of overt external pressures to conform, the liberal 'se constitue en police, il se réprime lui-même' ['polices himself, represses himself'] (212), masking the truth by superimposing 'bourgeois' terms such as 'crise' ('a passing phase') upon the situation, and employing 'un langage décent' ['respectable language']: 'on ne dit pas enculer mais homosexualité, pas: bander, mais érection et toujours celle des autres' ['you say homosexuality, not buggery, you don't say hard-on but erection, and always someone else's at that'] (221).

The link between oppression and language is clear, and is taken up in *C'est bizarre* when Rochefort insists on the need to 'vulgarize' her language, to break from that of the dominant ideology. In an imaginary dialogue in which she is asked if she endlessly 'polishes' (polisser) her work, she replies:

> Mais pas du tout oh là là, du reste ce serait plutôt: et le dépolissez. Ou même: dépolicez. Ce qui vient premier, c'est le langage poli; policé; de la cité, ou même de la police c'est pareil. Celui qui nous a été versé dans nos réservoirs (mémoires) depuis bébés. (CB, 132)

> [*Not at all, good grief it's more a case of un-polishing it. Or even: un-policing it. What comes first is polite language; policed, of the polis, or of the police it's the same thing. The language we've had poured into our reservoirs (memories) since we were babies.*]

Certainly the language employed by Christophe and Thomas is to the point: 'je triquais cela devrait aller sans dire' ['I had a hard-on, that should go without saying'] (215); or the punning (and almost untranslatable!): 'Cet hiver, le mariage en bloc, spécialement conçu pour les Grands Ensembles. Le prêt-à-enfiler. Le savoir-foutre dans le vent' [Announcing this winter's fashion, marriage en bloc, specially designed for housing estates: the off-the-peg-poke. Trendy savvey-shagging' (224).

The 'sex scene' itself, although commented on at length, is in no way explicit. Christophe states that the most interesting fact is that afterwards both men wondered what all the fuss had been about, adding rather coyly: 'je ne prétends pas que le reste ne le soit pas (dieu non) (il l'est, c'est un ravissement) j'essaye seulement d'être un peu pudique [. . .]' ['I'm not claiming that the rest isn't (God no) (it is, it's bliss) I'm just trying to be a little discreet'] (208). What we *can* see is an attempt to get away from stereotypical descriptions: Rochefort not only pulls apart the homo- / heterosexual binary, she also seeks to subvert a masculine/ feminine dichotomy as it relates to the portrayal of homo-eroticism. Writing on the representation of gay sex, Christopher Robinson points to the importance of inscribing femininity as 'a normal part of man's experience which the heterosexual code requires him to suppress'.[12] Christophe states that he will describe events in order to dismantle macho images of war and violence—'couper en herbe le cinéma guerrier avec assauts d'infanterie et charges de cavalerie' ['to undercut that sort of war-like cinema with its infantry assaults and cavalry charges'—and adds: 'Ce n'est pas ça du tout. Ce qu'il faut imaginer c'est la tendresse; le répit; la vérité mise à nue n'inspirait que douceur' ['it's not like that at all. You have to picture a scene of great tenderness; respite; the truth was revealed and it inspired only gentleness'] (207).

Rochefort's representation of sexuality breaks away from hierarchies or power-imbalances which can result from splitting the couple into a subject and an object of desire. A sense of fusion is communicated by images of incorporation: 'je me promène avec toi. Je suis tout mélangé avec toi'; 'je te bois' ['I walk with you. I'm a part of you'; 'I drink you'] (233), and by Christophe's repeated use of a first-person plural pronoun: 'je nous aimais' ['I loved us'] (222). Just before the couple make love Thomas quotes lines from Pierre Louys to Christophe: '"Quand il eut achevé, il mit doucement ses mains sur mes épaules, et il me regarda d'un regard si tendre, que je baissai les yeux avec un frisson"' ['"when he had finished he gently placed his hands on my shoulders, and he looked at me with such tenderness, that I shivered and lowered my eyes"'] (201). Although the source of the quotation is not identified in the text, the passage in fact comes from Part I of Louys's *Les Chansons de Bilitis*, 'Bucolique en Pamphylie', in a section entitled 'La Chevelure'. Thomas's quotation comes immediately after a passage which reiterates images of fusion and co-mingling:

> Je les [tes cheveux] caressais; et c'étaient les miens; et nous étions liés pour toujours ainsi, par la même chevelure la bouche sur la bouche, ainsi que deux lauriers n'ont souvent qu'une racine. Et peu à peu, il m'a semblé, tant nos membres étaient confondus, que je devenais toi-même ou que tu entrais en moi comme mon songe.[13]

> [*I stroked your hair, and your hair was mine, and thus were we linked together forever, by the same hair, mouth on mouth, just as two bay trees often share a single root. And little by little, so mingled together were our limbs that it seemed to me that I became you or that you entered me, like a dream.*]

Although the above passage actually refers to the eponymous Bilitis and a male lover, *Les Chansons de Bilitis* is perhaps best-known as a typical turn-of-the-century text treating lesbianism as a risqué and titillating subject. Rochefort's reappropriation of the work represents another example of subversive reframing or recontextualization.

Although Christophe and Thomas are referred to as Phaidros and Socrate, the Platonic line is taken one step further than in *Les Stances à*

Sophie, where we already saw that passion as a path leading to an absolute was transformed into a more pragmatic line, which saw desire as a route to freedom from oppression. Thomas initially cites Plato, 'c'est l'amour des idées à travers les apparences. . . à travers la beauté, dit-il en me regardant avec désespoir. C'est le seul amour véritable' ['it's the love of ideas in the form of appearances. . . in the form of beauty, he said, looking at me despairingly. It's the only true love there is'] (205), but subsequently admits that his recourse to Plato was just one more means of avoiding the truth: 'je socratais,—disciple félon! Socrate faisait mieux que discourir mais moi, tout dire et ne rien faire' ['I was reasoning like Socrates—treacherous disciple that I am! Socrates did more than talk but me, all talk and no action'] (217). Furthermore, the traditional pupil/teacher relationship which we associate with 'Greek love' is subverted. Although Christophe first turns to Thomas seeking knowledge, by the close of the text the roles have been reversed, and it is precisely Christophe's lack of intellectualizing which transforms him into the teacher of Thomas, the wordsmith whose very learning turns him away from action: 'corrompu par la saleté de culture!' ['corrupted by filthy culture!'] (216).

Printemps does not conclude with Thomas and Christophe's passion. Although Christophe appears to close his narration with a framing remark ('j'arrive à la fin de mon histoire' ['I'm coming to the end of my story'], p. 237), the final chapter comprises ten subsections, each dealing with 'loose ends' (or 'paquets' which he bundles up before moving on) concerning the various characters mentioned in his tale. In some respects, this pattern echoes that of *Les Stances à Sophie*, in which Julia's death marked the end of a personal relationship but the start of a new political awareness for Céline. In his analysis of their feelings for each other, Thomas points out to Christophe that true passion ('ce qui est vrai') is subversive: 'la liberté, elle, déborde, elle n'est pas le sexe mais la vie, elle entraîne beaucoup trop loin, elle mène à la politique alors ça devient sérieux' ['but freedom overflows, it's not sex but life, it takes you so much further, it leads you into politics, and that's serious stuff'] (225). For Christophe, sexuality becomes secondary to revolutionary politics, as Thomas, like Julia, is written out of the text, although it is suggested that the relationship will continue. Christophe returns home and decides to go back to school and take a 'bac technique'. His old plans, formulated with the anarchist Nicolas, to 'faire sauter les baraques' ['blow the place up'] are re-adopted, but now Christophe realizes that political action is more effective if undertaken from a position of knowledge, and an understanding of how the system works. As Nicolas says: 'Pour faire sauter n'importe quoi mon vieux il faut savoir ce que c'est au juste, et se trouver à portée' ['to blow anything up you have to know exactly what it is, and be up to the task'] (253). With the help of Nicolas, Christophe articulates his belief that passion cannot be separated from the wider sphere; that it is the manifestation of something which extends beyond the individual:

—Je ne sais pas dire ça mais il y a quelque chose d'important, ce qui était important ce n'est pas le sentiment et même pas la, la passion, c'est autre chose de plus, de plus fort et important qui nous dépasse, c'est la fureur, c'est. . . c'est la terre entière, c'est. . .
—La Révolution.
—Merci Nicolas. (266)

[*I don't know how to put it but there's something important, it wasn't the feelings that were important, and not even the, the passion, it's something else, something more, something stronger and more important that goes beyond us, it's rage, it's . . . it's the whole world, it's . . .*'
'Revolution.'
'Thank you Nicolas.']

'C'est la fureur': it is rage which fuels Christophe's political passion; rage against the injustices of a system which had sought to deny and devalue his feelings for Thomas. Rochefort has pointed to the importance of the fury which accompanies political awareness. In *C'est bizarre* she notes that the original title envisaged for *Printemps* was *Un certain état de fureur*, adding: 'd'ailleurs toutes mes tentatives de cette époque s'intitulent comme ça' ['besides, that was what all my efforts of the time were called'] (CB, 36). In *Les Petits Enfants du siècle* Josyane's younger brother, also called Nicolas, embodies the anger which was to be associated with political consciousness in the later text. Nicolas plans to become a 'Grand Assassin' (139); he scribbles furious lines in a notebook: 'Je tuerai mon père. Je tuerai ma mère. Je tuerai mon frère' ['I'll kill my father. I'll kill my mother. I'll kill my brother'] (140). Josyane too, although her anger is rapidly defused by the oppressive environment in which she evolves, at one stage recognizes the mobilizing potential of rage: 'la colère ça me parlait, ça me faisait bouger, c'était le seul truc qui m'aurait fait sortir de ma gelée et réchauffée, qui arrivait encore à me faire mal; et ça venait de loin; de toujours' ['anger said something to me, it got me going, it was the only thing that could have got me out of my frozen state and warmed me up, that could still upset me, and it came from far away and it had always been there'] (143). *Printemps* ends back in the 'parking' in which it began, with Nicolas and Christophe screaming their revolt ('merde, merde, merde, merde') to the HLM inhabitants: 'Ils se sont mis aux fenêtres, et ils ont vu que c'était le Printemps' ['they looked out of their windows and they saw that it was spring'] (270). *Printemps au parking*: the Prague spring, but also the spring of freedom, for as Thomas points out: 'la liberté, c'est le printemps de l'esprit' ['freedom is the springtime of the spirit'] (75).[14]

Christophe comes full circle, ending up physically where he began, but of course his spatial revolution is also a spiritual, political one. The spatial metaphor is one of many, and we can conclude this chapter with a brief examination of the ways in which the text, via the use of spatial imagery, represents a subversion of the concept of normality. Christophe left home aiming vaguely for an unidentified 'pays lointain' ['distant land']. Although the link is not established in the text we might note that homosexuality is commonly presented in exotic settings, both because other countries (Algeria, Morocco, etc.) provided Europeans with the opportunity for gay sex, and because representing gay sex in far-off lands was less hazardous than representing it in France itself. Christophe, however, as we have seen, goes nowhere in literal terms. Once he has acknowledged his love for Thomas, he realizes that he has already reached his hoped-for destination: 'C'est vraiment un pays lointain. . . Je me demandais ce que c'est un pays lointain. La frontière est imaginaire' ['It's really a distant land. . . I wondered what a distant land was. The frontier is imaginary'] (219).

State of mind is more important than physical location; the important journey is that which takes place within the individual. Once Christophe crosses the invisible frontier (a concept which, as we shall see in a later chapter, will be taken up in Rochefort's utopia, *Archaos*), his sense of liberation, of difference with relation to the society in which he lives, can only be articulated in extreme terms: he becomes an alien being from another planet. Standing embracing Thomas in the street, he states: 'on s'était mis à vivre au milieu de la rue autant dire qu'on avait changé de planète, on était des Martiens et des objets de curiosité c'est presque à dire des criminels' ['we'd begun to live in the middle of the street, you might as well say we'd changed planets, we were martians, we were curiosities which more or less amounts to saying we were criminals'] (196). As we saw in Chapter 2, a similar image is used in *Les Petits Enfants* when Josyane strives to explain to the young Nicolas how her relationship with Guido has opened her eyes to another way of being: 'je lui racontai que j'avais rencontré un habitant de la planète Mars. [. . .] Chez lui, tout le monde avait une âme, tout le monde se comprenait' ['I told him that I'd met an inhabitant of Mars. [. . .] Where he came from everyone had a soul and everyone understood one another'] (41).

The idea of a mental barrier is used again in *Printemps* in a metaphor which likens society to a zoo. To Thomas, Christophe's aimlessness and freedom signifies clearly that he is an escapee, and escape, as both learn, means changing one's own perceptions. As Thomas says: 'Les barreaux étaient à l'intérieur' ['the bars were on the inside'] (233). More than this, Christophe represents the 'homme normal'. To be 'normal' is, precisely, to have broken out of the frame, the story, the bars set up by society to contain and control. If Christophe decides to go to war against society, it is in order to break down the external controls which lead to the raising of internal (self-policing) constraints: 'Bien sûr, il y a toujours les barreaux dehors et c'est à ceux-là que j'en ai maintenant. Car en plus ils se tiennent, ceux de dedans sont un reflet de ceux du dehors tu vois ce que je veux dire?' ['Of course the bars on the outside are always there and it's those ones I'm mad at now. Because they reinforce each other, those on the inside are the reflection of those on the outside, you see what I mean?'] (257). In Plato's *Republic* the shadows cast upon the wall of the cave were mere reflections of an absolute realm of ideas. Here, once more, the absolute is translated into pragmatic politics.

Fabrice's mother despairingly wonders how it can be that her children are homosexual (her daughter, Zélie, is also gay) when both she and her husband are 'normal' (163). Initially, Thomas, drying Christophe's tears in public view, worries about whether his actions can pass off as normal, but after they have had sex for the first time, the situation changes. Now behaving normally means expressing their love without censure. Sitting with Thomas in a café, Christophe notes : 'Ça faisait bizarre de ne plus pouvoir se conduire normalement, on s'était déjà habitués à être normaux' ['It felt odd not being able to behave normally any more, we'd already got used to being normal'] (223). This redefinition of normality is reinforced later when Christophe informs Boubou, who is training to be a psychiatrist, that he will not be able to use his and Thomas's relationship as a case-study:

'En tant que psychiatre' ça relève pas de chez toi. Parce que c'est normal. Ce qui relève de chez toi, c'est quand ça n'arrive pas! C'est là qu'il y a du malsain [. . .]. Parce que c'est naturel d'aimer quelqu'un ·qui est bien, qu'il soit n'importe quoi. (243)

[*In your capacity as psychiatrist*' it doesn't concern you. Because it's normal. What does concern you is when it doesn't happen! That's when you're dealing with something unhealthy [. . .]. Because it's natural to love a good person, whatever he or she is.]

Early in his relationship with Christophe, Thomas, uttering the lyrics of a Bob Dylan song, points out, 'je vous dis les Temps n'ont pas fini de changer' ['I tell you the times are still a-changing'] (69). *Printemps* ends with two rebellious figures screaming their revolt. In Rochefort's *Une Rose pour Morrison*, a work which anticipated the 1968 events, the streets will be filled with thousands of like-minded revolutionaries.

CHAPTER FIVE

Une Rose pour Morrison

Que sera 1968? L'avenir n'appartient pas aux hommes et je ne le prédis pas. Pourtant, en considérant la façon dont les choses se présentent, c'est vraiment avec confiance que j'envisage, pour les douze prochains mois, l'existence de notre pays.

(Charles de Gaulle, Dec. 1967)

Sustained political satire targeting French society of the late 1960s, the incumbent president of France himself, and the Vietnam War; elements of a futuristic dystopia combining with an occasional foray into the fantastic; a quite dazzling, often erudite, and always humorous display of linguistic virtuosity: it is little wonder that *Une Rose pour Morrison*, 'petit canard dans une couvée de poussins' ['an ugly duckling'], was not, initially, easily classifiable or indeed identifiable as 'classic Rochefort'—'il ne ressemblait pas [. . .]. Ça ne rentrait dans rien. [. . .] Et il paraît que ce n'était pas moi' ['it wasn't like anything else [. . .] It didn't fit in anywhere. [. . .] And apparently it wasn't me'] (9).[1] Certainly the form has changed. The author's previous works centre on a first-person narrator's interaction with a restricted number of characters, and tell a tale of personal development and discovery. Now the cast of not quite thousands (forty-six human beings and three dogs by Rochefort's count) is complemented by a third-person narrator. The layering of tenses and accompanying splitting of perspective seen in earlier works is replaced by a unified past historic narrative. Although some of the characters do evolve, for the most part they are larger-than-life static figures who would not be out of place in a cartoon-strip or animated film. Characterization, such as it is, is restricted to action and speech, with next to no penetration into the 'inner life' of any character. Rochefort's usual strict adherence to realism is cast aside. And yet for all this, *Une Rose* remains a typical Rochefort text in so far as it is dedicated to an exposition and critique of oppressive socio-political mechanisms which are seen to stifle individual liberties. Humankind's capacity for resistance and survival in the face of domination is once more foregrounded with typical optimism (some might say idealism), and the links between passion and political action, established in *Les Stances à Sophie*, and developed in *Printemps au parking*, are further clarified. Most crucially, *Une Rose* once again reveals the importance of language as a potential threat, but also as a powerful subversive weapon in the hands of those who seek to fight back.

In this novel Rochefort launches an attack against what she perceives to be the flaws, indeed dangers, of the society in which she and her readers live, a society deemed to be ruled by an autocratic government which seeks to bind and control individuals to a party line, which wages or at best connives in the waging of war, and which has no place for individual creativity or expression. In some respects, *Une Rose pour Morrison* might be likened to a propagandist text, written very rapidly (the manuscript was completed in only twenty-four days) as a gut-reaction to what was perceived as an untenable situation, with a minimal time-lapse between its conception and publication, thereby ensuring its immediate contemporary relevance.[2] (It may be that the very propagandist nature of the work, which singles out a specific historical moment for attack, accounts for the relatively low sales figures—see Appendix.)

The principal vehicle for the author's critique is satire, and as a satirical work *Une Rose* must strike a chord with its readership; it must represent recognizable aspects of contemporary 1960s France. The text is thus set in Paris, with place-names comically altered: the Place de la Concorde becomes the dismal-sounding 'Place de la Miséricorde'; Boulevard Saint-Germain is replaced by 'Boulevard Saint-Vénérien' with its connotations of both sickness and venality, whilst the 'Champ de Marche' rings of militarization. As we shall see, the head of government, Sénile, is cast in the image of Charles de Gaulle. Aspects of daily life in France of the 1960s are easily recognizable: massive construction programmes (a Rochefort 'bête noire' as we know) are in progress, with shoddy building materials proving hazardous to the immigrant workforce. (It has been estimated that immigrant workers constituted approximately 6 per cent of the total population of France by 1968; poor materials in the building industry were a fact of life.)[3] Rochefort's linguistic play lends a sinister note to contemporary issues: Théostat, one of the text's central characters, refers to his deportation out of the centre of Paris in the 'Epoque Zupiste', a play on the acronym ZUP or 'zones à urbaniser à priorité' ['zones designated for priority urbanization'] (21), and reference is made to a 'Plan de Lavage Electoral Urbain et Orbain' (12), suggestive of both brainwashing and gerrymandering. Students are packed into overcrowded lecture-halls, and schoolchildren show signs of unrest and rebellion. Songs by Bob Dylan, to whom the text is dedicated, are sung in student bars, as is the fictitious 'Lendemain de Bombe' ['The Day after the Bomb'] (the first French A-bomb was exploded on 13 February

1960). Extending the scope of the satire to the USA, the text translates the Pentagon to the 'Pantygone', the CIA to the 'CHIA', Defense Secretary McNamara becomes 'Mac Connery'. The title itself alludes to the Vietnam War: Norman Morrison was the first US citizen to set himself alight (on the steps of the Pentagon) in protest against US military involvement in South East Asia.

Satire requires the presence of a stratum of contemporary reference in the text, but alongside the recognizable features of 1960s France there lies a second, futuristic, world more aligned with the genres of the dystopia and science fiction. This is a Paris which has become so polluted that citizens are obliged to wear 'respiratoires' (a neologism suggesting breathing-apparatuses); the university buildings are enclosed in a 'cloque de plastiglace' ['plastiglass bubble'] (17). We are in the presence of a totalitarian state: lecture halls are policed by armed guards who 'zap' students with ray-guns or beat them with batons as they leave classes. Bars are raided on a daily basis, and man-hunts organized to seek out dissidents. Citizens who sing forbidden songs may end their days in the 'Fosse Banale' ['Communal Pit'] (41). Philibert, in charge of construction work, struggles to master quadratic equations in order to align a machine-gun trajectory with maximum efficacy. State officials are aided by a sinister 'Service de Dissuasion' ['Dissuasion Corps'] and 'Milice de Répresseurs' ['Militia for Repression']. Students lured onto the 'Champ de Marche' by government tracts are ruthlessly felled by gunfire.

In common with Orwell's *1984* or Huxley's *Brave New World*, indeed as with many dystopic works, the society represented in *Une Rose* is rigidly hierarchical: Orwell's 'proles' have become Rochefort's 'serves'; Philibert is a 'Classe Trois' citizen, member of the 'tie-classe', inferior to 'Deux Bis', 'Un', or the elevated 'toxido-classe' with its play on both 'toxic' and 'tuxedo'. The Orwellian ministries of Love, Peace, Plenty and Truth have their equivalent in a group of 'Vénérables': Ravale ['Excoriator'], Ruines ['Ruins'], Sinistre ['Sinister'], Sanguinolle ['Gore'] and Décombres ['Debris']. Sexuality and thought are under state control. In *Brave New World*, Alphas and Epsilons are genetically engineered in the Central London Hatchery and Conditioning Centre in order that they may be integrated into specific social strata; here, the 'Ecole Prénuptiale' ['Pre-nuptial School'] trains young girls to be docile and compliant wives. Young men are seized in order to be milked of their sperm (by women with callused hands!) and women impregnated in a manner reminiscent of the Orwellian Artsem programme. The state employs 'psychophages' ['psychophagocytes'] to keep track of individuals' mental condition, whilst 'Opération Léthé', like Huxley's hypnopoedia, brainwashes the young.

The text, as we can see, comprises two related discourses or genres, juxtaposing known and unknown, 'now' and 'yet to come'. This combination of discourses should come as no surprise. Dystopias, after all, are always anchored in a stratum of recognizable reality. It is difficult to conceive of an example of the genre which did not include at least a minimal degree of the familiar; the whole point of the dystopia is to sound a cautionary and critical note: 'this is what our society will or could become'. *Une Rose*, however, perhaps differs from the norm in that its field of contemporary reference is extremely specific. Current events, or real figures like de Gaulle, are integrated into a futuristic world which clearly is not 'real', has not (or in the case of today's readers, did not), in fact, become reality. Construction programmes coexist with features of the text such as sleep-treatment which, whilst remaining within the bounds of the possible, nonetheless have affiliations with the genre of science fiction, belong to another world. There is, in other words, a collision of heterogeneous elements in the text: the real, historical present on which the satire relies, and a fictive future world which grounds the dystopic dimension (which itself, of course, has a satirical function). To complicate matters further, the text also introduces elements which break even more radically with any stratum of realism, which tend, in fact, towards the fantastic. Philibert, for instance, is attacked on his building-site by a strange, apparently sentient machine, the 'bécassin', and is then given some rather unorthodox first-aid:

> Il prit son pied dans un bécassin dont la partie supérieure, dentée, lui sauta à la figure et le mordit cruellement. [. . .] Le bécassin fut privé de dessert, et comme il adorait le sable, il se recognit sur ses pales, en grinçant. Les ouvriers cimentèrent comme ils pouvaient la moitié défigurée de Philibert, et lui recommandèrent de rester un quart d'heure sans faire un mouvement, pour que ça prenne. (13)

> [*He trapped his foot in a bécassin whose toothed upper part leapt at his face and bit him savagely. [. . .] The bécassin had to go without its dessert, and as it loved sand it grouched over its blades, with a grating sound. The workers patched up Philibert's disfigured half as best they could with cement and advised him to stay absolutely still for fifteen minutes so that the cement could harden.*]

The combining of different discourses, which we might call the satirical, the dystopic, and the fantastic, is such that the reader is constantly unsettled, unable to suspend disbelief and plunge into another world, quite simply because there is no one stable world with its own internal logic. This unstable form tends to elicit an intellectual rather than an emotional response: the text is not disturbing in the same way that a pure dystopia might be, although we should bear in mind that for the reader of 1966 threats of nuclear war and social unrest were realities rather than distant possibilities. Indeed, for the post-1968 reader, the work, especially as regards its emphasis on the student milieu as the source of eventual uprising, has a powerful prophetic quality (Rochefort subsequently described her text as a 'crise de prémonition' ['a premonitory crisis'], p. 10).

If today's readers perhaps do not feel quite the same chill of apprehension when reading *Une Rose,* they will respond to the text's sheer verve and sustained humour. Furthermore, however fragmented the text may be at the level of genres, linguistic play, whether in the form of neologisms or parody, serves to re-establish a level of aesthetic unity. Preceding chapters have already revealed Rochefort's belief that language lies at the core of oppression; that those in power may use words to conceal, label, delimit, and thereby control. The influence of language and the need to control it is a common topos in the genre of the dystopia, yet the majority of writers in the genre do not diverge from a standard language in their narration. Rochefort breaks from this pattern in the very writing *of* her text, which not only displays the force of humour and parody, but creates its own language in the form of a multitude of neologisms.

Monique Crochet has produced an excellent study of over one hundred and fifty neologisms in the text (there are more, as she acknowledges), combining a taxonomic survey with a brief assessment of the function of each grouping of neologisms, and it is not my intention to duplicate her material here.[4] What must be stressed is the fact that Rochefort's linguistic play is more than a ludic verbal joy-ride: the great majority of the neologisms serve a political function. A number of examples may serve to give readers at least an idea of some the processes at work: familiar words may be altered to point to deficiencies in the social situation, thus 'crottoirs' (43) for 'trottoir' with its suggestion of filth ('crotte'); 'enlisements dans la Néo-Milice' (11), combining the English 'enlist' and the French 'enliser' ('to be stuck or bogged down in'); or prayers offered up to the 'Saint Esfric' (58), pointing to the spiritual void at the centre of consumer society ('fric' meaning 'cash' or 'dough'). Philibert's wife, Girofle, like all young girls who have been through the 'Ecole Prénuptiale', suffers from an inability to enjoy sex. A humorous malformation of the imperfect subjunctive of 'recevoir' (correctly, 'reçût') thus combines a bawdy note with a more serious intention: 'dans la glace elle se trouva le teint brillant, et regretta qu'on ne reçusse pas ce soir' ['looking in the mirror she saw that her complexion was glowing and regretted that they would not be receiving/sucking again that evening']

111

(53). Borrowings from different languages are common: consumerism is undermined by references to 'Nice-Crime' for 'ice-cream' (85), 'vache-machine' (literally 'cow-machine') for 'washing-machine' (201). Séminolle, assistant to Ruines, takes part in the 'lèche-parties du Second Cercle' (46), a phrase suggestive of both the English 'party' and, on a metaphorical level ('lécher' meaning 'to lick'), the licking of parts—or 'arse-licking'. 'Mots-valises', or telescopings of several words, provide an alternative source of neologisms: the immigrant workers are referred to as 'portagnols' (13), combining 'Portugais' and 'Espagnol'; Marxists become 'vérolutionnaires' (36), combining revolution with the pox ('la vérole'); the 'general good' is translated into the self-seeking 'intérêt Vénéral' ('venal' translating as 'vénal') (119).

Unsympathetic characters are attributed individual linguistic mannerisms. Belette, a representative of the up-and-coming structuralism, speaks an incomprehensible babble of coined linguistics terminology: 'existéité' (20), 'référant' (used as a present participle, p. 21), 'vous dénotez' (21). His thesis itself bears the impenetrable title: 'La Banalité de la Parlition, Essai de Verbiologie Conarrative' ['The Banality of Oralition, an Essay on Conarratorial Verbiage'] (29). Belette's parodied intellectual precocity is accompanied by an emotional immaturity, signalled by a child-like duplication of syllables: 'il arriva chez sa Manman, manmangea, pipissa, externua, excetera, puis se remit à sa Thèse' ['he got home to his mummy-wummy, had his dindins and a pee-pee, expectorated and etceterated, then restarted work on his Thesis'] (29). The evil Séminolle is afflicted by a lisp, and his speech impediment is milked to maximum effect: 'la confience [conscience] est l'affaire du Vénérable Ravale de l'Infirmation et des Maffes Média, et de fes fix fent foifante-fix favants du Corps Pfychique' ['conthience ith dealt with by the Venerable Ekthcoriator in charge of Infirmation and Math Media, and by the thix hundred and thixthy-thix thpethialithts in the Pthychic Corps'] (48).

The creative manipulation of language is the mark of political consciousness, the capacity to step outside an existing system, perceive its underlying workings, and subvert them. Whilst the whole text which is *Une Rose* evidently bears witness to its author's 'prise de conscience', the ability to create and mould language is attributed primarily to one of the text's characters, the young university lecturer Sereine, whose series of speeches, which punctuate the text at regular intervals, will eventually incite her ever-growing audience to action. As we have seen, the text singles out and satirizes a specific historical period, and Sereine's first target is none other than de Gaulle, a man, ironically enough, known for his ability to use speech to maximum effect. As one biographer sums it up: 'De tous les hommes d'état contemporains, Charles de Gaulle fut celui dont le destin politique aura dépendu le plus constamment des mots' ['amongst all contemporary statesmen it was de Gaulle whose political destiny depended most consistently on words'].[5] Sereine prefaces her first lecture with a scathing reference to what she perceives as a ruling gerontocracy, bemoaning the fact that presidential figures are 'des gens vieux, qui ont oublié la vie' ['old people who have forgotten life'] (16). At the time *Une Rose* was published, de Gaulle was 75 years old and had been on the political scene for several decades. When a student, amusingly aghast at the thought of the president's continuing in office, enquires 'mais n'est-il pas mortel?' ['but is he not mortal?'], he is told that the leader will be deep-frozen ('grâce à un Emprunt National 3% indexé' ['thanks to a 3% National Loan']) and thawed out should the country need him (23). Not only do these elderly presidents remain in office for years, they are, Sereine informs her audience, 'atteints de préférence dans les organes conducteurs d'humeurs comme le foie ou les reins' ['diseased, preferably in the organs which conduct the humours, like the liver or kidneys'], perhaps an allusion to de Gaulle's prostate operation of 17 April 1964.

These are no more than preliminary gibes. The greater part of Sereine's lecture consists of a critique of presidential activities, for example:

> Durant son nouveau mandatement, ayant renforcé dans le précédent ses pouvoirs légiférants, il fera anticonstitutionnellement des ordon-nancementations présidenstabilisatrices qui seront référendomisées auprès de la surpopulation hyperconditionnalisée. (22)

> [*In the course of his new mandate, having reinforced his legislative powers in the previous one, he will anticonstitutionally carry out presidenti-stabilizing ordonenticements which will be referensodomized before the hyperconditionned overpopulation.*]

This extract, explicitly referring to Sénile, but of course implicitly targeting de Gaulle, allows us to pin the text's field of reference down to a specific historical point in time. Beyond this, the coded language of the neologisms establishes a strong bond of complicity between the author and her readers: being in the know, or getting the joke, effectively means that readers too have attained a certain critical distance. The reference to increased legislative power ('ayant renforcé dans le précédent ses pouvoirs légiférants') refers to de Gaulle's success in the referendum of 28 October 1962 in which he called for the presidential election to be decided by universal suffrage, securing a 'yes' vote of 61.8 per cent. This move was seen by many as symptomatic of the president's belief in his own right to rule, and his desire to increase presidential powers. Critics have noted that during this period de Gaulle showed a marked tendency to refer to the president as the leader of France as if such leadership operated outside parliamentary control.[6]

The neologisms employed are a compact and highly efficient means of attacking the existing régime. The referendum, de Gaulle's political trademark (as well as the 1962 vote on election by universal suffrage, the French people had been presented with referenda on the Algerian situation in the early 1960s), is singled out for attack via the humorous 'référendomisées', suggestive of sodomy (the people are, metaphorically, 'buggered' by the system). Later in the text we find a more sinister reference to the 'référendrome' (27), the neologism on this occasion alluding to the infamous 'vélodrome' (Vel' d'Hiv') or round-ups of Jews for deportation in 1942. Mention is also made of a past government operation, 'l'Opération Stadium' (111), and here the text strikes another prophetic note. Revelations published in *Libération* in 1974, subsequently taken up by the *Nouvel Observateur* and *Canard enchaîné*, suggested a plan had been drawn up in May 1968 to round up extreme left-wing militants in 'stades' in 41 French cities (as was later to happen after the fascist coup d'état in Chile in 1973). Initially planned for 24 May, the programme was apparently cancelled on 29 May.[7] Paradoxically, the fictive dystopia almost became an historical reality.

Sereine's lecture begins with a reference to the president's standing for re-election—'le président se représidentera' ['the president will represident himself'] (22)—again allowing us to situate the text's field of reference quite specifically. De Gaulle sought re-election to the presidency in 1965. The first round was held on the 5 December 1965, and de Gaulle was subsequently elected on the 19 December with a winning second-round vote of 54.5 per cent to Mitterrand's 45.5 per cent. Sereine goes on to allude to what we can identify as a particular speech made by de Gaulle. Asked by a student if 'le pays' ['the country'] cannot ultimately be identified with its citizens, she points out that this is sadly not the case, continuing:

> Tout conglomérat rendu suffisamment plasmique par des techniques appropriées de ramollissement prend une forme référendémentielle lorsqu'il est mis en présence d'un dilemme suffisamment interférent [. . .]. Dans le cas présent, où plutôt futur, la question sera: 'Préférez-vous la stabilité ou le désordre?' (24)

> [*Any conglomeration which has been rendered sufficiently plasmic by the appropriate softening techniques takes on a referendemential form when confronted with a suitably interfering dilemma* [. . .]. *In the present or rather future case, the question will be: 'Do you prefer stability or disorder?'*]

On the 4 November 1965, de Gaulle, one month before the presidential elections, and after an unusually protracted period of media silence, finally officially announced his candidature for the presidential election in a speech which came to be summed up in the words 'moi ou le chaos' ['me, or chaos']. Although in an interview with Michel Droit held on 15 December 1965 de Gaulle denied having said either 'moi' or 'chaos', he admitted this was indeed 'l'esprit du texte' ['the spirit of the text'], his 'all or nothing' rhetoric perhaps best summed up in the following extract:

> Que l'adhésion franche et massive des citoyens m'engage à rester en fonctions, l'avenir de la République nouvelle sera décidément assuré. Sinon, personne ne peut douter qu'elle s'écroulera aussitôt et que la France devra subir—mais cette fois sans recours possible—une confusion de l'Etat plus désastreuse encore qu'elle ne connut autrefois.[8]

> [*Should the people lend their unequivocal and overwhelming support to my remaining in office, the future of the new Republic will without doubt be safeguarded. If they do not, there can be no doubt that the Republic will collapse at once and that France will be subjected—and this time with no possible way out—to a non-separation of State powers more disastrous yet than any it has previously known.*]

Sereine (and beyond her Rochefort) deplores what she regards as the pseudo-democratic mechanism of the referendum with its 'yes' or 'no' agenda ('Préférez-vous la stabilitité ou le désordre?'). In the same lecture she sets her student audience homework based on a refusal to engage in dialogue: 'Constituer le réflexe de non réponse. Principe: toute question est une agression' ['Develop the non-response reflex. The principle being: all questions are a form of aggression']. This opposition to the Gaullist régime is captured in a series of exchanges between Xavière Gauthier and Marguerite Duras which took place some eight years later:

> M.D. Même si vous dites 'non', vous entamez le dialogue. C'était ça, les référendums gaullistes, la grande, grande escroquerie intellectuelle. 'dites-moi si vous me choisissez. . .'. Et on avait envie de lui dire: 'Mais on ne vous a rien demandé'. Tout le monde a marché.[9]

> [*M.D. Even if you say no, you're engaging in dialogue. That's what happened with the Gaullist referendums, that great intellectual swindle. 'Tell me if you are for me or against me. . .' And you felt like saying to him: 'But we haven't asked you anything.' And everyone went along with it.*]

Sereine's first lecture, with its references to 'la surpopulation hyper-conditionnalisée' and 'techniques appropriées de ramollissement', raises the issue of social conditioning via the channelling and controlling of information, and we can see here how the satirical and dystopic genres coexist in the text. On the one hand, references to a brainwashed population are to be read at a literal level within the futuristic dystopic world: citizens are subject to the monitoring of the 'psychophages' and the sleep-treatment of 'Opération Léthé'. Reading at another level, that of the purely satirical, these references reflect the well-documented media stranglehold of the Gaullist régime. The ORTF (Office de la Radio-diffusion et Télévision Française), for instance, was, during much of the 1960s, under the control of the Ministry of Information, and opposition leaders were given scant media coverage.[10] Michael Winock has described the régime's media control as a 'télécratie' ['telecracy']

> La censure, le droit de regard du Prince, l'intervention incessante du politique sur le responsable des programmes et de l'information: panoplie d'un pouvoir fort, incapable de croire aux vertus de la société civile, accumulant contre lui des réserves de frustrations, de refoulement, de désirs de dire interdits.[11]
>
> [*Censorship, the Head of State's prerogative to vet all material, incessant political interference vis-à-vis those responsible for programming and news-bulletins: all this was the panoply of a strong government with absolutely no faith in the virtues of civil society, a government which generated hostile reserves of frustration, repression, and forbidden desires to speak out.*]

So far, we have seen the attack on the Gaullist government function primarily by means of Sereine's neologizing lectures, but the text uses a second form of linguistic subversion—parody—when president Sénile himself rehearses his next public performance. (Rochefort maintained that during the writing of *Une Rose* she transcribed whole sections of de Gaulle's speeches for use in her text.)[12] The technique of capitalization which we first saw in *Les Petits Enfants du siècle* is used to full effect, highlighting well-known Gaullist terms and phrases, whilst the language of the president is further undermined via a process of accumulation. Elements which recur in de Gaulle's speeches throughout the 1960s appear in rapid succession: the familiar image of France as a ship (with, of course, de Gaulle at the helm), 'nous avons pris la vitesse de croisière' ['we've reached cruising-speed'], and an insistence on the marked improvement in the country's internal and external standing—the Republic is described as 'Maître de son Destin et sur la voie du Développement Intérieur et de l'Harmonie Extérieur Stable et Efficace' ['Master of its Destiny and on the way to Internal Development and an

External Harmony both Efficacious and Stable'] (81). De Gaulle's frequently reiterated references to the bad old days (usually associated with 'le régime des partis', the fragmented multi-party system) are echoed in Sénile's 'foin à présent de la Confusion, du Chaos et de l'Impuissance, foin!' ['And now, now I laugh in the face of Confusion, of Chaos, and of Impotence; I laugh in the face of it all!']. His stressing of the healthy economic climate he had promoted translates into Sénile's reference to 'Travail, Consommation, Production' and the all-important 'Produit National Brute [sic]' ['Gross—in every sense of the word—National Product'] (82).

De Gaulle's rather distinctive, ponderous rhetorical style is mimicked throughout Sénile's speech, for instance in the following anaphoric pronouncement: 'Quelle anarchie au commencement, quelle méconnaissance des vrais intérêts de Classe, quels tâtonnements, quelles erreurs, commises par des hommes de peu' ['What anarchy there was in the beginning, what failure to recognize true class interests, what gropings in the dark, what errors, committed by men of little account'] (81). The text may also take a Gaullist linguistic trademark and topple it into the absurd. One discernible trait of de Gaulle's 1960s speeches is his repeated image of the 'tête' or head of state: 'Ainsi devra demeurer cet élément capital de permanence et stabilité que comportent nos institutions, je veux dire la présence au sommet de la République d'une tête qui puisse en être une' ['And so this crucial factor contributing to permanence and stability within our institutions must remain, I mean the presence at the head of the Republic of a head of state who can truly be one'] (7 November 1962); 'Oui! La République veut que le peuple lui donne demain, plus tard et toujours, une tête qui en soit une' ['Yes! The Republic wishes that the people give it tomorrow, later, and always, a head of State who can truly be one'] (30 November 1965).[13]

This (rather bizarre) linguistic tic becomes in Sénile's speech a series of absurd rhetorical questions: 'Qui mieux qu'un pilote peut piloter l'avion? Qui mieux qu'un capitaine peut diriger le bateau? Qui mieux qu'un cavalier peut monter le cheval? Qui mieux qu'un chapeau peut couvrir la tête?' ['Who better than a pilot to pilot a plane? Who better than a captain to captain a ship? Who better than a rider to ride a horse? Who better than a hat to cover a head?'] (81). The passage, already tilting into the absurd, further undermines the presidential person with deflatory references to Sénile's receiving of serum injections prior to appearing on 'Mégavision', where he begins his actual speech with a detailed account of his recent bowel movements.

The creation of words and the parodic subversion of the words of others shows clearly that language is a weapon not only for those in power. The world of *Une Rose* is a world threatened by war, both the nuclear conflagration alluded to in the closing pages of the text, and the very real Vietnam War being waged as the text was written. But the war in the text is also a war of words. The society represented is a police-state, and that policing extends to language itself. The control of language is a common topos in dystopic literature. In Orwell's *1984* 'Newspeak' is developed with a view ultimately to preclude the very possibility of 'Thoughtcrime', any concepts which run counter to the prevailing ideology. 'B Vocabulary', a form of verbal shorthand comprising compound words, serves clear ideological aims; words become dissimulative tools, the political euphemism 'joycamp' masking the reality of 'forced labour', 'Minipax' standing for the Ministry of Peace (in fact War).[14] In *Printemps au parking* Thomas realized that words could serve to control and delimit aspects of reality; in *Une Rose* Rochefort develops further her critique of the dominant ideology's control of language. The usually unobtrusive narrator breaks from anonymity to deliver a harangue against state-employed 'verbologues' whose task is to defuse dangerous anti-government activities by investing them with names or labels:

> Ils avaient inventé [. . .] le Mot Chaos Intérieur pour supprimer les libertés, le Mot Stabilité pour se maintenir au pouvoir, le Mot Prospérité pour faire croire que c'était celle de tout le monde [. . .] le Mot Pays pour nier les citoyens, le Mot Monde Libre pour cogner sur le reste. (191)

> [*They had invented* [. . .] *the Word Internal Chaos to suppress freedom, the Word Stability to keep their hold on power, the Word Prosperity to make us believe that prosperity belonged to everyone* [. . .] *the Word Nation to deny the citizens, the Word Free World to beat up the rest of it.*]

True to the propagandist aims of the text, the highlighted capitalized terms in the above passage are all recognizable Gaullist terms.

Rochefort's critique extends beyond the targeted presidential figure to all those nameless individuals who employ a similar language: that of the dominant ideology. In *One-Dimensional Man*, Marcuse comments on the encroaching power of the bureaucrat in modern society (expressing views which those in many sectors of society today—not least the education system—will recognize all too well):

> Domination is transfigured into administration. The capitalist bosses and owners are losing their identity as responsible agents; they are assuming the function of bureaucrats in a corporate machine. Within the vast hierarchy of executive and managerial boards extending far

> beyond the individual establishment into the scientific laboratory and
> research institute, the national government and national purpose, the
> tangible source of exploitation, disappears behind the façade of
> objective rationality.[15]

Towards the close of *Une Rose* we find a stream of terms which clearly
echo Gaullist speeches, mouthed on this occasion by the 'bureaucrats', a
group previously identified as dangerous cogs in the state machinery: 'ces
vieux fœtus sont plus dangereux que vingt ministres. L'Appareil, c'est
eux' ['those old foetuses are more dangerous than twenty ministers. They
are the State Apparatus'] (119). The bureaucrats are alarmed by growing
signs of disturbance on the streets:

> Ces murmures spectraux évoquaient, pour les Bureaucrates, le
> Funeste Retour aux Errements Anciens, le Déséquilibre Budgétaire, la
> Faillite de la Monnaie, l'Incertitude, la Subordination Étrangère,
> l'Instabilité, le Chaos Intérieur et l'Impuissance Extérieure et la
> Retombée dans les Ornières du Passé. (207)

> [*These ghostly murmurings evoked, for the Bureaucrats, the Funereal
> Return to Bad Old Ways, Budgetary Imbalance, Monetary Collapse,
> Uncertainty, Subordination to Foreign Powers, Instability, Internal Chaos
> and External Impotence and a Tumbling into the Potholes of the Past.*]

Already alerted to the work of the 'verbologues', we are left to 'translate'
these phrases for ourselves.

Rochefort extends her critique further, beyond France to the USA,
specifically to the Vietnam War (which is never actually named).[16] At the
time of the text's composition some 200,000 US soldiers were in
Vietnam. In 1965, anti-war protests in America were at a peak: 15,000
young people demonstrated on the streets of Washington on the 17 April.
In the text, Amok, a deserter from the Vietnam War, reveals to his young
audience just how words can mask reality. The truth is obfuscated 'quand
on appelle par d'autres mots' ['when different words are used'] (105).
War becomes 'la Croisière de la Paix' ['Push for Peace'] or 'Protection de
la Paix' ['Peace Protection'] or 'aider les gouvernements amis' ['helping
friendly governments'] (105). Amok acts as translator of this Orwellian
'Newspeak': 'protecting bridges' means forcibly preventing citizens from
crossing them, and blowing them up in air-strikes if necessary. In a
powerful diatribe, Amok reveals the truth behind the jargon: 'j'ai protégé
des villages, et ils sont en paix pour toujours. Nous avons établi la paix
sur des forêts entières avec du napalm. [. . .] La paix s'étendait partout où
nous passions, la paix éternelle' ['I've protected villages and they are at

peace forever. We established peace over entire forests with napalm. [. . .] Peace spread everywhere we passed—eternal peace'] (106). Today's readers may be reminded of our own 'Newspeak', in which the death of civilians, for instance, becomes 'collateral damage'.[17]

As we shall see in subsequent chapters, Rochefort's texts of the late 1960s and the 1970s all reveal the influence of the emerging New Left and counter-culture.[18] Disillusioned with both capitalism and the authoritarian socialism typified by the Soviet Union, traditional left-wing thinking turned increasingly in the late 1950s to the anarchist tradition. The late 1960s saw the emergence of the counter-culture as a whole generation challenged society's values and institutions. Rochefort's *Une Rose* captures the mood of dissatisfaction and potential civic unrest which threatened many European countries in the late 1960s. More particularly, many of the ideas presented in the text coincide with those of one of the many non-aligned, left-wing groups which came to the forefront of politics at the time, the International Situationists.

This anti-authoritarian movement, which, alongside the more significant 'Mouvement du 22 mars', was to play a part in the events of May 1968, was born in July 1957, and had by the early 1960s gelled into a 'small, tightly knit group of revolutionaries devoted to forging a critique of *contemporary*, that is to say consumer, capitalism'.[19] Although public awareness of the group emerged most strongly subsequent to the publication of *Une Rose*, with the Situationists' highly publicized occupation of Strasbourg University students' union in November 1966 (the union was subsequently closed by court order on the 14 December), and after the publication in 1967 of two key works, Raoul Vaneigem's *Traité de savoir-vivre à l'usage des jeunes générations*, and Guy Debord's *La Société du spectacle*, the group's ideas had already been disseminated for some years via the magazine *Internationale Situationniste*, which was first published in 1958.[20] Both Debord and Vaneigem deplore what they perceive as a society which stifles individual creativity and passion. The 'spectacle' referred to in the title of Debord's principal work is described in Vaneigem's *Traité* as including the media, stereotypes, schemas and roles, 'explications toutes faites' ['ready-made explanations'], and 'sentiments contrôlés' ['controlled emotions']: all recognizable features of the world of *Une Rose*.[21] Christopher Gray defines the 'spectacle' as:

> A one-way transmission of experience; a form of 'communication' to which one side, the audience, can never reply; a culture based on the reduction of almost everyone to a state of abject non-creativity: of receptivity, passivity, and isolation.[22]

120

The Situationists were alert to the dangers of language control and manipulation: Vaneigem's insistence on the need to demystify language is closely aligned with Rochefort's own comments in *Une Rose*:

> Savoir vivre c'est savoir ne pas reculer d'un pouce dans sa lutte contre le renoncement. Que personne ne sous-estime l'habilité du pouvoir à gaver ses esclaves de mots jusqu'à en faire les esclaves de ses mots. De quelles armes chacun dispose-t-il pour assurer sa liberté? [. . .] décryptage de nouvelles, traduction de termes officiels ('société' devenant, dans la perspective opposée au pouvoir, 'racket' ou 'lieu du pouvoir hiérarchisé') éventuellement glossaire ou encyclopédie.[23]

> [*Knowing how to live means knowing how not to back down an inch in one's struggles against renunciation. Let no-one underestimate the cunning with which those in power force-feed their slaves full of words until they have made them slaves to their words. What weapons do each man and woman possess with which to secure their freedom?* [. . .] *Decoding the news, translating official terminology ('society' becomes, if we adopt a point of view opposed to that of those in power, 'racket' or 'site of hierarchized power') perhaps in the long run a glossary of terms or an encyclopedia.*]

Une Rose is an example of what has been termed an 'unstable dystopia', a form which has been associated particularly with women writers. In an unstable dystopia the prevailing dystopian vision is tempered by elements which hint at an eventual cessation of the nightmare and emergence into a better future.[24] In spite of the policing which operates at every level of society, *Une Rose* reveals the potential for subversive action, and closes on a revolutionary scene as all citizens, led by the young, pour onto the streets, children hurl documents from the windows of the offices of the bureaucrats, and police agents are murdered in the crowd. The double-agent Druise apparently succeeds in cutting the wires to the nuclear 'red button'. The final word of the text, 'COMMENCEMENT' ['START'], looks to a new future. But how does this happy ending come about? For the Situationists, the disaster of capitalist consumer society could be reversed only by means of tapping individual creativity and, above all else, passion. Rochefort, too, as we shall now go on to see, suggests that revolutionary action draws its strength from the awareness and love of the individual.

In *Printemps au parking*, Thomas indicates the power of analogy to Christophe: 'on ne comprend vraiment à fond que par analogie. [. . .] C'est une transposition du problème dans un autre système déjà connu' ['you can only really explain things by using analogy. [. . .] It's a process of transposing the problem into another system; one with which you are already familiar'] (84). After her initial onslaught directed against the president, Sereine goes on to deliver a series of subversive political speeches in the coded language of quantum physics: individuals become particles, political régimes translate into electron orbits. Sereine's speeches reveal that the author has at least a basic grasp of some of the principles of quantum physics. When, for instance, Sereine refers to 'points de résonance' ['sites of resonance'] at which electrons can jump orbit and change their energy state—by analogy, occasions when political dissidents can gain the upper hand, the weak become strong (60)—she is invoking quantum physicist Niels Bohr's discovery that 'electrons jump from one energy state to another in discontinuous "quantum leaps", the size of the leap depending on how many quanta of energy they have absorbed or given off'.[25]

The deciphering and explanation of Sereine's speeches need not be undertaken here; what is important is that once more language is used subversively, this time via the process of analogy. The reader of the text, like Sereine's audience, is forced to adopt an active reading mode far removed from the passive receptivity, the uni-directional communication, so criticized by the Situationists. Understanding the hidden message leads to the formation a self-selecting group of those who know, forming a strong bond of complicity between reader and author. Not everyone is up to the task. Government representatives, like the spy Cléoporte, receive a dose of their own medicine as language is used to dissimulate: words mean more, or something other, than they seem to. Cléoporte, who subsequently struggles in libraries to grasp the intricacies of theoretical physics and sends his superiors opaque reports, despairs at the polyvalence of language: 'Alors si chaque mot veut dire autre chose comment s'y retrouver?' ['If every word can mean something else, how are you supposed to work it out?'] (67). As Théostat rather unhelpfully points out: 'Faut savoir, c'est tout' ['You just have to know'] (67).

The relationship between revolutionary politics and passion sketched out towards the end of *Printemps au parking* becomes central to *Une Rose*. In his *Traité*, Vaneigem points to the potential which lies in each and every individual: 'Il n'est rien dans l'univers des choses monnayables ou non qui puisse servir d'équivalence à l'être humain. L'individu est irréductible; il change, mais ne s'échange pas' ['There is nothing in this world of goods, be they cash-convertible or not, which can be held as equivalent to human beings. The individual is irreducible; s/he changes, but cannot be exchanged'].[26] In *Printemps au parking*, Thomas expressed wonderment in the face of humankind's resilience: 'si même avec les moyens dont ils disposent [. . .] ils n'ont pas été foutus d'y arriver encore, avec tout le temps qu'on leur a laissé, à l'écraser, l'homme, est-ce que ça ne voudrait-il pas dire qu'il aurait la vie dure?' ['if they can't do it even with all the means at their disposal, if they haven't been able to crush mankind, in all the time we've given them, doesn't that suggest that man is pretty hard to get rid of?'] (231). Sereine, developing this notion, identifies an all-important force, 'l'Esprit': 'l'Esprit sera immortel. S'il ne l'était, il aurait depuis longtemps déserté ces lieux [. . .] et on n'en trouverait plus trace. Il a donc la vie dure' ['The Spirit is immortal. If it weren't it would have deserted this place long since [. . .] and we wouldn't find any trace of it. So the Spirit is pretty hard to get rid of'] (133).

Attempts to pin down and define 'l'Esprit' are bound to failure, for it is by its very nature ineffable, unnameable. Rochefort combines the discourses of quantum physics, philosophy and politics in an attempt to describe at least the qualities of 'l'Esprit', and, ultimately, seems to approach the realm of mysticism. (Here, too, the influence of the counter-culture, which turned increasingly to Eastern religions for inspiration, can be felt. As Roszak points out: 'Traditionally, the insights of the religion [Zen] have been communicated directly from master to pupil as part of an extremely demanding discipline in which verbal formulations play almost no part'.)[27] Lecturing on what she calls 'la téléologie Généralisée' ['Generalized Teleology'] (25), Sereine alludes to the existing political régime, stating that 'la fin d'un système clos est l'entropie' ['a closed system tends towards entropy'] (25), evoking on this occasion the Second Law of Thermodynamics (entropy) which states that 'all inanimate systems are destined to degenerate into chaos'.[28] 'L'Esprit', by contrast, appears to tend towards an absolute in an ever-expansive and all-embracing movement which characterizes human life itself: 'la fin de l'esprit est de dépasser les clôtures et de découvrir ce qui est plus grand que lui, et la fin de l'être de s'inscrire dans le système le plus large' ['the Spirit tends towards a surpassing of all boundaries and a discovery of that which is larger than itself, and Being tends towards its insertion in the largest system'] (25).

If 'l'Esprit' cannot be adequately labelled or named, it is at least clearly associated with a recognizable human quality, and that is love, or passion. Sereine, guru-like, ultimately reveals that 'l'Esprit' belongs 'au système le plus large, au Grand Système Inconnu et Inexprimable' ['to the largest system, the Great Unknown and Unutterable System'] which is 'Quelque Chose de Merveilleux' ['Something Wonderful'] (196), a phrase which finds its source in the love-making of Sereine and Théostat. It is when he lies next to Sereine that Théostat states: 'Il y a quelque chose de merveilleux ['There's something wonderful'] (92), and later, 'quand il y avait une spécialement mauvaise nouvelle, ils restaient là, l'un sur l'autre, ou l'un à côté de l'autre, et ils se taisaient, jusqu'à ce qu'arrive la Sensation qu'il y a Quelque Chose de Merveilleux' ['when there was particularly bad news they stayed there, lying on top of each other, or side by side, silently, until the Feeling of the presence of Something Wonderful came upon them'] (186).

If 'l'Esprit' is linked to love, it is also directly linked to politics, for it is associated with the capacity to step back from one's situation (change orbit), to adopt critical distance, which, as we have already seen, is for Rochefort crucially important: 'l'Esprit' arises alongside 'la Conscience' (130). Roszak points to the counter-culture's attempt to break from an objective, scientific world-view: 'In its place there must be a new culture in which the non-intellective capacities of the personality [. . .] become the arbiters of the good, the true, and the beautiful.'[29] Théostat, who, like Christophe in *Printemps au parking*, finds himself in a student milieu by pure chance, proves to be particularly gifted in what Sereine will term 'désystémantation' ['desystemization'] or 'départicipation' ['departicipation'], precisely because he adopts an intuitive mode of thought: 'Moi je ne sais rien dit Théostat, alors je ne peux pas penser. Je suis obligé de m'y prendre autrement' ['I don't know anything, said Théostat, so I can't think. I have to approach things differently'] (20). As Christophe became teacher to Thomas, so Théostat will prove to be a mentor to Sereine: 'Sereine disait que Théostat lui faisait tout comprendre' ['Sereine said that Théostat made her understand everything'] (186). It is Théostat who proves to be particularly adept in the art of 'extravagation', a skill Sereine tries to inculcate in her students as part of their homework in 'désystémantation', and which involves breaking free from rational thought: 'le processus du cerveau travaillant sans code a priori' ['the process whereby the brain works without any a priori code'] ; 'mettre le cerveau en roue libre' ['letting the brain free-wheel'] (60). The emphasis on intuition and the fact that 'l'Esprit' is 'Inexprimable', extra-linguistic, is central to the text's political dimension. Since language has been hijacked and corrupted, another dimension must be sought. As Druise recognizes: 'Ils ont volé nos mots et ils les ont tués. [. . .] Et à nous il reste ce qui n'a pas de mots' ['They've stolen our words and they've killed them. [. . .] And all we have left are things without words'] (56). 'Newspeak', after all, was able to make heretical thought impossible only 'at least as far as thought is dependent on words'.[30] In an early scene in the text, Sereine watches youngsters make love in a moment of communion as they shelter from a police raid in the cellar of a student bar, and points out that here is something totally alien to the trainee-'verbologue' Belette: 'quelque chose à quoi Belette ne comprendrait absolument rien' ['something which would be totally beyond the comprehension of Belette']; 'que le moindre mot casserait et disperserait' ['which would be smashed and dispersed by the least word'] (39).[31]

The link which *Une Rose* establishes between passion and politics is a common dystopic topos, though Rochefort brings to it a new dimension in her emphasis on the importance of the extra-linguistic and in her use of the language of analogy. In Orwell's *1984* sexuality is identified as a dangerous, potentially subversive force: 'the animal instinct, the simple undifferentiated desire: that was the force that would tear the Party to pieces'; 'the sexual act, successfully performed, was rebellion. Desire was Thoughtcrime'.[32] Fears of passion are such that the state aims to do away with sexual pleasure: 'We shall abolish the orgasm. Our neurologists are at work upon it now.' The force of such sexual pleasure is clearly demonstrated in *Une Rose*. When the young girl Triton experiences orgasm with Théostat, and is subsequently punished by an act of mutilation which precludes all future pleasure, she turns terrorist, channelling her fury into her politics and finally assassinating the president Sénile. Passion ultimately fails in *1984*; threatened by torture in the infamous Room 101 Winston will betray Julia, but in *Une Rose* it triumphs, exemplifying the International Situationists' belief that it is the driving force which will bind individuals together in a powerful movement based on genuine communication:

> La passion de l'amour porte en soi le modèle d'une communication parfaite: l'orgasme, l'accord des partenaires dans l'acmé. Elle est, dans l'obscurité de la survie quotidienne, la lueur intermittente du qualitatif. L'intensité vécue, la spécificité, l'exaltation des sens, la motilité des affects, le goût du changement et de la variété, tout prédispose la passion de l'amour à repassionner les déserts du Vieux Monde.[33]

> [*The passion of love bears within itself the model of perfect communication: orgasm, the acme of understanding between two people. It represents, in the darkness of daily survival, the intermittent light of the qualitative. Lived intensity, specificity, intense sensory pleasure, the motility of affect, the taste of change and variety, all these things predispose the passion of love to repassion the deserts of the Old World.*]

The Situationists expressed a deep distrust of Marxism as it had developed in the latter half of the twentieth century, rejecting it as yet another authoritarian bureaucracy. Both they and Rochefort suggest that political change must be founded not on classic Marxist notions but on the desire and creativity of the individual. Druise persuades the Marxist Vérole that he must abandon ideas of 'conditions objectives', a deterministic emphasis on praxis, and give the young their heads (and their beds) (56). In *Printemps au parking* we saw Christophe explain to Nicolas that his feelings for Thomas were secondary to 'la Révolution'. In *Une Rose* the same process takes place between Théostat and Sereine:

Théostat était étendu sur le petit divan, tout nu, et Sereine, nue aussi, lui tournait une mèche autour des doigts. Mais ce n'était par pour cela qu'il était si content. C'était pour autre chose, et il ne savait pas du tout quoi ni l'expliquer mieux que ça.—Je ne sais pas, dit-il à Sereine, qui le lui demandait. Il y a quelque chose de merveilleux, et je ne sais pas ce que c'est.
—Ce n'est pas de moi que tu veux parler?
—Non, dit-il avec simplicité. Mais tu fais partie. (92).

[*Théostat was lying on the small couch, quite naked, and Sereine, who was also naked, was playing with a lock of his hair. But that wasn't why he was so happy. It was because of something else, and he had no idea what it was, or how to explain it better than that.*
'I don't know,' he told Sereine, who was asking him to explain. 'There's something wonderful and I don't know what it is.'
'Isn't it me you're talking about?'
'No', he said simply, 'but you're part of it.']

Passion has the capacity to transcend individual concerns or relationships and open the way into the political arena. As Vaneigem stated, those who seek to change society should look to passion and seek to: 'étendre le moment de l'amour à tous ses prolongements, autrement dit de ne pas le dissocier ni des autres passions ni des autres projets' ['extend the moment of love in every possible direction, in other words not dissociate it from other passions or other projects'].[34] Théostat's insight into the political possibilities of passion subsequently informs Sereine's lecture on 'liaisons interparticulaires' ['interparticle liaisons'], in which she states that the coming together of 'particules hétérogènes' (those who stand outside the system; political dissidents) generates an energy greater than that of the sum of individual charges, producing a potential 'renversement d'équilibre' ['reversal of the balance of power'] (133). Love, in other words, leads to revolutionary mass-movements. Here, too, Rochefort's ideas are not so far removed from the realities of quantum physics. In *The Quantum Self,* Danah Zohar stresses the unique relational qualities of quantum systems:

> In any quantum system of two or more particles, each particle has both 'thingy-ness' and 'relating-ness', the first due to its particle aspect and the second due to its wave aspect. It is because of the wave aspect and what it allows to happen that the quantum systems display a kind of intimate, definitive relationship among their constituent members that doesn't exist in classical systems.[35]

This kind of internal relationship, which exists only in quantum systems, is known as 'relational holism': 'a whole created through quantum relationship is a new thing in itself, greater than the sum of its parts'.[36] Zohar, indeed, alluding to Plato's *Symposium* in which the love between the lover and the beloved creates a third thing that is the love between them, suggests that 'love is a particularly apposite example of relational holism'.[37]

The events of May 1968 were, as we know, spearheaded by the young, specifically by the student population, and the potential for unrest from this quarter was evidently clear to Rochefort, whose text strikes a particularly prophetic (or perhaps receptive?) note in this respect: the majority of the characters in *Une Rose* are either students or school-children. An awareness of the potential power (or danger, depending on one's perspective) of youth is expressed by both Druise, who wonders at their 'Esprit' ('D'où Cela leur vient-il?' ['where do they get It from?'], p. 40), and Philibert, who asks the same question, apprehensive (but also admiring) of the 'conscience' he sees 'dans chaque adolescent' ['in each adolescent'] (49). President Sénile is equally unnerved by this sector of society: 'Il n'y a guère que ce prurit de notre adolescence qui chatouille encore un peu le Pays' ['There's only this pruritus of our adolescents still irritating the Nation a little'] (82). This emphasis on youth certainly captures and mirrors the contemporary situation in France, at a time when 'une unité culturelle de jeunesse' cut across traditional party lines.[38] By 1968 student numbers has increased from 250,000 (in 1960) to 500,000; it is estimated that in 1966 some 33.9 per cent of the population was under 20 years of age, a result of the 1942 baby-boom.[39] Student unrest had already begun by the time Rochefort wrote *Une Rose*: in the autumn of 1965 the police were called in to deal with unrest at the student residence Anthony (some 20 minutes by train from the centre of Paris) as students demanded the right of free movement between male and female student residences.

In the world of *Une Rose,* schoolchildren, who have discovered that state brainwashing of the young is masked by claims that children are struck down by the illness 'Cervéole' (a play on 'cerveau' meaning 'brain' or 'mind', and 'rougeole', meaning 'measles', or 'variole', meaning 'small-pox'), form the 'Société Secrète pour la Réparation des Cervéolés' (181), with a view to standing alongside the student body. In 1968, highly politicized 'lycéens' all over France would form militant CALs or 'Comités d'Action Lycéens'. Though *Une Rose* has, as we have seen, much in common with *1984,* Rochefort's view of youth, as of love, remains fundamentally optimistic, and in this respect diverges from

Orwell's vision: in *1984* children readily join 'Spies', the party sector for the young, and participate in the Junior Anti-Sex League; Parsons is betrayed by his own child when he talks in his sleep. Rochefort's positive view of youth once again coincides with that of the Situationists who, whilst aware of the possible risks of complicity in the 'société du spectacle' ('le *teen-ager* porte les premières rides du consommateur' ['the teenager bears the first wrinkles of the consumer']), nonetheless saw the young as a driving force for the future:

> Et cependant, s'il se reprend, s'il sort du cauchemar, quel ennemi vont devoir affronter les forces de l'ordre? [Q]ue ne faut-il donc attendre d'une jeune génération [. . .] lâchée sur un théâtre d'opérations qui recouvre tous les aspects de la vie quotidienne.[40]

> [*But if he gets a grip, if he wakes from the nightmare, what an enemy the forces of order will have to confront. What can we not expect from a young generation released into the theatre of operations which covers every aspect of daily life.*]

But although the young predominate in the text, Rochefort suggests that disengagement from existing political systems, the capacity to gain new levels of awareness, is open to all. Perhaps the core of the optimism of this text consists in its insistence on, and belief in, change and movement; its opposition to all concepts of stasis. In an important episode in the text the young Triton, watching citizens emerge from the state-run 'cybernéma', expresses her contempt: 'Penser que les gens sont con au point de laisser mettre jusque-là!' ['To think that people are so bloody stupid as to sink that low']. Sereine, however, is quick to criticize this point of view: 'il ne faut pas penser en termes statiques [. . .]. Les gens, ça n'existe pas' ['you mustn't think in static terms [. . .]. "People" don't exist'] (166). In her next lecture she translates her claim into the language of physics, stating that 'en fait "les" particules ça n'existe pas' ['in fact "the" particles don't exist'] (197). Particles may be divided into two types: 'hétérogènes', or outside the system, and 'homogènes', within the system. With the help of an electron microscope, however, it becomes clear that even the 'homogènes' may have a heterogeneous core; given a boost of energy from other particles, or transported into a new situation, the 'particule homogène' may reveal a truly heterogeneous nature: in other words the most complicit citizen is open to change and dissidence. The people are not 'cons' but 'conifiés' (not bloody stupid but rendered so); thinking in static terms amounts to mimicking the reductive ploys of those in power, labelling or naming means precluding the possibility of change.

This point of view is, in fact, dramatized in the form of Philibert, the only character to show a marked development in the course of the text. Initially a compliant cog in the system, Philibert's desire for Sereine (and desire is, of course, not the prerogative of the young) produces dramatic changes in his outlook. Unable to concentrate on his work, he fears that he is treading a dangerous path: 'il pensait trop, pour son âge' ['he thought too much for his age'] (50). Philibert's passion effectively undoes the work of brainwashing which had taken place early in his life; as he fantasizes about Sereine, glimpses of his preconditioned life start to emerge, and the terms in which he expresses his metamorphosis echo Sereine's lecture on the capacity of all particles to become 'hétérogène': Mais qu'est-ce j'ai donc que m'arrive-t-il et de quelle étranges vies suis-je assiégé je ne suis pas normal! Et se sent soudain Philibert étrange, *hétérogène au monde* [. . .]' ['But what's wrong with me what's happening to me and by what strange lives am I being besieged I'm not normal! And so does Philibert suddenly feel strange, *heteregenous to the world*'] (100, my emphasis). Philibert, demoted in social rank, will go on to murder the Venerable Ruins.

From the passion experienced by the individual to the revolutionary mass-movement, *Une Rose pour Morrison* represents not only its author's, but a large sector of the French population's desire to overturn what was perceived as an autocratic, unparliamentary government. If the dominant system controls language, then according to Rochefort it is passion, that extra-linguistic force, which opens the way to the all-important 'privilege of consciousness', and it is just such a political lucidity which, in turn, makes possible a *new* order of language, a language of distance, of irony and satire—a language which is of course the hallmark of *Une Rose* itself. *Une Rose pour Morrison*, was born of, and encapsulates, the social and political tensions of the late 1960s. The prophetic nature of both Rochefort's writings and those of the International Situationists was to be revealed in the explosive events of May 1968.

CHAPTER SIX

Archaos, ou le jardin étincelant

> This is the one and only
> firmament. . .
> I am living in Eternity.
> The ways of this world
> are the ways of Heaven.
> (Ginsberg)

The predominantly dystopic *Une Rose pour Morrison* closes on a note of uncertain hope. While angry citizens take to the streets, the ex-Marxist Druise dies in his bid to dismantle the nuclear apparatus: 'A-t-il pu exécuter à temps l'ultime sabotage? On ne sait pas encore. On attend les nouvelles. L'Histoire nous le dira' ['Was he able to carry out the ultimate act of sabotage in time? We don't know yet. We're waiting to hear. History will tell us'] (219). History, in fact, was to reveal the limitations of the '68 uprising, but although revolutionary fervour rapidly gave way to reform, the New Left and counter-culture flourished in the early 1970s, spawning alternative lifestyles which gelled a literary project embarked upon some two decades previously. Rochefort's utopia, *Archaos, ou le jardin étincelant* (1972), was drafted as early as 1950, with a first version completed before the writing of *Le Repos du guerrier*. As we saw in Chapter 2 above, a further attempt was subsequently undertaken, only to be interrupted by *Les Petits Enfants du siècle*.[1] There is, it would seem, a time and a place for every utopia; Rochefort records the passage from an untenable oneiric vision to a viable project:

> There was too much dream and too gratuitous a dream. I had to have some links with reality [. . .] I think I finally succeeded in building a utopia because there were seeds outside at that moment—the communes and new ideologies of how to live together.[2]

Towards the end of this chapter the question of definition, and the interrelated issues of the function and feasibility of the utopia (is the

130

projected society more than an escapist dream, and does it matter?), will be discussed further, but for the moment we can consider the utopia as both a 'no place' or 'outopos', and a 'good place' or 'eutopos'. *Archaos*, like *Une Rose*, presents us with a huge cast of characters (the 'Gens d'Archaos' are conveniently listed at the start of the book), and similarly breaks with the realist genre. The satire which targets a specific socio-political period in France in *Une Rose* is replaced by an alternative utopian vision in which past, present and future collide; a vision which suggests that individuals have lived, and by extension might yet live together in harmony. *Archaos* takes its name from an eponymous fictitious kingdom existing some time between the end of the middle ages and the modern bourgeois and capitalist world: 'entre la fin des Temps Barbares et le commencement des Temps Barbares' ['between the end of the Barbaric Era and the start of the Barbaric Era'] (5). A 'no place', Archaos has been, so the text's Prelude informs us, deliberately expunged from history by the dominant ideology:

> L'examen des entrailles et des poubelles de l'Histoire, conjugué avec l'enquête du type 'à qui profite le crime' et un certain état de fureur révèlent qu'il s'agit d'effacements délibérés avec falsifications rétroactifs, effectuées sur l'ordre des diverses bandes de brigands qui se succèdent au pouvoir.

> [*An examination of the entrails and dustbins of History, carried out alongside a survey of the 'who stands to profit from the crime' variety undertaken in a certain state of anger reveals that it is a case of deliberate expurgations and retrospective falsifications carried out by order of various bands of brigands who successively come to power.*]

A group of alternative historians whose work is carried out amidst 'fumées diverses' ['various vapours'] (a nod to the psychedelic '70s) and generous measures of alcohol, are puzzled by an apparent lack of continuity in the received histories. The origins of contemporary social trends (we are left to work out that this refers to those subversive elements which characterize the counter-culture) simply cannot be traced: 'des événements postérieurs restent inexpliqués. Les coordonnées ne se rejoignent pas' ['subsequent events remain unexplained. The coordinates don't join up'] (5). *Archaos* represents the reconstruction of this lost realm, built up via a process (acknowledged as 'scientifiquement absurde' ['scientifically absurd']) of joining together the vanishing-points of the historical co-ordinates: 'nous obtenions ainsi une image par manque, une sorte de négatif' ['we thus obtained an image out of absence, a sort of photographic negative'] (6). Retrieved from the dustbin of history, the 'no place' is also a 'good place', although *Archaos*, like *Une Rose*, combines dystopic and utopic elements: the utopic society of Archaos emerges in the third part of the text, 'Les Heures de la Béatitude', having been preceded by the repressive régime of the king, Avatar, in Part I ('Le Roi Père'), and the more enlightened reign of his son Govan in Part II ('Le Roi Fils').[3]

The growth of the feminist movement gave rise in the 1970s to a resurgence of utopian texts written by women, and *Archaos*, with its emphasis on decentralized government, sexual freedom which aims to separate sexuality from notions of ownership and reproduction, and the valorization of the community, typifies the 'good place' represented in this body of texts.[4] Although this chapter will begin with an examination of the political and economic dimension of the text before moving on to consider the role of sexuality and religion, it is important to stress that these elements are necessarily linked: true to the agenda of the New Left with its focus on individual lifestyle and personal relationships, this is a text which suggests that political change, the transformation of the structures of society, are dependent upon a change of consciousness at the level of the individual.

As was noted above in Chapter 5, the traditional Left's growing disillusionment with authoritarian socialism gave rise to a change in attitude, and the New Left began espousing traditional anarchist principles. Following on from earlier figures such as Emma Goldman, many women were to be attracted to anarchist ideas, and a second wave of anarcho-feminism emerged in the 1960s and 1970s. As Marshall points out in his comprehensive history of anarchism:

> They [anarcho-feminists] argued that as women generally live on the boundaries of capitalism and yet are its most unfortunate victims, they have a remarkably clear insight into its nature. Their position makes them particularly aware of patriarchy in the family as well as in the State. To anarcho-feminists, the State and patriarchy are twin aberrations; they are both part of the fundamental social and psychological model of hierarchy and domination.[5]

Rochefort's comments on women's attraction to anarchist thought echo Marshall's observations: 'Bien qu'elles [les femmes] puissent en être contaminées, elles n'ont ni estime ni affection pour le pouvoir [. . .] car elles ont l'habitude de l'auto-gestion' ['although women may be contaminated by power, they neither value nor like it [. . .] because they are used to self-management'].[6] Her utopia represents a rejection of patriarchal and centralized power; the 'good place' which Archaos becomes is an anarchist society. Whereas *Une Rose* ends with what is

132

perhaps a popular conception of anarchy, with the destruction of the bureaucrats' files and Triton's act of individual terrorism, *Archaos* represents a more comprehensive vision, building slowly towards a good society which embraces all the key characteristics of anarchism: the common ownership of the means of production; the distribution of goods and services according to need; the destruction of the State and its replacement by voluntary associations; mutual aid; an abolition of any compulsion to work, and of punitive measures taken against criminal activities.[7]

As the text is set in a late medieval framework, initially under monarchic rule, there is no State as modern usage perhaps envisages the term. Nonetheless, if we consider the State, from an anarchist perspective, to be a coercive, punitive, exploitative and destructive entity, then the political regime of Part I approximates the modern concept.[8] The patriarchal Avatar wields absolute power.[9] Taxes are high, royal coffers brimming, wars waged for territorial gain are a commonplace, and subjects of the realm (including all the members of Avatar's family) are hurled into dank dungeons at the least provocation. Avatar's reign is brought to a close at the end of Part I when he rapes his own daughter, Onagre, and subsequently castrates himself, thereby losing the confidence of the people. Although the unseating of Avatar marks a step towards the 'good place', at this stage in the text the people continue to equate power with the phallus; they object not to tyrannical rule, nor indeed to the act of rape, but to the castration of Avatar, the symbolic divestment of power: 'On ne veut pas un roi sans queue!' ['We don't want a king without a prick!'] (144). Setting up a pattern of non-violence which is maintained throughout the text, the revolution which topples the king is strikingly low-key. Significantly, it is a woman, Avanie, wife of Avatar, who acts as spokesperson in confronting the king. Neither she, nor her son Govan, who is to succeed Avatar, seek power in their own name: 'Nous venons au nom du peuple' ['We come in the name of the people'] (145). As Rochefort points out, 'the women and the children take the power but don't exert it'.[10] Nonetheless, the notion that an individual can, and should, speak in the name of others, will also be undermined as the text proceeds.

Under the somewhat unorthodox rule of Govan (to be named Eremetus Premier), Part II sees the beginnings of decentralization and the erosion of the structures of power present under Avatar's reign. Anarchism is marked by its anti-hierarchizing tendencies. Economic and political decisions must work 'from the bottom up', so it is significant that Govan's first entry into the capital city of Trémènes takes place in the Basse-Ville, before the official investiture ceremony: 'Ainsi entra Govan [. . .] dans son règne par le bas' ['Thus Govan's rule began from the base'] (165). In *Printemps au parking* Thomas and his friends ponder the revolution to come:

> —Les bordels sont indispensables à la Révolution, dit Miguel, je l'ai toujours dit.
> —Le bordel aussi, dit Thomas. Le grand énorme fantastique bordel poétique avec accordéon, vodka, filles de joie, garçons de joie, vertige, pagaille, liberté, passions coupables! (232)

> [*'Brothels are indispensable to the Revolution,' said Miguel, 'I've always said so.'*
> *'Chaos too,' said Thomas. 'That huge gigantic fantastic poetic chaos/brothel complete with accordions, vodka, female prostitutes, male prostitutes, intoxication, disarray, freedom, and guilty passions!'*]

The 'bordel', both literal and metaphorical, is placed firmly at the centre of *Archaos*. Govan's first royal act consists of a visit to the city brothel, where the all-important anarchist principle of unanimity is instigated. The New Left insisted on the need to create counter-institutions and build a new society from the bottom up. Government, Govan legislates, will consist of a council, but this is no elite body; rather it represents what we might call a counter-council: the newly conceived law states that 'tout le monde doit se mêler aux affaires du Conseil' ['everyone must get involved in Council business'] (163). Politics are to be governed by personal relations. Turning the received image of the prostitute as paid purveyor of pleasure on its head, Govan decrees that Désirade, the brothel's 'madam', be responsible for judging the worthiness or otherwise of potential council members. The brothel becomes a site where pleasure, not cash, is exchanged:

> On légifère. [. . .] Mets au dos de la feuille que Désirade est instituée nécessité commune. Et obligatoire: 'Pour occuper une fonction dans l'Etat, ajoute ça, il faut être passé dans ses mains. Et y avoir donné satisfaction. On devra montrer un certificat, signé et authentique.' (158)

> [*Let us legislate.* [. . .] *Write on the back of the piece of paper that Désirade is hereby appointed a communal necessity. And that it is obligatory 'for anyone wishing to hold any State office—add that—that they pass through her hands. And that they must have given satisfaction. They'll have to show a certificate, duly signed and authenticated.'*]

Children, as we have already seen, and will see again in subsequent chapters, play a key role in Rochefort's work. Uncontaminated, or less contaminated, by the dictates and norms imposed by society, the young represent hope, and the possibility of change. The utopia that Archaos becomes emerges from the untroubled vision of the young Govan and his twin sister Onagre. Govan's rule is characterized by his blithe dismissal of abstract concepts such as honour, authority, and power, whilst his child-like literalism reveals the hypocrisy of empty words and promises. Informed by an alarmed treasurer that he cannot spend the royal treasure, which represents 'une remise purement symbolique' ['a purely symbolic sum'], and that he can buy nothing since all goods belong to him by right, Govan replies: '—Ce n'est pas logique. [. . .] qu'ayant de quoi je ne puisse et ceux qui peuvent n'ont pas' ['It's not logical that I've got the means but can't, and those who can haven't got the means'] (168). Observing that he has more than sufficient monies, Govan goes on to abolish taxes, and is soon to be found drinking in the Basse-Ville, distributing jewels to the people. After all, as he points out in typically literalist mode, has he not promised 'de faire le bien au peuple' ['to work for the good of the people'] (171)? Govan's reign will be characterized by a policy of non-aggression. When told that he must participate in the traditional 'joutes courtoises' ['courtly jousts'] in order to secure the allegiance of neighbouring monarchs, he expresses a preference for picking flowers. Territorial gain is regarded as unnecessary and wearisome, and three wars are studiously avoided.

Part III of *Archaos* marks a shift towards a truly anarchist regime. Under anarchism the abolition of the wage system and of exchange relations renders money redundant. Here, it is the abolition of money which comes first. Rochefort gives her utopia a helping hand in the form of a miraculous growth of wheat which leads first to the decree that bread is free, and thenceforth to the logical pronouncements that the wood needed to fuel the ovens is free, the woodsmens' axes and bellows free, and finally, inevitably, that 'tout est gratuit' ['everything is free'] (258). Wealthy merchants, not surprisingly, are far from content with Govan's legislative measures, but are unable to counter the child's rigorously literalist approach. The following exchange, reminiscent of Céline's exchanges with the bourgeois Philippe, typify the logical onslaught:

> —Qu'est-ce que vous faisiez?
> —Des échanges, Majesté.
> —Qu'est-ce qui vous empêche de continuer?
> —A quoi ça sert si on ne gagne pas d'argent?
> —A quoi ça sert de gagner de l'argent si tout est gratuit?
> —C'est ce qu'on est venu vous demander Majesté.
> —Excusez-moi, dit Eremetus. A quoi ça vous servait quand ce n'était pas gratuit?

—A acheter des choses.

—Les choses sont gratuites, dit Eremetus.

—Mais à quoi ça sert si on ne peut plus gagner d'argent?

—L'argent est gratuit, dit Eremetus.

—J'ai peur que nous ne nous comprenions pas, dit le prévôt. (261–2)

[*'What did you do before?'*

'We traded, your Majesty.'

'And what's stopping you from carrying on?'

'What's the point if we don't earn any money?'

'What's the point of earning money if everything's free?'

'That's what we've come to ask you, your Majesty.'

'Forgive me,' said Eremetus, 'but what use was it to you when everything wasn't free?'

'We could buy things.'

'Things are free,' said Eremetus.

'But what's the point if we can't earn money any more?'

'Money's free,' said Eremetus.

'I'm afraid that we don't understand one another,' said the provost.]

Once again, the political and economic dimensions are indissolubly linked to the personal. If all goods are free, then so too are people—free, that is, in the sense of belonging to no-one. Former councillors consequently find themselves deserted by their wives, whilst the country's army falls apart as the soldiers, also free, leave in droves. The socio-economic changes underline a central anarchist principle:

> But the crucial point is that the economic system must be in harmony
> with social relationships generally in the new order. As we have seen,
> these are to be relationships of solidarity among equals; each person
> will be bound by ties of sympathy to the rest, and will express that
> sympathy in acts of mutual aid.[11]

Govan counters the disgruntled burgomaster's observation that 'si tout est gratuit personne n'a rien' ['if everything is free no-one has anything'], by pointing out that the reverse is true if personal relations are strong: 'Tiens, pour nous c'est le contraire. Il est vrai qu'on s'aime bien, ça n'est pas pareil' ['You know, it's the other way round with us. It's true that we get on well, so it's not the same'] (263).

Govan's measures prove too much for those who are unwilling, or unable, to change their mentality, and the gradual emergence of the utopian society of Archaos is challenged by temporary dystopias which take the form of parodic representations of two authoritarian political

regimes held in equal abhorrence by those of anarchist persuasion: capitalism and communism. First, the disaffected burgomaster, Brimbalon,
unopposed by Govan, annuls the laws of Archaos, and declares Trémènes
'ville libre, franche et close' ['a free town, a closed tax-exempt zone'], in
which 'tout se paye' ['everything has its price'] (265). Legal sub-clauses,
in the form of a subversive list of clichés, underline the bourgeois
mentality at work:

> Tout se paye. [. . .] Toute peine mérite salaire, Pierre qui roule
> n'amasse pas mousse, Qui veut voyager loin ménage sa monture, Un
> bon tiens vaut mieux que deux tu l'auras, Mens sana in corpore sano,
> Les petits ruisseaux font les grandes rivières, L'argent n'a pas
> d'odeur, Qui vole un œuf vole un bœuf, Un sou est un sou, et Demain
> on rase gratis. (265)

> [*Everything has its price. The labourer is worthy of his hire, a Rolling stone
> gathers no moss, He who takes it steady travels far, a Bird in the hand is
> worth two in the bush, Mens sana in corpore sano, Little streams make big
> rivers, Money has no smell, He who steals a pin will steal a pound, Every
> penny counts, and Jam yesterday, jam tomorrow, but never jam today.*]

The subsequent reiteration of these clichés links the downfall of the newly
formed market-economy to the sterile mentality it represents. Theft in
Trémènes is punishable by death regardless of the object stolen, since 'qui
vole un œuf vole un bœuf'. An escalation of criminal activity ensues:
'Aussi valait-il mieux carrément voler le bœuf tout de suite, et on ne s'en
privait pas' ['So it was as well to steal a pound/ox straight off, and that's
exactly what people did'] (270). The system, it is suggested, is
undermined by its own internal logic. Anarchists believe that political and
judicial authority is not the remedy for social disorder, but rather its
cause. In the rest of Archaos, where no punitive authority exists, theft is
unknown. Trémènes soon begins to fall apart under the joint pressures of
soaring inflation and crime, whilst growing numbers of citizens join the
(non)-council by secretly visiting the brothel and giving pleasure. And not
just any citizens. In the eyes of the New Left, revolutionaries could be
identified as all those who broke with the dominant ideology and led
subversive lifestyles (typically, the hippies and commune-dwellers of the
counter-culture). Where Marxists identified the proletariat or urban
working-class as the only agents of revolutionary change, the anarchists
took a different view: 'they used terms like "proletariat" to refer indis-
criminately to factory workers, artisans, peasants, down-and-outs and so
forth—anyone not included in the ruling stratum of capitalists and state
functionaries.'[12] Trémènes, true to the anarchist agenda, is gradually
undermined by just this sector of the population:

La fraction citadine du Conseil, réunie chez Désirade, se compta, et
constata qu'elle comportait principalement les ribauds et les femmes
de mauvaise vie, les garnements de la Basse-Ville, les mitrons, des
célibataires (qui eût osé, marié, faire état d'un certificat de fornication
adultère?), les veuves, les musiciens, les blanchisseuses, les jongleurs
les funambules et les lunatiques, un bossu, un écolier, et l'idiot
Catarsis—soit à quelques nuances près la lie de la population urbaine
[. . .]. (267)

[*The city-dwellers on the Council, who gathered at Désirade's, took a look
at themselves and noted that they consisted principally of bawdies and
women of ill-repute, hoodlums from the slums, baker's boys, bachelors (who,
if married, would have dared to instance a certificate of adulterous
fornication?), widows, musicians, laundry women, jugglers and tight-rope
walkers and lunatics, a humpback, a schoolboy, the idiot Catarsis—in other
words more or less the dregs of the urban population.*]

The failed market-economy rapidly gives way to a second parodic and
dystopic representation, this time of a regime at the opposite end of the
political spectrum, that is, communism. Evidently the sequence of events
is significant: Rochefort parodies Marxist notions of dialectical
materialism, although in *Archaos* the highest stage of social development
is to be anarchism, not communism. Anarchists, unlike classical Marxists,
reject violent struggle and the dictatorship of the proletariat as acceptable
means of transition to social change, recognizing in this a dissonance
between means and ends.[13] Accordingly, the revolutionary Jérémias's lust
for confrontation ('la victoire est une vierge, l'avoir c'est la perdre!'
['victory is a virgin: to have her is to lose her!'], p. 295) is comically
deflated when he is met by Govan and Avanie bearing a bouquet of
roses—the archetypal '70s 'flower-power' statement—and showing more
interest in quaffing ale than in retaking the city of Trémènes. Like
Brimbalon's reified bourgeois proverbs, Jérémias's pronouncements have
all the hollowness of clichéd overuse: '— En finir avec la tyrannie, et
établir la justice et l'égalité' ['Let's put an end to tyranny and establish
justice and equality'] (287); '—Nous vendrons chèrement notre vie'
['We'll sell our lives dearly'] (287); 'vous êtes venu [. . .] paré de toutes les
séductions de votre caste' ['you have come here adorned with all the
enticements of your caste'] (288). The revolutionary, like the arch-
bourgeois, is reduced to caricatural status.

Whereas Avanie and Govan had spoken for the people at the close of
Part I, the shift towards true anarchism is marked on this occasion by a
refusal to accept even this degree of hierarchy: when Jérémias insists that
he speaks 'au nom du peuple' ['in the name of the people'], Govan

enquires mildly, 'pourquoi, il est muet?' ['why, are the people dumb?']
(287). Anarchists preach abstention from politics and an avoidance of all
the structures of the State, including the path of parliamentary elections.[14]
When Jérémias (whose takeover bid is studiously ignored by Govan)
stands for elections, he is the only candidate. The Marxist notion of the
distribution of wealth is subsequently parodied as each and every object
and individual in Trémènes is laboriously counted: 'Et ce n'était pas
facile, car nombre de cela bougeait, on pouvait compter deux fois une
casserole prêtée, une poule courante, une femme volage, et ne parlons pas
des personnes, agitées comme des puces' ['and it was no easy task, for a
lot of it was on the move, a lent saucepan could be counted twice, as
could a running hen or a flighty woman, not to mention people, who were
continually coming and going'] (297). Unsurprisingly, Jérémias soon
gives way and enters the council by giving pleasure to Avanie.

After these two dystopic interludes, Archaos reaches the final stages of
its economic and political development towards anarchism. True to the
anarchist (and in this case Marxist) vision of the abolition of the division
of labour, the country's tanners cut their hours but agree to spin wool and
teach their skills to others, whilst the refuse-collectors becomes masons
who in turn dabble in bakery. The commune-dwellers of the counter-
culture recognized the problems relating to the distribution of tasks: 'In
practice, of course, there is considerable bitching and neglect, resentment
and guilt. Long ago a man with much experience in communities told
me, "If you figure out who is going to carry out the garbage, everything
else will seem simple."'[15] In the light of this, it is apt indeed that Jérémias
finds himself in the (even less desirable) post of 'vidangeur' ['cesspool
emptier'] (306). The division between town and country is breached as
farmers refuse to work, and city-dwellers are obliged to take their place.
As each group learns the tasks of the other, they gradually become
indistinguishable. Although the situation is far from perfect—'C'était un
peu le désordre. Des choses qui n'intéressaient pas grand monde étaient
faites très au dernier moment par ceux qui n'en pouvaient plus [. . .]' ['It
was a bit chaotic. Things that no one was very interested in were done at
the last minute by those who couldn't stand it any more'] (309)—the new
society bears witness to the anarchists' belief that the productive capacity
of any society is much greater than it appears under capitalism, which
dictates that production be driven by profit rather than need. The people
of Archaos make do, eat less, work 'que pour répondre aux besoins de la
vie—et non de la mort; non plus pour emplir divers gouffres sans fond
tels coffres seigneuriaux et marchands, ou parades d'orgueil, ou festins
destinés à nourrir plus que la chair la vanité ou quelque manque de l'âme'
['only to satisfy the needs of everyday life, not death; and not to fill
various bottomless coffers belonging to merchants or overlords, or to

show off, or to lay on feasts whose purpose was to feed vanity or some emptiness of the soul rather than bellies'] (315). New energy is released by the changes wrought: 'quantité de métiers jadis nécessaires croyait-on, tels geôlier, exempt, vérificateur, releveur, vérificateur de releveur, juge, avocat, greffier, comptable, prêteur, bourreau, laquais, etc., etc., tombèrent en désuétude [. . .] libérant des énergies fraîches pour des tâches plus utiles' ['a whole lot of jobs previously thought indispensable, like jailers, officers of the watch, auditors, meter-readers, meter-reader supervisors, judges, advocates, bailiffs, accountants, loan sharks, hang-men, lackeys, etc., etc., became obsolete [. . .] releasing new energies for more useful tasks'] (309). Archaos functions according to two primary laws, renamed 'propositions' in order to dispel any notion of authority or hierarchy: 'tout est gratuit' ['everything is free'], and 'tout le monde fait ce qu'il veut, et à la grâce de Dieu' ['everyone does what they want, trusting to God'].[16] Self-regulation and peer-pressure replace judicial authority: 'il suffit de laisser passer le temps: les gens comprennent tout seuls si on ne les brusque pas' ['you just have to wait a bit: people get the message all by themselves if you don't rush them'] (311). The literal 'bordel', centre of the council of pleasure-givers, which eventually comprises almost the entire population of Archaos, becomes a symbol for the new anarchist society: 'Comme dit le proverbe: bordel n'est pas mortel. Tandis que l'ordre, l'est' ['chaos is not fatal, but order is'] (320).

Political and economic considerations form only one strand of *Archaos*. Human relationships and spiritual needs must also be accommodated in Rochefort's anti-authoritarian utopian vision, and here, too, the text moves towards a synthesis in Part III. Under Avatar's patriarchal reign religious principles are equated with an oppressive regime; authoritarianism operates at both a spiritual and a political level, a point succinctly conveyed by the zeugma in the following passage:

> Ce roi-ci était atteint d'une dévotion aigue, qu'il entendait répandre sur un peuple ignorant, encore imparfaitement illuminé par la vraie foi. Des clochers s'élevèrent, ainsi que les impôts. Les gens courbèrent un peu plus l'échine. (11)

> [*The king was a deeply devout man, and he intended to disseminate this devoutness to an ignorant people as yet imperfectly enlightened by the true faith. Bell-towers soared as did taxes. The people bowed their heads a little lower.*]

In the blinkered vision of the monarch, sexuality and spirituality are mutually exclusive, antagonistic forces. No sooner is a male heir secured than Avatar develops a puritanical distaste for matters of the flesh. Gongs are sounded in the royal dwelling to signal the approach of the king, permitting all those of the female sex to keep their distance. Erostase, a priest with a fearsome reputation, is called in to cleanse the royal household of sin. The excesses of Avatar's religious fervour are conveyed via a humorous accumulation of potentially sexually-related verbs:

> Regarder un objet vertical était péché, ou bien un objet creux; [. . .] les chasseurs virent l'horreur de bander des arcs; le boulanger se surprenant à pétrir sa pâte rougit, et ne fit pas le pain, le bûcheron n'abattit pas sa hache, le potier ne fit pas de dedans à son pot et le batelier n'enfonça point la rame ni le charpentier la cheville, le toit s'effondra, tuant deux paysans qui filèrent droit en enfer car elle bourrait une oie et il pilait du grain. (38)

> [*Looking at a vertical object, or indeed a concave object, was a sin;* [. . .] *the hunters saw the horror of tautening their instruments; the baker blushed when he caught himself kneading his dough and stopped making bread, the woodcutter no longer wielded his tool, the potter no longer made insides for his pots and the ferryman no longer thrust in his oar nor the carpenter his dowel, and the roof collapsed killing two peasants who went straight to hell because she was stuffing a goose and he was pounding rape-seed.*]

Unsurprisingly, Avatar's rule is marked by misogyny. Onagre, Govan's twin sister, is recalled from banishment merely in order to secure land by marrying a neighbouring prince. Avatar claims absolute authority over his daughter: 'Je vous ai donné la vie. [. . .] elle m'appartient' ['I gave you your life. [. . .] it belongs to me'] (48). As Avanie points out: 'c'est un malheur de naître femme [. . .]. Nous ne sommes que des monnaies d'échange' ['being born a woman is a hard lot [. . .]. We're just a form of currency'] (44).

Archaos works towards a dissolution of the binary polarization of sexuality and spirituality, and points to the dangers facing those who would deny their sexuality in the name of religious faith. Tempted by Onagre, Erostase dies (after a brief flirtation with flagellation) in what is according to his own beliefs mortal sin, though not before, in a moment of high farce and irony, a final spasm sends his crucifix flying through the air to kill Onagre's unwanted intended. The puritanical priest remains trapped between the world of the living and the dead, struggling to hide a mighty erection. 'Une stase', appropriately enough, is a medical term referring to a circulatory problem or congestion of the blood. . .[17] The sexual and political dimensions of the text remain closely linked. A society's political regime cannot be separated from its sexual mores: 'an authoritarian society with a repressive morality encourages the psychological disorders which lead to rape, murder and assault'.[18] King Avatar, striving to suppress his sexuality in the name of his religious principles, leads a dual existence. His repressed puritanical self is doubled by Avatar the bestial marauder who eats raw flesh and ravishes the country's maidens in his secret second life. Ultimately his split persona leads to his downfall. His auto-castration is the product of his own authoritarian morality ('it is better for you to lose one part of your body than for the whole of it to be thrown into hell', Matthew 5:29). As Rochefort points out: 'les représentants de la moralité patriarcale tombent dans leurs propres pièges' ['the representatives of patriachal morality are caught in their own traps'].[19]

Although utopian projects tend to present themselves as universal, one man's vision of heaven can be a woman's vision of hell. Singling out what she identifies as a rampant misogyny and, especially, 'misopédie' (her coinage) in the tradition, Rochefort comments on the failures of the genre:

> Pour ce que je connais, il me semble que les inventeurs de ces tentatives désespérées d'organiser le bonheur en société y trimballent, à leur insu évidemment, leur solide esprit de caste, et la plus idéale justice oublie toujours une classe dans un coin.[20]

> [*As far as I can see it seems that those who come up with these desperate attempts to design a harmonious society cart their robust caste mentality around with them, without even realizing it of course, so the most ideal system of justice always leaves one class or another forgotten in a corner.*]

The sexual freedom which characterizes *Archaos* extends to all members of society without exception: the symbolic 'bordel' is no male sanctum. Early in Part II, Govan ensures that all citizens, women and children included, are treated on equal terms when he creates a 'bordelle' and 'bordelet'. Indeed, far from being forgotten in a corner, the children in Rochefort's utopia are the very instigators of a sexual revolution which runs alongside, indeed is the prerequisite for, political change. It is the archetypal love of the reunited twins, Onagre and Govan, which releases sexual energies in Avatar's repressed household. Shortly after Onagre's return from banishment, the nurse Litote is to be seen enjoying sex with both the page Filet-Mignon and Avanie herself. For the first time, the notion of sin is undermined as Avanie reflects upon the sexual pleasure she has discovered: 'Elle demanda à sa foi naïve si c'était là péché. Sa foi naïve lui répondit ceci: ce lieu qui n'a d'autre destination que le plaisir, Dieu nous l'aurait-il créé pour en même temps nous le défendre? C'est un cadeau de Dieu, conclut-elle' ['She asked her simple faith if this was a sin. Her simple faith replied thus: would God have created a part of the body whose only function is to give us pleasure if He then intended to forbid us that pleasure? It's a gift from God, she concluded'] (43).

In Rochefort's view, sex, 'that is the desire, longing, feelings and emotions that are really connected with sexual energy', has been weakened and transmogrified by oppression, alienation, social obligations and the traditional nuclear family. *Archaos* represents the author's vision of liberated or unbound sexual energy, a vision characterized by what she refers to as 'polysexuality'.[21] Although many feminist utopias of the 1970s, and indeed earlier examples of the genre such as Charles Fourier's *Le Nouveau Monde amoureux*, envisaged an abolition of the traditional nuclear family and promoted same-sex relations (usually female), Rochefort's emphasis on child sexuality and her approval of incest places her on the radical fringes of the genre.[22]

Although Govan, via his incestuous relationship with Onagre, plays a central part in the initial unleashing of sexual energies, his main function (and in this Rochefort is perhaps guilty of adhering to stereotypes) is to implement economic and political changes, whilst Onagre is largely associated with the realm of a redefined spirituality. Far from suffering from the effects of a polarization of sexuality and religious faith, Onagre represents a position of synthesis: the convent of Trémènes which she heads is modelled upon the city brothel; the twins she bears to Avatar, Copula and Fornicato, who are born locked in sexual embrace, may be condemned by Rome, but go on to found their own religious orders. Rochefort has stated that *Archaos* 'is a book about how to desire without power'.[23] Just as Avanie persuades the battling Jérémias to lay down his arms, so Onagre effects a dramatic change in the artist Héliozobe, who, like Erostase, falls victim to a conflict between what is termed 'le Haut et le Bas' (literally, the top and the bottom).

Starting out as the stereotypical phallus-driven male ('zob' is slang for penis; 'helios' indicates the sun, or spiritual dimension), Héliozobe struggles with his sexual feelings for Onagre once she becomes head of the convent of Trémènes, believing her to be untouchable: 'J'en aime une, qui ne peut aimer sur Terre' ['I love a woman who cannot partake of earthly love'] (231). Unable, like Avatar and Erostase before him, to reconcile his divided self, Héliozobe initially sublimates his sexuality; his paintbrush, in effect, acquires a phallic status: 'il aspirait douloureusement à toucher son âme immortelle par les voies de l'esprit, et à cet effet faisait passer toute son énergie d'amour, à défaut de l'autre dans l'instrument à cela propre: son pinceau' ['painfully, he sought to move her immortal soul via the spirit, and to this end, since he lacked the use of the usual instrument, he channelled all his passionate energy into his paintbrush']

(227). Later, we shall see that Héliozobe's triptych represents a 'mise en abyme' of the utopic sexual vision of *Archaos*, but it is an earlier work, a mural depicting heaven and hell painted with Onagre, which first indicates the gradual breakdown of the binary divide. Little by little, the two panels, representing angels and demons, become indistinguishable:

> Et à mesure qu'ils grignotaient les murs, démons et damnés liés dans les tortures revêtaient des expressions de plus en plus extatiques, et ressemblaient davantage à Onagre; Gloires et Chérubins dardaient de plus sombres regards. Et enfin Dieu Lui-Même eut les traits d'Héliozobe. (227–8)

> [*As they gradually spread across the walls, demons and damned souls united in torture assumed ever more ecstatic expressions, and looked more and more like Onagre, whilst Glories and Cherubs glared with increasingly sombre miens. And finally, God Himself took on the appearance of Héliozobe.*]

Before the two-panelled mural can give way to the synthesis symbolized by the triptych, Héliozobe undergoes a final 'cure' at the hands of Fornicato. Marshall observes that 'a conservative, quietist and authoritarian tendency in the Pauline Church in Rome' traditionally stands in opposition to anarchism.[24] Fornicato, significantly, recognizes that Héliozobe's problem, his 'division de l'être' ['split self'], is caused by 'le Mal de Saint-Paul' ['the sickness of Saint Paul', that is, the division between the spirit and the flesh] (353). Rochefort does not pull her punches in signalling her opposition to what she identifies as authoritarian religion, as Onagre's words (doubtless shockingly blasphemous in the eyes of many readers) clearly reveal:

> Christ est mort seul. Eli l'a vraiment abandonné—Eli, pourquoi l'as-tu abandonné? Tu as laissé Paul s'asseoir sur lui avec ses grosses fesses de soldat romain qui aspiraient à être chevauchées, tu l'as laissé parler à sa place avec sa grosse bouche romaine qui aspirait à être foutue [. . .]. Tu as permis à la haine de la chair de couvrir la voix du Dieu de trente ans qui parlait de l'amour. (392)

> [*Christ died alone. Eli really did forsake him—Eli, why did you forsake him? You let Paul sit on him with his big Roman soldier's buttocks, those buttocks which were just longing to be straddled, and you let him speak in His place with his big Roman mouth which was just longing to be fucked [. . .]. You let hatred of the flesh drown out the voice of the thirty-year-old God who spoke of love.*]

The final utopic vision of sexuality which emerges in Part III of the text has three fundamental characteristics. Firstly, the notions of sin and shame give way to a desire for transparency: 'on montrait tout. On ne cachait absolument rien' ['we revealed everything. We hid absolutely nothing'] (389). Onagre confesses her incestuous love for Govan; Erostase admits his love for Onagre and emerges from the basin in the convent of Trémènes in which he had been concealing his importunate erection; Héliozobe declares his true feelings for Govan, and Jérémias his love of Avanie. Secondly, *Archaos* anticipates many later feminist utopias of the 1970s in its separation of sexuality from any exclusive ties or notions of ownership. Writing on sexual relations in feminist utopias Lefanu cites Sally Miller Gearhart's *The Wanderground: Stories of the Hill Women* (1979) as a typical example: 'There are no words more obscene than "I can't live without you."'[25] In a similar vein, Rochefort's Govan learns to accept, even to admire, his sister's desire for Héliozobe: 'Que tu es belle, sans moi. Je ne savais pas que tu existais en dehors de moi. C'est beau. [. . .] j'aime ton désir de lui' ['You're so beautiful without me. I didn't know you existed outside me. It's beautiful. I love your desire for him'] (229). Ursula le Guin's *The Dispossessed* (1974), a utopia much admired by Rochefort, represents sexual desire which precludes a power-based objectification of the other: the language spoken in the utopian Anares 'lacked any proprietary idiom for the sexual act'; verbs denoting sexual congress are neutral and take only a plural verb: 'it meant something two people did, not something one person did, or had'.[26] Héliozobe comes to adopt a similar stance: 'tu confonds aimer avec posséder. Aimer c'est être possédé' ['you're confusing love with possession. To love is to be possessed'] (361). His passivity, and renunciation of what we might call teleological sex (where orgasm is the desired end-point), typifies Rochefort's aim to reverse traditional cultural symbols:

> One of the ways to recreate culture is to change the symbols. This is what I tried to do in *Archaos*, for example [. . .]. The poor penis has been taken as a symbol of power, but for me this is a perversion of the symbolism of the penis. [. . .] The phallic aggressiveness is destroyed in the first part of the book and then, in the utopian parts, there is no longer any link at all between the phallus and aggressiveness. Instead, the penis becomes symbolic of waiting, almost passivity, of invitation.[27]

The people of Archaos are not restricted to penetrative sex: they touch, contemplate, make love at a distance. Sexual relations are summed up by what comes to be called 'le désir désirant' ['desiring desire'], a term which effectively removes all notions of a subject and object of desire, and whose present participle stresses the importance of passive waiting. A final proposition is drafted: 'Toute âme qui marche sous le ciel et rencontre sur son chemin le désir qui la désire et humblement l'attend, y répondra, dans le cadre de la Loi XVI et sous le regard de Dieu' ['All souls which walk beneath the firmament and encounter the desire which desires and humbly awaits them will respond to that desire, as stated in Law XVI and under the watchful eye of God'] (372).[28] Once again we can see the influence of the counter-culture at work. Those who write about the communes which proliferated in the US and many Western countries in the 1970s are quick to point out that, contrary to popular belief, sex was always something more, or other, than random meaningless relationships; that '"making love" need not refer to orgasmic, genital sexual activity. The idea is not orgy but an ambience of loving, and, indeed, erotic interpersonal contact among a variety of unrelated people.'[29]

The counter-law relating to the 'désir désirant' includes the all-important phrase 'et sous le regard de Dieu' (372): in Rochefort's utopia sexuality is conjoined with spirituality. Two further aspects of the text must be considered if we are to arrive at a full understanding of the author's vision: the character Anastème, and Héliozobe's triptych 'Le Jardin Étincelant'. Classic anarchist thinkers had little time for organized religion: 'they saw the Church as aligned with the State, and the priest anointing the warrior and king. [. . .] The traditional image of God as an authoritarian father-figure was anathema to them, and they felt no need for a supernatural authority to bolster temporal authority.'[30] Anastème, orthodox bishop of Archaos, represents precisely this authoritarian strand of Christianity. Horrified at the thought of a communist takeover, he urges Govan to claim back the city of Trémènes, and invokes the power of the Church: 'Et quand même: en droit tu es roi, c'est moi-même qui t'ai chrémé, et rien ne vaut contre le chrême, surtout pas le temporel' ['Besides, you're king by right, I anointed you myself, and nothing can stand against that chrism, least of all anything of this world'] (280). Govan's appeal to the commandment not to kill is fobbed off with a healthy dose of hypocrisy: 'mais nous t'aurions absous évidemment' ['but of course we'd have given you absolution'] (280). As the text unfolds, Anastème is increasingly alarmed by the steady march away from orthodoxy. Finally, the outraged bishop identifies the problem: Archaos is beset by 'la dangereuse hérésie de l'esprit libre' ['the dangerous heresy of the free spirit'] (395). True to his name—'un anathème' is an excommunication pronounced on heretics or enemies of the Catholic faith—Anastème sends for the Inquisition.

The allusion to heresy, and to that particular heresy, is crucial. As the influence of the established Church in the Middle Ages grew, many underground movements which sought to challenge the power of both State and Church emerged. One of these was the heretical sect of the Free Spirit, which first appeared towards the close of the 12th century in Islamic Spain, spreading throughout Christian Europe towards the end of the 13th century, before emerging into full view in the 14th century. The links with *Archaos* are clear. Adepts of the sect, which has been referred to as a form of 'quasi-mystical anarchism', rejected private property, were sexually promiscuous, and opposed the institution of marriage. More significantly, they claimed to be filled with the Holy Spirit and thereby incapable of sin, beyond the jurisdiction of both State and Church.[31] Once again, links with the counter-culture can be established. Marshall indicates the continuity of thought which cuts across the centuries to the 1970s: 'A modern version of the cult of the Free Spirit, with its stress on the total emancipation of the individual and call for universal peace and love, can be even recognized in the counter-culture of the Sixties this century'; whilst Cohn refers to 'an eroticism which, far from springing from a carefree sensuality, possessed above all a symbolic value as a sign of spiritual emancipation—which incidentally is the value which "free love" has often possessed in our own times'.[32]

And the influence of the heresy of the Free Spirit extends further. The tripartite structure of *Archaos* reflects the sect's belief that a Third and Last Age, an earthly paradise (hence 'Les Heures de la Béatitude'), would succeed the Ages of the God and Christ ('Le Roi Père', 'Le Roi Fils'), whilst the all-important proposition 'tout le monde fait ce qu'il veut, et à la grâce de Dieu' ['everyone may do as they wish, trusting to God'] echoes the adepts' belief that individuals, embued with grace, were free from the authority of both the State and organized religion. Finally, it can be demonstrated that Héliozobe's triptych 'Le Jardin Étincelant' is modelled on Hieronymous Bosch's *The Garden of Earthly Delights* (also called *The Millennium*), and that Rochefort was aware of the interpretation of some critics, notably Wilhelm Fraenger, who argued that Bosch painted his triptych for a patron of the Free Spirit sect, and indeed may have been a member himself. Several elements now enter into play in our reading: the extra-textual artwork; Fraenger's rather maverick interpretation of Bosch's triptych as a visual representation of the beliefs of the sect of the Free Spirit; the text of *Archaos* itself, more specifically the thematic representation of sexuality and spirituality; and the descriptions within the text of Héliozobe's own triptych. Although a detailed analysis is beyond the scope of this study, the following discussion will seek to point up the principle characteristics of the interplay between the various strands, and to complement the more extensive work already carried out by Isabelle Constant in *Les Mots Étincelants de Christiane Rochefort*.[33] Summing up the intermeshing of inter- and intratextual elements, it can be suggested that

Rochefort's utopic vision is based, at least in part, upon Bosch's *The Garden of Earthly Delights* as interpreted by Fraenger, and that Héliozobe's triptych stands as a 'mise en abyme' of the utopic vision which emerges in Part III of *Archaos*.

As in Bosch's *Garden*, the left-hand panel of Héliozobe's triptych represents the Garden of Eden:

> Le péché a commencé lorsque Adam et Eve ceints de feuilles essayèrent de fuir le regard de leur Créateur. Non pas avant. Sur le premier volet je représenterai Dieu dans sa jeunesse, assis dans les Paradis les mains tendues bénissant l'homme et la femme embrassés ravis d'amour sous Ses yeux. (366)

> [*Sin began when Adam and Eve, girded with leaves, tried to flee the watchful eye of their Creator. Not before. The first panel of the triptych will show God in his youth, sitting in Paradise with his hands outheld as he blesses the man and woman embracing, transported by love before His eyes.*]

Gibson indicates that in Bosch's triptych 'God himself is much more youthful than his white-bearded counterpart on the outer wings, and represents the deity in the guise of Christ, the second person of the Trinity.'[34] According to Fraenger the choice of the Christ figure reflects the Free Spirit sect's views in its suggestion of an absence of sin: 'all thought of the Fall is outweighed by the certainty of salvation as vouchsafed by the Son of Man.'[35] Héliozobe's plans for the panel clearly reveals a similar standpoint. His Garden of Eden will represent the beliefs which subtend the sexual spirituality, or spiritual sexuality, which emerges in the third section of the utopia: the people of Archaos, as we have seen, replace all notions of sin, shame, and secrecy with a desire for openness; the 'désir désirant' is blessed by the deity ('sous le regard de Dieu'). It is important to note that Héliozobe's description of his triptych is followed by a second, more detailed version which conveys a markedly different point of view; that of the hostile outsider who condemns both the triptych, and by extension, the values and mores of Archaos which it represents (383–5). To the anonymous external critic of Archaos, Héliozobe's triptych is both blasphemous and highly offensive, and the second description concludes with a withering assessment of the triptych's creator, which, by extension, applies equally to Rochefort herself:

> Le talent, la fantastique imagination et le délire, dû sans doute à la démence, de l'artiste, porterait cette œuvre aux cimes du génie si elle n'était tout un entier blasphème, que l'on doit soustraire aux yeux du profane. (385)

[*The artist's talent, fantastical imagination and frenzy, doubtless attribut-
able to insanity, would elevate this work to the very heights of genius were
it not for the fact that it is utterly blasphemous and should be withheld
from the sight of the profane.*]

The two descriptions of the triptych not only constitute 'mises en abyme'
of the central themes in *Archaos,* but also of two potential responses to the
work: complicity, or hostility. The reflexive device tacitly invites readers to
acknowledge their own standpoint, to condone or condemn Rochefort's
utopic vision. Furthermore, the first description, which anticipates
Héliozobe's painting, differs in detail from the second description of the
completed work: Héliozobe, for example, plans to depict his Adam and
Eve 'embrassés' ['embracing'], whereas the completed panel represents
the couple in a pose which seems closer to the quiet passivity of the 'désir
désirant': 'étendus sur le côté, face à face, non entrelacés, leur mains se
tenant' ['lying on their side, face to face, not entwined, holding hands']
(384). In both cases Rochefort alters the original triptych to suit her
needs: Bosch's panel represents Adam and Eve sitting and kneeling
respectively.

The central panel of Héliozobe's triptych again owes much to Bosch.
Gibson observes that 'the central panel [of Bosch's *Garden*] is heightened
by the clear and even lighting, the absence of shadows, and the bright,
high-keyed colours'.[36] Héliozobe's panel is similarly described as
'extrêmement lumineux et coloré' ['very bright and highly coloured']
(383). A profusion of water, flowers and fruit appear (or are reported to
appear) in both works. At the bottom right-hand side of Bosch's work a
youth is depicted thrusting flowers into the rectum of his companion.
Héliozobe's panel represents two characters who can be identified from
previous textual references as Govan and Héliozobe engaged in anal
intercourse. The panel is filled, as is Bosch's, with naked couples engaged
in sexual acts. To the orthodox interpreter this panel represents sinful
sexuality and stands as a mid-point between heaven and hell: as in the
Roman de la Rose it is a false paradise. This is the view taken by both the
mainstream critics of Bosch's triptych and those outsiders who identify in
Héliozobe's panel figures 'abandonnés à tous les péchés charnels' ['given
over to all the sins of the flesh'] (383). The unorthodox Fraenger,
however, whose interpretation is premised on the claim that Bosch's
triptych represents the views not of the orthodox Church but of the
Brethren of the Free Spirit, regards the central panel as 'a Utopia, a
garden of divine delight'; 'not an exposure of sinful humanity, but the
joyous representation of Paradise as it was in the times of Adam and as it
will be again under the aegis of a new Adam'.[37] The reader who approves
Rochefort's vision adopts a similar stance: the world of Archaos is a

heaven on earth. Links with the 1970s persist: Gibson, who discounts Fraenger's reading, acknowledges that the central panel can be regarded as 'a sort of universal love-in'.[38]

Once more Rochefort deviates significantly from the original triptych. Héliozobe's work includes 'une bulle transparente posée sur une vasque parmi des dauphins' ['a transparent bubble resting on a basin of water amidst dolphins'] in which 'deux très jeunes enfants se tiennent enlacés' ['two very young children are entwined'] (384). Bosch's triptych includes a similar sphere in the same location at the lower left-hand side of the panel, but the couple enclosed within it are not children. Commenting on the Garden of Eden panel in Bosch's *Garden,* Gibson observes:

> The marriage of Adam and Eve by a youthful deity occurs frequently in Dutch manuscripts of the fifteenth century, and illustrates the moment when he blessed them, saying in the words of Genesis I.28: 'Be fruitful and multiply, and replenish the earth and subdue it [. . .].'

Gibson goes on to state that the absence of children in the central panel signals the fallen state of mankind, as sexual acts are divorced from reproduction.[39] In Héliozobe's triptych, as in the textual world of *Archaos,* far from representing the fruit of sin-free sexuality, children are themselves portrayed as fully sexual beings. Indeed, earlier in the text Anastème takes umbrage with Onagre's subversion of the Genesis edict: 'Et nous Te demandons la grâce d'être part de cette beauté, afin que Tes autres créatures y soient baignées comme nous, Amen' ['And we ask for Your grace that we may be part of this beauty so that Your other creatures may be bathed in beauty like us, Amen'] (372):

> 'Remplissez la Terre, et l'assujettissez,' voilà ce qu'Il a dit. Pas: 'Baignez-y.' Fais envoyer cette infamie à Rome, ils vont nous expédier des juges cette fois. (372).

> [*'Be fruitful and multiply, and subdue the World,' that's what He said. Not 'Bathe in its beauty.' Send word of this vile blasphemy to Rome, this time they'll send the Inquisition.*]

Where feminist utopias of the 1970s typically engage with problems of child-care and education, Rochefort's utopia bypasses the issue by representing children as human beings undifferentiated from adults.

The interpretation of the triptych's central panel as a heaven on earth can inform our understanding of another facet of *Archaos,* and that is the departure from realism. Govan and Onagre are still children by the close of the text; Jérémias ages only during his brief excursion to the lands outside Archaos; only two characters, Anastème and Ganidan the equerry, die. The secret of eternal life, so we are told, lies in the elixir of life concocted in Part I by the court scientists, and tossed dismissively into the moat by a depressed Avatar. For those who bathe in, or drink, the waters, time apparently stands still. Govan, however, provides a second explanation—'c'est parce que nous aimons au-delà de toute mesure' ['it's because our love knows no bounds'] (427)—and although his statement is never discussed, it is consistent with the beliefs of adepts of the Free Spirit:

> To have the Holy Spirit incarnated in oneself and to receive the revelation which that brought—that was to rise from the dead and to possess heaven. A man who had knowledge of the God within himself carried his own heaven about with him. One had only to recognise one's own divinity and one was resurrected as a Spiritual, a denizen of heaven on earth.[40]

Ganidan and Anastème die because they fail to embrace the sexual spirituality of the utopic world.

Both of these readings (magic potion or Free Spirit faith) indicate the manner in which readers of *Archaos* may seek to recuperate non-realist elements of the text by interpreting them within a specific historical framework, regarding them, that is, as representations of the medieval mind-set. The same process can be applied to the 'mage' ['magus'] Analogue, who can observe the outside world in a magic 'source', or the enchanted forest of Féline which swallows up and spits out those who enter it. Other fantastic incidents can be interpreted symbolically, for instance the melting of the snows when Govan and Onagre are reunited, or the magic rose bush which assumes something of a peripatetic existence (roses traditionally symbolizing passion). Other elements, such as Erostase's capacity for flight, or Govan's ability to metamorphose into a cat and talk to rats, are perhaps more resistant to recuperative readings. Perhaps we should not seek to recuperate. Rochefort's incorporation of the fantastic not only intersects with the late-medieval time-scale, it is also typical of the spirit of the 1970s:

> Unlike the classic anarchist thinkers, who as heirs of the Enlighten-ment looked to reason and science to bring about progress, the gurus of the counter-culture rejected the 'rationality' and 'objectivity' which had been so debased by the dominant culture in its attempts to justify war, poverty and injustice. The pendulum swung in the other direction, towards a reinvigorated spirituality, towards subjectivity, feelings, sensations, play, mysticism, and magic.[41]

Rochefort explicitly opposes an over-reliance on rational thought:

> Le rationalisme a tué la pensée intuitive. Celle-ci est sans arrêt opprimée, délaissée. Le rationalisme, c'est l'incarnation du principe de concurrence, de compétition, c'est 'ou toi, ou moi'. Dans la pensée occidentale, comprendre c'est détruire les autres.[42]
>
> [*Rationalism has killed intuitive thinking. Intuition is ceaselessly oppressed and cast aside. Rationalism is the incarnation of the principle of competition, of rivalry, it's 'you or me'. In Western thought to understand is to destroy others.*]

Archaos embodies the author's rejection of what she perceives to be the dominant culture's mind-set: 'la dimension délirante, qui fait tant défaut aux rationalisateurs [. . .] on ne fera rien sans non plus' ['nothing can be accomplished without that wild irrational element which rationalizers lack so badly']; 'l'utopie sera défoncée, ou ne sera pas' ['utopia will be stoned, or will be nothing at all'].[43]

Returning to the triptych after this brief digression, we can see that Héliozobe's right-hand panel represents hell, and that the second description paints a picture which is very similar to Bosch's vision:

> L'Enfer, très sombre, montre, dans un décor de ruines et d'incendie semé d'étranges machines de métal, toute la gamme des tortures que l'imagination délirante de l'artiste a su concevoir, et que des monstres sémi-humains sémi-mécaniques infligent aux pauvres damnés nus et frissonnants livrés à leurs cruautés. (383)
>
> [*Against a background of ruins and fire strewn with strange metal machines, hell, very dark, depicts the whole range of tortures that the artist's delirous imagination could conceive, tortures which half-human and half-mechanical monsters are inflicting upon the poor naked shivering damned souls subjected to their cruelty.*]

The first description, provided by Héliozobe, guides our interpretation: 'le dernier volet sera les pays que j'ai traversés' ['the last panel will represent the countries I have travelled through'] (366). Earlier in the text an exchange between Jérémias and Héliozobe, both of whom leave Archaos then return, had revealed the sterility of those lands which lay beyond the boundaries of Archaos, and which, by extension, did not share the utopia's beliefs and values: 'Que penses-tu d'un univers pour lequel Archaos n'existerait pas? / —C'est de là que je viens, dit le moine. C'est la mort' ['"What do you think of a universe for which Archaos doesn't

exist?" "That's where I've come from," replied the monk. "It's death"']
(344). Hell, in other words, is whatever is not Archaos. Spatial or
geographical references in the text can assume a metaphorical dimension.
The Brethren of the Free Spirit did not regard heaven and hell as places
of punishment or reward located in an after-life. Rather, heaven and hell
are 'transferred to the inner experience of each individual, as ever-present
reality'; 'the Brethren of the Free Spirit did in fact hold that heaven and
hell were merely states of the soul in this world.'[44]

Towards the end of *Archaos*, as enemy armies threaten to annihilate the
country, Govan makes a similar point: 'Archaos est dans nos cœurs, ou si
l'on préfère dans nos esprits, ou si l'on préfère dans nos peaux. C'est là
qu'il existe, est vivant, et peut être sauvegardé' ['Archaos is in our hearts,
or if you prefer in our very spirit, or if you prefer in our blood. That's
where it exists, where it's alive, and where it can be protected'] (420).[45]
Rochefort takes us back to the optimism which threatened to undermine
State oppression in *Une Rose pour Morrison*, in which Sereine lectured on
the eternal presence, and undying strength, of the intangible 'Esprit':
'L'Esprit sera immortel. S'il ne l'était, il aurait depuis longtemps déserté
ces lieux [. . .] et on n'en trouverait trace. Il aurait donc la vie dure' ['The
Spirit is immortal. If it weren't it would have deserted this place long
since [. . .] and we wouldn't find any trace of it. So the Spirit is pretty
hard to get rid of'] (*Une Rose*, 133).

Archaos ends with an intense, lyrical description of countless nameless
individuals kneeling as if in prayer, but also caught up in sexual ecstasy,
waiting with infinite patience for an unspecified event. The voices of two
lovers emerge, reiterating the necessity for patience: 'Mais c'est un long
ascèse, ne l'oublie pas. Tu risques d'être là pour un bon moment. J'ai
autant de patience que de désir. Ils te blesseront, ils te feront mal' ['But
it's a long asceticism, don't forget. You may well be there for quite some
time. My patience is as great as my desire. They'll hurt you, they'll do you
harm'] (445). The significance of these rather enigmatic closing pages is
clarified by a passage located on the fly-leaf of the original Grasset
edition, and signed 'Les Archaotes':

> On ne s'occupait pas de vous: vous étiez si loin, si morts, on vous
> avait oubliés. Mais aujourd'hui il nous semble qu'il y a des change-
> ments: vous cahotez de plus en plus, votre univers a des ratés: de
> nouveau le monde existe après si longtemps. Vous avez produit des
> enfants de vie, une nouvelle fois. Et déjà ils vous regardent, de leurs
> yeux résolus et rêveurs, ouverts comme des pièges: ils attendent que
> vous tombiez. Le temps est revenu de donner signe, le temps revient
> de s'en remettre au désordre, au hasard, et tout spécialement au
> plaisir. Jouir est la réponse, dans un premier temps, le reste en

découle, et sera donné par surcroît. Nous, nous sommes là encore, à genoux, et nous vous attendons au prochain tournant de l'Histoire. Ce ne sera plus très long.

[*No-one was paying any attention to you: you were so far away, so dead, you'd been forgotten. But today we think things are changing: your universe is hiccuping along, it's misfiring: after such a long time the world is alive once again. Once again you have given birth to children of life. And they are already looking at you, with determined and dreamy eyes, open like traps: they're waiting for you to fall. Once again the time has come to give a sign, once more it is time to give yourselves over to disorder, to chance, and most of all, to pleasure. In the first instance pleasure is the solution, everything else will follow, and it will be given. And we are still there, kneeling, we are waiting for you at the next turn of History. It won't be long now.*]

From this we can suggest that the people of Archaos represent all those individuals who, across the centuries, from the Brethren of the Free Spirit to the youth of the counter-culture of the 1970s, take a stand against the dominant ideology. Returning to the definition of the utopia, we can now suggest that Archaos can be regarded as a metaphorical realm which transcends time and place. The utopic realm represents any 'good place' in which a spirit of subversion exists and persists. It is a 'no place' because it is, in a sense, every or any place in which the combative spirit eternally present in humanity manifests itself, a point which is succinctly conveyed by the combination of tenses in Rochefort's own description of Archaos as a society 'où nous pourrions vivre si les choses s'étaient pas déroulées autrement' ['where we could live if things hadn't turned out differently'].[46] Archaos is also a 'no place' because the dominant ideology will always seeks to deny, or recuperate, subversive factions: the countries which lie outside Archaos, symbolic representations of the dominant ideology, consistently deny the very existence of the potentially dangerous utopia: 'Archaos n'existait pas en dehors d'Archaos' ['Archaos did not exist outside Archaos'] (359).

Whilst we can interpret *Archaos* metaphorically, the question of feasibility nonetheless remains. Is the society depicted mere pie-in-the-sky, 'utopic' as colloquial usage envisages the term; can, or could, Rochefort's vision serve as a blueprint for contemporary life? The answer, if we restrict ourselves to the question of viability, is no. Quite apart from the magical, non-realist dimension of the text, Archaos is a pre-industrial society, and Rochefort herself acknowledges the sleight of hand she has performed: 'Qui ne s'en est pas donnés, des facilités? Moi je me suis dispensé de l'industrie, carrément, ce n'était pas intentionnel mais c'était plus commode que du béton à mettre en poudre' ['Who hasn't made life a little easier for themselves? Me, I got rid of industry altogether, I didn't mean to but it was easier than having to blow everything up'].[47] And even if we disregard this problem, does the anarchism which forms the very heart of *Archaos* have a place in the modern world? Is it not, as some critics have claimed, 'a backward looking, pre-industrial ideology' which 'depicts a radical future' but ultimately presents a vision which 'depends on social mechanisms that flourished in the simpler and more stable communities of the past'?[48] Even the communes of the counter-culture which inspired Rochefort's writing faced numerous, often insurmountable, problems: the principle of unanimity tended to lead to a breakdown of decision-making; economic stability was rarely attained, and members of communes were often obliged to draw on personal savings or social security; only those communities with extremely restricted numbers ultimately stood any chance of survival.[49] Nonetheless, even though anarchism and the communes may no longer represent alternative ways of living today if we take 'alternative' to mean 'replacement', they may yet have a part to play. As Marshall points out (and his words apply equally to the counter-institutions of the counter-culture):

> The aim of anarchist practice is no longer to overthrow capitalism and the state directly, but immediately to create a space in which individuals may develop alternative styles of life, and perhaps in the longer term to subvert contemporary society by the contagion of these lifestyles.[50]

This very process of subversive 'contagion' is played out in Rochefort's text. The geographical entity which is Archaos is in a state of flux. The people from neighbouring lands who congregate on the frontiers to watch the 'mistères', plays which re-enact the changes which have taken place in Archaos from the time of Avatar, begin to desert their homelands: 'C'était une frontière active, celle d'Archaos. Elle corrodait. Elle rongeait. Elle avançait. D'elle-même' ['Archaos had an active frontier. It corroded. It gnawed its way forward. It advanced. All by itself'] (402).[51] Archaos impinges on the repressive regimes surrounding it, just as the counter-culture, perhaps, left its mark on the dominant ideology of the 1970s.

The fact that *Archaos* cannot serve as viable blueprint for society does not, in any case, mean that it should be dismissed as mere whimsy. In her search for a definition of the utopia, Levitas suggests that we should look beyond a restrictive focus on the question of feasibility: 'the problem of limiting utopia to the "possible world" is that it conflates the categories of hope and desire'. The utopic text need not express a viable alternative vision of society; it may express no more, or less, than 'a desire for a better way of being and living', Levitas's chosen definition for the genre.[52]

The strength of *Archaos* lies in its capacity to reveal flaws in the prevailing system (or 'way of being and living') by representing a counter-image, or negative image, of contemporary society. In this, it can be compared to the very counter-institutions which inspired Rochefort to finally record her vision of utopia:

> As an attempt to define an alternative society, the communes of the counter culture have more coherence as a set of choices made to avoid the dystopian spectre of the dominant society than as a positive program. But whatever their initial motivation and despite all their shortcomings, they perform the indispensable utopian task of proving a model of an alternative society, and showing 'what of human nature has been lost'.[53]

Utopias, even if they are 'impossible worlds', may serve to criticize, or reveal gaps in any given society:

> The utopias current in a society tell us much about the experience of living in it, because they tell us in a way that we cannot directly ascertain where the felt absences are in people's lives—the spaces, that is, that utopia offers to fill, whether in fantasy or reality.[54]

In 1972 Rochefort was finally optimistic enough, after some two decades' waiting, to believe that *Archaos* could be written, and would not, perhaps, be so divorced from reality as be dismissed as mere fantasy. Society, however, was to change, and as Levitas points out, 'utopia is a social construct which arises [. . .] as a socially constructed response to an *equally* socially constructed gap between the needs and wants generated by a particular society and the satisfactions available to and distributed by it'.[55] As the hopes and dreams of the counter-culture waned, so Rochefort's perception of those gaps in society was transformed. Only six years after the publication of *Archaos*, her desire for change was to be expressed in a more pragmatic, and more pessimistic, manner:

> Bon alors en ce moment l'utopie, ce serait: pas de CRS en tenue de combat au coin des rues, Aldo Moro largué vivant [. . .], quelques infarctus (ti?) aux sommets, pour souffler, que les paras quand ils sautent montent au ciel au lieu de descendre, de l'eau propre, et que la merde arrive pas plus haut que le menton, y compris des personnes petites. De façon qu'on ait le temps un peu, de réfléchir et de devenir moins bête. Après on verra à se lancer dans des utopies plus compliquées, sans classes et sans pouvoir, pour une fois. Tant pis si vous me trouvez optimiste.[56]

Archaos, ou le jardin étincelant

[*Okay now, today, utopia would consist of the following: no armed police in combat gear on street corners, Aldo Moro released alive* [. . .], *a few heart-attacks in high places to give us a bit of breathing space, paratroopers going up to the heavens instead of down when they jump, clean water, with the shit rising no higher than our chins, including little kids' chins. So that we have a little time to think and become less idiotic. After that we'll see about rushing headlong into more complex utopias, classless and power-free ones for once. And if you think I'm an optimist, well tough.*]

CHAPTER SEVEN

Encore heureux qu'on va vers l'été

Et malgré les menaces du maître
sous les huées des enfants prodiges
avec des craies de toutes les couleurs
sur le tableau noir du malheur
il dessine le visage du bonheur
(Prévert)

Caught up in the imaginary universe of the forgotten kingdom of Archaos, we may easily lose sight of the fact that the twins Govan and Onagre, the catalyzing forces at the centre of Rochefort's utopia, are mere children. Children, after all, are not fully-fledged human beings. They cannot lay claim to the same sexual, political, and social rights as adults. Or can they? *Encore heureux qu'on va vers l'été* (1975), more than any of Rochefort's previous works, shifts the focus of attention firmly onto the child. From the anarchy of *Une Rose pour Morrison,* in which politically-conscious young schoolchildren stood alongside the student corpus, to the anarchism of *Archaos,* it is children who once again take to the streets in *Encore heureux,* but this time they keep right on walking. Starting on a small scale with the flight from school of a disaffected class of thirteen-year-olds, the text charts the exponential growth of a mass-exodus, as the nation's youngsters attempt to break free from adult-imposed values and institutions, and head for the promised land of the south.

The status of 'the child'—Rochefort typically questions the very label—was evidently something of a preoccupation for her at this time. Once she had completed the opening sections of *Encore heureux,* she broke off work in order to write *Les Enfants d'abord* (1976), an essay on children's rights, before returning to the novel.[1] *Les Enfants d'abord* is an angry piece of writing, frequently controversial in the radical nature of its demands, for example the right to vote, to work, and to express sexuality on demand, that is, regardless of age. Rochefort's sources, listed in a brief bibliography, include familiar anti-establishment names which were adopted by the counter-culture in the 1970s, such as David Cooper, Ivan Illich, Wilhelm Reich, and R.D. Laing. Writing in her habitual colloquial register, Rochefort puts her case for children's rights vigorously, if not always rigorously. Although the essay came in for considerable criticism, condemnations on the grounds of the impracticable and excessive nature of Rochefort's proposals and claims tended, in some cases at least, to be tempered by a degree of praise for her obvious engagement: 'Tant mieux si la générosité l'emporte sur le bon sens, si la tendresse et l'indignation vitupèrent à l'aveuglette! Ses outrances mêmes confèrent à ce pamphlet un accent de sincérité qui force la sympathie, sinon toujours la conviction' ['If generosity prevails over common sense, and if tenderness and indignation lash out haphazardly, so much the better. It is the very excesses of this pamphlet which give it a note of sincerity which inevitably elicits our sympathy, if not our agreement'].[2]

Rochefort's prime target in *Les Enfants d'abord*, as in previous works, is capitalist consumer society, represented as an inhuman machine which takes in, remodels, then churns out quality-controlled human beings who will ideally take their docile place in the rigid hierarchical social structure. Children are identified as an oppressed class which, unlike other disadvantaged groups (notably 'les femmes et les non-blancs' ['women and non-whites']), has yet to assert itself and be recognized: 'De tous les opprimés doués de parole, les enfants sont les plus muets' ['Of all the oppressed groups which have a voice, it is children who remain the most silent'] (ED, 7). Rochefort suggests that the powers that be have a vested interest in machine-tooling the young, tomorrow's citizens and consumers, from an early age, eradicating their innate vivacity and autonomy. To this end, children are systematically deprived of legal, civic, and economic rights; forced into a state of dependence which is rapidly internalized. The family (itself a cog in the machine), and medical, psychiatric, educational and legal institutions all come under attack as Rochefort seeks to lay bare the mechanisms of oppression and outline a putative charter for the child.

At the root of the problem lie the twin issues of definition and identity. Children, Rochefort informs us, are created by adults, who as participants in a dominant–dominated relationship, cannot but impose their own perspective:

> L'observateur modifie l'observé. Cette loi est spécialement valable en sciences humaines, et dans le cas d'une relation de pouvoir l'indétermination peut aller dans les 100%. Cela veut dire: l'observation est *impossible*. On ne connaît que les enfants-des-adultes. (ED, 47)

> [*The observer modifies the observed. This law is particularly applicable to the human sciences, and when a relation of power is involved the margin of error can be as great as 100%. In other words, observation is impossible. Only children as defined by adults are recognized.*]

'The child', in other words, is yet another socially-engineered category; children are made and not born: 'L'enfance est une institution, non un fait' ['childhood is an institution, not a fact'] (ED, 39). If any steps forward are to be made, Rochefort believed, adults must stop defining children from their own perspective, stop, that is, seeing them as proto-adults, 'des humains inachevés mentalement et physiquement' ['mentally and physically incomplete human beings'] (ED, 48):

> Pour nettoyer les yeux adultes, il faudrait prendre à peu près le contre-pied de l'idée reçue: les enfants sont plus complets, ils sont solides, héroïques (voir à quoi ils résistent!), adroits, capables, graves, profonds, leur intelligence est vaste et déliée, ils sont subtils et malins, ils savent se débrouiller, surtout seuls, etc. (ED, 49)

> [*In order to open adults' eyes one would more or less have to turn received ideas on their heads: children are more complete, sturdy, heroic (just consider what they're up against!), skilful, capable, serious, profound, their intelligence is vast and unbridled, they are subtle and cunning, they can cope, especially on their own, etc.*]

It is precisely this new vision of the child which Rochefort sets out to represent in *Encore heureux*.

Given that *Les Enfants d'abord* and *Encore heureux* were written contemporaneously, it is not surprising that the two texts should share a great deal of common ground, and indeed, the cross-over of material is striking. To cite just a few examples: *Les Enfants d'abord* includes a lengthy section (ED, 131–9) deploring the medicalization of so-called deviant behaviour: 'tout ce qui dit pas papamanman quand on appuie sur le ventre. Tout est médicalisable et tout se traite' ['anything that doesn't say daddymummy when you press its tummy. Anything can be medicalized and treated'] (ED, 138). This process of institutionalization is represented in *Encore heureux* by the character Lucrèce, a thirteen-year-old. The reader initially learns that Lucrèce 'avait été mise au vert, après ce qu'on appelait pudiquement une "maladie"' ['had been put out to grass after what had been coyly referred to as her "illness"'] (60). An allusion to the girl's sexual desire soon clarifies the nature of the 'illness': 'Mais les garçons, quatorze et onze ans, étaient un peu jeunes pour le goût de Lucrèce. A moins qu'elle n'eût changé, à la suite des électrochocs' ['But eleven- and fourteen-year-old boys were a little young for Lucrèce's taste. Unless she'd changed after the ECT'] (60). We follow Lucrèce's progress through the text, from her sexual encounter with the young adult Mann (143), to signs of her political awareness as she recognizes spies in a meeting of children (186), to her naming of her prior institutionalization:

'J'ai déjà été deux fois dans des asiles de fous, bien qu'ils les appelaient pas comme ça' ['I've already been in lunatic asylums twice, though that's not what they called them'] (213). A section in the essay on legal dependency (ED, 101–12), in which children's rights to vote are discussed in some detail, translates in the fiction to a single line within a dialogue between a group of children: 'Droit de vote à douze ans!' ['Votes for twelve-year-olds!'] (185). Similarly, a section focusing on economic rights in *Les Enfants d'abord* (ED, 141–55) becomes a brief reference to two of the children's desire to support themselves financially: 'Ils voulaient bien travailler, ils pouvaient parfaitement être coursiers cyclistes, voire coureurs cyclistes' ['They wanted to work, they could perfectly well be bicycle couriers, or even racing cyclists'] (216). A lengthy diatribe directed against IQ tests (ED, 121–31) is reduced to an exchange between children and schoolteachers in *Encore heureux* (154).

Although a detailed comparison will not be undertaken here, clearly a familiarity with both texts raises a number of questions: does the fiction succeed in conveying Rochefort's often extreme views more forcefully than the work of non-fiction? Is 'showing' more persuasive than 'telling'? Do the characters in *Encore heureux* become mere ideologues? Some of these points will be raised again below. For the moment, we can consider one area in which a knowledge of *Les Enfants d'abord* serves to clarify our reading, and that is the representation of those societal agents who oppose the runaways. In *Encore heureux* the forces of 'good' and 'evil' are sharply polarized: children, and non-aligned adults (women, the elderly, those who live alternative lifestyles, for example in communes) are set against those adults who have become unthinking cogs in the State apparatus, and of course, the governing agents themselves. The latter are not characterized in any way. Names are markedly absent, replaced by capitalized titles denoting functions or abstract status. Thus, early in the text, we find Mann challenged by 'la Conseillère' ['the Guidance Counsellor'], who loses even the specificity of her function in the following sentence: 'Nous manquons d'imagination, dit le Pouvoir. Il faut toujours s'attendre à tout' ['We lack imagination, said The Powers That Be. One must always be prepared for any eventuality'] (12). Media reports in the form of newspaper articles and television broadcasts refer to the 'Responsable de la Préparation à la Vie' ['Agent Responsible for the Preparation for Life'] (149), or 'les Autorités' ['the Authorities'] (145). Critics of the text have singled out the author's black-and-white representation, and have objected specifically to the lack of characterization of the forces against which the children react:

> If in earlier novels Rochefort excelled in representing the archaic, oppressive social and economic structures which incarcerate youth,

161

and in defining their linguistic manifestations, here she makes no real effort to present the negative aspects of modern civilisation, as if its evil were implicit in the labels 'Le Pouvoir' and 'Le Système'. There-fore, the rebellion of the young depicted in the novel seems unjustified and even gratuitous.[3]

To some extent this is a valid criticism; certainly a knowledge of *Les Enfants d'abord* does clarify Rochefort's use of anonymity and capitalization in the novel. However, the work of fiction does itself go some way toward explaining the use of these devices. In the opening pages of *Encore heureux* the reader can, in fact, see the very process of capitalization at work, as two of the runaways, Régina and Grâce, reflect upon the school they have left behind:

—Ils en avaient tous marre!
—Sauf nous. Nous on revenait là tous les matins, lâchement.
—Qui ça nous? au fait?
—Ben je me le demande qui ça nous, en définitif. Un beau traître ce Qui-Ça. Il est installé là et il nous fait faire des choses emmerdantes. (18)

['They were all fed up!'
'Except for us. We went back there every morning, like cowards.'
'Who is this "we"?'
'That's true. I wonder who "we" are, when it comes down to it. A real snake in the grass that Who-We. He's settled in there and makes us do bloody awful things.']

The shift from lower to upper case ('qui ça' to 'Qui-Ça') signifies a calling into question of agency and responsibility. It conveys the idea (admittedly rather obliquely) that individuals may act unquestioningly according to externally imposed dictates; that values and thought-systems may all too easily be internalized. To employ familiar Rochefort terminology, it points to a lack of 'conscience'. This device is taken up again later in the text in an exchange between the two girls and an old man who is about to lose his farm to mechanization:

—Je les déteste! déclara Grâce.
—Qui ça? dit le vieux.
Qui-Ça. Qui-Ça, du fond des temps, remontait, sous la forme d'un bulldozer [. . .]. (83)

[*'I hate them!,' Grace declared.*
'Who they?' asked the old man.
Who-they rose up from the depths of time, in the form of a bulldozer.]

Here, again, capitalization is employed to express an anonymous external agency whose workings remain unseen, and unchallenged, by the individual. Significantly, the literal bulldozer figures metaphorically in *Les Enfants d'abord* in a passage which makes Rochefort's meaning quite clear:

> Le monde où nous naissons—la société industrialisée—est [. . .] une Entreprise mondiale d'exploitation des choses, bêtes, et gens, par un petit nombre de personnages [. . .] tous adultes, mâles, et blancs [. . .] qui, à force d'éliminer les plus faibles, ont concentré et concentrent sans cesse davantage dans leurs mains les biens et les pouvoirs. [. . .] *Bien qu'ayant conservé une forme à peu près humaine, ils sont en train de devenir aujourd'hui une force aveugle, une abstraction régnante, un grand ordinateur servi par des vestons interchangeables. Cette Force Aveugle avance droit devant elle comme un bulldozer,* en s'emparant de tous les matériaux et de toutes les énergies terrestres, qu'elle exploite à son profit afin d'avancer encore et dévorer des énergies, afin d'avancer encore. (ED, 15–16, my italics)

> [*The world into which we are born—industrialized society—is a global Enterprise geared to the exploitation of things, animals, and people, controlled by a small group of individuals, all of them adult, male and white, who, by eliminating the weakest, have concentrated and continue to concentrate goods and power in their hands. Although they have more or less maintained a human face, they are now in the process of becoming an indiscriminate force, a reigning abstraction, a gigantic computer served by interchangeable grey suits. This indiscriminate force ploughs ahead like a bulldozer, seizing all earthly goods and energies, which it exploits to its own advantage so it can advance yet further and devour more energy, so it can advance yet further.*]

If Rochefort chooses to represent those in power as nameless functions, it is in order to suggest that society's rulers are progressively dehumanized. The capitalization in *Encore heureux* is employed to represent faceless power, the 'grey suits', bureaucracy, reification. It should be interpreted as a linguistic marker of social and political entropy:

> Ainsi va leur rêve de Meilleur des Mondes, planifié et sans bavures, où plus rien ne bouge dans un cercle parfait de production/consommation (avec au milieu un petit circuit spécial: profit). L'entropie et la paix sociale. (ED, 129)

> [*And there you have their Best of all Possible Worlds, regulated and flawless, where nothing moves any more, frozen in a perfect cycle of production and consumption (with a small closed circuit for profit in the middle). Entropy and social harmony.*]

163

Grasping Rochefort's reasons for employing this device is essential to a full understanding of the text. In *Une Rose pour Morrison* we saw the young lecturer Sereine denouncing the stasis of the existing political regime: 'la fin d'un système clos est l'entropie' ['a closed system tends towards entropy'] (*Une Rose*, 25). 'L'Esprit', it will be recalled, was by contrast characterized by process and change. *Encore heureux,* too, is built around the opposition of two key elements: entropy or stasis, and energy or process. *Les Enfants d'abord* stresses the idea that societal forces seek to deplete, rein in, the innate energy or life-force of the young child: 'on usera le temps où il est réduit à l'impuissance pour lier ses énergies et ses désirs' ['the time during which he is reduced to a state of helplessness will be used to bind his energies and desires'] (ED, 16). Schooling, the nuclear family—all the 'corps constitués' which come under attack in the essay—conjoin to break the spirit of the child: 'Il s'agit de casser. Casser physiquement la fantastique machine à désirer et à jouir' ['They're out to break; to physically break that amazing machine built to desire and experience pleasure'] (ED, 115). The flight of the children in *Encore heureux* represents the means whereby energy may be restored and deployed. Where society represents 'l'arrêt, l'extension d'un pouvoir sur un territoire' ['stasis, the extension of a certain power over a given territory'], the children stand for process: 'eux, ils marchent' ['they are on the move'].[4] With movement comes a restoration of life: David, one the children, is endowed with 'une beauté surhumaine' ['a supernatural beauty'] (172); a child who walks into a police station in the closing paragraph of the text is 'surhumainement belle, et fière' ['supernaturally beautiful, and proud'] (219); all the children who take to the roads manifest vigour and strength: 'leur extraordinaire énergie émerveillait, ils étaient proprement infatigables' ['people marvelled at their extraordinary energy, they were quite simply indefatigable'] (195).

Process and energy are more than thematic concerns. Perhaps the most arresting aspect of *Encore heureux* is its structure, which marks a new departure in Rochefort's writing. In previous works, plot is largely unilinear, restricted to a single spatio-temporal dimension in which the protagonists evolve. This pattern changes with *Encore heureux*. Rochefort has stated that the original framework for the text was a dialogue, and, indeed, in the opening pages the focus falls almost exclusively on the direct speech of two characters, Grâce and Régina. Having interrupted her writing in order to complete *Les Enfants d'abord*, however, Rochefort then switched to a structure based on a web, or network.[5] As the text unfolds, more and more characters are progressively introduced, their trajectories periodically intersecting as they head for the south in a dispersed, but accumulative, mass movement. Thus Jean-Marie is described hiding in church (38), before the focus shifts back to the two girls; he is next seen with Manuel (54), while Grâce and Régina continue their journey. Lucrèce is briefly identified as an escapee (60), then reappears with Mann (144), then Grâce, Régina and David (187). Anaïs and Arthur are reported missing in a newspaper (77); they are next seen with the adult 'helper' Mélanie some seventy pages later (146), then with Mélanie and Amélie (152). A beautiful boy is seen outside a bakery by Régina (75). Later identified as David, he is next seen with Agnès (91), then Grâce and Régina (101); he is then joined by Ben, Sara and Lucrèce (188), and finally by Régina, Grâce and Lucrèce in the closing pages. The effect of this structure upon the reader is extremely powerful. Constant plot-shifts as an ever-increasing cast of characters appear, meet, cross paths, and reappear later in different locations, convey a strong sense of process and momentum. The structure of the text, in other words, perfectly reflects the thematic concern with energy and growth.

If the network structure is instrumental in conveying the momentum of the children's flight, it also influences the fictional representation of adults, especially parents. *Les Enfants d'abord* condemns the majority of adults as 'des outils inconscients qui exécutent une commande sociale' ['unthinking cogs executing a social programme'] (ED, 18). Rochefort is uncompromising in her claim that adults have a responsibility to disengage themselves from this role: 'Finalement, est-ce qu'on peut avoir pitié d'un qui vous mène au charcutier, sous prétexte qu'il a les yeux bandés? Qu'il arrache son bandeau, merde. Il a des mains' ['When it comes down to it can you feel pity for people who lead you to the slaughterhouse, just because their eyes are bound? Bloody hell, why don't they rip the blindfold off? They've got hands haven't they?'] (ED, 66). Clearly this is not as simple as it sounds. To act differently one must have choice, and the prerequisite of choice is insight into the processes in which one may be unwittingly caught up. Rochefort alludes to 'la douloureuse question de l'aliénation, et de la responsabilité humaine' ['the painful issue of alienation and individual responsibility'] (ED, 32), but fails to suggest just how adult awareness might come about.

In *Encore heureux* the parental situation is presented more optimistic-ally, and more constructively. The dramatic growth in the number of runaways is met by progressively extreme sanctions. The text becomes increasingly dystopic, with a sustained use of militaristic vocabulary: the 'Responsable de la Préparation à la Vie' draws up a 'Plan Etourneaux' and organizes phone-taps (149); a 'Corps Spécial des Jeunes', sounding all too reminiscent of the Nazi Youth League, is formed. A Vichy-like militia declares open season on children: 'les bruits de la formation de Milices par les Bourgeois, et d'ouverture prochaine de la chasse aux Errants' ['rumours about the formation of Militias by middle-class citizens, and a declaration of an open season on Runaways' (173). Some parents begin to come out in support of their children; a demonstration calling for the return of the runaways is disrupted by a dissident group of parents shouting 'ne nous les rendez pas' ['don't give them back to us'] (179). The text suggests that when, and if, pushed far enough—here, by the tenacity of the young—the subtlety of the 'Force Aveugle' will give way to a blatant wielding of power, and an extremism that will raise parental awareness. Once a clear-cut 'them and us' situation emerges, individual responsibility and 'conscience' are precipitated. The growth in parental awareness is analogous to Philibert's change of allegiance in *Une Rose pour Morrison*, or indeed to the ever-expanding boundaries of Archaos: change is always possible.

Theme and structure are tightly interwoven with respect to the representation of adults. On a thematic level, the network ties in with images of war and resistance. Safe houses are set up by friendly adult forces who help smuggle the children on their journey south; a system of signals and secret codes is organized, as more and more escapees enter the relative safety of a 'réseau de soutien' ['support network'] (167). The network structure initially excludes adults, who side with the State. As *Les Enfants d'abord* puts it, reiterating the military terminology: 'Les parents collabos sont les fantassins de la Force Aveugle' ['Parents who collaborate are the foot-soldiers of the Indiscriminate Force'] (ED, 65). In *Les Enfants d'abord* Rochefort stresses the need for adults to enter into a joint struggle with their children against the State mechanisms, calling for a 'stratégie horizontale de lutte, entre classes solidaires abolissant le rapport de verticalité' ['a horizontal strategy for our struggles, joining together like-minded classes and abolishing any vertical power structures'] (ED, 77–8). The structural network of *Encore heureux* constitutes just such a model of horizontality. Parents in the text remain absent and invisible whilst they remain within a hierarchical system, joining the network only in the closing stages of the work.

One of the hierarchical structures which both *Encore heureux* and *Les Enfants d'abord* strongly rejects is that of the education system. Before looking at this issue more closely, a possible source, or indeed two sources, for Rochefort's use of the network structure can be identified. The bibliography in *Les Enfants d'abord* includes texts by Ivan Illich and David Cooper, both of whom refer to a network in the context of education. Illich, seeking an 'educational revolution', proposes as an alternative to the existing framework of education 'an educational network or web for the autonomous assembly of resources under the personal control of each learner'.[6] Cooper, who also seeks radical changes in education, calls for 'as massive a drop-out of teachers and pupils as possible' (the overlap with *Encore heureux* is striking), and proposes 'a totally de-hierarchized mobile structure that is in continuous revolution'.[7] This is precisely the structure we find in *Encore heureux*, whose structural and thematic emphasis on process and change may remind us of the anti-Stalinist Maoist call (taken up by many during the 1970s) for a constant calling into question of the permanence and validity of all institutions.[8]

Although *Encore heureux* does not focus specifically upon new proposals for the education system—Illich's and Cooper's network seems rather to have inspired Rochefort's structural design—it is the school system which forms the basis of the runaway children's discontent: the text opens with the teacher Mlle Bell's laconic dismissal of the 'Cinquième D', the class of thirteen-year-olds to which Grâce and Régina belong: 'Je sais que vous êtes une classe pas intéressante' ['I know you're not a very inspiring class'] (5). *Les Enfants d'abord* criticizes the educational institution as one of the State's most powerful tools, used to control and mould the young. Children, increasingly numerous and well-informed, represent a growing threat to the establishment, which, it is suggested, will do all in its power to prevent a re-enactment of May '68: 'comment faire que ça n'arrive plus jamais?' ['what can be done to ensure that it never happens again?'] (ED, 60). The essay goes on to claim that schools both reflect and seek to perpetuate the hierarchical structures of society.[9] Both works, essay and fiction, single out the system's treatment of those children who are academically weak. *Les Enfants d'abord* deplores what the author regards as a damaging selection process: 'ils coincent les lycéens dans des "réformes scolaires" de plus en plus élaborées qui quadrillent les enfants, ils nettoyent l'école des enseignants dangereux' ['they ensnare schoolchildren in ever more complex "educational reforms" which control these children, they purge schools of dangerous teachers'] (ED, 61). The children who take to the roads in *Encore heureux* are, at least initially, drawn exclusively from the lower academic streams. A brief examination of the French education system at the time may cast further light on the specific cultural references in both texts.

Before 1958 the educational establishment in France was far removed from what we would recognize as a fully comprehensive secondary system. Children aged eleven could either remain in the primary sector until the school-leaving age of fourteen, take a qualifying examination and enter 'cours complémentaires' ['supplementary classes'], allowing them to leave school at fourteen with a slightly higher qualification, or enter a lycée with a view to completing the Baccalauréat at eighteen and thereby proceed to tertiary education. The first major reform was instigated in 1959 by Berthoin, who sought to insure that all eleven-year-olds would transfer into a true secondary system. The CEG, or Collège d'éducation général, would replace prolonged primary classes; the examination previously required for entry into the 'cours complémentaires' would be removed, and a two-year 'cycle d'observation' would be set up: children, in other words, would be monitored until they were thirteen years old, whereupon they could transfer from the CEG to the lycée. 'Classes de transition' were to be set up in both the CEGs and the lycées for children who were academically less able, and who would previously have been excluded from the secondary system. However, although the aim was to allow for the possibility of a transfer out of the 'transition' into the mainstream, it has been suggested that the reform may in fact have exacerbated the problems of selection:

> The creation of such transition classes, however, tended to reinforce what was still a blatant division in the secondary system since the majority of them were attached to the CEGs. These institutions also ran the majority of the short study courses whilst the *lycées* monopolised those courses which led to the better qualifications. Not surprisingly, three times as many of the children in the higher social categories went to the *lycées* than went to the CEGs.[10]

The fact that different curricula operated in the CEGs and lycées further impeded the possibility of transfers. Focusing primarily on children of weak academic standing, *Encore heureux* refers specifically to 'transition' classes, that is to those groups which would be most affected by the process of orientation, the term used to describe the guidance provided, and more importantly the decisions made, about each pupil's academic progression from class to class. Two of the runaways, Agnès and Thierry, express their apprehension: 'Pas ce tortillon au creux de l'estomac. Pas la transition. Pas l'année prochaine' ['Not that knot in the stomach. Not the transitional class. Not next year'] (93). It is noted that most of the runaways come from such classes: 'le mal frappe principalement les Transitions' ['it is principally the transitional classes which are experiencing difficulties'] (118). Some parents suggest that streams are based on a false perception of intelligence: 'Et une enfant intelligente comme ça est en Transition!' ['A clever child like that in Transitional!'] (200). The State's attitude to such children is clear: they are dismissed as dunces: 'Le Responsable de la Préparation à la Vie venait de déclarer que seuls les cancres avaient déserté' ['The Agent Responsible for the Preparation for Life had just announced that only the dunces had deserted'] (149).

The next major reform came in 1963 with Fouchet's attempt to locate all children leaving primary in one school, the newly established CES (Collège d'enseignement secondaire), which would include classes from the 6ème to the 3ème (approximately eleven- to fifteen-year-olds). The growth of the CESs was rapid, but the older CEGs remained, especially in sparsely populated regions, well into the 1970s, as did the lycées. Although published in 1975, *Encore heureux* refers exclusively to the CEGs. The CESs did not signify a shift to a truly comprehensive system. The process of orientation remained in force. First, at the end of primary, pupils would be directed into one of the three tracks operating in the CES: Modern I, Modern II, or Transition III, these tracks representing descending levels of academic difficulty. Although this initial orientation was supposed to replace the selection process, observers of the system have noted that this was not necessarily the case:

> Political critics of the system see orientation as a covert form of selection under a more acceptable name. The numbers oriented towards a particular track or institution may fluctuate not according to the interests and abilities of the children, but are dependent on the future needs of the economy.[11]

Such criticisms are echoed in *Les Enfants d'abord*: 'L'école a fidèlement évolué, ou muté, en harmonie profonde avec les besoins de l'Industrie et de ses services. [. . .] elle est sa pépinière de matériel humain adéquat' ['Schools have faithfully evolved, or mutated, in close harmony with the needs of Industry and its services [. . .] schools are Industry's breeding-ground for appropriate human resources'] (ED, 114). It has been suggested that the orientation procedure may suffer from more than the dictates of industry. Halls notes that 'teachers may be infected by middle-class values to an undue extent and will orient those children whose social background reflects those values into higher streams'.[12] In fact, very few children in the CESs moved from Transition III to Modern II at the second stage of orientation (thirteen years). And whereas children in the higher streams would go on at fifteen to either a lycée or technical college, those in the Transition tended to leave school inadequately qualified. Most entered pre-vocational classes; some entered classes preparing for apprenticeships. The employment situation in France in the mid-seventies was such that the future for the under-qualified was bleak. The rate of unemployment for students holding the BAC rose from 10% in 1973, to 20% in 1977. For those holding vocational qualifications such as the CAP (Certificat d'aptitude professionnelle) or BEP (Brevet d'études profes-sionnelles), the figures increased from 8% (1973) to 21% (1977). Those with no qualifications were hit hardest, with unemployment figures rising from 15% to 38%.[13] Halls's observation that 'it is little use steering young people into blind alleys or to enter forms of education that will lead to non-existent jobs' is echoed by a young teacher in *Encore heureux*: 'je me demande pourquoi ils s'acharnent tant à les conserver pour après les foutre à la poubelle' ['I wonder why they work so hard to keep them when they just dump them on the rubbish-heap afterwards'] (13).[14]

Objections to the education system in the text are not restricted to the spontaneous flight of the children. A single mother has opted out of state education, preferring to educate her son at home (70). Later in the work, two parents change allegiances and decry the school system. The father of Sophie (a child who does not feature in the work, but whose named presence serves to emphasize the growing numbers of defectors) is seen on television screaming 'A bas l'école-poubelle' ['Down with dead-end schools'] (179), whilst the father of Olivier (another new name) writes indignant letters to the 'Responsable':

> Comment se fait-il que tant d'enfants brillants, comme mon fils, ne le soient qu'en dehors du programme? C'est peut-être vos programmes qui ne vont pas. Et je commence à me demander si mon enfant n'apprend pas davantage depuis qu'il a quitté vos bancs. Vu le sort que vous lui destinez dans la société de, il raya [. . .]. (149–50)

> [*Why is it that so many highly intelligent children, like my son, only shine outside the school system? Maybe it is because there is something wrong with your programmes. I am beginning to wonder if my child has not been learning more since he left your establishment. Given the future you are offering him in this society full of, he crossed the last word out* [. . .].]

The next school reform was contemporaneous with the writing of *Encore heureux* and *Les Enfants d'abord* (although it only began to come into force in 1977). In 1975 Haby set out to abolish once and for all the differences between the CEGs, CESs, and lycées by setting up a single secondary institution, the 'collège', supposedly an unstreamed, truly mixed-ability school. Pupils would follow the same programme for two years (the 'cycle d'observation'), extra classes being provided for both the strongest and the weakest students, and would then choose options at the end of the second year when they entered the 'cycle d'orientation'. In spite of this apparent shift towards a comprehensive system, selection and streaming remained in force, either covertly—for example by placing in one class pupils drawn from more academically-inclined feeder-schools— or overtly, via the re-emergence of the 'transition' under a different name: 'In any case the reform itself foresaw the necessity for grouping together the very weak in what was formerly the *classe de transition* and was now to be called the *classe allégée*.'[15] The categorization of the academically weak comes in for strong criticism in *Les Enfants d'abord*:

> Ils ont glissé dans l'ombre des sections spéciales aux noms charmeurs (pour ne pas choquer les malheureux parents), et variables comme le vent (les parents pigent vite), de perfectionnement à rattrapage à

faible à accueil, vraiment charmant celui-là (on suggère: Limbes), et
on ne les voit plus [. . .] ils ne troubleront plus les classes studieuses,
ils ne troubleront plus Adieu. (ED, 128–9)

[*They've slipped away into the obscurity of special classes with beguiling
names (so as not to shock the poor parents), names which change every two
minutes (the parents catch on quickly), from finishing to remedial to weak
to reception, that one's particularly charming (why not Limbo), and they're
never seen again [. . .] they won't bother the high achievers, they won't
bother anyone any more, Goodbye.*]

Once again, critics note that pupils, overwhelmingly those from the lower
social classes, were all too often guided too early out of mainstream
'collège' studies into pre-vocational and vocational classes.[16] Once a
choice was made at the young age of thirteen (the age of many of the
runaways in *Encore heureux*), there could be no going back:

Vers les 13 ans dans les Conseils de classe se décide la voie d'où
désormais (ère Haby en France) on ne pourra plus revenir. Une sorte
de grand couteau à découper nommé abusivement 'mathématiques' est
l'instrument de séparation du matériau, dans le sens vertical. (ED, 118)

[*When children are about 13 years old the class Advisory Boards decide
which path they will follow (the Haby era in France), a path from which
there is no going back. It is 'Mathematics'(as it is inappropriately called), a
sort of giant carving knife, which is used to carve up the human material
hierarchically.*]

Different Baccalauréat study programmes were undertaken in the lycées.
The section which devoted the most time to mathematics, section 'C', was
the most prestigious, providing as it did by far the greatest percentage of
students who would go on to sit the competitive 'grandes écoles' entrance
examination.[17] The flight from school in *Encore heureux* begins with the
'transitions', spreading to programmes which initially exclude the pure
maths students: 'il [le mal] se propage dans les A [literature], les G
[economics], les D [maths and natural sciences], et quelques CET
[Collège d'enseignement technique]. Les B [economics and social
sciences] et les C [maths and physics] sont totalement épargnés' ['the
problem is spreading into the A, G, and D streams, as well as some
CETs. The B and C streams are totally unaffected'] (118). By the end of
the text, however, the mass movement has spread:

Albert E. fut le premier honorable C à rejoindre les forces de la
désertion, donnant tort au Responsable de la Préparation à la Vie. Au-
dessus des Quatrième, ce furent les génies mathématiques qui
dropèrent. (194)

[*Albert E. was the first member of the honorable C stream to join the deserting troops, thereby proving the Agent Responsible for the Preparation for Life wrong. Above the fourth year it was the mathematical geniuses who were dropping out.*]

The desertion of the 'C' section further challenges the elitist, segregating structure of the education system. The children who join the (horizontal) network leave a system which channels them into different, diverging, streams. Orientation in *Encore heureux* becomes voluntary and uni-directional: all the children head south.

In *Les Enfants d'abord* Rochefort stresses the need to speak not for, but as, a child, in order to escape adult-imposed definitions. Adults who lack 'conscience' are differentiated from 'ancien enfants' ['former children'] (ED, 8) amongst whom she numbers herself: 'on ne parle pas du dehors, "sur" les enfants, on parle de dedans, et de soi' ['we don't speak as outsiders, "about" children, we speak as insiders, and about ourselves'] (ED, 8). Children must, above all, be seen as subjects and not objects. But what of Rochefort's fictional work? And what precisely does speaking as an 'ancien enfant' entail? Although much of *Encore heureux* is given over to dialogue, Rochefort's desire to represent the child as subject may be considered to be partially undermined by intrusive narratorial comments which recur throughout the work. Although the children in the text do speak for themselves, their limited point of view and knowledge is brought to the reader's attention by the presence of an omniscient speaking subject. Narratorial omniscience is flaunted when, for example, the thoughts of a supermarket guard who refuses to allow un-accompanied children onto the premises are carefully explained: 'on n'a pas à donner des raisons au peuple, pense sans le penser le garde n'ayant pas en tête qu'il est du peuple aussi, n'ayant rien en tête, que la mission dont il est investi' ['we're not here to explain things to the people, thought the guard unthinkingly, not grasping the fact that he was part of the people, not thinking at all, except about the mission with which he'd been entrusted'] (91). The presence of the omniscient narrator, who quite clearly speaks for Rochefort herself, is still more intrusive when a long section of dialogue between adults is signposted for the reader:

—Ça oui, dit une autre mère (alliée).
[. . .]
—Mais ça ne peut tout de même pas continuer comme ça il faut que ça cesse! (non allié)
—On ne peut quand même pas les laisser faire ce qu'ils veulent (non allié) (199–200)

172

[*'Yes, that's true,' said another mother (ally).*
[. . .]
'But things can't just go on as they are, it's got to stop!' (non ally)
'They can't just be left to do what they like' (non ally)]

One authorial intervention is particularly striking. In the course of their travels the children arrive at a castle. A letter addressed to the government, signed by 'une partie de la population' ['part of the population'], is then cited in the text, and immediately followed by the passage below:

lut la vieille dame. Elle trônait sur un haut fauteuil. Non, recommence, c'est pas ça.
—Et croyez bien que je suis d'accord avec ce pamphlet, dit-elle. D'ailleurs c'est moi qui ai payé l'imprimeur, un Hollandais. Elle avait une mantille noire sur ses cheveux blancs, coiffés en rouleaux, et une robe mauve avec un châle violet. Et elle trônait sur un haut fauteuil. Non, retire le fauteuil. Mais elle va se casser la gueule.
—Leurs gens n'entreront pas chez moi [. . .]. Merde, qui a retiré mon fauteuil? (188)

[*read the old woman. She was enthroned on a tall armchair. No, start again, that's not right.*
'And believe me, I agree with every word of the pamphlet,' she said. 'Besides, it was I who paid the printer, a Dutchman.' She was wearing a black mantilla over her white hair arranged in coils, and a mauve dress with a purple shawl. And she was enthroned on a tall armchair. No, take the armchair away. But she'll smash her face in.
'Their people will not gain entry into my home [. . .]. Shit, who's taken my armchair away?']

The voice of what appears to be Rochefort herself, writing and deleting her own text at will ('recommence, c'est pas ça'; 'non, retire le fauteuil'), strikes a bizarre and dissonant note. Such intrusive authorial self-consciousness may be dismissed as rather self-indulgent whimsy. More generously, it may be interpreted as a deliberate means of calling into question another faceless anonymous power, that of the omniscient author. Seen as such, it becomes a parodic, reflexive, device signalling Rochefort's desire not to become yet another manifestation of the 'Force Aveugle'.

Although authorial or narratorial intrusions of this kind need not undermine Rochefort's attempt to disengage herself from an adult-centred representation of the child, there is no doubt that they do shift the focus of attention away from children as subjects in their own right. This process is aggravated when comments are directed at the children themselves, for example when Régina's and Grâce's exploration of sexuality is glossed by a narratorial voice which the reader—especially the reader who is familiar with *Les Enfants d'abord*—recognizes as the author's: '[elles] se contemplèrent interminablement s'extasièrent de plaisir planant à ses extrêmes, *on est sans limites à cet âge*' ['they gazed at each other unendingly revelled in an ecstasy which sent them soaring from reality, *at that age you are without limits*'] (57, my emphasis). On this occasion, the interpretive gloss serves merely to emphasize the divide between the child who acts, and the adult who knows; between object and subject.

This split between doing and knowing raises further questions about the status of the child, specifically about the extent to which children may be deemed themselves to have insight into the mechanisms of oppression, to have their own 'conscience'. We have already seen in previous works that one of the key signs of 'conscience' is the ability to parody or mimic, an ability which manifests itself in various forms in *Encore heureux*. Parody, or playing the system at its own game, may take the form of role-play. When a law is passed forbidding children to appear in public places unaccompanied, complicit adults pass off stray children as their own by mimicking authoritarian adult–child relationships. By playing at the bullying father, Mann persuades hostile observers that a young girl is under his care:

> —Je t'ai dit: pas de bonbons, commença-t-il en approchant des caisses.
> —Alors achète-moi des caramels, gémit-elle aussitôt.
> —Quand je dis non c'est non, arrête tes comédies Caroline s'il te plaît.
> —Pourquoi tu veux pas, pleurnicha-t-elle, régressant d'un bon lustre mais personne ne verrait l'invraisemblance, les enfants sont infantiles. (95)

> [*'I told you, no sweets,' he began, as he approached the tills.*
> *'Buy me some toffees then,' she whined straight away.*
> *'When I say no I mean no, please stop making a scene Caroline.'*
> *'But why won't you,' she snivelled, regressing a good few years but no-one would see how implausible the scene was, all children are childish.*]

Few would question the capacity of (some) adults to engage is such parodic role-play, but what of children? Is their mimicry also to be interpreted as a conscious means of subverting or challenging the adult point of view? Grâce and Régina reveal a talent for the parodic mode:

—Nous sommes incompréhensibles. Ma pauvre fille je ne te comprendrai jamais, tu l'as entendu celle-là?
—Je me demande, parfois, comment tu a pu sortir de moi. (A vrai dire moi aussi je me le demande, entre parenthèses.)
—Les enfants sont d'étranges petits animaux.
—Aussi faut-il les dresser, dès leur plus jeune âge. (30)

[*'We are incomprehensible. My poor child I will never understand you, have you heard that one?'*
'Sometimes I wonder how you could possibly be mine.' (Incidentally, quite honestly I wonder too.)
'Children are strange little creatures.'
'So you have to train them, from a very young age.']

Significantly, this exchange is preceded by an important incident. When Grâce and Régina appropriate a doll's pram in which to carry their possessions, they realize that the object renders them (metaphorically) invisible: nice girls who play with dolls are scarcely likely to be identified as deviant runaways. The girls subsequently draw up a rule: 'utiliser à fond leur connerie' ['make full use their asininity'] (29). The use of the doll's pram is not a planned tactic but a fortuitous event; as Régina says: 'le hasard pense pour nous' ['chance is thinking for us'] (29). Rochefort seems to be suggesting that the children gain insight as a direct result of their flight; that their eyes are opened by their experience of freedom. This reading nonetheless begs certain questions. Do we not hear Rochefort speaking through (and for) her characters? Does 'the average' child really have the capacity to challenge adult views in this manner?

We perhaps need to reassess just what Rochefort means when she states that adults should speak as, and not for, children. What she actually appears to be doing in both essay and fiction is articulating that which the child merely feels. In other words, she consciously appoints herself, as enlightened adult, as spokeswoman for the child. This reading is supported by the closing words of *Les Enfants d'abord*, where Rochefort draws a clear distinction between experience and the articulation of experience: 'Si ce qui est dit là [. . .] aide à formuler ce qui n'est que ressenti, à légitimer l'expérience, et à changer le regard depuis toujours jeté, du haut vers le bas, sur les enfants—alors bon, ça va. Salut' ['If what is said above [. . .] helps to put into words what is only felt, helps to legitimize experience, and to change the manner in which children are always seen, from a great height looking down, then great, that's fine. Cheers'] (ED, 188). The problem, however, still remains. Rochefort may criticize adult-imposed views of the child, 'l'enfant-des-adultes' ['the child as defined by adults'] (ED, 48), but does she not merely offer up a new creation: 'l'enfant-de-Rochefort' ['the child as defined by Rochefort']?

The reader's perception of the question of voice—who speaks?—in *Encore heureux* is inevitably coloured by a familiarity with *Les Enfants d'abord*. Narcissistic intertextuality is such that children in the fiction may speak words which are explicitly the author's in the essay. Thus we find an exchange concerning the role of mothers in *Encore heureux* which directly picks up on the author's discussion in *Les Enfants d'abord* (pages 77–8):

> —J'aime ma mère, soupira Blaise. C'est mon malheur.
> —C'est comme ça qu'elle t'a, dit Emmy. Ces créatures sont les exécutrices des basses œuvres.
> —Mais elle en est la victime, dit Blaise.
> —Qu'elle le sache alors, dit Emmy, hautaine. Toute l'information est à sa portée. (193)

> [*'I love my mother,' sighed Blaise. 'More's the pity.'*
> *'That's how she keeps a hold over you,' said Emmy. 'Those creatures do all the dirty work.'*
> *'But she's a victim of the system,' said Blaise.*
> *'She should be aware of it then,' said Emmy haughtily. 'She has access to all the necessary information.'*]

The problem of voice does not stop here, for the children in *Encore heureux* can be seen to articulate ideas which originate in other texts. Grâce and Régina, playing at adults (thereby complicating matters further!), comment on a passing adult and child: 'Voyez cette personne grande accrochée à la main d'une personne petite, qui pourrait marcher seule: elle est en train de l'empêcher d'être heureuse' ['See that big person clutching the hand of that little person, who could walk alone: she's in the process of stopping that child from being happy'] (75). The example of the reluctant hand-holder can also be found in *Les Enfants d'abord*, where it is, of course, Rochefort who speaks in her own name (pp. 86–7). But the intertextual network extends further still: the same incident can be located in David Cooper's *The Death of the Family*:

> Take a very ordinary situation between parent and child. Parent walks down the high street holding his child's hand. At a certain point there is a necessary breakdown of reciprocity—the parent holds the child's hand but the child no longer holds the parent's hand.[18]

Following a slightly different intertextual pattern, the figure of the uncle occurs in the same three texts. In *Les Enfants d'abord* the uncle is metaphorical, representing any chance encounter which might liberate the child from adult views:

Un seul oncle farfelu de passage réussit sans y penser à foutre par terre tout un édifice d'abêtissement [. . .]. L'oncle peut être une rencontre de vacance, d'autres enfants, le ciné, une chanson, la rue, les événements socio-politiques. (ED, 97)

[*A casual encounter with an eccentric uncle is all it takes to stuff up a whole structure geared to reducing people to imbecility [. . .]. The uncle could be someone met on holiday, other children, the cinema, a song, the streets, socio-political events.*]

The uncle becomes literal in *Encore heureux* where we see Régina tell Grâce of her uncle Hugues who would 'shut off' or 'die' in adult company:

Je mourais subitement. C'est Hugues qui m'a montré. L'oncle fou. Il faisait ça avec sa mère c'était le seul moyen de la faire taire elle arrêtait pas une seconde ça le rendait dingue, alors il mourrait, comme ça il n'entendait plus. Tu fermes tout, et tu pars, il disait. (24).

[*I would die suddenly. It was Hugues who showed me how. My mad uncle. He did it with his mother it was the only way to shut her up she wouldn't let up for a second it drove him crazy, so he died, that way he didn't hear any more. You shut everything down, and you leave, he said.*]

Once again, Régina, the child, in effect performs an act of ventriloquism, articulating a scenario which originates with Cooper:

[T]he conversation switched to issues of institutional work problems [. . .] and this became a defensive chatter that became less and less meaningful to me [. . .]. I found myself becoming more and more kinesically frozen and could scarcely think—much less concentrate [. . .]. So [. . .] I died to the situation.[19]

In each of these examples Rochefort's desire to maintain the child as subject appears to be jeopardized. Ultimately the voice, or voices, which speak in the text remain those of adults, albeit adults who challenge the system.

One further area remains to be discussed and that is utopia. In the previous chapter we saw that utopian texts could serve a range of functions: the fictional world could represent a viable blueprint for the future; it might express the author's hopes, rather than expectations, for a better society; it could serve to criticize the status quo; it could constitute

177

a less tangible expression of desire. Clearly, *Encore heureux* differs from *Archaos* in that the world it portrays is situated firmly in contemporary 1970s France with its attendant socio-political problems. It does, however, engage with the idea of the outopos, or 'no place'. From an early stage the fictional world is split into two distinct realms or parallel realities: as a prefatory page describes it, 'le monde de la réalité' ['the world of reality'], that is the world of adults, and 'un monde de rêve, et complice des enfants' ['a dream world, on the children's side']. The text introduces the science fiction topos of an alternative reality: when Régina sees Mann watching her as she leaves the school precinct, she believes she hears a voice acknowledging 'on ne vous reverra plus en ce monde' ['you will never be seen again in this world'] (20). Grâce and Régina discuss their apparent shift to a new spatio-temporal dimension: 'On a glissé sur une dimension, c'est sûr' ['We've crossed into another dimension, that's for sure']; 'peut-être qu'on est vraiment invisibles?' ['maybe we're really invisible?'] (26). In the closing stages of the text, blank pages with a single line of text suggest that the children have truly vanished: 'Mais où sont-ils, ces enfants non accompagnés?' ['But where are the unaccompanied children?'] (197); 'Où sont-ils?' ['Where are they?'] (209). However, although the idea of an alternative world is used, this world is not a literal one: the children have not 'beamed up' to another galaxy. Rather, the new world or 'no place' operates metaphorically. Like the planet Mars in *Printemps au parking*, it represents a new way of seeing, and being, free from externally-imposed views and restrictions.

In *Les Enfants d'abord* a fictitious letter signed 'vos filles et fils, trop heureux' ['your all too happy sons and daughters'], outlines the gap between adult- and child-centred definitions of happiness:

> Votre idée de notre bonheur, qui ne vous appartient même pas mais vous fut dictée, n'est pas forcément la nôtre. Vous devriez nous demander avant de nous rendre heureux. Peut-être préférons-nous être vivants. (ED, 36)

> [*The idea you have of our happiness, which does not even belong to you but was dictated to you, is not necessarily ours. You should ask us before you make us happy. Maybe we'd rather be alive.*]

The alternative reality of *Encore heureux*, the 'monde de rêve', is a world in which happiness is defined and experienced by the child. When Régina utters the titular words 'Encore heureux qu'on va vers l'été. C'est notre veine' ['It's a good thing we're heading for summer. Lucky for us'] (significantly omitting the subjunctive), we are told that these were 'ses dernières paroles, dans le monde des adultes' ['her last words in the adult world'] (11). In the adult world, time, like everything else, is commodified, regulated and controlled ('la disparition du Temps est le plus grand mystère policier de l'époque' ['the disappearance of Time is the biggest mystery of our epoch'] ED, p. 84), especially as far as the young are concerned: 'les mouvements des enfants sont limités à l'intérieur de ce complexe temps-espace contrôlé' ['the movement of children is limited within this regulated spatio-temporal complex'] (ED, 44). In an interview focused primarily upon *Les Enfants d'abord* Rochefort equates freedom with space: 'la liberté, c'est quelque chose qui ressemble à l'espace' ['freedom is something which resembles space'].[20]

The new spatio-temporal dimension discovered by the children in *Encore heureux* is precisely a variable, unregulated realm: '—Ici, on a tout le temps devant nous. / —Et tout l'espace. / —Tout l'espace-temps' ['"Here we've got all the time in the world in front of us." "And all the space in the world." "All of space and time."'] (32). The resented selection process or orientation of the school system is replaced by a willed disorientation which represents freedom from the oppressions of society: 'je ne me sens pas perdue je me sens sauvée, dit Régina. Je me sens comme si une porte s'était ouverte. Une porte invisible, dans la haie' ['I don't feel lost, I feel saved,' said Régina. 'I feel as if a door's been opened. An invisible door, in the hedge'] (33). Picking up on the nautical image of the title *Les Enfants d'abord*, Grâce and Régina imagine themselves to be the sole survivors of a sinking ship (33).

The metaphorical 'no place' inhabited by the children shares features which we saw in the previous chapter. When Grâce and Régina build an altar to celebrate nature, the blurring of spatio-temporal dimensions reminds us of the status of Archaos as a past paradise which, paradoxically, has yet to be realized: '—Les archéologues s'interrogent, quelle civilisation passée a laissé ces traces? / —C'était une civilisation future, messieurs!' ['"The archaeologists confer, what past civilization has left these traces?"/"It was a future civilization, dear sirs!"'] (47). As was the case with *Archaos*, the outopos is also a eutopos or 'good world', marked by a deregulation of desire. In *Les Enfants d'abord* Rochefort suggests that adults fear the unbound libido of the young, writing off any manifestations of sexual desire as aberrations. Passion is subject to a strict process of delimitation: 'arrangé par zones. Décent. Habillé. Ici pas là, tout à l'heure pas maintenant' ['organized into zones. Decent. Fully clothed. Here, not there, later, not now'] (ED, 187). Rochefort picks up on the image of the garden which was so central to *Archaos*: in adult society child sexuality is like a weedless garden in which the lawns are neatly trimmed and the trees pollarded: 'Tout à l'envers de ce qu'on sent, qui est le jardin des délices' ['Quite the opposite of what we feel, which is the garden of earthly delights'] (ED, 187). In *Encore heureux* David finds freedom in the garden of an unoccupied house, expressing his liberation in a masturbatory act: 'il s'est livré à lui-même impunément à la face du soleil' ['he gave himself up to himself with impunity, there in the sunlight'] (92). The garden is both a real physical space and, like Bosch's Garden of Earthly Delights, a figurative representation of desire:

> Dans la joie d'être seul, sans maîtres guettant et surprenant et engluant de honte, il leur a craché à la figure et puis il est parti, pour aller plus loin encore. Mais quoi de plus loin, qu'est-ce qui peut être plus loin que ce jardin qui fait planer, jardin à lui, jardin comme lui. (92)

> [*In the joy of being alone, without any masters spying and taking him by surprise and making him feel trapped in his guilt, he spat in their faces and then left, to go still further. But what could be further, what could be further than this garden which made him soar beyond reality, his garden, a garden in his image.*]

The alternative world of the young extends beyond this literal garden: all of the characters find a new freedom of sexual expression, and an escape from categorization—Grâce and Régina; Jean-Marie and Manuel; and two young lesbians labelled 'les maudites' ['the accursed ones']. The very categories of sexual difference are broken down. Régina and Grâce describe David as 'une petite Aphrodite', and David, inscribing another science-fiction topos, that of another planet, another species, states: 'Vous n'êtes pas des filles, [. . .] vous êtes, Nous sommes des mutants!' ['You're not girls, [. . .] you're, We're mutants!'] (148). As was the case in *Archaos*, sexuality is separated from anatomy: when Lucrèce questions David's claims to womanhood ('je suis une fille, dit David'), indicating his penis, David replies: 'Ça ne veut rien dire. [. . .] La question n'est pas là' ['That doesn't mean anything. [. . .] That's not the issue'] (213).

The 'no place', which is also a 'good place', is a world in which children can escape adult definitions. As a utopian text, *Encore heureux* is clearly both an expression of desire and a criticism of contemporary society, but is it also a blueprint for the future? Is Rochefort actually suggesting that freedom can only be attained via a mass exodus of the young, or should the children's exodus to the south be read meta-phorically? Some critics of the text certainly read the tale of flight *à la lettre*, decrying Rochefort's escapist fantasies and 'false solution of a retreat to nature': 'Has the confused political and social legacy of May '68 finally coalesced into a massive wish to *escape* (rather than destroy) the "société de consommation"?'; 'the answer to the problem of school indoctrination may not be for every child to take to the roads of France and trust to Chance and Nature'.[21] This literal, 'blueprint' reading is perhaps influenced by various aspects of the text: the specific contemporary references to the education system may discourage a metaphorical interpretation, as may allusions to the issue of personal safety: Grâce and Régina are stalked by two men in a car; David suffers an attempted rape; the government is compelled to issue warnings: 'les mauvais traitements et brutalités à enfants sont passibles de poursuites' ['ill-treatment and the abuse of children are liable to prosecution'] (178).

The ambiguity of the text, which appears to be both a real call to flight and a metaphorical expression of freedom, a spiritual rather than a literal journey, is compounded by its conclusion—or rather by alternative conclusions. The first ending appears to advocate dropping out from society, and in this it reflects one trend of the counter-culture, that of the 'hippie' who chooses to disengage from politics and seek an alternative lifestyle. Towards the end of the text Grâce and Régina make it to the south and join a thriving commune. Children, naked or daubed in bright colours, learn to make their own shelters from earth and straw, and eat in communal kitchens. Here too, however, the play of real or metaphorical readings remains. Whilst the commune appears to be tangible enough, it is again suggested that the children have somehow entered a new spatio-temporal realm. They make their way to the commune 'ayant passé sous la frontière invisible, effacée des cartes scolaires et officielles, mais jamais des âmes, jamais' ['having crossed the invisible frontier, wiped from school and official maps, but never ever from souls'] (205). We seem to be back in the land of Archaos, in uncharted territory. The status of the commune, which can be interpreted as both a real and/or metaphorical expression of desire and freedom, remains undefined. In some respects this is a static ending. The setting up of the commune marks an end to the all-important notion of process ('on *va vers* l'été') which had driven the text up to this point. The reader may be left with some unanswered questions. The commune, as an alternative structure, is all very well, but we may be left wondering what the end to summer will bring. After all, the swallows which appear earlier in the text may migrate, but they do so on a seasonal basis.

This, however, is only one ending, marking the conclusion of the journey of most of the central characters: Mann, Lucrèce, Grâce, Régina and David. But not all of the children make it to the south, and the recapture of two of them, Agnès and Thierry, constitutes a second ending to the text. Although they return to their families, Agnès and Thierry have discovered a fighting spirit. They refuse to be separated, and refuse equally to accept conditions which they had previously submitted to without question. The authorities are obliged to take steps to control the student unrest which ensues from attempts to return the two escapees to school; Agnès's mother is forced to consider some harsh realities, like the contraceptive pill (217). This ending might be considered to reflect another dissident strand of the 1970s, that of the more politicized New Left. Like Christophe in *Printemps au parking*, Agnès and Thierry return to the system, but do so with a new-found political awareness. Rather than drop out, they will fight the system from within. Utopia, in this case, becomes a state of mind.

Finally, the closing page of the text offers the reader a third ending. The authorities decide to lure children back to their homes by granting a mock amnesty, and the text closes with a beautiful child of indeterminate sex entering a police station of her/his own free will. Dazzled by the vision, officers are stunned into a respectful silence. Some bow. The officer in charge is faced with a dilemma: 'A l'intérieur le Secrétaire appelait en hâte les Autorités Centrales, pour savoir qu'est-ce qu'on fait, si on le prend ou si on le rend à la Nature' ['Inside, the Secretary quickly called the Central Authorities to ask for advice on how to proceed, whether the child should be taken, or released into the wild'] (219). We are, once again, on the borderlines of science fiction. The child is described as though it were a member of an alien species. The question of release or capture is a familiar sci-fi topos: is the alien being to be returned to its planet (or ship)? Rochefort closes her text on an optimistic note. Whichever choice is made, the two previous endings have already indicated that the child, and those which might follow, will no longer be a compliant victim of oppression.

Reading the critical material, it is clear that Rochefort touched a nerve with *Encore heureux*. Unlike *Archaos*, this utopian work elicited strong responses from critics, whose comments strikingly reveal their own partisan standpoints: *Encore heureux* is, for example, labelled 'a one-dimensional fantasy'; we are told that 'Rochefort effectively evokes in her reader a reactionary response the effect of which is to render attractive the return to hierarchical and traditional value-systems'.[22] Perhaps the key to such responses lies in the very indeterminacy of the work: the uneasy co-existence of literal and metaphorical readings; the presence of multiple endings; the astringent social criticism. As the narrator of *Encore heureux* points out, referring to the recaptured Agnès and Thierry, society is quick to anabolize subversive elements: 'La grande Autruche travailla à avaler ce pavé, comme tant d'autres' ['The giant Ostrich settled down to swallow this obstruction, as it had swallowed so many others'] (216). Unlike *Archaos*, *Encore heureux* cannot be neatly pigeon-holed into a tidy category; critics may damn it as 'utopic', but they fall short of the static label 'utopia'. It is perhaps this resistance to literary recuperation which makes the work particularly successful as a piece of social criticism.

CHAPTER EIGHT

Quand tu vas chez les femmes

> An attentive observer of life may still easily recognize how the custom of
> unnumbered generations, in connection with the passive role with which
> woman has been endowed by Nature, has given her an instinctive
> inclination to voluntary subordination to man [. . .]. Under the veneer of
> polite society the instinct of feminine servitude is everywhere discernible.
> (Richard von Krafft-Ebing, *Psychopathia Sexualis*, on Masochism)

Towards the end of *Encore heureux qu'on va vers l'été*, just after the
denunciation of society's ostrich-like ability to digest and consequently
regulate 'precocious' sexuality, is a question which is never answered:
'Mais la sexualité, l'amour si on veut, où sont ses limites, et qui peut les
fixer?' ['But what about sexuality, love if you like, where are its limits, and
who can set them?'] (216). Returning to fiction after a seven-year gap
(during which *Les Enfants d'abord* and the 'anti'-autobiography *Ma Vie
revue et corrigée par l'auteur* were published), Rochefort takes up the
unanswered question in *Quand tu vas chez les femmes* (1982). In 1958,
sensitive souls had been shocked by the portrayal of what we might term
a psychological sado-masochistic relationship in *Le Repos du guerrier*.
Over two decades later, Rochefort plunges us into the world of s-m sex,
complete this time with whip-wielding Mistresses and wild masturbatory
orgies. The text, which was at least partly inspired by a conference in
New York on the rights of s-m women, asks serious questions: where to
draw the line? individual liberty at what cost? It is also, as Rochefort
acknowledged, 'carrément une farce' ['an out and out farce'], in which
'toutes les partouzes finissent en tartes à la crème' ['all the orgies turn into
slapstick'].[1] Adding to the reader's difficulties, Rochefort breaks with the
pattern of previous texts by returning to a problematic first-person
narrative. *Une Rose pour Morrison*, *Archaos*, and *Encore heureux*, all
narrated in the third-person, leave little room for ambiguity with respect
to authorial point of view. Readers might agree or disagree with
Rochefort's polemical position; might indeed, as was the case with some
critics of *Encore heureux*, disagree whilst acknowledging the integrity of

the author's principled stand, but there can be little doubt as to just what that stand is. *Quand tu vas* raises the interpretive stakes. Not only is the narrator, Bertrand, a psychoanalyst (a profession consistently derided by Rochefort); he is also an author in his own right:

> S'est en effet enflé jusqu'à devenir un ouvrage d'importance, de reste tournant décidément au journal intime (très)—qu'ai-je, désormais, à perdre? En vérité au point où je suis je devrais dire: au testament. Que vous avez présentément sous les yeux. (117)

> [*It has expanded into a significant work, which is in the process of becoming something of a (very) personal diary—what have I got to lose now? Truth to tell, given the stage I've got to, I should rather say it's become. . . a last will and testament. Which you are reading at this very moment.*]

A potentially unreliable, undoubtedly ego-maniacal, psychoanalyst as narrator; a world which questions the very definitions of reality and illusion, in which performance, lies, paradox and role-play are part and parcel of the masochist's life, *Quand tu vas chez les femmes* may be a mere 125 pages long, but it is perhaps the author's most challenging work.

The novel presents us with a range of props and ritual humiliations, but just how well does Rochefort know her s-m, and how are we to respond to Bertrand's escapades? Initial impressions might incline the reader towards a parodic interpretation: the author has surely plunged into an absurd world of caricature, in which a man with a whip up his arse lurches from beatings to orgies, becomes a whip-insertion trendsetter (an anal-retentive of a novel kind), whilst experiencing quasi-mystical moments of ecstatic transcendence. And yet, though the text undoubtedly does topple over into parody, a base-line of realism remains. In her recent publication *Françoise Maîtresse*, Annick Foucault, s-m Mistress-turned-author, describes a typical day's work in which a client (not 'psychan-alyste' but 'avocat') parades 'harnaché, engodé, avec un collier à pointe sur [les] couilles et tenu en laisse dans la rue' ['in a harness, complete with dildo and a studded collar around his balls, led through the streets on a lead'].[2] Bertrand's experiences are perhaps not so extreme. Judging by some of the practices described by Foucault, it could be said that he had got off lightly.

Although Foucault's text is primarily a description of various s-m practices, it does on occasion strike a more theoretical note, and when it does, Foucault looks to a particular text: Gilles Deleuze's *Présentation de Sacher Masoch*, which is both an introduction to the work of Masoch and an analysis of the aetiology and structures of masochism (to which

Masoch gave his name).[3] There are striking parallels between Rochefort's *Quand tu vas* and Deleuze's work. Looking first at the broad picture, Deleuze indicates that Masoch's sexual preferences include 'se faire chasser' ['being hunted']; 'se faire infliger des châtiments, des humiliations et même de vives douleurs physiques par une femme opulente en fourrure et au fouet' ['being punished, humiliated and even suffering extreme physical pain at the hands of a buxom whip-wielding woman in furs'].[4] Rochefort's narrator wistfully recollects 'la nuit des chasseresses' ['the night of the huntresses'], an occasion from his past when his (now estranged) wife Malaure and her partner Maude, 'vêtues [. . .] d'épaisses fourrures' ['wearing thick furs'], organized a man-hunt, complete with live ammunition (82). Deleuze notes that Masoch's role-plays include 'se travestir en domestique' ['dressing up as a maid']:[5] the final pages of *Quand tu vas* find Bertrand firmly ensconced in his Mistress's kitchen, resplendent in his (French?) maid's uniform: 'revêtu du mignon tablier à festons coquettement noué derrière, porté sans autre, dans lequel je me trouvais irrésistible' ['wearing a cute little frilly apron with an alluring knot at the back, worn with nothing underneath it, in which I found myself quite irrésistible'] (94). Bertrand's initial humiliation will be at the hands of the whip-brandishing prostitute Macha, and although his elected Mistress favours tight jeans over furs, her name, as so often in Rochefort's work, is telling. Pétra, a feminized form of Peter, reflects Bertrand's elevation of his Mistress to the founding figure in his Church of Pain, a point made clear when she is first formally introduced (to both the prostitutes and the reader): 'escomptant par mon humble attitude indiquer où je la situais dans mon église. / —Pétra, dit l'Ange, et tendit la main' ['relying on the fact that my humble attitude would signal where I situated her in my church. / "Pétra," said the Angel, holding out her hand'] (53).[6] And if the prostitutes in *Quand tu vas* prove not to have hearts of gold, Pétra will similarly be revealed to be the woman with a heart of stone. After all, as Deleuze points out regarding the masochistic relationships in Masoch's œuvre: 'L'apprentissage se fait avec des femmes de pierre' ['Apprenticeship is undergone at the hands of women of stone'].[7] These similarities, of course, need not reveal anything more than a casual knowledge of the subject on Rochefort's part: after all, furs and whips have become something of a cliché, along with handcuffs and thigh-boots. The parallels, however, extend further, and whilst they do not necessarily confirm Rochefort's familiarity with Deleuze's work, they do suggest a shared perception and articulation of the subject. They also provide a foundation upon which degrees of parody may be built.

As a psychoanalyst, Bertrand is an enthusiastic self-exegete who in the course of the text offers up tempting aetiological insights into his masochistic tendencies. We are informed of a distant, patriarchal father who considered his son to be too soft, too feminine; a man who carried out his conjugal duties with considerable reluctance, preferring to dissipate his young wife's family fortune on prostitutes. In a moment of role-reversal which situates the reader as analyst, Bertrand offers up a fantasy dating from his childhood: 'Autour de mes dix ans j'eus le fantasme que mon père m'enculait. Il me rentrait dedans par-derrière bien à fond, et nous jouissions ensemble en beuglant' ['When I was about ten years old I had a fantasy in which my father was buggering me. He entered me from behind, deep inside me, and we came at the same time, bellowing'] (109). This fantasy and the interpretation Bertrand then provides, is explicitly linked to the narrator's masochism: 'et voilà pourquoi votre fils est muet planté là dans la rue vide. Vide d'Elle' ['and that is why your son stands silent and alone in an empty street. Devoid of Her'] (109).

Bertrand's, and thus of course Rochefort's, proposed aetiology can once again be read in the light of Deleuze's work, more specifically his revision of Freud. In his paper 'A child is being beaten', Freud analyses six cases of 'beating phantasies' (Freud's spelling in this instance indicating unconscious material), representations of humiliation which may take various forms: 'The situation of being beaten [. . .] may go through the most complicated alterations and elaborations; and punishments and humiliations of another kind may be substituted for the beating itself.'[8] For Freud, phantasies of this sort represent punishment for incestuous (Oedipal) desires: 'The boy's beating-phantasy is therefore passive from the very beginning, and is derived from a feminine attitude towards his father. It corresponds with the Oedipus complex just as the female one [. . .] does.'[9] Reinterpreting Freud, Deleuze claims that it is in fact the father-figure who is being humiliated and beaten in such phantasies : 'le masochiste se fait battre; mais ce qu'il fait battre en lui, humilier et ridiculiser, c'est l'image du père, la ressemblance du père, la possibilité du retour offensif du père' ['the masochist allows himself to be beaten; but what he gets beaten in him, what he gets humiliated and ridiculed, is the image of the father, the possibility of the destructive return of the father'].[10] If we now turn to Bertrand's own interpretive work, a clear parallel with Deleuze's position emerges. At first, the narrator's insights seem to point to a desired identification with the father:

> Je crois, il me semble, c'est parce qu'il est la Loi. Ce n'est pas lui. C'est la loi poussé à son extrême, je ne le désire pas, je veux que la loi sévisse dans sa rigueur, c'est la loi que je désire, parce qu'elle est. (109)

> [*I think that it is because he is the Law. It's not him. It's the law pushed to extremes, I don't desire him, I want the law to impose itself in all its rigour, it's the law I desire, because it is there.*]

Bertrand, however, goes on to suggest that the fantasy actually represents a form of revolt (much as Geneviève's passivity in the face of Renaud's aggression in *Le Repos du guerrier* represented the means whereby she could neutralize the power-dynamic):

> Et, est-ce même sexuel? C'est le ravissement par la toute-puissance, l'amour de l'inéluctable. Le désir en place de la fuite impossible. L'érotisme du double-bind: acculé = enculé? ma façon de révolte: la pure acceptation. (109)

> [*And is it even something sexual? It's being ravished by the all-powerful, it's the love of the ineluctable. Desire replacing an impossible flight. The eroticism of the double-bind: no exit = rear entry? my way of rebelling: pure acceptance.*]

Here, we are very close to Deleuze, who identifies Masoch as one of two representatives of 'grandes entreprises d'une contestation, d'un renversement radical de la loi' ['major contestatory works, works which represent a radical reversal of the law'] (the other being Sade).[11] Deleuze highlights the paradox which lies at the centre of masochism: the submission and apparent passivity of the masochist is, in fact, derisory. Challenging Freudian interpretations, Deleuze states that the masochist is endowed with a huge ego and lacks super-ego. In the beating phantasy, the super-ego is externalized and overturned; paradoxically, the beater ultimately serves the ends of the ego of the beaten: 'la même loi qui m'interdit de réaliser un désir sous peine d'une punition conséquente est maintenant une loi qui met la punition d'abord, et m'ordonne en conséquence de satisfaire le désir' ['the same law which forbids me to realize a desire under threat of punishment is now a law which puts the punishment first, and orders me to satisfy the desire which arises from it'].[12] Punishment, in other words, becomes the necessary precondition for pleasure:

> Chaque fois que l'on considère un phantasme ou un rite masochistes, on est frappé par ceci: la plus stricte application de la loi y a effet opposé à celui qu'on aurait normalement attendu (par exemple, les coups de fouet, loin de punir ou de prévenir une érection, la provoquent, l'assurent).[13]

> [*Each time we consider a phantasy or masochistic ritual, we are struck by the fact that the most severe application of the law has the opposite effect of what we might have anticipated (for example, the lash of the whip, far from representing a punishment or preventing an erection, provokes it, indeed guarantees its presence).*]

The masochist attacks the law (represented by the father in Bertrand's fantasy) by pushing it to its logical conclusion (in Bertrand's own words: 'ma façon de révolte: la pure acceptation'). To bow (in this case literally) to the law, is thus to contest it:

> Nous connaissons tous les manières de tourner la loi par excès de zèle: c'est par une scrupuleuse application qu'on prétend alors en montrer l'absurdité, et en attendre précisément ce désordre qu'elle est censée interdire et conjurer.[14]

> [*We are all familiar with the ways in which the law can be subverted by an excess of zeal: it is by means of a scrupulous application of the law that we can reveal its absurdity, and expect to witness the very disorder which it is supposed to prohibit and avert.*]

Reading *Quand tu vas* in this light points towards a sympathetic perception of Bertrand as a positive figure, one who, like so many of Rochefort's protagonists, contests patriarchal law. And yet, whilst there can be little doubt as to the presence of a serious, and if we follow Deleuze, accurate, stratum in the representation of masochism in the text, and a positive interpretation of Bertrand, it is equally true that Rochefort moves away from this base-line into parody. Bertrand's tortured family history is just too good to be true, a psychoanalyst's dream, with a mother dying young and three strict aunts bringing up a lonely boy: Bertrand is quick to inform us of his 'réflexe enfantin d'obéissance durement acquis sous les regards d'acier de mes tantes éducatrices' ['instant obedience instilled in childhood, painfully acquired under the steely gaze of my pedagogic aunts'] (13). Psychoanalytic clichés abound, absurdly recontextualized. When Bertrand, whip still firmly in place, worries about his bowel-movements, kneeling above the toilet-bowl 'de peur de voir, sorti de ma bouche, ce qui n'avait pas d'issue à l'autre bout' ['terrified that I might see that which could not issue forth from one end emerging from my mouth'] (42), his fears are allayed by recollections of his early potty-training (the ultimate psychoanalytic cliché): 'ayant acquis dans mes très jeunes ans le pouvoir de me refuser: mes tantes, indignes de mes offrandes enfantines, ne tolérant pas que je me vautre à mon gré' ['having learned to deny myself at a very young age: my aunts, unworthy recipients of my childish offerings, would not tolerate any self-indulgence on my part'] (43). As he points out, surely with a degree of self-consciousness and self-parody: 'ce sont des événements qui vous marquent à vie' ['such events mark you for life'] (43).

This, of course, is the key question faced by the reader: just how self-conscious *is* Bertrand? Is he the subject or the object of the parody; a spokesman for the author, or her foil? If we consider further parallels between Deleuze and *Quand tu vas*, we can see that in every case an informed degree of realism provides a foundation for baroque parodic constructions, whose intentional source (Bertrand? Rochefort?) is often hard to locate. Placing the maternal figure at the centre of masochism, Deleuze identifies rebirth as a recurring theme in Masoch's œuvre, in which female figures help to make a new man of the male masochist:

> Que signifie ce thème constant dans les romans de Masoch: Tu n'es pas un homme, je fais de toi un homme. . .? que signifie 'devenir un homme'? Il apparaît que ce n'est pas du tout *faire comme le père*, ni prendre sa place. C'est au contraire en supprimer la place et la ressemblance, pour faire naître l'homme nouveau. [. . .] Devenir un homme signifie donc renaître de la femme seule, être l'objet d'une seconde naissance.[15]

> [*What is the significance of this recurrent theme in Masoch's novels: You are not a man, I am making a man of you. . .? what does 'becoming a man' mean? It would seem that it is not at all a matter of acting like the father, nor of taking his place. On the contrary, it is a matter of suppressing his place and any resemblance to him in order that the new man may be born. [. . .] Becoming a man thus means being born again from woman alone, being the object of a second birth.*]

When Bertrand returns to the prostitutes to have his whip removed, he becomes both child-bearer (more of which below) and new-born infant: 'souriant délivré, le nouveau-né c'était moi' ['delivered, smiling, I was the new-born infant']; 'contemplant ma jeune mère [Macha, the prostitute] de mes yeux mouillés de reconnaissance—tu es ma jeune mère retrouvée' ['gazing upon my young mother [Macha], my eyes moist with gratitude: "You are my young mother, I have found you again"'] (55). On this occasion the potentially serious theme is deflated by outside points of view: the delivery-team, Pacha, Elise and Pétra herself, respond to Bertrand's lyricism with bursts of hysterical laughter. Bertrand will plead to have his appendage reinserted, noting that its presence makes him less macho (less like his father?). Hampered by the whip, his aggressive driving style becomes 'une conduite toute en souplesse', whilst his manful stride is similarly transformed: 'j'avais pris une démarche amortie, proprement féline, contrastant avec le pas martial de jadis, qui m'ajoutait en grâce ce qu'elle me retranchait en virilité—bref j'étais un autre homme' ['I'd adopted a cautious, feline gait, quite different from my previous military stride, and what I lost in virility, I gained in grace: in short, I was a different man'] (63). Another blow against patriarchy, or mere comedy? Perhaps both. A serious point is made about Bertrand's masculinity, but the vision of Bertrand cutting holes in his car upholstery in order to accommodate the protruding object belongs to the world of farce. And is Bertrand himself aware of the humour? As retrospective narrator of his own tale (tail), is he responsible for the bathetic description of his over-delicate perching on the edge of seats in polite company, 'qui pouvaient passer pour des préciosités à des regards étrangers. Ou pour des hémorroïdes réluctantes' ['which might have seemed mere affectation to a stranger's eyes. Or a sign of recalcitrant haemorrhoids'] (63)?

Deleuze identifies two central male figures in Masoch's work: Cain and Christ. Both are associated with the sign of the cross, interpreted by Deleuze as a symbol of crime and suffering, but also as marking out the bearer as the mother's favourite: Cain's killing of Abel signals a break with any resemblance to the father, whilst with the figure of Christ:

> La ressemblance du père est de nouveau abolie ('Pourquoi m'as-tu abandonné?'). Et c'est la Mère qui met le Fils en croix. [. . .] C'est moins le Fils qui meurt, que Dieu le Père, la ressemblance du père dans le fils.[16]

> [*Any resemblance to the father is once more abolished ('Why have you forsaken me?'). It is the Mother who puts the Son on the cross. [. . .] It is less a case of the Son dying than God the Father, the resemblance of the father in the son.*]

Identical imagery is employed when the prostitutes break off their routine, temporarily ignoring Bertrand: 'Maman. Warum hast du mir verlassen. Mais c'est fini maintenant Mère chérie' ['Mummy. Warum hast du mir verlassen. Now it is finished, my darling Mother'] (9). Bertrand's allusions to Christ are sustained throughout the text, often in rather unusual contexts: 'je marchais mon châtiment, je portais ma croix où il fallait et dans la rue Saint-Denis. Vers le Golgotha des Lombards, avec mes deux laronnes' ['I walked out my punishment, I bore my cross wherever I had to, in the rue Saint-Denis, heading for Golgotha des Lombards, accompanied by my two thieves'] (as he is led down the street, complete with whip, by the two prostitutes, p. 19); 'on m'enfonça une couronne sur la tête, d'épines' ['a crown was thrust onto my head, a crown of thorns'] (at an orgy, p. 79); 'épinglé au tableau noir comme un vilain insecte, crucifié' ['pinned to the blackboard like some nasty insect, crucified'] (confronted by Pétra in a lecture-hall, p. 121); 'Es ist vollbracht' (humiliated in front of his students, to whom he lectures on the Oedipus complex in matriarchal societies!, p. 122).

Deleuze identifies a strong element of idealism, a desire for trans-cendence, in Masoch's work: 'dans la soumission à la femme, dans les tourments qu'ils [Masoch's heroes] subissent, dans la mort qu'ils connaissent, il y a autant de moments d'ascension vers l'Idéal' ['in their submission to women, in the torments they suffer and the death that they know, one can identify as many moments of ascension towards the Ideal'].[17] Foucault, too, indicates that:

> Quand on est maso, on est forcément mystique. La pratique vous met dans un véritable état de lévitation. Votre esprit est comme chamboulé, renversé. Vous vous retrouvez comme dans une bulle, ailleurs, en dehors du temps. Le mystique se mutile ou se flagelle pour Dieu, le maso pour un homme qu'il déifie. L'un est religieux, l'autre est païen. Mais l'idée de transcendence existe dans les deux pratiques.[18]

> [*When you're a masochist, you're inevitably a mystic. The practices you carry out put you in a veritable state of levitation. Your mind is turned upside down, topsy-turvy. You feel as though you're in a bubble, somewhere else, outside time. Mystics mutilate or flagellate themselves for God; masochists do it for a man they deify. One is religious, the other pagan. But the idea of transcendence is there in both sets of practices.*]

In his (not infrequent) rapturous moments, Bertrand, never one to do things by halves, evokes a bewildering range of deities: 'Ha. Serpent soleil dieu. [. . .] Je cours à la vitesse de la lumière, je disparais de ma propre conscience' ['Aha. Serpent sun god [. . .] I run at the speed of light, I disappear from my own consciousness'] (as he trots on all fours around the prostitutes' room, p. 8); 'le serpent! Satan-Kundalini-Quetzalcoatl' (musing upon the strange nature of his own meditations, p. 91).

As in *Archaos*, though under rather different circumstances, spirituality and sexuality are reunited. As he thrashes the architect Kuntz-Lopez (no mean acrobatic feat, as he does so with his own inserted whip) Bertrand enters 'un délire mystique' ['a mystical delirium'], assuming the role (in his own eyes at least) of dervish (77). While fellow-practitioners form a masturbatory circle, 'des sexes jaillis hors de leurs fourreaux de cuir et maniés à haut régime' ['penises thrusting out of leather pouches, being pumped at high speed'], he experiences a moment of liberation and primordial passion which, as he puts it in his inimitable manner 'évoquent pour moi la Communion des Saints' ['brings to mind the Communion of Saints'] (77). Again, the serious co-exists alongside the parodic. Bertrand's mysticism goes too far (but how far is too far?) and is, moreover, undermined by other characters in the text. A lengthy lyrical

191

reflection on attaining 'le satori' (a bit of Zen Buddhism thrown in for good measure) prompts a cutting rejoinder from one of the prostitutes: 'Il déconne complètement dit Elise' ['He's talking absolute crap.'] (20).

For the reader, the problem of intentionality remains. Bertrand's language is marked by puns, for example his evocation of the Holy Ghost (at an orgy): 'tout se passait dans un complet silence, qui ne laissait filtrer que des souffles. J'inspirais' ['everything happened in total silence. Only the sound of breathing could be heard. I was an inspiration.'] (75). His highly figurative language both reflects his preoccupations ('je tremblais comme un vibro-masseur' ['I was trembling like a vibrator', p. 49]), and provides a constant source of humour: 'Je tranche dans le tas humain comme un couteau dans le pâté, comme un navire toutes voiles dehors je fond de mon étrave le brouhaha mondain. Je fais le partage du silence, tel Moïse celui des eaux' ['I cut through the mass of human beings like a knife through pâté, like a ship with all sails hoist I plunge my prow through this wordly hubbub. I part the silence, just as Moses parted the waves'] (24). Do we laugh at, or with, Bertrand; admire his authorial skills, and thence his disengagement in self-mockery, or view him as the butt of Rochefort's own parodic intents? Moments of explicit self-consciousness on Bertrand's part may push us towards the former reading. On several occasions the narrator pauses in order to comment on his own use of language, positioning the reader as addressee: 'à la queue leu leu si vous me permettez celle-là' ['head to tail, if you'll excuse the pun'] (78); 'si navire je suis alors aussi peu maniable qu'un pétrolier géant' ['if I'm a ship then I'm as difficult to manoeuvre as a giant petrol tanker'] (commenting on his own metaphor, p. 25); 'si on peut formuler ainsi' ['to coin a phrase'] (37). Some questions will remain in the reader's mind. Should we attribute the humorous misquotation of St Paul to Bertrand, or to Rochefort: 'ah combien Paul dit vrai: je fais le bien, que je ne veux pas, et je ne fais pas le mal, que je veux' ['how very true St Paul's words are: I do the good which I do not want to do, and I do not do the ill which I want to do'] (25)?

The narrator's ambiguous status as both authorial whipping-boy and reliable representative emerges clearly in the text's ludic thematization of fetishism, a trait which Deleuze identifies as characteristic of masochism.[19] In *Quand tu vas* the status of the whip as fetish is signalled both by its capitalization—Bertrand refers to his appendage with some reverence as 'l'Objet' (55)—and by the narrator's own interpretive comments. Returning to the prostitutes in order to have the whip restored, Bertrand states: 'Dans une illumination je le compris: je l'avais métaphorisée' ['In a blinding flash I understood: I'd metaphorized it'] (54). Playing with the idea of 'lack' which links fetishism and penis envy, Rochefort leads her readers through a series of comic scenes in which a more serious point emerges: the inversion of gender stereotypes. Certainly Nietzsche's pronouncement, which gives the novel its title—'Are you visiting women? Do not forget your whip!'—is given a gender-twist: Bertrand will indeed take his whip, but not quite in the manner, nor for the purposes, Nietzsche had envisaged![20] When the whip is first inserted, Elise comments: 'Elle fait corps avec toi. C'est comme si tu étais né avec' ['It's become a part of you; it's as if you were born with it'] (20). Bertrand, too, comes to believe that the tail (metaphorically represented by the whip) is a natural part of the human anatomy: 'après tant de millions d'années, finalement la Sélection Naturelle a estimé que la mise en rancart de la caudalité avait été une erreur' ['after so many million years Natural Selection has finally decided that ditching the tail was a mistake'] (79). Leaving the prostitutes for a literary party he states, deadpan, 'j'avais un cocktail' (21). The pun will not be lost on those who, like Rochefort, are fluent English-speakers!

Playing on the Freudian equivalence of penis and baby (the little girl who suffers from penis envy desires first a penis, then, by a process of displacement, a baby, from her father), Rochefort gives Bertrand the female role as he 'gives birth' to the whip: 'elle leva le rasoir. Je me couvris de sueur. [. . .] Respire par petits coups [. . .] Pousse! Mais pousse donc!' ['she raised the razor. I broke out into a sweat. [. . .] Pant [. . .] Push! Push for goodness sake!'] (53).[21] Provided with an insight into the female lot, Bertrand is not a happy man. As one of the prostitutes remarks: 'Les hommes ont vraiment pas de couilles dit Chantal, heureusement que c'est pas eux qui accouchent' ['"Men really have no balls", said Chantal, "it's just as well they're not the ones who have to give birth"'] (53). In Bertrand's scheme of things, 'lack' becomes associated not with woman but with all humanity, signalling a further breaking down of psycho-analysis-inspired gender stereotypes. The removal of the whip, which represents both baby and absent penis, brings on a bout of post-partum depression:

> Cette absence, en moi. Ce manque! La nostalgie. Telle une femme dont l'amant est parti, je me sentais vacant. [. . .] Ce morceau de leur corps intime perdu pour toujours, qu'il leur faut perdre encore en le sevrant de leur sein [. . .]. Comment supportent-elles cette castration? (56)

> [*This absence I feel inside me. This lack! Nostalgia. Like a woman whose lover has gone, I felt empty. [. . .] That intimate part of their body lost forever, a part which they have to lose a second time when weaning begins [. . .]. How can they bear such castration?*]

The restoration of the whip leads to Bertrand's discovery of the solution to humanity's problems: 'je rêvais comme une femme comblée. Le serais-je donc? Aurais-je découvert ce qui manque à l'homme et que son activisme de devant faut lui procurer' ['I was dreaming like a satisfied woman. Maybe I was one? Had I discovered what men lack, what they have to procure by means of full-frontal activity?'] (73). The serious and the parodic again join forces, as Bertrand, punning on the phrase 'révolution permanente', and simultaneously invoking the all-important notion of changing man which we have seen lies at the heart of the counter-culture, plans a short work lauding the therapeutic benefits of anal penetration: 'J'exaltais dans mon petit placet les bienfaits éthiques de la pénétration permanente, envisagée comme source et racine d'une révolution intérieure' ['My little petition sang the praises of the moral advantages of permanent penetration, which I envisaged as the source and foundation of an inner revolution'] (69). Whilst Bertrand's whimsical notions are evidently absurd, they do, nonetheless, send up the Freudian notion of female 'lack'.

As always, the reader is not permitted to settle into a straightforward reading. Bertrand's philosophical ruminations are repeatedly undermined by the pathos of one-liners: 'il n'y a pas de meilleur endroit pour penser que des chiottes' ['there's no better place to think than the crapper'] (after the passage on post-partum depression, p. 56); 'j'écrivais couché sur le ventre' ['I wrote lying on my stomach'] (after his exposition on anal penetration, p. 69). As should by now be clear, the reader-author contract in *Quand tu vas* is constantly called into question via the ambiguous status of the text's narrator. Indeed, it could be said that the contract constitutes the text's unifying theme. Deleuze emphasizes the contractual nature of the masochistic relationship: 'il faut que les amours [. . .] soient réglées par des *contrats* qui les formalisent, qui les verbalisent' ['trysts must be regulated by *contracts* which verbalize and formalize them'].[22] Since the 1980s, as Foucault reveals, contracts in France may be facilitated by the Minitel service.[23]

Whatever the nature of the contract, the relationship is based on consent. Following from this, both Deleuze and Foucault stress that contrary to popular belief a sadist and a masochist would never choose to come together: 'Jamais un vrai sadique ne supportera une victime masochiste. [. . .] Mais pas davantage un masochiste ne supportera un bourreau vraiment sadique' ['A genuine sadist could never tolerate a masochistic victim, anymore than a masochist would tolerate a truly sadistic torturer']. As Deleuze says, the old s-m joke, 'masochist: "hurt me"; sadist: "no"', is fundamentally flawed; the term sado-masochism a misnomer: 'sado-masochisme est un de ces noms mal fabriqués, monstre sémiologique' ['sado-masochism is one of those misnomers, a semio-logical freak'].[24] Foucault, following similar lines, points to the need to differentiate between the sadist and the 'bourreau à maso'. The sadist has no interest in consent; sadist and masochist operate in mutually exclusive territory: 'Le sadique et le masochiste sont, l'un et l'autre, maîtres de leurs fantasmes respectifs. Voilà pourquoi ils ne peuvent se compléter' ['The sadist and the masochist are each masters of their respective fantasies. That is why they cannot complement each other'].[25] What is more, within the maso-bourreau relationship, it is the masochist who is very much in charge: 'c'est la victime qui parle à travers son bourreau'; 'c'est lui qui la forme et la travestit, et lui souffle les dures paroles qu'elle lui adresse' ['it is the victim who speaks via his torturer'; 'it is the victim who trains the torturer, who gives her her role and whispers the cruel words with which she then addresses him'].[26]

In many respects Bertrand and the reader of *Quand tu vas* share a common lot: both strive to interpret correctly the nature of the relationship with an authority-figure (Rochefort, 'bourreau de lecteur'; the prostitutes and Pétra, chosen Mistresses of the narrator), and both experience some difficulty in differentiating performance from reality. Although there are times when the reader perceives Bertrand to be the master of his own tale, a self-conscious and self-parodic narrator, this impression is weakened considerably in those scenes which represent Bertrand's interactions with his Mistresses, when, in other words, alternative points of view offset that of the narrator. It becomes clear to the reader that both the prostitutes and Pétra are working to their own agendas, and that the narrator's ability to identify a base-line of reality, to grasp levels of role-play and performance, is inadequate. This pattern emerges from Bertrand's first visit to the prostitutes. As the scene unfolds, the reader rapidly realizes that Macha and Elise are experiencing some difficulty in playing their part: 'Tu sais que des choses comme toi ça ne devrait pas exister? Je parle sérieusement' ['You know, creatures like you shouldn't exist. I'm serious'] (8). Of course such a statement already leads us into a vertiginous mirror-gallery: is the expressed distaste 'real', and if it is, does the paradox of masochism not set up humiliation as the masochist's goal? And which is worse (or better)—real or feigned indifference?

Like the reader, Bertrand is repeatedly impelled to question just what 'serious' means. When Macha, dismissing her client's request for stiletto heels on the grounds that these are damaging to the health, plays hopscotch on Bertrand's back (in flat soles), performance and reality are once more foregrounded: 'quand on a des talons de toute façon tu ne supportes pas qu'on te monte dessus, il faut faire semblant. Ce n'est pas sérieux' ['in any case you can't bear it when we stand on you in high heels; we have to pretend. It's make-believe'] (14). The maso-bourreau contract appears to have broken down. Although Bertrand is aware of the importance of the contract—'Le corps, o.k., elles en font ce qu'elles veulent, enfin ce qu'il faut c'est le contrat, mais penser, ça, pardon, ce n'est pas leur affaire' ['Okay, they can do what they like with my body, at least they can do what has to be done, that's the contract, but thinking, excuse me, but that's outside their remit'] (16)—his anti-feminist views, which emerge clearly in this scene, are strongly challenged. When the prostitutes break off their routine in order to chat about the pros and cons of woollen socks required for cross-country skiing, their offhand remarks—'regarde moi ce con' ['just look at that bloody idiot'] (9)—point to a genuine disinterest which Bertrand misguidedly strives to interpret in a positive light, mistaking real sentiment for performance: 'leur négligence était jouée, ah elles sont fortes' ['their indifference was a role; they're so clever'] (11).

Adding a further level to the interpretive game, this early scene is open to an autobiographical reading.[27] When Rochefort first showed her writing to her husband, her efforts were dismissed by a curt remark which, given the author's repeated references to the incident, obviously made a lasting impact: 'ma pauvre fille, tu ferais mieux de raccommoder des chaussettes' ['my poor girl, you'd be better off darning socks'].[28] Now, in a fitting gesture of revenge, Bertrand, arch anti-feminist, is left alone in his corner bemoaning his Mistresses' neglect: 'on me laisse sécher dans mon coin comme une vieille chaussette, non, moins qu'une chaussette, les chaussettes ça les intéresse' ['I'm left shrivelling up in a corner like an old sock, no, less than a sock, they're interested in socks'] (10). Bertrand objects to the creative autonomy of the prostitutes: 'On me trahit. On ne suit pas les règles. On invente on inaugure on prend des libertés. On s'offre de l'imagination' ['I'm being betrayed. The rules are being flaunted. They're being creative, they're taking liberties. They're using their imagination'] (15), but as the women point out, 'les temps changent, mon petit' ['times have changed, mate'] (16). Rochefort went on to become a writer; Elise and Macha plan a forthcoming publication (15). Later in the text, Bertrand's wife will take a similar course of action. Amused by the gender role-reversal which has relegated Bertrand to Pétra's kitchen, Malaure echoes Macha's comments on the changing times: 'C'est quand même énorme, l'Histoire' ['History's pretty amazing']; 'les femmes sont forcément plus intelligentes que les hommes aujourd'hui' ['obviously women are more intelligent than men these days'] (124–5). Like the prostitutes, Malaure anticipates her own creative venture and the annulment of another sort of contract: 'je n'ai pas besoin de toi [. . .]. A propos, j'ai demandé le divorce. J'ai finalement trouvé ma voie. [. . .] Je vais écrire nos mémoires' ['I don't need you [. . .]. By the way, I've filed for divorce. I've finally found my vocation. [. . .] I'm going to write our memoirs'] (124–5).[29]

The prostitutes, working to a feminist agenda, do not play the game; or at least not the game which Bertrand wants them to play. As far as this contract is concerned, the masochist is quite clearly *not* in control. Bertrand misreads his relationship with Macha and Elise when he misinterprets genuine indifference as role-play. With Pétra he will make the opposite mistake: his 'bourreau' will indeed play a part, but Bertrand will fail to see that the role of Mistress is a role at two removes, a convenient mask to hide behind whilst Pétra follows her own agenda: that of investigative reporter. The reader may be alert to Pétra's motives from an early stage: her very first exchange with Bertrand, at the famous 'cocktail', is limited to the taking of a photograph of the narrator complete with whip (32). When Bertrand's pursuit begins in earnest, he clearly believes that he calls the shots, indeed his initial response is one of apprehension on behalf of his supposed protégée: 'Je ne crains pas d'ordinaire, mais là . . . L'angoisse—qu'elle fût trop jeune et débutante, et que les implications extrêmes de mon offre lui échappassent' ['Normally I'm not afraid, but in this case . . . My main worry—that she was too young and too naive, and that she was unaware of the extreme implications of my offer'] (48). This reaction is wholly inappropriate. At this and every ensuing meeting, whilst Bertrand becomes ever more embroiled in a wholly imaginary relationship, a false contract, Pétra's career takes precedence. When Bertrand prostrates himself at her feet, Pétra seeks information about various architectural carbuncles (50); while an s-m orgy rages around her, she elicits information about the participants (81); when Bertrand tells her that she has become the catalyst of s-m society, her (honest) response is not taken seriously: 'Elle, bien sûr, elle riait, quand je lui sortais des choses pareilles, ça l'amusait' ['Of course she laughed, when I came out with things like that she found it funny'] (99).

As was the case with the prostitutes, Bertrand cannot distinguish reality from performance. When he declares himself Pétra's slave, he is in earnest, but fails to grasp that Pétra's indifference is equally genuine, that he and she are, in a sense, not dancing to the same tune:

Je m'y trainais comme au pèlerinage, après elle. Nous avions à présent un modeste public de trois personnes—ils nous prenaient pour un théâtre! les niais. Si bien piégés dans le spectacle qu'inaptes désormais à en distinguer la Réalité nue sous leur nez. (48)

[*I dragged myself there as if I were on some pilgrimage, following her. By this stage we had a modest audience of three—they thought we were performers, the naive fools! They're so caught up in the spectacle that they can't recognize bare Reality under their noses.*]

197

The term 'spectacle' is significant, for it takes us back to *Une Rose pour Morrison* and the International Situationists, who, it will be recalled, include stereotypes, role-play, schema, and false sentiment in their definition of the spectacle, opposing these to passion, or sincere love (see above, Chapter 5). Here the very definition of sincerity is called into question. Bertrand's passion is real enough, but his partner's is not. To the outsider, the narrator is merely making a spectacle of himself. Although Bertrand is slow to grasp the imbalance in his relationship, he does gain a measure of insight into his situation in two key scenes, both of which involve mirrors. The first scene of disenchantment takes place at the orgy held at the home of the architect Kuntz-Lopez:

> Par surprise affronté au grand miroir où sur le coup je ne me reconnus pas, une seconde je m'étais pris ma parole pour un Autre. L'apparition, polo noir et le reste nu où s'érigeait ma seconde nature [. . .] avait quelque chose de si extrême, symbolique, mythique, résurgent, tombé d'un Ailleurs d'un Jadis et d'un Autrement, en disjonction totale et d'une telle évidence que je me frappai moi-même d'effroi sacré. (79)

> [*Suddenly confronted with the big mirror in which all at once I failed to recognize myself, for one second, good grief, I thought I was an Other. The apparition clad in a black polo neck and naked from the waist down, with my second nature thrusting forth [. . .] was so very extreme a vision, so symbolic, mythical, resurgent, hailing from some other Place, some other Time, some other Way, [. . .] that my own image filled me with a sacred awe.*]

For a brief moment Bertrand believes in his own transfiguration, but when he sees Pétra reflected in the mirror, fully-clothed and clearly set apart from the chaos before her, the illusion is broken: 'brutalement toute l'affaire m'apparut par ses yeux [. . .] *du spectacle*' ['with brutal clarity I perceived the whole business through her eyes [. . .] *a spectacle*'] (80, my italics). The masochist requires validation, and Pétra fails to reflect back the necessary image.[30] The contract between them is void. The second disillusionment comes towards the end of the text when Bertrand is reduced to abject slavery as Pétra's domestic help:

> 'Servez le thé, et des toasts.' Service, avais-je dit. Vous nettoyez tout ça, répondit-elle. Tranquille. Celle-là ne jouait pas. Je n'y connaissais rien. Ce n'était pas ma partie. Je n'avais jamais eu à le faire, je veux dire pour de vrai—sans le miroir-Autre. (95)

> [*'Serve the tea and toast.' 'At your service,' I said. 'And tidy all that up,' she replied. At peace. She wasn't playing games, not her. I didn't know what was going on. It wasn't what I was used to. I'd never had to do it, I mean for real, without the Other there as mirror.*]

The paradox of masochism re-emerges. Bertrand's own role-play—a performance which ironically precipitates genuine emotion—is nullified in the absence of his Mistress's confirmatory gaze. Bertrand is faced once more with the harsh reality of the one-sided contract; he performs alone on an empty stage.

Like the prostitutes, Pétra the avenging angel teaches Bertrand a tough lesson about the female lot: 'j'appris que la synchronisation d'un petit déjeuner est une prouesse d'organisation [. . .]. Comment les femmes ne sont-elles pas poussées dans l'engineering au lieu de flétrir leurs cerveaux dans le fond des offices?' ['I discovered that synchronizing breakfast is a remarkable organizational feat [. . .]. Why is it that women aren't encouraged to take up engineering, instead of dulling their brains in the depths of offices?'] (93). The middle-class psychoanalyst soon bears signs of the exhaustion of the working-class: 'La fatigue me dota peu à peu de cet air d'hébétement qui m'apparentait aux travailleurs' ['Tiredness gradually lent me a dazed expression which made me look like a member of the working-class'] (96). By the close of *Quand tu vas* Pétra has extracted further information about his fellow-sufferers from Bertrand: 'Elle s'asseyait dans l'auto, elle demandait: qui sera là? [. . .] Elle me retournait sur le gril, délicatement, avec des pincettes [. . .]. Toutes les trahisons mes frères, c'est moi.' ['She sat in the car and asked: "Who'll be there?" [. . .] She roasted me on the spit, delicately, turning me with tongs [. . .]. All those betrayals, my brothers, it was I'] (118–9). Various articles appear in the press, denouncing exploitative figures such as Kuntz-Lopez. Like Malaure, Pétra abandons Bertrand in favour of a woman, heading off on the ultimate symbol of masculinity, the 'grosse moto noire, luisante de vernis et de chromes' ['the big shiny black motorbike with gleaming chrome-work'] (107). Bertrand remains in the kitchen, gazing at a complete photographic record of his masochism stuck to the fridge door–a warning, perhaps, of journalistic scoops to come.

Masochism is an enterprise fraught with difficulty, not least because 'real' feeling or sexual pleasure must be elicited by means of 'false' suffering. The maso-bourreau contract is ultimately a piece of theatre, and as Foucault indicates: 'Le théâtre n'est pas la réalité, et il ne s'agit pas de briser un individu, ni psychologiquement, ni physiquement. Au contraire, il faut jouer au mal pour ne pas le faire' ['Theatre is not reality and it's not a matter of breaking someone, either psychologically or physically. On the contrary, you have to simulate suffering in order not to inflict it.'][31] Bertrand's suffering marks the failure of the contract, but his suffering is relative. Rochefort explores, and deplores, the pain which results from an abuse of power; a situation in which one party exploits a helpless victim. Three examples of non-consenting and non-contractual relationships are represented in *Quand tu vas*. Macha and Elise recall with distaste the 'flic chef dans un supermarché' ['head cop in a supermarket'] who humiliates young boys caught shoplifting by forcing them to undress in his office. The 'flic' seeks punishment at the hands of the prostitutes, but does so for the wrong reasons: 'Parce qu'il bandait, pas parce qu'il fouillait les mômes' ['Because he had a hard-on, not because he was frisking kids'] (14–15). Ironically, the man's guilt is real, and punishment deserved. Paradoxically, punishment elicits pleasure:

> —Faut-il qu'ils se sentent coupable, dit Elise.
> —Et il y a de quoi. Ils le sont.
> —Malheureusement ils se le sentent jamais au bon endroit. (15)

> [*'They have to feel guilty,' said Elise.*
> *'So they should. They are guilty.'*
> *'Unfortunately they never feel it in the right place.'*]

Rochefort's second target is the architect Kuntz-Lopez, erector of glass pyramids and similar monstrosities. Like the supermarket guard, Kuntz-Lopez is an abuser of power, building substandard housing ('boîtes à peuple' ['boxes for people'], 'clapiers' ['hutches']) in the suburbs, and using his profits to buy himself illegal immigrant labour: 'des esclaves véritables, au XXe siècle. De jeunes et solides garçons d'importation, gérontophores et servants, servants de servant' ['real slaves living in the twentieth century. Sturdy young boys imported from overseas, bearers of the aged and slaves, slaves of slaves'] (86). The difference between s-m theatre and true guilt is highlighted when Kuntz-Lopez suffers a beating at unknown hands, and is photographed (it is implied by Pétra) 'les fesses à l'air' ['with his arse in the air'] (122). Kuntz-Lopez does his best to put on a brave face, but Bertrand realizes that the punishment may have hit home: 'et content? Pas sûr; c'était du vrai, pour une fois ce n'était pas du théâtre de salon' ['and was he happy? Not necessarily; it was real, for once it wasn't salon theatre'] (123).

From small-scale exploitation through more extensive social injustices, Rochefort progresses to her third and most important target: the whole-sale State-backed violence exercised under totalitarian régimes. Deeply disturbed by angry cries of 'SS Nazis' which had disrupted the s-m conference she attended, Rochefort seeks to draw a clear dividing-line between such abuses and the consenting victim-bourreau s-m relation-ship.[32] The issue is first raised when the prostitutes refer to concentration camps: 'T'as l'air de ton cadavre. Si on était dans la nature je te ferais creuser ta tombe. Comme au camp. A la copine: on joue au camp' ['You look like your corpse. If we were out in the country I'd make you dig your own tomb. Like in the camps. To her pal: let's plays at camps'] (11). Bertrand expresses an unease ('mais non ça ne me plaît pas! ça ne me plaît aucunement!' ['no, I don't like it, I don't like it one little bit!'] p. 11), which is to grow as the text unfolds. Although he jokes with fellow-masochist Kavel about such camps, Rochefort's narrator begins to question just where lines should be drawn: 'Qui sait? Et où est au juste la différence?' ['Who knows? Where precisely does the difference lie?'] (26). At another soirée hosted by socialite Plato Tzottos, mention of a concentration camp 'pour jouer', complete with 'barbelés miradors baraquements interrogatoires à l'aube blême and the like sauf je crois chambres à gaz, enfin pas encore' ['barbed wire, sentry towers, barracks, bleak dawn interrogations and the like, everything but gas chambers as far as I know, at least not yet'], run for paying guests in south London, provokes a crisis of conscience:

Et dont je ne savais que penser. Je ne savais quoi en penser. Je ne savais pas. Je ne pouvais décider, si nous étions inscrits, eux là-bas, et nous ici, dans un même champ historique, une chaîne causale, une conséquence. (101)

[*And I didn't know what to think about it. I just didn't know what to think. I didn't know. I couldn't decide, if we were inscribed, them over there and us here, in the same historical field, part of a causal chain, logically linked together.*]

Bertrand finds the answer to his question when he is inadvertently caught up in a demonstration disrupted by the neo-military JASC ('Jeunes Au Secours de la Civilisation' ['Youth Mission to Save Civilization']). Beaten up by baton-bearing youth, Bertrand has a revelation: 'Non, nous n'appartenons pas au même. Vous tenez de la haine et moi, je tiens de l'amour. De l'amour seul je peux recevoir le sacrement de la souffrance, le péché et le rachat' ['No, we don't belong to the same group. You represent hatred and I represent love. Only love can give me the sacrament of suffering, sin and salvation'] (112). But just how satisfactory an answer is this? Certainly a boundary is set up between consenting, contractual s-m violence and that of the totalitarian régime or neo-fascist organizations, but does this figurative frontier do any more than differentiate between the *nature* of the two phenomena? The text makes a descriptive point, but does it make a prescriptive one too? Does Bertrand, or Rochefort, set limits to the freedom of expression? To answer this question we need to work through the complex thematic constellation in *Quand tu vas* which centres on liberation and militancy.

At the cocktail party Bertrand is quick to differentiate between true liberation and the mere 'snobisme' of followers of fashion: 'ils sont tous libérés bien sûr qui ne l'est, mais la question c'est les limites et moi je n'en ai pas' ['of course they're all liberated, who isn't, but the real issue has to do with limits, and I don't have any'] (23). In certain circles sexual liberation is little more than a means of scoring points on the socialite-scale: 's'étonner n'est pas de bon ton, chacun connaît tout donc n'est surpris de rien, il n'est pire disgrâce par ici que de passer pour normal' ['it's bad taste to show surprise, everyone is well-versed in everything and so surprised by nothing, there's no bigger disgrace around here than to appear normal'] (24). As Bertrand quips with some irony, his whip suits the company, 'étant de chez Kermès' (24). The narrator's first public appearance soon makes him something of a trendsetter—'avais-je fais école? Je me voyais me répandre comme un feu de brousse, une épidémie' ['had I started a trend? I saw myself spreading like a brush-fire, an epidemic'] (79)—and it is here that he, and the reader, run into difficulties: should the stream of replicant anal-inserters be condemned, or recognized as 'a good thing' for s-m? The first question which arises is: are Bertrand's followers 'for real'? Foucault distinguishes between true s-m sexuality and the 'salon snobs' whose pale imitations belong to the world of cliché (or 'spectacle'):

> La mode 'sadomaso' a engendré beaucoup de faux-semblants qui exaspèrent les puristes. L'émotion ne s'apprend pas. [. . .] Lorsqu'on est ainsi, il n'existe nul stéréotype. Il n'y a plus de loi. Juste un art. Un masochiste ne se plie pas aux caprices inconsidérés des frimeurs. On connaît les petits snobs du sadomasochisme, et leurs images sont le plus souvent héritées d'*Histoire d'O*: cul nu sur la moleskin, ils se baladent dans des soirées spécialisées, ou dans un bistrot parisien, avec leur chien et leur chienne en laisse.[33]

> [*The 's-m' trend has given rise to a lot of fakes which infuriate the purists. The emotion involved isn't something which can be learned. [. . .] When you're like that, there are no stereotypes. There is no law. Just an art. A masochist does not submit to the thoughtless whims of show-offs. The little s-m snobs are well known, and they usually get their image from The Story of O: naked arses on fake leather seats, they parade about at their specialized soirées, or some Parisian bistro with their dog or bitch on a lead.*]

Imitation may in such cases be the most insincere form of flattery, but does it do the s-m cause an injustice, or does it rather constitute a step towards genuine liberation? Bertrand's response to the trend which he precipitates is rather ambiguous. On the one hand, his open display of his appendage is a source of pride: 'J'étais une Première' ['I was a first']

(115). Furthermore, his reflections may on occasion remind the reader of
the utopian sexuality envisaged in *Archaos*. Bertrand picks up the image
of pushing back frontiers (see Chapter 6): 'Et nous, nous nous
dévoilerons. Il me plaisait d'être un tel objet, qui, d'être seulement posé là,
attisait les feux au-dedans, et ouvrait au-dehors les frontières' ['And we
will disclose ourselves. I was happy to be that way, to be someone whose
mere presence stoked the inner fires and opened up frontiers'] (68). The
importance of openness in sexuality is echoed later in the same scene: 'Et
je me prenais à songer: si le monde était tout entier ainsi, peuplé d'êtres
qui se troublent constamment l'un l'autre et ne se cachent point!' ['And I
began to dream: what if the whole world was like this, peopled with
individuals who constantly moved one another and never concealed
themselves'] (69). But perhaps such sentiment is utopic in the negative
sense of the term. More realistically, sexual trends are open to risks which
Bertrand later articulates:

> On parlait de nous. Nous étions passés dans les mœurs. Portés au
> registre des nouveaux gadgets du sexe. En promotion. Nous
> supplantâmes bientôt dans les bruits d'alcôve la scatophagie, qui
> jusque-là menait dans la course-au-plus-libéré, qui ne mange pas la
> merde est un enfant de chœur c'est bien connu. L'un n'empêche pas
> l'autre direz-vous, mais la mode a ses têtes et procède par exclusive.
> Nous pouvions d'ores et déjà ambitionner de figurer, chiffrés, dans les
> enquêtes prochaines de courageux hebdomadaires. (116)

> [*We were being talked about. We had become a part of daily life. Added to
> the list of new sex toys. On special offer. Soon we had supplanted
> scatophagy in the rumour-mill which had up until now led the race-to-see-
> who-is-most-liberated, if you don't eat shit you're a little choirboy as
> everybody knows. The two aren't mutually exclusive, I hear you say, but
> trends have their favourites and are highly selective. Already we could
> aspire to a slot in the next set of surveys carried out by plucky weekly
> magazines, duly reduced to a set of statistics.*]

Like the precocious sexuality in *Encore heureux*, or the 'labelled',
institutionalized homosexuality in *Printemps au parking*, s-m becomes
another meal for the society-ostrich to digest. True passion, 'ce qui est
vrai' (to use Thomas's words), becomes regulated and controlled via
commercialization.[34]

Inasmuch as he perceives the dangers of institutionalization, Bertrand
is set against another character in the text, Gilles-Henri, 'petit activiste' ['a
little activist'] (29). When the press of the extreme right condemn the
growing trend—'Ils ne se cachent même plus' ['They're not even doing it

behind closed doors any more'] (87)—Gilles-Henri praises Bertrand for what he (wrongly) interprets as the narrator's 'in your face' militancy. Bertrand, however, is a trendsetter and militant malgré lui. Like Pétra and the prostitutes, he follows a strictly personal agenda. His display was motivated by love, and not by a desire to shock: 'si [. . .] je m'en suis allé en ce lieu entre tous exhiber mon ignominie, c'est parce qu'Elle y serait, et qu'Elle devait m'y voir' ['if I went there to display my ignominy to the world it was because I knew She would be there and She would see me'] (88). Gilles-Henri becomes the target of parody as he struggles to work out an appropriate line-up for the March of the Oppressed: 'Alors ça donne, as-tu un papier? hommes homo-maso, femmes homo-maso—ou hommes hétéro-maso? Qu'est-ce qui fait le plus d'oppression, maso, ou homo?' ['Okay, so that gives us . . . have you got some paper? gay male masochists, followed by gay female masochists—or should that be straight male masochists? Which group is more oppressed—the masochists or the homosexuals?'] (90). The narrator explicitly condemns the activist's stance:

> Personne ne veut connaître du malheur d'à côté, on ne veut savoir que du même. [. . .] Le malheur-autre porte ombrage, il gêne, il fait concurrence, chaque malheur se veut tout seul occuper tout le terrain, les malheurs se font la guerre d'extermination. La souffrance de A insulte la souffrance de B car elle aspire à rogner de son territoire, B doit lui dénier l'existence. La souffrance de A menace la souffrance de B qui menace la souffrance de A, et voilà pourquoi votre militance est muette. (90–1)

> [*No one wants to know about other people's problems, they just want to know about problems like theirs. Others people's problems cause offence, they're embarrassing, they vie with one's own problems, each problem wants to be centre stage, problems fight to the death. A's suffering is an insult to B's suffering because it tries to encroach on its territory, so B has to pretend it doesn't exist. A's suffering threatens B's suffering which threatens A's suffering and that is why your militancy fails.*]

It comes as no surprise that Gilles-Henri, by the close of the text, will have adopted the cropped hair-cut of the neo-military group (123). Bertrand recognizes the dangers of a militancy which merely replicates the hierarchies of the dominant ideology.[35] On this occasion the narrator, dubbed 'anar' by Gilles-Henri, sounds very like Rochefort herself, who, as we know, insists on the importance of the horizontal struggle of oppressed groups. Indeed, in a wonderful twist of authorial self-consciousness, the above passage is followed by Bertrand's musing observation:

'Parfois je me demande qui pense mes pensées? Elles ne sont plus miennes, m'ont échappé' ['Sometimes I wonder who is thinking my thoughts. They're not mine any more; they've got away from me'] (91). A wink to the reader from an author who realizes that her own voice has intruded perhaps rather too forcefully?

We know by now what liberation is not. It is not the insincere imitation of the salon snob, nor is it the institutionalized labelling of capitalist society, nor yet the hierarchical re-categorization imposed by the militant. So just what is the way forward? Bertrand takes violent exception to Gilles-Henri's writings in the marginal press on 'ce qui se dénomme aujourd'hui "minorités sexuelles", et du "droit à tous les désirs"' ['what are currently referred to as "sexual minorities", and "the right to desire"'] (30): the expression 'minorités sexuelles' is deemed to be little more than a 'cauchemar syntaxique' ['syntactic nightmare']; the phrase 'droit au désir' regarded as 'un monstre grammatical, sémantique, ainsi que métaphysique, et aussi physique' ['a grammatical, semantic, metaphysical and physical monster']. Bertrand's insistence that desire is 'ce qui outrepasse, et transgresse, et transcende' ['that which goes beyond, which transgresses and transcends'], amounts to saying that desire and sexuality quite simply do not belong in the realm of legislation, that society ultimately has no rights to a say in the sex-life of the individual. This stance, if it is Rochefort's own—and the text's satirical undermining of Gilles-Henri's point of view reinforces such a reading—is deeply problematic. The text appears to be suggesting that sexuality stands, and should remain, outside the mechanisms of society; that sexuality is the one true force, as indeed it was in *Une Rose pour Morrison,* which can combat oppression. Paradoxically, sexuality becomes a liberating force, rather than itself in need of liberation; so-called oppressed minorities become liberated freedom fighters.

This is an idealist stance which ignores the very real social injustices which prevail in society. The harsh reality is that individuals do not live in a utopian world in which sexual tendencies can be exercised in freedom. Bertrand rails against homosexual marriages and similar struggles for equality before the law ('la mode insane de réclamer des droits de tout' ['the insane trend whereby people claim the right to do everything and anything'] p. 30), but the law—however regrettably in the eyes of some—does exist, and legislative inequalities cause very real hardships. Bertrand insists on the radical nature of desire itself: 'L'interdit, voilà mon territoire, et l'opprobre, la nourriture dont je m'empoisonne, ce n'est pas un gouvernement qui peut le changer en confiserie par décret' ['The realm of the taboo, that's where I operate, disapproval is the stuff I poison myself with, and it's not the government that's going to make everything nice and palatable just by passing a few laws'] (30). But surely a middle-ground must be sought between institutionalization and a self-satisfied revelling in the transgressive nature of one's own sexuality? For the masochist or gay man or woman who has no choice in the matter of his or her sexuality, the argument that pleasure stems from the very illicitness of the activity will seem truly inadequate. Ultimately, *Quand tu vas* inevitably obfuscates the issue of setting limits to desire. Bertrand fleetingly ponders the rights of the JASC organization—'les JASC réclamaient le droit de porter des armes (fallait-il les mettre dans notre cortège, au titre du droit à tous les désirs?)' ['the JASC claimed the right to carry weapons (should we include them in our procession, in the name of the right to all desires?)'] (91)—but the logic of the text is such that there can be no answer: 'real' desire is deemed to be that which transgresses, therefore it stands outside the law and cannot be subject to legislation; any desire which reinforces the dominant ideology (such as the desire to bear arms and fortify social mores) is not 'real' desire.

'J'aime ces jeux, qui obligent à garder un contrôle parfait des niveaux de mensonges' ['I like these games which force you to maintain a perfect control over the layers of lies'] (28). The words are Bertrand's, but they could equally be Rochefort's. Attempts to stabilize levels of interpretation, to identify a base-line of reality, to disentangle Bertrand's point of view from his creator's, leads the reader of *Quand tu vas* into a discomforting hall of mirrors. The narrator's point of view is undermined by his excesses, but Bertrand is himself master of his own extremes, and he has all the speaking parts. In an imaginary dialogue the narrator, assuming the voice of God with typical immodesty, reveals the extent of his self-consciousness—and perhaps echoes the sentiments of the disoriented reader:

> —Et si je t'abandonnais? Te laisser choir une bonne fois, en ayant marre à la fin des grands airs que tu te donnes et de tes prétendus défis et de ton théâtre et toutes tes insanités? (71)

> [*'What if I left you? Let you drop once and for all, having got sick and tired of your airs and graces and your supposed challenges and all your play-acting and all your craziness?'*]

Bertrand's perspective is also challenged by the views of other characters, but of course as writer of the account we read, it is he who represents the very people whose words denigrate him. As Foucault points out, the ultimate pleasure for the masochist lies in anticipation: 'Le masochiste repoussera toujours le passage à l'acte. Il aura besoin d'écrire, de programmer et d'imaginer les scènes qu'il va vivre' ['The masochist will always delay the moment of action. He will need to write, to programme and to imagine the scenes he is going to play out'].[36] In the words of Deleuze: 'Les scènes masochistes ont besoin de se figer comme des sculptures ou des tableaux, de doubler elles-mêmes des sculptures et des tableaux, de se dédoubler dans un miroir ou un reflet' ['Masochistic scenes have to freeze like paintings or sculpture, they have to mirror sculptures or paintings, to split into twin images in a mirror or a reflection'].[37] *Quand tu vas* is built around precisely such scenes: Bertrand and the prostitutes; literary cocktail; orgy chez Kuntz-Lopez; soirée Tzottos; Bertrand caught up in a demonstration; Bertrand alone in Pétra's kitchen. Once the narrator's adventures are over, what better way to recapture the titillation of suspense than to recreate them in writing? To write one's own downfall and humiliation: the ultimate masochistic pleasure.

And what of the reader of *Quand tu vas*? We, like Bertrand, strive to differentiate real from role, but are we, too, victims of a false contract? Author–reader, husband-wife, and maso-bourreau: all contracts which are called into question in the text. One more remains: that of analyst and analysand. Do we, like Bertrand in his masturbatory sessions with Malaure, find titillation in the reading act? Bertrand points to the parallel between analyst and prostitute: his clients pay him just as he pays Macha and Elise (113). Both contracts end in failure: Bertrand finally abandons his clients. *Quand tu vas* closes with Bertrand laughing at the divine comedy of life: 'Je ris de la première fois depuis que j'existe, je ris de tout, je ris ma vie entière. Le monde, cette plaisanterie divine, je ris aux larmes' ['I laugh for the very first time since I came into the world, I laugh at everything, I laugh out my whole life. The world, this divine comedy, I laugh until I cry'] (126).[38] Perhaps this is our best response to the comedy of the world of *Quand tu vas*. The text continues:

> Et que faire?
> Le chocolat. (126)

> [*What next?*
> *The chocolate*]

'Être / faire chocolat': 'to be done out of something; to get swindled / rooked / cheated out of something'. The analyst is he who knows; perhaps we too are punters, seeking, but not finding, an answer to our questions.

CHAPTER NINE

La Porte du fond

> Je suis arrivé à la demeure.
> Au fronton, on avait gravé:
> LE DEVOIR DE TOUT SURVIVANT EST DE SURVIVRE
> et à part ça il n'y avait pas le moindre
> fronton, et le 'on' est une figure de style.
> (Rochefort, *Le Monde est comme deux chevaux*)

Throughout her writing career Rochefort sought to give a voice to those whose freedom is restricted, whether they be women (*Les Stances à Sophie*), gay men (*Printemps au parking*), or those perceived to be on the outer margins of the sexual spectrum (*Quand tu vas chez les femmes*). One group proved to be an abiding concern, and that was children (*Les Petits Enfants du siècle, Encore heureux qu'on va vers l'été, Les Enfants d'abord*); and it is the child who once again stands at the centre of Rochefort's last novel, *La Porte du fond* (1988). In common with many of her previous works, *La Porte* represents both the destructive nature of interpersonal relations marred by an abuse of power, and an alternative vision of reciprocity and sexuality as life-giving, liberating forces. Once again, Rochefort seeks to trace the roots of oppression back to what she identifies as nefarious institutions: the traditional nuclear family; the Church; and the medical establishment, in this case in the form of classic Freudian psychoanalysis. Stylistically, the novel bears many of the hallmarks which we have come to associate with Rochefort's writing practice, and, more specifically, with her use of the first-person narrative: a break with standard French; a first-person narrator of questionable reliability; and the presence of parallel structures which prompt readers to engage with ethical issues and reflect upon their own values and preconceptions. Less typically, readers face a new challenge in the form of a highly fragmented, a-chronological representation of events: the text divides into nine sections, splitting into a further sixty-three subsections; although a chronological base-line charts the narrator's life from childhood to adolescence, this linear strand is disrupted by proleptic incursions into various periods in her adult life. *La Porte du fond* proved to be Rochefort's last novel, and it is appropriate, indeed, that at the age of seventy-one, after some thirty years of championing the rights of oppressed groups, she should have turned to what is perhaps one of contemporary society's most pressing concerns, child sexual abuse.

The 1980s saw the publication of a number of books on child sexual abuse which set out to debunk existing thoughts on the subject. Anna Salter sums up the situation in a textbook aimed primarily at practising mental health clinicians:

> The literature on child sexual abuse in this century has often held victims and their mothers responsible for the sexual abuse, particularly in the case of incest, frequently with little mention of the role of the offender. Attributing responsibility to the child was more prevalent in the early part of the century, although there is literature in the '80s that continues this tradition. Holding the mother and non-offending family members responsible has been more frequent in the past 30 years, and is currently the dominant position in the field of incest cases.[1]

Judith Herman's *Father–Daughter Incest* outlines two prevailing myths which shift the onus of responsibility away from the offender: the myth of the 'Seductive Daughter' (the precocious, sexually-provocative child, the 'small temptress'), and the myth of the 'Collusive Mother' (the 'frigid, unloving wife') who is deemed to be complicit in the abuse.[2] Whilst *La Porte du fond* undermines both of these myths, it also seeks to represent the complexities and moral ambiguities surrounding the family dynamic (father–child, mother–child, father–mother).

In what is perhaps still the best-known novel representing child sexual abuse, Nabokov's *Lolita*, the eponymous twelve-year-old 'nymphet' apparently initiates the sexual relationship with her step-father Humbert Humbert:

> Frigid gentlewomen of the jury! I had thought that months, perhaps years, would elapse before I dared to reveal myself to Dolores Haze; but by 6 she was wide awake, and by 6.15 we were technically lovers. I am going to tell you something very strange: it was she who seduced me.[3]

Locked into the first-person perspective of the highly articulate Humbert, the reader of *Lolita* gradually becomes aware that this 'Seductive Daughter' is, in fact, far from being a consenting partner in an equal relationship, though she may well be sexually precocious. Increasingly, the reader strives to acquire distance from the abuser's point of view, reading 'against the grain'. *La Porte du fond* reverses the situation, confronting us with the 'victim's' perspective of events (although as we shall see later, we may have occasion to read 'against' this narrator too). At no point do we gain access to the father's thoughts; indeed, such is the narrator's contempt, she would rather ponder the nature of 'les coccinelles cabossées qui ne peuvent plus voler et n'importe quoi vivant sur la Terre' ['damaged ladybirds which can't fly and any other living creature on Earth'], than seek to delve into the psyche of her abuser.

By denying us any access to the father's point of view, Rochefort effectively precludes any possibility of sympathy with a figure who condemns himself by his very words and deeds. Far from suggesting that the child is in any way seductive, *La Porte* charts the father-offender's deliberate programme of subversion and manipulation, and the young narrator's constantly renewed struggle in the face of his unsolicited advances. Taking advantage of the young girl's innocence (the narrator is barely eight years old when the abuse begins), the abuser-to-be sets about undermining the moral code of Catholicism in which his daughter has been raised, proclaiming that sin is no more than an invention, and a belief in God less desirable than blatant hedonism: 'moi [. . .] en tout cas je crois au plaisir' ['as for me, one thing's for sure: I believe in pleasure'] (48). The 'fameux stratège' ['famous stategist'] has an impressive arsenal at his disposal; his manipulative endeavours run the gamut from bribery, to the provision of salacious literature, to more subtle emotional power-plays, for example his first attempt to lure the child into a closer physical relationship:

> Tu as manqué de tendresse . . . (il attend). L'austérité, ce n'est pas bon . . . On perd l'habitude des caresses et après . . . C'est comme ça qu'on devient comme ta grand'mère . . . Ce serait bien dommage . . . Tu ne mérites pas ça. (50)

> [*There hasn't been enough tenderness in your life . . . (he waits). Austerity isn't good for people . . . They get out of the habit of being caressed, and then . . . That's how they end up like your grandmother . . . That would be a real shame . . . You don't deserve that.*]

More crucially, he takes advantage of the strong mother–daughter bond, playing off mother against daughter by casting the former in the role of 'bad cop' ('chez les flics, il y a toujours le gentil, et le méchant' ['with the police there's always the good cop and the bad cop'] (45), whilst assuming for himself the part of the understanding father. A slap in the face, administered, significantly, by the mother on the occasion of the first meeting between child and father (the latter returns after deserting the family seven years earlier), assumes a symbolic status, heralding the gradual deterioration of the mother–daughter relationship. Although the child's love for her mother diminishes, enough of this primary bond remains for the father to use emotional blackmail in the form of the repeated threat that should the child reveal the truth, her mother would throw herself from the nearest window. On only one occasion does the father attempt to use force, but the psychological acuity of his manoeuvrings is such that the child is helpless: as she points out, 'les cordes à l'intérieur c'est vicieux' ['inner chains are nasty things'] (163). Clearly, we are a long way from the myth of the 'Seductive Daughter'.

Although *La Porte* recounts and represents the young child's resistance and struggle to survive, the speaking voice, as it was in *Les Stances à Sophie* (and more problematically in *Les Petits Enfants du siècle*), is that of the 'escapee', in this case that of the adult who has extricated herself from the oppressive father–child relationship, and looks back upon it with that all-important critical distance or 'conscience'.[4] Rochefort makes full use of narrative devices we have already encountered to undermine the offender's position. Contrapuntal ironic asides, for example, serve to highlight the iniquities of the father's stance, just as they revealed the growing chasm between Céline and Philippe in *Les Stances*:

—Et dis-moi, qu'est-ce qu'il te reste à perdre maintenant?
C'est vrai c'est déjà perdu. Mes illusions.
—D'ailleurs on n'y peut plus rien, ce qui est fait est fait on ne revient pas en arrière.
Puisqu'il le dit.
—Ou alors il n'aurait pas fallu que tu commences du tout.
Que 'je' commence.
—Nous sommes embarqués dans le même bateau tous les deux, que tu le veuilles ou non.
Un à la barre l'autre aux fers.
—Si c'est ça qui te dérange les liens du sang ces vieilles lunes je peux te rassurer: c'est pratique courante dans les familles.
Rassurée. (63)

['*So tell me, what have you got to lose now?*'
True enough, it's already lost. My illusions.
'*In any case, nothing can be done about it, what's done is done, you can't go back.*'
If he says so.
'*Maybe you shouldn't have started in the first place.*'
'*I*' *shouldn't have started.*
'*We're both in the same boat now, whether you like it or not.*'

One at the helm, the other in chains.
'If that's what's bothering you, family ties, that's old hat I can assure you,
it's common practice in all families.'
That's alright then.]

La Porte du fond is both savagely ironic and, surprisingly, given the subject-matter, extremely funny. As we have seen in previous chapters, most especially Chapter 2, humour and irony are powerful devices, serving to entice the reader into complicity. Perhaps more importantly in this text, both serve to emphasize the strength of the speaking subject: whereas the young child was helpless, the adult is empowered. This is not a work about a victim. Rochefort, significantly, concludes her text with a section entitled 'Le Survivant'. It may be that some readers experience discomfort in the face of such narratorial detachment: are knowing irony and glib humour really appropriate? If they do, then they will find that Rochefort pre-empts and challenges their reservations. Towards the close of the text, the narrator puts the case for the survivor: 'Perdez illusion bonnes gens, assis dans la croyance que les malheurs passés doivent labourer la mémoire la vie durant, comme si c'était un devoir d'encore et encore les payer' ['Cast off your illusions you good people who firmly believe that past misfortunes must inevitably come back to haunt one's memory all life long, as if one had to pay over and over again'] (238). No victim, she will resist the self-flagellation of enduring suffering, 'la combine profitable qui est: on est prié de continuer à s'opprimer soi-même quand il n'y a plus personne pour le faire' ['the profitable little scheme which states that members of the public are politely requested to continue to oppress themselves when there is no-one else there to do it for them'] (238).

It is, perhaps, ironic that Rochefort, so opposed to bulldozing tactics, should confer upon her own narrator a voice of such apparently unimpeachable authority. By anticipating the reader's response, the author leaves little room for alternative views. When relating a period in the abuse when she decided to stop struggling and bow instead to her father's sexual advances, the narrator once again pre-empts possible responses:

Là je sens que vous allez me jeter la pierre: ça n'est pas bien alors ça c'est vilain. [. . .] A cela, chères dames, je ferai la réponse évangélique: j'aurais voulu vous y voir tiens. Aux messieurs je dirai seulement de balayer derrière leur porte. (87)

[*At this point I sense that you're going to accuse me: that's not nice, that's wicked.* [. . .] *To which I reply, dear ladies, in the evangelical manner: I'd like to have seen you in the same situation. To the gentlemen, I merely suggest that they put their own house in order.*]

Adopting the moral high ground in this fashion is potentially problematic. If only abuse victims can judge the narrator's stance, then the reader's freedom to respond to the text is curtailed: readers who wish to distance themselves from the narrator's point of view must refuse the role of addressee. One can only assume that those readers who have suffered abuse may well adopt a more critical stance than those who have not. Furthermore, the attitude expressed by Rochefort's narrator necessarily has implications for the author's own ethical stance: if only abuse victims can speak with authority, then by what right does Rochefort herself write of sexual abuse? When *La Porte* was first published, some critics automatically assumed that it was an autobiographical work.[5] The Livre de Poche edition which succeeded the Grasset text, however, comes with a disclaimer: 'Toute ressemblance avec qui que ce soit serait purement fortuit, et due principalement à ce que dans nos sociétés uniformisées tout le monde se ressemble' ['Any resemblance to any individual is purely accidental, and due principally to that fact that everyone is much the same in these uniform societies in which we live'].

Disclaimer notwithstanding, if we look to *Ma Vie revue et corrigée par l'auteur* (1978), we can see that there are clear echoes of Rochefort's own life in *La Porte*. The concierge Babet who is affectionately recalled on several occasions by the narrator of *La Porte* is also named in *Ma Vie*: 'Je me souviens de la Briance limpide et pleine de gardons[. . .]. Et de la grosse Babet, qui ne saura jamais ce qu'elle m'a donné' ['I remember the clear waters of the Briance full of roach [. . .]. And big Babet, who will never know how much she gave me'] (*Ma Vie*, 287). The dubious and unsuccessful business ventures of the father are similarly alluded to in both texts: 'Je me souviens quand mon père faisait fortune tous les soirs, et était ruiné tous les matins. Ou l'inverse' ['I remember when my father made his fortune every evening, and was bankrupt every morning. Or the other way round'] (*Ma Vie*, 110); 'un truc sinistre comme recouvrements allez donc expliquer ce que ça recouvre (à part un paquet de fric par-ci par-là et pleins de pots, et plus souvent rien du tout et des scènes à travers la porte)' ['a dubious venture like "collection", you tell me what's being collected (apart from a wad of cash here and there and a whole load of vases, and more often than not nothing at all and scenes in the other room)'] (66–7). Whether *La Porte* is, or is not, autobiographical, is a question which will in all probability never be resolved. What is certain is that by setting up her narrator as the voice of authority, Rochefort raises questions about both her own status—abuse victim or not?—and that of her text—fiction or autobiography?

Ma Vie revue et corrigée par l'auteur records another significant memory which is echoed in *La Porte*: 'Je me souviens de la peine que j'ai eue au départ à distinguer entre le Bien et le Mal' ['I remember the trouble I had in the beginning trying to distinguish between Good and Evil'] (*Ma Vie*, 96). Although, as we have seen, the voice of the narrator in *La Porte* is that of the enlightened adult, Rochefort does suggest that such clear-sightedness may be preceded by a period of moral ambiguity. Early in the text the narrator pauses in order to reflect and comment upon her own act of narration. Distance and irony, a knowing tone ('ces airs d'avoir toujours su d'avance' ['that impression of having always known in advance']), are acknowledged as entertaining: 'ça fait du style [. . .] avec recul et le recul c'est l'art' ['that's style, and style with retrospection, and retrospection is art'] (37). The reality, however, is that for some time the young child could not distinguish good from bad; the simplistic 'doer' and 'done to' polarization simply did not exist: 'Donc, d'avance, j'étais bête. Et lui, non il n'avait pas l'air, à l'arrivée, de l'araignée tissant patiemment ses toiles pour sa petite mouche' ['So before, I was ignorant. And no, at the outset he didn't seem like the spider patiently spinning its web to catch its little fly'] (37). Only gradually did the Prince become the Ogre; the understanding father metamorphose into the spider spinning his web. In Chapter 7 (*Encore heureux qu'on va vers l'été*) we saw how a blatant wielding of power might serve to precipitate resistance and a clear 'them and us' situation. The narrator of *La Porte* records the same process: 'Si j'ai vu, ce n'est pas par mes propres lumières, c'est grâce à lui, mon père' ['If I came to see, it wasn't because of my own insight, it was thanks to him, my father'] (59). Rochefort suggests that those placed in a position of power will inevitably abuse that power: 'Quand on a la veine d'occuper une position élevée, on ne peut pas s'empêcher de s'en servir pour avoir ce qu'on veut' ['When you're lucky enough to be in a position of power, you can't help using that position to get what you want'] (59). Unable to sustain a waiting game, the father loses his subtlety and the complicity of the narrator, and the phoney war consequently gives way to genuine conflict: 'Les deux côtés s'étaient rejoints. Au seul lieu possible: sur le front' ['The two sides had joined up. At the only possible location: the battlefront'] (64). The knowing voice of authority can emerge only once the battle-lines have been clearly delimited.

  La Porte is unusual—and courageous?—in pointing to the early period of moral ambiguity which characterized the father–child dynamic. Subsequent references to the abusive situation, however, are perhaps more controversial. Although Rochefort at no stage suggests that the child either solicited or approved her father's actions, the text nonetheless represents the abusive situation as one which necessarily precipitates a loss of innocence. When, for example, the narrator seeks to win her mother's love by giving in to her father's desire, her increased manoeuvring power is offset by a loss of purity: 'Mon plateau de balance était un rien moins bas. Je n'étais plus la pure victime, j'étais aussi la salope' ['The scales had tipped a little way in my favour. I was no longer the un-adulterated victim, I was the tart as well'] (89). It is suggested that the absolute innocence of the victim is itself a myth: 'L'innocence du faible, qui y croit? Ne dit-on pas que, ce qui lui arrive, il l'a quelque part cherché? Lui-même, certain dans son cœur que non, n'est pas exempté de doutes—au fait, légitimes: entièrement innocent, il serait mort' ['Who believes in the innocence of the weak? Isn't it said that they get what they somehow asked for? And they themselves, even though they know in their heart of hearts that that isn't true, still have some doubts—and legitimate ones at that: if they were entirely innocent, they'd be dead'] (21).

As we have seen, although Rochefort undoubtedly undermines the myth of the 'Seductive Daughter', she also seeks to represent something of the complexities of the father–child dynamic, and the same is true of the mother–child relationship. Although the myth of the 'Collusive Mother' blames the mother for the initiation of child sexual abuse by pointing to, especially, maternal absence and/or the withholding of sexual relations from the husband, writers such as Herman and Salter stress that respons-ibility must lie with the father. Salter notes that 'maternal dysfunction or absence provides the opportunity in the same manner that a family on vacation provides the chance for a burglar to rob them and implies the same degree of culpability'.[6] Taking a similar line, Herman condemns those who would support the husband's claims to marital 'rights': 'It is this attitude and entitlement—to love, to service, to sex—that finally characterizes the incestuous father and his apologists.'[7] *La Porte* is con-sonant with such views. At no stage does the narrator blame her mother for her absence from the house. Although she refers to her mother's reluctance to engage in sexual relations ('Ce gentleman m'avait voici longtemps informée qu'elle "n'aimait pas ça"' ['The gentleman had long since informed me that she "didn't like doing it"']) she glosses this remark with heavy irony: 'Bien forcé donc le malheureux n'est-ce pas qu'il aille chercher ailleurs' ['So naturally the poor soul was forced to look elsewhere'] (133).

If the mother cannot be held responsible for the initiation of the abuse, can she be blamed for allowing it to continue? This issue, in fact, remains unresolved within the text, whose structure both emphasizes the powerful mother–child bond, and prompts the reader to question the mother's position: did she even know that the abuse was taking place? The text opens with the report of a conversation held between the narrator and her mother some twenty years after the narrator has left home, on which occasion the mother refuses to discuss past events: 'Il y a des choses qu'on ne dit pas' ['Some things are best left unsaid'] (17) and 'On ne parle pas de ces choses' ['Some subjects aren't open to discussion'] (18).

For the first time, the narrator wonders if her mother was as blind as she had believed: 'Car enfin—pour la première fois cette pensée se formait chez moi—ne savait-elle pas? Et—oh mon dieu!—n'avait-elle pas toujours su?' ['Because in the end it occured to me for the very first time: didn't she know? And—oh my God!—hadn't she known all along?'] (19). Significantly, this expression of doubt is preceded in the text by a statement of forgiveness: 'Ce n'est pas notre faute' ['It's not our fault'] (13). What is unclear, however, is whether this statement precedes, in chronological terms, the narrator's new-found suspicions. Does she forgive in spite of her doubts, or before these arise?

Faced with the textual ambiguity which arises from the alinear present-ation of events, and thereby deprived of the authority of the first-person narration, readers find themselves reading the ensuing text with critical alertness: the mother's apparent blindness is constantly questioned; her guilt, or otherwise, becomes the focus of reflective attention. Guilt, furthermore, is very much a two-way street with respect to the mother–daughter relationship. The powerful bond between mother and child is underlined by the circular structure of the text: *La Porte* not only opens but also ends with the narrator facing her mother. Informing her that the father has died, the narrator cannot quite conceal her glee: 'j'ai tenté de me composer un visage qui, au moins, ne choquât point sa veuve [. . .]. Je crains de n'y être pas parvenue tout à fait. Et qu'elle ait aperçu, sous son masque mal ajusté, le sourire du survivant' ['I tried to arrange my features in such a way that my expression wouldn't shock the widow [. . .]. I'm afraid I might not have been altogether successful. And that she may well have spotted, behind the ill-fitting mask, the smile of the survivor'] (242). Survival, however, comes at a high price: the child's love and respect for her mother diminishes, and her unannounced departure from the family home is perceived by her as a betrayal, albeit a necessary one. The narrator's frequently reiterated references to herself as an unnatural child or 'monstre' underline her feelings of guilt with considerable poignancy: 'Ah, je ne suis pas née monstre' ['I wasn't born a monster'] (33); 'malade de pitié mais pour rien au monde, non! je ne reviendrai car: ma vie! ma vie! et que monstre je sois mais quoi que valût cette vie c'était une vie et je n'acceptais plus que parce que j'aimais, l'on me tue' ['sick with pity but I won't come back at any price because my life's at stake! my life! and if I'm a monster then so be it, but whatever this life was worth at least it was a life and I could no longer accept the fact that just because I loved her I should pay with my life'] (98).

Clearly, the role of the mother is far from straightforward, and the reader's response is further complicated by Rochefort's representation of the three-way dynamic linking the child with her two parents, and of the parents' own status within the traditional nuclear family. If we assume that the mother was aware of the abuse, should she be blamed for allowing it continue? Early in the text the narrator hands her mother a letter which stresses society's role: 'lui laissant une lettre de douze pages où j'exposais limpidement le misérable rôle des mères dans la société patriarcale' ['leaving her a twelve-page letter in which I set out in clear terms the wretched role of mothers in patriarchal society'] (12). Recent works note that mothers may fail to report abuse for various reasons: fear of social ostracism, of single parenthood, or of physical abuse.[8] Furthermore, research suggests that mothers in traditional patriarchal households, in which women have a submissive role, are less likely to report abuse. Interestingly, the family situation in *La Porte* is not typically 'traditional': the mother has already experienced single parenthood (and therefore fears the loss of her 'model family' all the more), and it is she who is the principal breadwinner. However, the dynamics within the family, particularly the attitude of the mother, are significant. Introduced in the section 'Une femme capable' ['A capable woman'] as a headstrong, independent woman, she nonetheless appears to a large extent to be in thrall to her husband: 'Sa femme n'a pas fait un pli je l'ai vue avec horreur tomber sous sa coupe' ['His wife didn't bat an eyelid; horrified, I saw her fall under his spell'] (32). In a one-to-one relationship with her husband, she remains more than able to stand up for herself. When, for instance, the narrator decides to stop carrying out household tasks, the mother balks at her husband's inactivity: 'Et sa femme regimbe: "Je ne suis tout de même pas ton boy"' ['And his wife balks: "I'm not your slave, you know"'] (176). She will stand against the husband, but not the father:

—Pourquoi tu lui demandes pas à lui d'en faire un peu aussi, je lâche, courageusement, il a plus de temps que *nous*—avec appui sur le 'nous' exprès, nous toi et moi, dans le même sac. Et lui dans l'autre, celui des cossards.
—Qui, lui? Dire papa ça t'écorcherait la bouche? (177)

[*'Why don't you ask him to do something too,' I blurted out courageously, 'he's got more time than us'—with deliberate emphasis on the 'us', us, as in you and me, in the same boat. And him in the other one, the layabouts' boat.*
'What do you mean, "he"? Is it too painful for you to say dad or what?']

Although the reason for this ambivalent stance is never spelled out, it is suggested that the daughter's status as child is a major factor influencing her mother's attitude: 'Mais elle disait rien, jamais rien, ah elle ne me causait pas comme à une personne celle-là non, j'étais une môme et que je le reste, bien que je l'étais de moins en moins' ['But she never said anything, not a single word, she didn't speak to me as if I was a person, oh no, I was a kid and I should stay that way, although in fact I was becoming less and less of a kid'] (178). Rochefort returns us to an issue raised in previous chapters: the call for solidarity between oppressed groups; the importance of a horizontal struggle. The need for mothers to recognize a common cause and stand by their children is expressed in *Les Enfants d'abord*:

> Nous ne serons pas libres sans votre aide, et vous n'aurez pas votre liberté sans la nôtre. Lorsque [. . .] vous nous parlerez de personnes à personnes, d'opprimés à opprimés, seulement là nous pourrons affronter ce qui nous ligote ensemble.[9]

> [*Without your help we will not be free, and you will never win your freedom without ours. When [. . .] you speak to us as equals, as one oppressed person to another, then and only then will we be able to face up to the thing that chains us together.*]

Significantly, the words 'on ne parle pas de ces choses', employed specifically in the context of child sexual abuse in *La Porte*, refer in *Les Enfants d'abord* to the broader issue of a common struggle:

> Des complicités qui se nouent quelquefois, des protections mutuelles contre les abus de l'autorité, restent cachées, n'éclatent pas jusqu'à la conscience d'une même oppression. Dans la plupart des cas c'est le silence, 'on ne parle pas de ces choses', la famille d'ailleurs c'est le lieu du non-dit.[10]

> [*Complicities which are sometimes formed, mutual protection against abuses of power, remain hidden; they only burst into view when awareness of a common oppression arises. In most cases there is silence, 'some things are best left unsaid', besides the family is the place where things remain unsaid.*]

Seen in this light, child sexual abuse is merely a symptom—although obviously an extreme one—of a more pervasive process of oppression. By pointing the finger at what is presented as a dangerous societal institution, the nuclear family, Rochefort raises the issue of individual responsibility with respect to both mother and father. How are we to interpret the narrator's exculpatory statement early in the text: 'Tout ça n'est la faute de personne jusqu'à Adam et Eve inclus, avant je ne sais pas' ['None of all this is anybody's fault right back to and including Adam and Eve, before that I don't know'] (12)? Although *La Porte* encourages the reader to view the father as the responsible adult and guilty party, it is also suggested that once established, the traditional nuclear family engenders an abuse of power: 'L'infamie d'état, donnée cadeau à tout homme qui épouse et engendre, pour qu'il en use à son gré' ['Officially recognized depravity, presented gratis to every man who marries and has children, for him to use as he pleases'] (29). The abusive father becomes a mere pawn in the system: 'Il n'a pas pu se retenir d'être le plus fort. Il était prisonnier lui aussi là-haut dans son aire et n'en pouvait pas descendre' ['He couldn't stop himself being the most powerful. He was a prisoner too up there in his eyrie, and he couldn't climb down'] (59). Although Rochefort's suggestion that patriarchal households may be more likely to engender abuse is undoubtedly accurate, it is regrettable that she fails on this occasion to clarify the extent to which parents should be held responsible for their actions. A fictitious letter in *Les Enfants d'abord*, written from the child's perspective and directed at parents, makes the point which should perhaps have been made in *La Porte*:

> Vous n'êtes pas à cent pour cent dans le camp des opprimés, même si un pouvoir vous opprime ailleurs: vous exercez chez vous le seul qui vous est permis. Une part de vous, celle qui a signé la délégation de pouvoirs, est passé de l'autre côté'.[11]

> [*You are not one hundred per cent in the camp of the oppressed, even if you yourself are being oppressed from another quarter: you exercise the only power permitted to you. Part of you, the part which has agreed to the delegation of power, has gone over to the enemy camp.*]

Rochefort's attack on patriarchal institutions nonetheless forms an important part of her vindication of the child, and her second target is traditional Freudian psychoanalysis. Reading Freud some years after she has left home, the narrator is incensed by what she perceives as an attempt to shift the onus of responsibility away from the offending adult and onto the child: 'Naturellement c'est encore la faute des mômes, les vieux s'en sortent toujours blancs comme neige' ['Needless to say it's the kids' fault again, adults come out of it whiter than white'] (13). Rochefort's attack finds its source in the work of Jeffrey Masson, to whom *La Porte* is dedicated, and whose work *The Assault on Truth* (*Le Réel escamoté*) is acknowledged at the end of the novel.[12] A brief exposition of Masson's critical stance is required in order to grasp Rochefort's rather allusive references. In 1886, Freud delivered a paper in which he claimed that neuroses originate in sexual traumas undergone during early childhood or infancy. According to this formulation, the repressed memories of childhood abuse may be reawakened at puberty, giving rise to neurotic symptoms. In *The Aetiology of Hysteria,* Freud states quite unequivocally that real sexual abuse lies at the root of later neurotic symptoms:

> I therefore put forward the thesis that at the bottom of every case of hysteria there are *one or more occurrences of premature sexual experience,* occurrences which belong to the earliest years of childhood but which can be reproduced through the work of psychoanalysis in spite of the intervening decades.[13]

This early theory, which came to be known as the 'seduction' or 'trauma' theory, was not to enjoy a long life-span.[14] Between 1887 and 1903 Freud came increasingly to believe that his patients' tales of premature sexual experiences were in fact fantasies, or the memories of fantasies. By 1905 he had publicly retracted the 'trauma theory'. In its place came the 'drive theory', postulating an innate infantile sexuality and centring on Oedipal fantasies: in the case of the female child, incestuous wishes for the father which formed a normal part of sexual development. Masson and others have condemned what they perceive as dangerous intellectual cowardice on Freud's part: bowing to public pressure and a reluctance to accept that so many fathers might be abusers, Freud turned the tables on the victims, the reality of whose traumatic experiences was henceforth denied.[15]

Rochefort's familiarity with Masson's work is revealed in two sections of *La Porte*: 'Qu'est-ce que je serais devenue' ['What would have become of me'] (13–20), in which the narrator rejects central aspects of Freud's drive theory, and 'Divan à ressorts' ['Spring-loaded-couch'] (130–2), describing her experience of theory put into practice in a (brief) session with a psychoanalyst. With typical scathing humour, the narrator first sets out to debunk a central aspect of the Oedipus complex: penis envy (a process we have already encountered in a rather different context in *Quand tu vas chez les femmes*). Stripping the concept of any symbolic value by yoking it to a list of coveted material acquisitions (a gift-wrapped penis) the narrator forcefully conveys her derisive attitude, effectively dislodging this linchpin of the Oedipus complex:

> Je tombe sur l'envie du pénis. Que je n'ai pas vous pouvez me croire. Non? Bon, c'est votre problème. Moi j'ai envie d'un cheval, d'une décapotable bleue, d'un trois-mâts, de patins, d'un piano, de génie, et d'un tas d'autres choses, toutes rigoureusement non symboliques et votre pénis c'est encore la charrue devant les bœufs, non mais qu'est-ce que c'est ces gens qui savent mieux que moi ce que je veux et pour qui ils se prennent? (14)

[*I come across penis envy. You'll just have to believe me when I tell you I don't have it. No? Fine, that's your problem. Me, I want a horse, a blue convertible, a three-master, skates, a piano, genius, and a whole load of other things, all of them strictly real, not symbolic, and you and your penis are just just one more example of putting the cart before the horse. What is it with these people who know what I want more than I do, and who the hell do they think they are?*]

The Oedipus complex itself is then dismissed with similar briskness: 'Ayant fait ma colère j'expédiai leur pénis par le fond derrière leur œdipe' ['Once I'd thrown my tantrum I binned their penis along with their Oedipus complex'] (14). The problem does not lie in the narrator's unconscious; it stems from the reality of the father's abusive behaviour:

Nom de dieu qu'est-ce que je serais devenue s'il n'y avait pas eu papa!
Ce salaud.
Je venais de m'économiser une psychanalyse.
Papa était une ordure. (14–15)[16]

[*God in heaven what would have become of me if it hadn't been for dad!
The bastard.
I had just saved myself the cost of some psychoanalysis.
Daddy was a piece of shit.*]

In 'Divan à ressorts' the narrator's reservations about psychoanalysis are proven to be well-founded. Few details about the circumstances of her meeting with the analyst are provided, but we can infer that after a period in hospital the narrator is persuaded by the medical staff to seek help in curing what has been diagnosed as an hysterical symptom of shortness of breath: 'Dyspnée. Origine "hystérique"' ['Shortness of breath: hysterical in origin'] (131). Following the pattern of traditional Freudian analysis, she is invited to free-associate, and invents a nightmare in which she is being pursued by a man. The analyst's response follows predictable lines: 'Vous désiriez qu'il vous attrape dit-il, omettant le point d'interrogation' ['You wanted him to catch you, he said, minus a question-mark'] (130). When the narrator points out that not only had she invented the particular episode, but that the man in her past had, in fact, caught her (in other words when she stresses the reality of the event) she is presented with the anticipated Oedipal interpretation: 'Rêve, rêverie [. . .] le fantasme est toujours l'expression d'un désir' ['Dream or daydream, a fantasy is always an form of wish-fulfilment'] (130).

The analyst's next contribution highlights another aspect of Freud's later stance which is strongly criticized by Masson: the concept of psychic reality: 'Ce qui compte c'est comment vous avez vécu cet amour' ['What matters is how you experienced this love'] (130). In the context of his rejection of the 'trauma theory' Freud pointed to 'the certain insight that there are no indications of reality in the unconscious, so that one cannot distinguish between truth and fiction that has been cathected with affect'.[17] In the *Introductory Lectures on Psycho-Analysis* he restates his belief that female children's reports of sexual relations with their fathers are fantasies, adding: 'Up to the present we have not succeeded in pointing to any difference in the consequences, whether phantasy or reality had had the greater share in these events of childhood.'[18] In an earlier section of the novel, 'Les Bienfaits du malheur', the narrator of *La Porte* directs her ironic criticisms at the concept of psychic reality: 'La notion, fort en honneur, de "réalité psychique" (ou irréalité de la réalité): les désastres, ce n'est rien, tout est dans comment on prend ça' ['The very popular concept of "psychic reality" (otherwise known as the unreality of reality): disasters are unimportant; what matters is how you react to them'] (91).[19] In 'Divan à ressorts' the analyst's suggestion that the reality of the abuse is of little consequence proves to be the final straw. The narrator flees, effecting a rapid cure of her symptom of breathlessness by sheer dint of hard running.

The impact of the first-person narrative perspective once again plays an important part in the reader's response to these sections. Having had access to a first-hand account of the horrors of the narrator's struggle against sexual abuse, we are, in a sense, 'set up' to respond negatively to the analyst's apparent indifference to the reality of the past situation. His refusal to believe in the abuse confirms the father's claim that the narrator's story would be discredited: 'Je dirai que c'est toi qui l'as cherché et c'est moi qu'on croira, pas toi. On ne croit pas les enfants' ['I'll say that it was you that came looking for it and it's me they'll believe, not you. People never believe what children say'] (102). The narrator is disempowered by both father and analyst. It is no coincidence that she expresses her doubts about seeing a psychoanalyst in terms which link the two figures of authority: 'Où fallait-il que j'en sois rendue pour atterrir chez cet acharné d'amour filial, *j'avais lu papa Freud pourtant*' ['What must I have come to, to land up with this filial love fanatic, *it wasn't as if I hadn't read my daddy Freud*] (131, my italics). Yet in some respects the narrator's point of view is unnecessarily extreme. As the facts are presented, an adherence to the drive theory would seem to preclude any possibility of belief in the reality of child sexual abuse. In fact, the two are by no means mutually exclusive. Furthermore, Rochefort's minimalist portrayal of the analytic 'session' borders on the caricatural. It is to be hoped that practising analysts today would approach the subject with rather more circumspection.[20]

This last remark, however, touches on a crucial issue. Although the drive theory is not incompatible with a belief in the reality of child sexual abuse, it has been suggested that in terms of psychoanalytic practice, Freud's later theory could have a pernicious effect. Even though the analyst may claim that pragmatic and psychic reality cannot be differentiated, to confront the client/patient with this claim may well give rise to seriously detrimental repercussions:

> To tell someone who has suffered the effects of a childhood filled with sexual violence that it does not matter whether his memories are anchored in reality or not is to do further violence to that person and is bound to have a pernicious effect. A real memory demands some form of validation from the outside world—denial of those memories by others can lead to a break with reality, and a psychosis. The lack of interest in a person's store of personal memories does violence to the integrity of that person.[21]

In addition, Herman points out that Freudian theories might contribute to the perpetuation of another dangerous myth: that children lie about sexual abuse.[22] The damaging consequences of this myth are dramatized later in the text when Jason, a male abuse victim, tells of his reluctance to speak out about his father's abuse: 'Et me tenir devant lui bien serré: l'affection. Mais d'où j'étais placé je pouvais la mesurer son affection. Seulement j'étais le seul au courant et si j'avais cafté je me serais fait appeler œdipe' ['Holding me tightly in front of him: proof of his affection. Except that from where I was sitting I could measure the extent of his affection. But I was the only one in the know, and if I'd told, I'd just have had Oedipus thrown in my face'] (225). Of course if children's reports of sexual abuse are dismissed as fantasy, the abuser avoids both detection and punishment. The narrator of *La Porte* finds peace only when her father dies.[23] The 1990s have, of course, witnessed a further development with the recognition of the so-called False Memory Syndrome. In an ironic twist, analysts and therapists are now accused alongside their patients, whose memories of sexual abuse are rejected as concoctions of fantasies confused with facts.

In Part I of *Archaos* we saw Rochefort's rejection of patriarchal Christianity. The same target is isolated in *Les Enfants d'abord* ('Le conditionnement judéo-chrétien est toujours là [. . .]. Dieu s'appelle la Morale et dit la même chose: bien, mal, soumission à la loi du père ou faute' ['Judeo-Christian conditioning is always present [. . .]. God is Morality and both say the same thing: good, evil, submit to the law of the father or you're guilty']²⁴) and *La Porte du fond*. Although Rochefort does not cite any sources in this instance, her criticisms are closely aligned with the work of writers such as Florence Rush and Alice Miller. In her condemnation of Freud's shift of position, Miller points to the dangerous power exerted by the Fourth Commandment: Freud, she suggests, retracted his trauma theory because of his reluctance to stigmatize fathers as abusers.²⁵ Miller goes on to equate the individual father with God the Father, seeing in both 'an autocratic ruler [who] demands perfect obedience'.²⁶ In *La Porte* the parallel is brought out when the young narrator attempts to recite the Lord's Prayer: 'Notre Père! Qui êtes aux cieux! Que votre volonté soit faite! Merde. Sur la Terre comme au ciel, merde!' ['Our Father! Who art in heaven! Thy will be done! Shit. On earth as it is in heaven, shit!'] (83). A similar dilemma is faced when she attends confession:

> Donc j'entre dans la boîte et si vous n'êtes pas au courant le premier mot à dire c'est: 'Mon Père'—merde. Le deuxième: 'Pardonnez-moi'—et de quoi s'il vous plaît! Le suivant: 'J'ai péché'—ça va pas non? Et enfin: 'C'est ma fautes [*sic*]'—c'est le bouquet! Alors j'ai glissé discrètement de là et le mec a pas entendu un son. (83)

> [*I enter the confessional and if you're not familiar with the set-up the first thing you have to say is 'Father'—shit. The second thing is 'Forgive me'— and for what, I ask you! And then, 'I have sinned'—you're kidding or what? And finally, 'Mea culpa'—well that's the limit! So I slipped discreetly out of there and the guy never heard a sound.*]

Miller cites the story of Job as a typical example of an autocratic F/father's arbitrary exercising of power and demand for obedience.²⁷ In *La Porte,* the narrator draws a similar parallel: 'Je devins dépouillée comme Job [. . .]. Donné repris repris repris repris' ['I was stripped of everything, like Job [. . .]. Given taken taken taken taken'] (139). Her words (referring to her father's withdrawal of the gifts with which he had sought to bribe her) echo Job's submission to the Father:

> At this Job stood up and rent his cloak; then he shaved his head and fell prostrate on the ground, saying: Naked I came from the womb, naked I shall return whence I came. The Lord gives and the Lord takes away; blessed be the name of the Lord. (Job 1: 20–22)

One of the narrator's attempts to cope with the abuse takes the form of role-play, and her varied repertoire includes the proverbial 'Femme vertueuse'. Believing that she might defuse the situation by producing 'le

Théâtre de la Perfection' (playing the perfect woman: 'Qui peut trouver une femme vertueuse?' ['Who can find a virtuous wife?'] p. 144), she underlines the fact that patriarchal attitudes find their roots in the Bible with typical humour and irreverence:

> Et que fait-elle la Femme Vertueuse, sur le lieu du crime? 'Elle met la main à la quenouille'? 'Ses doigts tiennent le fuseau'? ainsi dit le Livre, Proverbes, 31, 19, qu'est-ce que c'est cochon ce bouquin vu du dessous, et je suppute que dans son enfance aux sources même du patriarcat elle y était si ça se trouve passée au droit de cuissage la pauvre môme, qui sait si ce n'est ce qui l'a acculée à la Vertu. D'une poigne de fer. (145)

> [*And what precisely is this Virtuous Woman doing at the scene of the crime? 'She puts her hands to the distaff'? 'Her fingers grasp the spindle'? so says the Holy Book, Proverbs, 31, 19, what an incredibly smutty book it is seen from a certain angle, and I dare say that in her childhood, close to the very sources of patriarchy, she fell prey to the droit du seigneur poor kid, who knows if that's not what drove her to her Virtuous ways. Guided by a grip of iron.*]

Rochefort's subversion of Christianity is more subtly conveyed by her use of religious imagery. More specifically, she reminds readers of the religious roots of patriarchy by bringing together references to the Bible and sexual abuse. Referring to 'l'infamie' (the father's abusive behaviour), the narrator describes its abrupt appearance and devastating conse-quences in terms of Old Testament plagues: 'Sa survenance est comme les sauterelles, les épidémies de peste: elle apparaît' ['It arrives like locusts, plagues: it just appears'] (29). The punishment meted out by the father is superimposed upon that inflicted by the Father. Alluding to a future period when she would feel able to talk about her experiences, the narrator highlights religious hypocrisy by juxtapositioning incest and religious ceremony: 'Des temps viendraient [. . .] où, quand on m'aura [*sic*] trop échauffé les oreilles avec des Le Père, La Mère très extrêmement Majuscules et Sacrés, je laisserai [*sic*] tomber paisiblement dans le bénitier avec un bon sourire:—Moi, j'avais un père incestueux' ['The time would come when after years of ear-bending on the subject of Mother and Father complete with sacred capital letters, I would calmly drop the following words into the font with a happy smile: "I had an incestuous father you know"'] (169).

In *The Best Kept Secret,* Rush singles out Christian and Judaic laws which stated that children were deemed to be the possession of their fathers.[28] The rape of a young girl, she points out, was considered not as a crime upon the person of the girl, but as an infringement upon the father's rights of ownership: 'If a man took an unbetrothed girl's virginity without her father's permission, the culprit had infringed upon another man's property, committed a civil crime which could be erased by payment to the father.'[29] Herman, following similar lines, notes that the biblical incest taboo did not extend to father–daughter relations because such a form of abuse did not involve the violation of another man's property:

> What is prohibited is the sexual use of those women who, in one manner or another, already belong to other relatives. Every man is thus expressly forbidden to take the daughter of his kinsmen, but only by implication is he forbidden to take his own daughters. The patriarchal God sees fit to pass over father–daughter incest in silence.[30]

The modern day equivalent of such patriarchal notions of ownership and possession is exemplified in *La Porte* by the abusing father, whose language is rapidly stripped down to a stark statement of power: 'Tu m'appartiens. Tu me dois la vie (son sale style pompeux). Je peux faire de toi ce que je veux. Je peux te violer comme je veux. Tu vois?' ['You belong to me. You owe me your life (his lousy pomposity). I can do what I want with you. I can rape you when and if I want. See?'] (197). Avatar, we might recall, addresses his daughter in similar terms: 'Je vous ai donné la vie, dit le roi [. . .]. Elle m'appartient' ['I gave you life, said the king [. . .]. It belongs to me'] (*Archaos*, p. 48).

Whether the focus falls on the individual father or on patriarchal institutions, *La Porte* clearly suggests that the child is not responsible for the sexual abuse, if by this we mean that she can neither be blamed in any way, nor called to account as either instigator or willing participant. Rochefort, however, is treading a potentially hazardous path, for if we consider the word 'responsible' to indicate a capacity to consent, a degree of moral autonomy, then *La Porte*—and indeed the whole corpus of the author's work—insists on the responsibility of the child. To grasp this distinction we need to examine another dimension of the text, the narrator's relationship with her uncle Paul, and it is here that textual structures play a crucial part. As was suggested above in Chapter 2, *La Porte* bears some similarity to *Les Petits Enfants du siècle* as regards the representation of a sexual relationship between an adult and child: Josyane and Guido; the narrator of *La Porte* and her uncle Paul.

From the narrator's point of view, as for Josyane, her relationship with her uncle is unequivocally a positive one. Her uncle is the only person who tries to see things from her perspective, and the first individual with whom she can establish any meaningful degree of communication. It is he who asks the crucial question 'ça va?' ['are you okay?'], and listens 'comme s'il se souciait vraiment de ma réponse' ['as if he was genuinely interested in my reply'] (146). When the response comes in the negative, the narrator glories in this first breaking of silence, stating, albeit a little ironically, 'ça c'est du dialogue' ['now that's dialogue'], and 'une grande confidence. Ma première' ['a huge secret shared. My first one'] (147). The uncle is thus set up in strong contrast both to the abusive father, who imposes his point of view, and to the mother, who apparently fails to see ('j'habite un monde d'aveugles' ['I live in a world full of blind people'] p. 133), and fails equally to pick up on the narrator's distress signals. The only exchange the narrator can establish with her mother is the 'dialogue de muettes' ['dialogue of the dumb'] (176–8). Whereas the father threatens the child with incarceration ('je peux te faire enfermer chez les fous' ['I can have you locked up in an asylum'] p. 205), Paul recognizes her as the only sane member of an insane household: 'Ils veulent m'emmener chez le psychiatre. Et tu sais, une fois là . . . —Quoi? mais ils sont dingues! C'est eux qui le sont oui, y a pas plus sain esprit que toi!' ['"They want to take me to a psychiatrist. And you know, once you're there. . ." "What? they're crazy! They're the crazy ones, you're the sanest person I know!"'] (183).

When the relationship develops beyond the platonic it is Paul who initiates the change, but immediately bows to the narrator's request to allow her to make any subsequent physical overtures, thereby reversing the father–daughter situation. Only two pages after uncle and niece declare their mutual love, the abusing father explicitly separates love and desire: 'Il n'y a aucun rapport entre ça et les sentiments. Les sentiments c'est de l'illusion. Ça, c'est la réalité, retiens l'idée elle pourra te servir' ['There's no connection between that and emotions. Emotions are just illusions. This is what's real, bear that in mind, it might come in useful'] (185).[31] The father, identified as the spider, the Ogre, Caesar, Hitler, ruler and possessor, is set against Paul, dubbed the narrator's 'chemin de la rédemption' ['path to redemption'] (219). Whereas the father shatters the integrity of the narrator's person, the uncle restores her to wholeness: 'Mais: il y avait un autre monde. A celui-ci j'appartenais non en pièces détachées, mais au grand complet' ['But another world existed. In this world I was complete, not a whole lot of body parts'] (219). Furthermore, intertextual allusions to both *Archaos* and *Les Enfants d'abord* inscribe Paul as a positive figure.

In Chapter 4 we saw that Christophe, setting out to discover a 'pays lointain', discovered through his love for Thomas that a literal journey was unnecessary, that the boundaries which had to be crossed were those of inner prejudice. Paul expresses his feelings for the narrator of *La Porte* in similar terms: 'Comme, comme un pays. Perdu oublié. Où tu me ramènes' ['Like, like a country. Lost, or forgotten. A country you take me back to'] (194). The narrator herself refers to the relationship in terms of a lost paradise reminiscent of the sin-free world of Archaos: 'un paradis [. . .] très inconforme, avec permission de goûter au fruit de l'Arbre de Vie' ['a very unconventional paradise where you're allowed to taste of the fruit of the tree of life'] (195).[32] The relationship between uncle and niece is further described by the narrator in terms which remind us of the utopic *Archaos*, where sexual relationships were characterized by the passive and non-orgasmic 'désir-désirant': 'l'inassouvissement en fût la règle et je dirai aujourd'hui l'essence, cette force qui nous tenait embrassés me transportait dans une réalité radicale' ['unfulfilled desire was the rule and today I'd say was the very essence of the relationship, this force which kept us in each others' arms transported me into a radically different world'] (219). Finally, in Chapter 7 we saw that in *Les Enfants d'abord* the figure of the uncle assumed a metaphorical status, representing a liberating chance encounter which could free the child from adult-imposed views ('Un seul oncle farfelu de passage réussit sans y penser à foutre par terre tout un édifice d'abêtissement' ['a casual encounter with an eccentric uncle is all it takes to stuff up a whole structure geared to reducing people to imbecility]' p. 97).

By establishing this powerful contrast between the two relationships—father and daughter; uncle and niece—Rochefort prepares the reader to accept a position which is made explicit later in the text: 'Le malheur n'est pas le sexe. Et pas non plus l'inceste. Le malheur c'est le Patron' ['It's not sex that's the problem. And it's not incest. The problem is Power'] (226). Readers are faced with a difficult choice: either they must accept the narrator's point of view, and thus disregard the incest taboo, or they must consciously read against the grain of the text, rejecting the narrator's point of view as they may reject Josyane's view of her sexual relationship with Guido in *Les Petits Enfants du siècle*.[33] Either way, they are forced to confront their own ethical stance. More than this, readers are invited to accept a position we have already encountered in previous chapters: that the child, although a minor, is responsible; that she has the capacity, and the right, to consent in a sexual relationship. This point of view is emphasized in an exchange between Paul and the narrator, in the course of which the uncle expresses doubts which are probably shared by the reader, whose response Rochefort thus once again pre-empts:

—Toi tu n'es pas, moi je suis. . .
—Adulte, grand, fort, averti. Responsable! Et moi je suis petite faible ignorante pure naïve candide. . .

228

—Non non n'en jette plus, essaye-t-il en vain de me couper le sifflet mais je suis fâchée.

—Nous ne sommes pas égaux hein? et toi tu m'as détournée pervertie dépravée corrompue. . .

—Pitié, pouce! je m'incline. Devant la richesse de ton vocabulaire. (208)

[*'You aren't, and I am. . .'*
'Grown up, big, strong, experienced. Responsible! And I'm just small weak ignorant pure naive ingenuous. . .'
'Enough, stop,' he tried to cut me off but I was angry.
'We're not equal, right? and you've led me astray, perverted me, depraved me, corrupted me. . .'
'Stop, truce! I give up. I submit to the wealth of your vocabulary.']

Although the position adopted by the narrator towards incest is an extreme one, it is consonant with Rochefort's own views as witnessed in *Archaos* (Onagre and Govan), and expressed in *Les Enfants d'abord*, in which she laments the fact that incest, which in itself should not be condemned, necessarily involves an abuse of power in the context of parent–child relationships:

On ne parlerait pas de l'inceste parents–enfants, car il n'est qu'un cas particulier de la relation adulte–enfant qui est l'une des plus riches lorsqu'elle est vraiment réciproque, on n'en parlerait pas, n'était-ce ce sacré rapport de forces. [. . .] Manifeste ou non, le rapport de pouvoir est là, dès lors l'inceste est du viol. Dommage.[34]

[*Parent–child incest would not be an issue, because it is merely a specific example of the adult–child relationship in general, which is one of the richest relationships there is, when it is really reciprocal. It would not be an issue were it not for the damned question of power. Overt or not, that power imbalance is there, and because of it incest becomes rape. Pity.*]

The views of the narrator in *La Porte* articulated in the exchange with Paul echo those expressed by the author in *Les Enfants d'abord*, in which she objects to the legal notion of 'détournement de mineur' ['corruption of a minor']:

Les délits et crimes commis contre les enfants sont définis par les adultes, non par les enfants qui les ont subis. Ainsi, avec meurtre et sévices, on trouve: 'attentat à la pudeur'—non *sa* pudeur, et 'détournement de mineur', *le mineur fût-il consentant.*[35]

[*Offenses and crimes committed against children are defined by adults, not by the children who have suffered them. Thus we find 'indecent assault' alongside murder and cruelty. Not 'assault on child x'. And we find 'corruption of a minor', even when that minor is a consenting party.*]

Rochefort places the reader of *La Porte* in an invidious position. To read against the narrator in *La Porte* is to be situated on the side of those who, like the father and psychoanalyst, claim to know what is best; those who impose their point of view and thereby disempower the child.

The reading of this dimension of *La Porte* is, however, more complex than has so far been suggested. It may be that we read against the narrator not because we bring to the text prejudices concerning incest or the appropriate age of consent, but because we feel that the narrator fails to perceive the situation correctly. Our resistance to the first-person perspective may be based on two factors: extra-textual information and, more crucially, certain intratextual elements. Writers on child sexual abuse point out that one of the consequences of abuse may be the sexualizing of the abuse victim's interaction with other adults. Salter suggests that victims of abuse frequently trade sex for affection or even confuse the two. The behaviour of an adult who accepts a sexual relationship in these circumstances is deemed to be inappropriate. Bearing this information in mind, the narrator's relationship with her uncle may be seen not, as she suggests, as one between equals, but of a child who has been scarred by abuse, seeking affection which should have been freely given. The fact that the narrator's thoughts when she is with her uncle turn to Babet, the concierge who had given her the unconditional love she failed to receive from her parents, supports this line of approach: 'Je le fais adosser à l'énorme tronc, j'enfouis ma figure dans sa poitrine. Voilà. Je suis bien. Il y avait si longtemps [. . .]. oh Babet' ['I make him lean up against its huge trunk, and I bury my head against his chest. There. That's good. It's been so long [. . .]. oh Babet'] (192). However, we must also remember that the narrator, as (consenting) adult, looking back on the relationship, still perceives it as beneficial.

Reading against the narrator in the case just examined means bringing extra-textual knowledge to bear, but what if the text itself allows such a reading? So far it has been suggested that the narrator's views are also the author's. In fact, readers may distinguish between the narrator and implied author of the text; they may, in other words, identify the narrator as unreliable. Textual structures do, indeed, invite readers to compare father and uncle, but the consequences which can be drawn from the comparison are highly ambiguous, and the uncle's words and actions may be interpreted in a more sinister light. When Paul refuses to drive into the countryside with his niece on the grounds that the sexual nature of the relationship would develop as a consequence, does he reveal a genuine desire to prevent this development, or is he, like the father, afraid of possible legal repercussions?[36] After all, the father too stops short of sexual intercourse—'Il n'y a que les brutes et les idiots qui consomment entièrement' ['Only idiots go the whole way']—and his motives are revealed by the narrator: 'Ouais, et les malins ne laissent pas de traces' ['Yes, and the smart guys don't leave any traces'] (72). The narrator's uncle states he loves her, but so does the father—'Je t'aimais tu sais' ['I loved you, you know'] (236). Again, the text invites a comparison of the two relationships, but does the parallel emphasize the difference between the two male adults, or hint at their similarity? Both characters state that they cannot stop themselves from relating to the child in a sexual manner: 'Je ne devrais pas t'aimer de cette façon mais je n'y peux rien' ['I shouldn't love you this way but I can't help it'] (208, the uncle); 'Moi, dit-il, j'ai besoin de ça. C'est plus fort que moi que veux-tu. C'est ma façon de t'aimer si tu tiens à des enjolivements' ['I need it, he said, it's stronger than I am, what do you expect. It's my way of showing you that I love you, if you go for such sentimentalities'] (205, the father).

If doubts are not initially raised by these parallels, then they may well be raised retrospectively, at that point in the reading when an outside view of Paul is supplied for the first time. When the relationship has been uncovered, Paul's wife provides a stunning indictment of her husband: 'Et si tu crois que tu es la première ah ah je le connais moi je vis avec pour mon malheur c'est un coutumier du truc la chair fraîche il aime ça même on l'a déjà pris la main dans le sac' ['And if you think you're the first, well guess again! I know him, I live with him more's the pity, he's always at it, he likes them young, that's what he's after, he's even been caught at it!'] (231). Whilst it may be that we are intended to read against this point of view, to perceive this as the misguided view of yet another adult, there is little doubt that the remark affects our interpretation of events. Throughout the text it is the father who has been referred to as 'l'Ogre', yet here Paul is suddenly revealed as the man with a taste for 'chair fraîche'. All at once, his previous acceptance of a passive role ('C'est tout à fait délicieux' ['It's quite delicious'] p. 193) may be perceived not in terms of a beneficial reversal of roles but as a perverted pleasure. Where Paul's confession that he was a thoroughly nasty piece of work ('Un sale type. Je drague. Je rend ma femme malheureuse et je m'en tape' ['I'm a nasty piece of work. I chase women. I make my wife miserable and I don't give a damn'] p. 194) may initially be read as an indication of his openness, it may retrospectively be perceived as a manipulative abnegation of responsibility (this is what I'm like; the choice is yours).

As we can see, *La Porte* is open to a reading which inculpates the uncle alongside the father as an abuser, and a subtle one, of his position. The problematic notion of responsibility is forcefully brought to our attention: should the relationship with Paul be considered in terms of intention or consequence; from the point of view of the uncle and his dubious motives, or from that of the narrator, who stresses the beneficial effects of the relationship? Is the child responsible, as she claims, and able to consent in a sexual relationship with an adult, or should she, as criminal law might suggest, be protected from her own immaturity? In *Les Enfants d'abord*, Rochefort suggests that protection for the child is acceptable only when actively solicited: 'Quand on aura besoin de protection, on vous appellera' ['When we need help we'll ask for it'] (110). In *La Porte*, however, we see all too clearly that abusers, or oppressors, may quite simply prove to be too strong or, more worryingly, too subtle, to be resisted. Whilst it is all very well to suggest that those in power will inevitably show their hand, will push their luck too far, and thereby precipitate an awareness in the oppressed which can, in turn, start the struggle for freedom, we are perhaps left wondering whether this is always necessarily the case, and whether oppression might not operate more subtly, and thereby more effectively in many cases.

CONCLUSION

Looking Forward to Rochefort
Discourse, Identity, Truth

The final section of the introduction to this study pointed to the centrality of language in Rochefort's work. By this stage the reader should also be aware that language is linked to another key theme explored in the novels, and that is identity. Throughout the preceding chapters we have seen how Rochefort's protagonists, particularly women, children, and those whose sexuality goes against societal 'norms', seek to escape the oppressive dictates of what the author refers to as the language of the dominant ideology. The struggle against such prescripted and thus prescriptive language is primarily a struggle against imposed identities, against what Rochefort refers to as labels, schemata, ready-made 'histoires'. Although Rochefort uses the terminology of class struggle and ideology, I would like to close this study by suggesting that her work lends itself to an analysis articulated around discourse, or more accurately, discourses, the power of which, as Michel Foucault has famously claimed, permeates society, criss-crossing it in a network of power-relations which cannot be laid at the door of a single so-called ruling-class.[1]

Considered from this perspective, Rochefort's texts can be seen to demystify and oppose the circumscriptive and exclusionary nature of dominant discourses. Children are represented as more, or other, than the medical, legal, and educational discourses which seek to deny their sexuality and curb their autonomy. The medical discourse which would represent independent women as neurotic, if not crazed, as beset by an unresolved Oedipus complex or suffering from a worrying penis envy, is undermined alongside the legal discourse which would criminalize gay men. Reading Rochefort in terms of discourse would also allow us to conceptualize a central aspect of her work, and that is resistance to oppression. Mills points out that although the concepts of ideology and class focus on oppressive power relations and the centrality of 'the revolutionary subject', the source of such revolutionary action may be difficult to locate:

It is sometimes hard to understand how subjects can develop a revolutionary consciousness, how they can resist oppression. Foucault argues that resistance is already contained within the notion of power: 'Where there is power there is resistance.'[2]

Discourses and the power relations from which they stem, and which they represent, 'produce forms of subjectivity and behaviour rather than simply repressing them'.[3] Such a process is manifested throughout Rochefort's work, from the very first struggle between Renaud and Geneviève in *Le Repos du guerrier*, to the young child's revolt against her father's abuse in *La Porte du fond*. Unfortunately, these are areas which must be explored further at some future time. I would like to limit myself here to opening up the discussion as it relates to two key aspects of Rochefort's work: first, her representation of sexuality, and second, her apparent belief in the existence of a transcendent truth.

As we have seen, Rochefort's texts contest both essentialist and hetero-sexist approaches to sexuality. More than this, I believe that her writing can be aligned with, and indeed anticipates, a body of theory and political practice which emerged in the late 1980s: Rochefort's work, I would suggest, is thoroughly 'queer'. A broad definition reveals from the outset that most, if not all, of Rochefort's protagonists might be designated 'queer':

> In its latest incarnation, and as it is deployed by 'queer activists' and 'queer theorists,' the term 'queer' signifies not only those who mark themselves as gay or lesbian, but anyone whose proclivities, practices, or sympathies defy the strictures of the dominant sex/gender/sexual identity system.[4]

Queer theory and politics, which emerged as a reaction against the entrenched identity politics of gay and lesbian studies and politics in the 1970s and early 1980s, are, like Rochefort's own work, 'marked by a resistance to being labelled, a suspicion of constraining sexual categories, and a greater appreciation for fluidity of sexual expression'.[5] Queer theory seeks to dismantle and reveal the workings of the binaries of the dominant sex-gender system whereby subjects must identify themselves as either male or female, either masculine or feminine, either straight or gay. Any and all identity labels are regarded with suspicion: to identify oneself as 'gay', be it in the name of affirmatory politics and collective action, is inevitably to replicate the dominant discourse's move to define what is 'normal' and what 'deviant'; it leads to the exclusion and repression of difference; it imposes normalizing judgements on desire.[6] Any identity constructions 'function as templates defining selves and behaviors and therefore excluding a range of possible ways to frame the self, body, desires, actions, and social relations'.[7]

Read in the light of such statements the 'queerness' of Rochefort's work is striking. We might, for example, recall the androgynous Rafaele in *Le Repos du guerrier*; the insistent rejection of the identity-tags 'lesbian' and 'gay' in *Les Stances à Sophie* and *Printemps au parking*, or the 'mise en abyme' in the latter text representing an unpredictable, zigzagging desire; the fluidity of the polysexuality of *Archaos* which seeks to embrace any and all (consensual) expressions of desire; the young boy David's rejection of the label 'male', or Régina's and Grâce's rejection of the category 'female' in *Encore heureux qu'on va vers l'été*. Rochefort's characters experience a desire which operates beyond sex or gender identity categories. 'Normal' is no longer a term set up in opposition to 'deviant'; 'normal' is quite simply the expression, and fulfilment, of desire. One further point should serve to situate Rochefort's writing in the 'queer' camp. An insistence on identity categories may lead to a dangerous re-hierarchization, a 'my-group-first identity politics' or 'turf war'.[8] Whilst this scenario is played out most obviously in *Quand tu vas chez les femmes*, in which the proposed March of the Oppressed leads to parodic attempts to line groups up in order of the severity of oppression suffered, the dangers of identity politics are revealed as early as *Les Enfants d'abord*, in which Rochefort calls for a coalition between children and women. For 'queer' theorists, as for Rochefort, political action need not, and indeed must not, result in the re-establishment of hierarchical power structures. As Phelan suggests in *Playing with Fire: Queer Politics, Queer Theories*: 'diversity of identities must necessitate chains of articulation, not reflect familiar hierarchies of oppression'.[9] The insistence on such horizontal political coalitions runs throughout Rochefort's work.

One phrase is repeated several times in Rochefort's novels, and that is 'ce qui est vrai' ['what is real/true']. This phrase, usually linked to the experience of passion, refers more broadly to those areas of human experience which, in some way, exceed or escape from society's dominant discourses, break free from any labels or categories. But can truth exist beyond language? Certainly it appears that Rochefort's work parts company with Foucault on this matter: 'truth, for Foucault, is not something intrinsic to an utterance, nor is it an ideal abstract quality to which humans aspire'.[10] Truth is not transcendent but political; it is the product of discourses which operate in any society, discourses which promote certain forms of knowledge as true whilst excluding others as false. Perhaps it is Rochefort's awareness of this that leads her to employ the language of science fiction in so many of her works, for truth as she conceives it cannot exist in our society, our world. Thus truth in

Rochefort's novelistic universe can be found on the alien planet Mars (*Les Petits Enfants, Printemps au parking*); it operates in another dimension (*Encore heureux, Archaos*). In the final analysis it may be that Rochefort is an idealist, a utopist, but utopia, as we have learned, need not be regarded merely as an impossible dream: it may, quite simply, point to a better way of living, a hope for the future.

The narrator of *La Porte du fond*, herself the author of a play with the same title, reflects upon the disastrous opening-night audience's response (a silent, rapid exit): 'On les avait pris en traître. On ne leur avait pas tout mâché d'avance. Plutôt, on leur savait gré d'avoir, à notre expériment-ation sur eux, si clairement répondu, et donné leur verdict: "On ne parle pas de ces choses"' ['We'd caught them off guard. We hadn't spoon-fed them. In fact, we were grateful to them for having responded so clearly to our little experiment, for having given their verdict: "Some things aren't open to discussion"']. By luring readers into agreement or disagreement, by repeatedly precipitating an examination of our beliefs, forcing us to confront our values, preconceptions, acts of categorization, and our very language, Rochefort's writing leads us along a path towards 'conscience' and truth.

For forty years Rochefort spoke out on controversial issues. I hope that this study will help to cultivate a more enlightened audience for her work.

Appendix

THE NOVELS OF CHRISTIANE ROCHEFORT: SALES FIGURES

The following figures were supplied by Grasset and Livre de Poche, 1996:

Title and publication date	Grasset sales	Livre de Poche sales	Total sales
Le Repos du guerrier (1958)	*126,000*	*845,000*	*971,000*
Les Petits Enfants du siècle (1961)	*66,000*	*1,480,000*	*1,546,000*
Les Stances à Sophie (1963)	*93,000*	*561,000*	*654,000*
Une Rose pour Morrison (1966)	*24,000*	*38,000*	*62,000*
Printemps au parking (1969)	*56,000*	*266,000*	*322,000*
Archaos, ou le jardin étincelant (1972)	*40,000*	*69,000*	*109,000*
Encore heureux qu'on va vers l'été (1975)	*57,000*	*215,000*	*272,000*
Quand tu vas chez les femmes (1982)	*27,000*	*52,000*	*79,000*
La Porte du fond (1988)	*80,000*	*42,000*	*122,000*

Total sales figure for 9 novels: 4,137,000.

Notes to Chapters

All books are published in Paris unless stated otherwise.

Notes to Introduction

1. Radioscopie de Jacques Chancel avec Christiane Rochefort (Radio France: 1976).
2. All translations in this volume are the author's.
3. *Dictionnnaire Bordas de littérature française*, ed. H. le Maître (Bordas: 1994). *Le Repos du guerrier* is identified as Rochefort's first novel in both *French Women Writers: A Bio-Bibliographical Source Book* eds E. Sartori and D. Zimmerman (New York & London: Greenwood Press, 1991) and *The New Oxford Companion to Literature in French*, ed. P. France (Oxford: Clarendon Press, 1995), as well as all articles on Rochefort to date. *Cendres et or* is the only one of Rochefort's novels not held by the British Library or listed in the Library of Congress catalogue.
4. Although the title-page bears the word 'roman', the first person pronoun clearly refers to Rochefort herself, as references to the authorship of *Le Repos du guerrier* (p. 67) and *Archaos* (p. 69) indicate.
5. M. Herz, 'Christiane Rochefort', in *French Women Writers: A Bio-Bibliographical Source Book*, pp. 369–70.
6. For further details of the French feminist movement in France, see C. Duchen, *Feminism in France* (London, Boston & Henley: Routledge, 1986).
7. J. Forbes and M. Kelly, *French Cultural Studies* (Oxford: Oxford UP, 1995) pp. 144–5.
8. Raymond Williams, *Keywords: A Vocabulary of Culture and Society* (London: Fontana, 1976), cited in A. Easthope *Literary into Cultural Studies* (London and New York: Routledge, 1991), p. 76. For a useful discussion of the shifting definitions of popular culture in France, see B. Rigby, *Popular Culture in Modern France* (London & New York: Routledge, 1991).
9. J. Forbes and M. Kelly, op. cit., p. 144.
10. D. Strinati, *An Introduction to Theories of Popular Culture* (London and New York: Routledge, 1995).
11. Ibid. p. 165. For a full discussion and critique of Gramsci's concept of hegemony, see pp. 165–75.
12. J. Fiske, *Understanding Popular Culture* (London & New York: Routledge, 1989). For a critique of populist approaches to cultural studies, see Strinati pp. 255–60.
13. M. Atack and P. Powrie (eds), *Contemporary French Fiction by Women* (Manchester: Manchester UP, 1990), p. 3.

14. A. Jardine and A. Menke, 'Exploding the issue: "French" "Women" "Writers" and "the Canon"?', *Yale French Studies*, no. 75, 1988, p. 256.
15. E. Marks and I. de Courtivron, *New French Feminisms* (Brighton, Sussex: The Harvester Press, 1981), pp. 184–5; C. Arsène, 'The Privilege of Consciousness' [interview with Rochefort], in E. Marks and G. Stamboulian (eds), *Homosexualities in French Literature* (Ithaca & London: Cornell UP, 1979), p. 102.
16. J. Savigneau, 'Médicis: Christiane Rochefort pour *La Porte du fond*', *Le Monde*, no. 1330, 23 nov. 1988, p. 46.
17. Herz, op. cit., p. 377. Herz inexplicably omits Nilsson, Loffredo and Holmes from her rather eclectic survey of criticism (and alters Ophir's name to 'Offrir').
18. Atack and Powrie, op. cit., p. 4.
19. Marks and de Courtivron, op. cit., p. 183; M. Crochet, 'Entretien avec Christiane Rochefort', *French Review*, vol. 54, no. 3 (1980–1), p. 428.
20. V. Quinn, 'Literary Criticism', in A. Medhurst and S. Munt, *Lesbian and Gay Studies: A Critical Introduction* (London & Washington: Cassell, 1997), p. 43 and p. 50.
21. Fiske, op. cit., p. 139.
22. Easthope, op. cit., p. 58.
23. Fiske, op. cit., p. 130.
24. Crochet, art. cit., p. 431.
25. Arsène, op. cit., pp. 102–3.
26. Rigby, op. cit., p. 7.
27. Forbes and Kelly, op. cit., p. 265.
28. D. Ager, *Sociolinguistics and Contemporary French* (Cambridge & New York: Cambridge UP, 1990), p. 218.
29. Forbes and Kelly, op. cit., pp. 265–6.
30. Fiske, op. cit., p. 106.
31. For a discussion of the 'bande dessinée' and popular singer-songwriters, see Kelly and Forbes, op. cit., p. 145, and pp. 248–51.

Notes to Chapter 1

1. D. Aubier, 'Christiane Rochefort: *Le Repos du guerrier*', *Esprit*, no. 27, 1–6 jan.–juin 1959, p. 372.
2. Radioscopie de Jacques Chancel avec Christiane Rochefort.
3. 'L'Écriture c'est la distance', interview with J. Hurtin, *Magazine littéraire*, no. 111, avril 1976, p. 10.
4. Rochefort includes a sample of hostile criticism in her autobiographical *Ma Vie revue et corrigée par l'auteur* (Stock, 1978), pp. 246–7.
5. For a discussion of Geneviève's problematic negotiation of sexuality and social values, see I. de Courtivron, '*Le Repos du guerrier*: New Perspectives on Rochefort's Warrior', *Esprit créateur* 19, no. 2, 1979, pp. 23–35.
6. Like *Le Repos du guerrier* the film is set against a background of political despair, although Geneviève and Renaud, unlike Juliette and Michel, fail to find an answer in sexuality: 'Avant toute la "génération perdue" de l'après-guerre, la Juliette de *Et Dieu créa la femme* est consciente de l'effondrement

secret de la vieille société. L'avenir se déroule sur une toile de fond de guerre froide et d'épouvante atomique. Alors, comme d'autres filles de son âge, Juliette se raccroche, désemparée, à la folle sensualité de la vie qui brûle, de la jeunesse éperdue qui l'embrase'. G. Guilleminault, *Le Roman vrai de la IIIe et IVe république*, deuxième partie 1949–58 (Robert Laffont, 1991), p. 1101.

7. Interview by M. Hirsch, M. J. Green, & L. A. Higgins, *Esprit créateur*, vol. 19 no. 2, 1979, pp. 111–12.
8. Ibid., p. 112.
9. Interview with J.-C. Perrier, 'Avez-vous été scandalisé par *Le Repos du guerrier*?', *Quotidien de Paris*, no. 1571, 11 déc. 1984, p. 19.
10. Hirsch, Green and Higgins, art. cit, pp. 112–13.
11. *Histoire d'O* (Société Nouvelle des Éditions Jean-Jacques Pauvert, 1954). All references are to the 1989 Livre de Poche edition. In the summer of 1994, Dominique Aury, then 87 years old, admitted to being the author behind the pseudonym. See Régine Deforges, *O m'a dit*, (Pauvert, 1995).
12. J. Benjamin, *The Bonds of Love: Psychoanalysis, Feminism, and the Problem of Domination* (London: Virago Press, 1990; first published by Pantheon Books, New York, 1988). Some of the material in this chapter has already been published in a more comprehensive form in my article '"A la guerre comme à la guerre": a reappraisal of Christiane Rochefort's *Le Repos du guerrier*', *Forum for Modern Language Studies*, vol. 31 no. 3, 1995, pp. 233–45.
13. Benjamin, op. cit., p. 53.
14. Ibid., p. 62.
15. Ibid., p. 58.
16. Ibid., p. 79.
17. Ibid., p. 72.
18. In a Radioscopie interview of 1976 (see above, note 2), Rochefort, commenting on her essay on children's rights, *Les Enfants d'abord* (1976), pointed out that her interest in the oppression of children went right back to *Le Repos du guerrier*, citing Geneviève as an example of a child still oppressed by her mother.
19. De Courtivron identifies this incident as a key point in the text. For her, Geneviève's capitulation is a positive acceptance of sexual desire, 'une libération à la jouissance'; not passivity but 'ouverture' and 'diffusion' (art. cit., pp. 27–35).
20. Benjamin, op. cit., pp. 53–4.
21. Hurtin, art. cit., p. 9.
22. Paolo Fabbri, *Monteverdi*, translated by Tim Carter (Cambridge: Cambridge UP: 1994), pp. 65–6.
23. Cocteau's play includes a police superintendent, a clerk of court, and an interrogation scene, whilst the film version comes complete with hit and run, safe house, anonymous letter, coded messages, trial and police inspector.
24. D. Aubier, art. cit., p. 374; A. Quereuil, 'Le Roman féminin aujourd'hui et l'amour', *Revue Général Belge*, 96 no. 4, avril 1960, p. 106.
25. J. McMahon, 'What Rest for the Weary', *Yale French Studies*, no. 27, 1961, p. 131.
26. F. Nietzsche, *Thus Spoke Zarathustra* (Harmondsworth: Penguin Classics, 1982), p. 91. The quotation comes from the section 'Of Old and Young Women'.

27. Anton Chekhov, *Plays*, translated and with an introduction by E. Fen (Harmondsworth: Penguin Books, 1972), p. 245. First published 1897.
28. Geneviève's guilty recognition that she has metaphorically killed Renaud is taken up in an image which can again be tied to *Histoire d'O*: 'Vais-je me changer en statue de sel?' (9). When O's lover leaves her, she equates desertion with guilt: 'Elle se sentait [. . .] comme les statues de sel de Gomorrhe. Car elle était coupable. Ceux qui aiment Dieu, et que Dieu délaisse dans la nuit obscure sont coupables puisqu'ils sont délaissés' (op. cit., p. 163).
29. Aubier, art. cit., p. 372.

Notes to Chapter 2

1. See Philip Thody's edition for a general introduction to the work, aimed at the British A-level market: *Les Petits Enfants du siècle* (Harrap Modern World Literature Series, 1982), pp. vii–xxv. For articles which highlight the text as a useful classroom tool, see M. P. Schmitt and A. Viala, '*Les Petits Enfants du siècle* de Christiane Rochefort. Compte rendu d'un exercice de lecture active en Première', *Le Français aujourd'hui*, no. 40, déc. 1977, pp. 31–42; C. Thiré, '*Les Petits Enfants du siècle*, ou la thématique du quotidien', *French Review*, vol. 67, no. 4, 1994, pp. 580–90; V. Kibedi, 'Christiane Rochefort, *Les Petits Enfants du siècle*: quelques suggestions pour une lecture en classe', *Rapports*, 54, 1984, pp. 157–9.
2. Jean Hurtin, 'Christiane Rochefort: l'écriture c'est la distance', p. 10; Rochefort, *Ma Vie*, pp. 256–64.
3. *Ma Vie*, p. 260.
4. H. Winchester, *Contemporary France* (Harlow, Essex: Longman Scientific & Technical, 1993), p. 44. (The net figure of 6.6 million comprises 14 million births, 9 million deaths, and 1.6 million immigrants.)
5. Ibid., p. 166.
6. Ibid., pp. 187–8.
7. *Ma Vie*, p.176.
8. Winchester, pp. 39–40. During the nineteenth century, France's population grew from 28 million to 40 million, an increase of approximately 43%, compared with Germany, whose population rose from 22 to 63 million (an increase of 186%), or Britain, with a growth of 16 to 40 million (an increase of 150%), over the same period.
9. Ibid., pp. 47–8. The 1995 'allocations familiales' monthly benefit figures, which are not income-related, are as follows: for a family with 2 children, 665F (approximately £79); for three children, 1,578F (£188); four children, 2,370F (£282); five children, 3,222F (£383); six children, 4,074F (£484); for each subsequent child, 852F (£101). The Rouvier family, with 11 children, could have expected a monthly sum of approximately £989. Figures are taken from Dominique and Michèle Frémy (ed.), *Quid 1996* (Robert Laffont, 1995), p. 1549.
10. Hurtin, art. cit., pp. 10–11.
11. *Ma Vie*, pp. 10–12.
12. Malcolm Offord, *Varieties of Contemporary French* (London & Basingstoke: Macmillan, 1990), p. 121.

13. Ibid., pp. 110–11.
14. Thody, op. cit., p. xix.
15. *Rouge*, 23 juillet 1977.
16. Kibedi, art. cit., p. 157.
17. Thody, op. cit., p. xiv.
18. Rochefort, *C'est bizarre l'écriture* (1970), p. 34.
19. J. Rothenberg, '*Les Petits Enfants du siècle*, Rochefort's Angry Comedy', *Modern Languages*, vol. 69 no. 4, Dec. 1988, p. 249.
20. M. M. Bakhtin, *The Dialogic Imagination: Four Essays By M. M. Bakhtin*, edited by Michael Holquist, translated by Caryl Emerson and Michael Holquist (Austin: University of Texas Press, 1981), p. 304.
21. Ibid., pp. 305–6.
22. C. Arsène, 'The Privilege of Consciousness' [interview with Rochefort], in *Homosexualities in French Literature*, ed. G. Stamboulian and E. Marks (Ithaca and London: Cornell UP, 1979), p. 103.
23. Rochefort points out that the Lefranc family was not intended to represent an ideal, specifically because of Ethel's attitude to sexuality: 'I presented in the communist family a kind of reformist position; it was a beginning. They were not sexist, for example—the boys and girls shared the housework. But even though they were of good will and not intolerant, I wouldn't recommend this type of family. The little girl was very puritanically raised, so she is rigid. They are pretty heavy on children, this communist family.' M. Hirsch, M. J. Green, and L. A. Higgins, 'An Interview with Christiane Rochefort', p. 119.
24. Thody, op. cit., pp. xxii–xxiii.
25. *Ma Vie*, p. 260, and p. 119.
26. Thody, op. cit., p. xxii.
27. Flaubert, *Madame Bovary* (Garnier-Flammarion, 1979), p. 189.
28. Ibid., pp. 96–7.
29. Ibid., p. 96.
30. Ibid., p. 72.
31. Rothenberg, art. cit., p. 251.
32. Rothenberg notes that 'the capital letters are the only clear indication of irony in these passages', but fails to clarify whose irony: Josyane's or Rochefort's (art. cit., p. 252).
33. *Ma Vie*, p. 277.
34. *Ma Vie*, p. 277; Hirsch, Green and Higgins, art. cit., p. 112.
35. *Madame Bovary*, p. 79.

Notes to Chapter 3

1. For a discussion of the links between the song and Rochefort's text, see C. Owen, 'Christiane Rochefort's *Les Stances à Sophie*: From Prescription to Script', *Romance Studies*, Winter 1991, vol. 19, pp. 91–103.
2. Crochet: 'Est-ce que le livre *Les Stances à Sophie* est jusqu'à une certaine mesure autobiographique?' Rochefort: 'Oui, c'est le seul. J'ai été mariée quatre ans et c'était vraiment une erreur du même type que celle de Céline'. M. Crochet, 'Entretien avec Christiane Rochefort', p. 432.
3. Rochefort, *Cendres et or* (Editions de Paris: 1956). All references will be indicated in the text by the letters 'CO'.

4. M. Hirsch, M. Green and L. Higgins, 'Interview with Christiane Rochefort', p. 109.
5. C. Arsène, 'The Privilege of Consciousness', p. 107.
6. M. Cardinal and A. Leclerc, *Autrement dit* (Livre de poche, 1988), p. 156. First published by Grasset, 1977.
7. Crochet, art. cit., p. 429.
8. For a fuller analysis of consumerism in *Les Stances*, see L. Penrod, 'Consuming Women Consumed: Images of Consumer Society in Simone de Beauvoir's *Les Belles Images* and Christiane Rochefort's *Les Stances à Sophie*', *Simone de Beauvoir Studies*, vol. 4, 1987, pp. 159–75.
9. Rochefort expressed a similar distrust of marriage shortly after the publication of *Les Stances*: 'Entre honnêtes gens, il n'y a pas de contrat'; 'on appelle provisoirement "amour" le besoin d'être rassuré', J. Demornex (interview), *Elle*, no. 1320, 1964, p. 33.
10. For a discussion of Godard's film in relation to *Les Petits Enfants du siècle*, see M. Hirsch, M. Green, and L. Higgins, 'Rochefort and Godard: 2 or 3 Things about Prostitution', *French Review*, vol. 52, 1979, pp. 440–8.
11. Engels, *The Origins of the Family* (London: Penguin Classics, 1986), p. 102. First published 1884. Hirsch, Green and Higgins (see previous note) explore the relationship between Engels and *Les Petits Enfants du siècle*.
12. A. Leclerc, *Parole de femme* (Grasset, 1974).
13. H. Marcuse, *One-Dimensional Man* (London: Routledge and Kegan Paul, 1964) p. 73.
14. H. Pedneault, interview with Rochefort, *La Vie en rose*, avril 1985, p. 24.
15. Rochefort stresses, and values, the irrational, or force of passion, to a much greater extent than Plato. In the *Phaedrus* image of the soul as a winged chariot, reason—the charioteer—remains in control, and seeks to curb the horse representing appetite or desire (just as reason subdues desire in the tripartite soul of *The Republic*).
16. In his study of *Quand tu vas chez les femmes*, Barbro Nilsson suggests that Céline's concept of love is similar to that of Renaud in *Le Repos du guerrier*—an idealist concept ('amour absolu') which stands in opposition to the 'amour néo-bourgeois' represented by both Geneviève and Philippe. See *Le Mot chien n'aboie pas* (Stockholm: Almqvist & Wiksell, 1990), pp. 14–62.
17. J. Hurtin, 'L'Écriture c'est la distance', p. 11.
18. G. Griffin, *Heavenly Love? Lesbian Images in Twentieth-century Women's Writing* (Manchester and New York: Manchester UP, 1993), pp. 41 and 125.
19. Arsène, op. cit., p. 105. Significantly, although Rochefort was herself bisexual, her work has recently been categorized as 'lesbian' writing. See Christopher Robinson's *Scandal in the Ink* (New York: Cassell, 1995). See the Conclusion (below) for another approach to Rochefort's horror of categories and 'labels'.
20. Arsène, op. cit., p. 106; Rochefort goes on to suggest that Céline's attitude to men will be radically altered as a result of her experience: 'I would say that now Céline would have a stronger tendency to love women than before. She will not exactly become a lesbian, but will have a much lower threshold of tolerance for men than before. [. . .] It's exactly what happened to me. [. . .] I became more and more intolerant, I put up with less and less from men. That's Céline afterward. That is, she will not be intolerant towards women who are not her oppressors, and she will be intolerant towards men.'

21. F. Martel, *Le Rose et le noir* (Seuil: 1996), p. 47.
22. Arsène, op. cit., p. 104.
23. Crochet, art. cit., p. 433.
24. Arsène, op. cit., p. 104.
25. Ibid., pp. 108–9.
26. Ibid.
27. Hirsch, Green and Higgins, art. cit., p. 109.
28. This conclusion is also to be found in *Cendres et or*, as Juliette expresses her intention to recommence her life alone in her parting letter to Etienne: 'Je sais maintenant que la solution honnête, point différente pour une femme et pour un homme, est d'assurer sa voie par ses propres moyens, et de demander à un autre que l'échange des bons sentiments, et non "l'échange des bons procédés". Je vais donc partir. Je vais vivre seule et travailler' (182).
29. Crochet, art. cit., p. 430.
30. Arsène, op. cit., p. 102.

Notes to Chapter 4

1. A (slightly altered) version of this text was subsequently published in Canada under the title *Journal de printemps: récit d'un livre* (Montréal: Éditions l'Étincelle, 1977). References to the Grasset edition will be prefaced in my text by the letters 'CB'.
2. See F. Martel, *Le Rose et le noir,* pp. 72–3. Martel's comprehensive account of homosexuality in France from the late 1950s to the present day is an invaluable guide. For an analysis of changing literary representations of homosexuality in French literature, see Christopher Robinson's *Scandal in the Ink.*
3. Rochefort states that her narrator had no name in the first, 1964, version of *Printemps* (CB, 31). Only when she began to rewrite the text towards the end of November 1968, did the name come to mind: 'Je raccommodais donc, rapidement [. . .] et, tiens, Christophe a attrapé un nom chemin faisant sans y penser comme par distraction' (CB, 61). In memory of the Stonewall riots, the gay Pride celebrations now take place annually on the last weekend of June. Starting out in Paris on 25 June 1977 as a demonstration attended by some 400 gay men, the French Pride celebrations (held on June 22) are this year, 1996, expected to attract some 100,000 participants. (*L'Evénement du jeudi,* no. 607, 20–26 juin 1996, pp. 22–31).
4. It should be noted that 'marcher à la voile et à la vapeur' is a slang expression meaning 'bisexual', 'AC/DC'.
5. The term 'pédé', originally a derogatory term, was taken up in a spirit of subversion by gay men in the early militant years of the 1970s. By the end of the decade the term 'gay' was widely used. See *Le Rose et le noir*, p. 70 and p. 122. In Dominique Fernandez's *La Gloire du paria* (Grasset, 1987), Marc, representing a young generation of homosexual men for whom the term 'gay' signals an end to social ostracism, criticizes his older partner Bernard's use of the word 'pédé': 'Bernard, tu m'avais promis que tu n'emploierais

plus jamais ce mot entre nous, même pour rire. Surtout pour rire, se reprit-il' (81). Bernard, suffering from AIDs and seeking self-definition as transgressor and outlaw, suggests that for many people AIDs provides the perfect opportunity to reveal their true feelings, previously masked: 'Et tu crois que tous les connards du quartier ne vont pas sauter sur l'occasion de nous jeter à la figure une insulte qui leur démange le fond de la gorge depuis vingt ans?' (pp. 81–2). For a discussion of Fernandez's text, see Robinson's *Scandal in the Ink,* especially p. 58, pp. 118–19, pp. 122–26, pp. 128–30, pp. 132–4.

6. Arsène, 'The Privilege of Consciousness', p. 105.
7. H. Marcuse, *Eros and Civilisation* (London: Ark Paperbacks, 1987), especially Chapter 10, 'The Transformation of Sexuality into Eros'. First published in England, 1956.
8. T. Roszak, *The Making of a Counter Culture* (London: Faber and Faber, 1970), p. 15. For a full discussion, see Chapter 1, 'Technocracy's Children', and Chapter III, 'The Dialectics of Liberation: Herbert Marcuse and Norman Brown'.
9. Ibid., p. 14.
10. F. Martel, *Le Rose et le noir,* p. 165.
11. Rochefort remarked that she received praise for her treatment of Thomas's and Christophe's sexual relationship: 'As for myself, I see no relationship between a specific physiology and what I write. Except a relationship of knowledge. I know the woman's body better than the man's. But the imagination does everything. The proof is that in *Printemps au parking* I described two men making love. Nobody has criticized it from the point of view of what they do. On the contrary, everyone said, "How do you know about that?" I was quite pleased, I must say. I didn't make any gross errors. How do you know about that? Imagination, what else.' See Arsène, op. cit., pp. 109–110.
12. Robinson, *Scandal in the Ink,* p. 246.
13. Pierre Louys, *Les Chansons de Bilitis* (Éditions Albin Michel, 1894), p. 81. Louys's text is something of a 'spoof'. The author claims that one M. G. Heim discovered the tomb of Bilitis, the walls of which were engraved with the songs which comprise the text. Real names and places are alluded to, for example Part II, 'Elégies à Mytilène' (Mytilène was the real chief city of Lesbos), centres on Bilitis's lesbian relationship with Mnasidika, a real figure whose name can be found in the works of Sappho, but there is no historical record of Bilitis's existence. I am grateful to Dr Clemence Schultze of the Department of Classics at Durham University for her help in this matter.
14. The link between left-wing revolutionary politics and gay rights is by no means self-evident. As Martel points out, political groups in 1968 were often reluctant to embrace the cause of homosexual rights: 'Les mouvements gauchistes reposaient sur des théories politiques générales, à visée universelles. L'intrusion de situations irréductiblement particulières (les femmes, les jeunes, les homosexuels. . .) ne pouvait que les déstabiliser.' *Le Rose et le noir,* p. 38. For a full discussion of political groups and the gay rights movements, see Chapter 1, ' "Je m'appelle Guy Hocquenghem" ', and Chapter 5, 'L'explosion militante'.

Notes to Chapter 5

1. Rochefort's foreword to the 1983 Livre de Poche edition, 'Lettre d'introduction pour un petit canard', p. 9. (All references are to this edition.)
2. For Rochefort's comments on the rapid completion of her text, see Hurtin, 'L'Écriture, c'est la distance', p. 11.
3. See L. Joffrin, *Mai 68* (Seuil, 1988), p. 149, and M. Winock, *Chronique des années soixante* (Seuil, 1987), p. 123.
4. M. Crochet, 'La Création lexicale dans *Une Rose pour Morrison* de Christiane Rochefort', *Modern Philology*, May 1984, pp. 379–94.
5. J. Lacouture, *De Gaulle* (Seuil, 1969), p. 8.
6. See H. Tint, *France Since 1918* (London: B.T. Batsford, 1970), pp. 168–9, and M. Larkin *France Since the Popular Front* (Oxford: Clarendon Press, 1988) p. 283.
7. A. Delale and G. Ragache, *La France de 1968* (Seuil, 1978), p. 132.
8. Charles de Gaulle: *Discours et Messages. Vers le terme*, tome IV, jan. 1962–déc. 1965 (Plon, 1970), p. 401.
9. Duras and Gauthier, *Les Parleuses* (Minuit, 1974), p. 107.
10. Larkin, op. cit., p. 290.
11. Winock, op. cit., p. 89 and p. 91.
12. Hurtin, art. cit., p. 11.
13. Charles de Gaulle: *Discours et messages. Vers le terme*, tome IV, jan. 62–déc. 65, p. 42, and p. 405.
14. See Orwell, 'The Principles of Newspeak', *1984* (London: Penguin Books, 1989), pp. 312–26. Originally published in 1949.
15. Marcuse, *One-Dimensional Man*, p. 32.
16. The closing page of *Une Rose* alludes to the US Defense Secretary McNamara, renamed 'Mac Connery' (219). Significantly, Roszak singles out McNamara as a typical cog in the technocracy: 'In the present generation, it is second- and third-level figures like McNamara who are apt to be technocrats par excellence: the men who stand behind the official facade of leadership and who continue their work despite all superficial changes of government. McNamara's career is almost a paradigm of our new elitist managerialism' (op. cit., p. 12, footnote 5).
17. For an analysis of this phenomenon, see Marcuse's *One-Dimensional Man*, Chapter 4, 'The Closing of the Universe of Discourse'.
18. For two invaluable expositions of the New Left and counter-culture see T. Roszak *The Making of a Counter-Culture*, and P. Marshall, *Demanding the Impossible: A History of Anarchism* (London: HarperCollins, 1992), Chapter 35, 'The New Left and the Counter-Culture'.
19. C. Gray, *The Incomplete Work of the Situationist International* (London: Free Fall Publications, 1974), p. 84.
20. R. Vaneigem, *Traité de savoir-vivre* (Éditions Gallimard, 1967); G. Debord, *La Société du spectacle* (Buchet-Chastel, 1967).
21. Vaneigem, op. cit., pp. 132–3.
22. Gray, op. cit., p. 7.
23. Vaneigem, op. cit., p. 104.
24. See G. Bouchard, 'Les Utopies féministes francophones', *Revue Francophone de Louisiane*, part 4, Spring 1992, and S. Lefanu *In the Chinks of the Machine:*

Feminism and Science Fiction (London: The Women's Press, 1988), especially Chapter 8, 'The Vicissitudes of Love'.

25. Danah Zohar, *The Quantum Self* (London: Flamingo, 1991), p. 14. Zohar draws on developments in quantum mechanics in order to establish a new model of personality and human beings' place in, and relation to, the universe, seeking to supersede previous models which she suggests are based on a traditional mechanistic concept of science.
26. Vaneigem, op. cit., p. 114.
27. Roszak, op. cit., p. 133.
28. Zohar, op. cit., p. 67.
29. Roszak, op. cit., p. 50.
30. Orwell, op. cit., p. 312.
31. Crochet (art. cit.) singles out the caricatural treatment of Belette whom she identifies as a representative of the rising fashion for semiotics in France: 'Les termes théoriques particuliers à la linguistique et à la sémiotique sont développés jusqu'à l'absurde' (394). Belette should also be seen in the broader context of his role as trainee 'verbologue' who is in the pay of the government, and who, as wordsmith, is opposed to the revolutionary movement. Belette's distaste for Sereine's lectures is explicitly linked to his pro-government status: 'il n'avait rien écouté du cours et [qu']il répondrait oui au référendrome' (27). When slapped by Théostat, his political leanings are communicated in a humorous image: 'sa peau était molle, et claquait comme un drapeau nationaliste' (28).
32. Orwell, op. cit., pp. 71, 132, and 280.
33. Vaneigem, op. cit., pp. 258–9.
34. Ibid., p. 263.
35. Zohar, op. cit., p. 80.
36. Ibid., p. 95.
37. Ibid., p. 84.
38. Joffrin, op. cit., p. 314.
39. Ibid., p. 42 and p. 148.
40. Vaneigem, op. cit., p. 230.

Notes to Chapter 6

1. In 1958, Rochefort stated that the hero of her next novel would be named Eremetus (Govan Eremetus is one of the central characters in *Archaos*), and that the creation of the character was inspired by her own painting of a young prince. She adds: 'je l'ai commencé [le roman] il y a huit ans (j'ai divorcé pour avoir le temps d'écrire. Je l'ai refait trois fois. [. . .] Maintenant, il a huit cent pages. C'était si long que, pour changer, j'ai écrit d'une traite *Le Repos du guerrier*.' See E. Mora, 'Christiane Rochefort: le roman, ça doit être une improvisation totale', *Nouvelles littéraires*, no. 1629, 20 nov. 1958, p. 6.
2. M. Hirsch, M. Green, and L. Higgins, 'An interview with Christiane Rochefort', p. 114.
3. Ruth Levitas notes the emergence of a mixed genre in women's utopic writing: 'recent novels frequently contain alternative dystopian futures as well

as eutopian ones, as warnings of what may come about if appropriate action is not taken.' *The Concept of Utopia* (London: Philip Allan, 1990), p. 172.

4. For analyses of characteristic features of contemporary feminist utopias, see Guy Bouchard, 'Les utopies féministes francophones', *Revue francophone de Louisiane*, Part VI, Spring 1992; Sarah Lefanu, 'Dreams of Elsewhere: Feminist Utopias', *In the Chinks of the World Machine* (London: The Women's Press, 1988), pp. 53–70; Joanna Russ, 'Recent Feminist Utopias', in M. S. Barr (ed.) *Future Females: A Critical Anthology* (Ohio: Bowling Green University Popular Press, 1981), pp. 71–85. See also Frances Bartkowski's *Feminist Utopias* (Lincoln and London: University of Nebraska Press, 1989), especially the introduction, pp. 3–19, and Chapter 4, 'The Houses of Women: Christiane Rochefort's *Archaos, ou le jardin étincelant;* and E. M. Broner's *A Weave of Women'*, pp. 111–30.

5. Peter Marshall, *Demanding the Impossible: A History of Anarchism* pp. 556–7.

6. Rochefort, 'J'ai perdu mes utopies', *Magazine littéraire*, no, 139, 1978, p. 42.

7. David Miller, *Anarchism* (London and Melbourne: J. M. Dent & Sons Ltd, 1984), p. 51.

8. The State is regarded as coercive to the extent that it enacts restrictive laws and other measures which are necessary not for the well-being of society but for its own preservation; punitive, because it inflicts excessive penalties on those infringing laws, whether or not these laws are justified in the first place; exploitative, because it uses powers of taxation and economic regulation to transfer resources from producers of wealth to its own coffers or into the hands of privileged economic groups; destructive, because it enlists subjects to fight wars whose only cause is protection or aggrandizement of the State itself. See Miller, op. cit., pp. 6–7.

9. Rochefort, like Thomas More in his *Utopia,* selects her names with care. For a comprehensive analysis of proper names in the text, see I. Constant, *Les Mots étincelants de Christiane Rochefort* (Amsterdam & Atlanta: Rodopi, 1996), pp. 56–69.

10. Hirsch, Green and Higgins, art. cit., p. 115.

11. Miller, op. cit., p. 53.

12. Ibid., p. 86. Miller further notes Marx's own definition of the 'lumpen-proletariat', a class consisting of 'vagabonds, discharged soldiers, discharged jailbirds, escaped galley-slaves, swindlers, mountebanks, *lazzaroni*, pick-pockets, tricksters, gamblers, *maquereaus*, brothel-keepers, porters, *literati*, organ-grinders, rag-pickers, knife-grinders, tinkers, beggars' (p. 86, footnote 26).

13. Ibid., pp. 12–13, 87 and 90.

14. Once a political party is formed it has to engage in electoral politics, and consequently has to adjust its platform to reflect the current views of its working-class supporters, which bear the imprint of the dominant capitalist ideology. There ensues an inevitable shift from a radical to a more moderate position. See Miller, p. 90.

15. Judson Jerome, *Families of Eden: Communes and the New Anarchism* (London: Thames and Hudson, 1974), p. 243.

16. Constant points out that this 'proposition', and the name of the capital city Trémènes, links the text to Rabelais's Abbaye de Thélème, whose order live by the rule 'Fays ce que voudras'. There is, however, a crucial difference:

whereas the society of Archaos seeks to be all-inclusive, the 'Abbaye' permits entry only to an elite body (op. cit., pp. 106–7).

17. Constant restricts herself to the observation that the name Erostase combines the words 'extase' and 'érotisme', op. cit., p. 21.
18. Marshall, op. cit., p. 648.
19. P. Venault, 'Un Roman historique-utopiste-optimiste', *Magazine littéraire* no. 69, oct. 1972, p. 31.
20. Rochefort, 'J'ai perdu mes utopies', p. 42.
21. C. Arsène, 'The Privilege of Consciousness', p. 104.
22. For a comparison of Rochefort's *Archaos* and Fourier's *Le Nouveau Monde amoureux*, see Constant, op. cit, pp. 112–49. Constant points out that although Fourier's utopian vision shares many features with Rochefort's, he drew the line at both incest and child sexuality.
23. Hirsch, Green and Higgins, art. cit., pp. 114–15.
24. Marshall, op. cit., p. 75.
25. Lefanu, op. cit., p. 64, citing Gearthart, *The Wanderground* (Watertown, Mass.: Persephone Press, 1979), p. 4.
26. *The Dispossessed* (New York: HarperCollins, 1974), p. 53. Rochefort expresses her admiration for Le Guin's utopia in 'J'ai perdu mes utopies', p. 43.
27. Hirsch, Green and Higgins, art. cit., p. 113.
28. For a discussion of the 'désir désirant,' see Constant, op. cit., pp. 177–9.
29. Jerome, op. cit., p. 134.
30. Marshall, op. cit., p. 74.
31. See Norman Cohn, *The Pursuit of the Millennium* (London: Mercury Books, 1962), especially chapters VII and VIII, 'An Elite of Moral Supermen (I) and (II)', pp. 149–94; Marshall, op. cit., pp. 87–9.
32. Marshall, op. cit., p. 89; Cohn, op. cit., p. 152.
33. Constant's study of *Archaos*, which was published after this chapter was drafted, confirms the importance of the Bosch triptych. See especially Chapter 1, 'Roman et représentation visuelle. *Archaos* et le triptyque', pp. 13–39. Rochefort refers to Bosch on two occasions in *Ma Vie revue et corrigée par l'auteur*: p. 40 (under the rubric of 'favourite painters'), and p. 104: 'je me souviens du *Jardin des délices* entre deux avions'. The artist is first alluded to in her short story *Le Fauve et le rouge-gorge* (Fayard, 1955) in the form of a mysterious spirit named 'Yeronimous Holbein' (a combination of Bosch and Hans Holbein) who is called up during a séance. For a reading of Bosch's work in relation to the Heresy of the Free Spirit, see Wilhelm Fraenger, *The Millennium of Hieronymous Bosch* (London: Faber & Faber, 1952), trans. E. Wilkins and E. Kaiser. In his *Hieronymous Bosch* (London: Thames and Hudson, 1973), Walter Gibson notes that 'although most scholars object vigorously to Fraenger's thesis, it has received widespread attention in the public press and popular magazines', p. 10. For a recent intertextual appropriation of Bosch's triptych, see Nicholas Salaman's novel, *The Garden of Earthly Delights* (London: HarperCollins, Flamingo, 1994). Salaman, like Rochefort, bases his work on Fraenger's interpretation of the triptych.
34. Gibson, op. cit., p. 92.
35. Fraenger, op. cit., p. 45.
36. Gibson, op. cit., p. 80.

37. Fraenger, op. cit., p.11 and p.14. Cohn indicates that nakedness and promiscuity in the rituals and meetings of the Free Spirit Brethren indicated a restoration of a state of innocence preceding the Fall; a coming of the Third Age or heaven on earth, op.cit., p. 191.
38. Gibson, op. cit., p. 80.
39. Ibid., p. 92.
40. Cohn, op. cit., p. 181.
41. Marshall, op. cit., p. 544.
42. P. Venault, art. cit., p. 31.
43. Rochefort, 'J'ai perdu mes utopies', p. 43.
44. Fraenger, op. cit., p. 83; Cohn, op. cit., p. 180.
45. Links can be established once again with Le Guin's *The Dispossessed*: one of the characters cites the words of Odo, leader of the revolution which founded the utopian Anares: 'The Revolution is in the individual spirit, or it is nowhere. It is for all, or it is nothing. If it is seen as having an end, it will never truly begin' (p. 359).
46. Venault, art. cit., p. 31.
47. Rochefort, 'J'ai perdu mes utopies', p. 43. Rochefort draws a comparison with Le Guin's *The Dispossessed*: 'Anarès est une économie de pénurie, et je suis à mettre dans le même sac: pénurie de biens matériels, abondance de biens relationnels, on ne peut rien faire à moins, l'important c'est de changer l'être.'
48. Miller, op. cit., pp. 175–6.
49. Ibid., p. 159.
50. Marshall, op. cit., p. 149.
51. For a discussion of the function of the 'mistères,' see Constant, op. cit., pp. 127–34.
52. Levitas, op. cit., pp. 7 and 190.
53. Keith Melville, *Communes in the Counter Culture* (New York: William Morrow & Co. Inc., 1972), p. 32.
54. Levitas, op. cit., p. 189.
55. Ibid., pp. 181–2.
56. Rochefort, 'J'ai perdu mes utopies', p. 43.

Notes to Chapter 7

1. P. Venault, 'l'Enfance et l'utopie', *Magazine littéraire* no. 103–4, sept. 1975, p. 77. In spite of the chronology of writing, the novel was in fact published in advance of the essay. References to *Les Enfants d'abord* in my text will be prefaced by the letters 'ED'.
2. G. Rolin, 'Quand les bébés voient rouge. . .', *Le Monde*, 13 fév. 1976.
3. S. Dijkstra, *French Review*, vol. 50, no. 1, 1976–7, p. 203.
4. Venault, art. cit., p. 78.
5. Ibid.
6. Ivan Illich, *Deschooling Society* (Harmondsworth: Penguin Books, 1973), p. 74. (The World Wide Web would, today, meet many of Illich's criteria.)
7. David Cooper, *The Death of the Family* (London: The Penguin Press, 1971), p. 76.

8. In 1958 Mao Zedong criticized Stalin and his party for allowing the Soviet Union to stagnate under an excessively centralized command structure which effectively precluded political activity, and criticized also the fact that institutions brought under communist control were subject to a process of reification, accepted as having permanent and universal validity. Revolution, according to Mao Zedong, must be continuous.

9. For a revealing first-hand account of life in a French secondary school in the early 1970s, see Nelcya Delanoë's *La Faute à Voltaire* (Seuil, 1972). Delanoë cites a text distributed amongst the staff of several lycées by like-minded teachers seeking change in the system. The views expressed here, as elsewhere in Delanoë's account, are closely aligned with Rochefort's: 'Notre bonne conscience de profs repose sur un sacré mensonge: "ils" auraient besoin de notre savoir pour vivre. Mais on leur apprend seulement, en réalité, à tenir leur place dans une hiérarchie, on leur donne seulement les raisons de se résigner à ne pas vivre' (*La Faute*, p. 32).

10. H. D. Lewis, *The French Education System* (London: Croom Helm, 1985), p. 35.

11. W. D. Halls, *Education, Culture and Politics in Modern France* (Oxford: Pergamon Press, 1976), p. 91.

12. Ibid. Delanoë gives a highly critical account of the 'conseils de classe' during which decisions are made about the academic future of each pupil. See *La Faute à Voltaire*, Chapter XI, 'Retour de vacances'.

13. J. E. Flower, ed., *France Today* (London: Hodder & Stoughton, 1993), p. 159.

14. Halls, op. cit., p. 92.

15. Lewis, op. cit., p. 46.

16. Ibid., p. 64.

17. Ibid., p. 83.

18. Cooper, op. cit., pp. 17–18.

19. Ibid., p. 131.

20. Radioscopie de Jacques Chancel avec Christiane Rochefort, 1976.

21. Dijkstra, art. cit., p. 203; B. Wright, 'Down with School', *TLS* no. 3838, 3 Oct. 1975, p. 1152.

22. Dijkstra, art. cit. p.203.

Notes to Chapter 8

1. H. Pedneault, interview with Rochefort, *La Vie en rose*, avril 1985, no. 25, p. 26.

2. Annick Foucault, *Françoise Maîtresse* (Éditions Gallimard; série Digraphe 1994), p. 42.

3. G. Deleuze, *Présentation de Sacher Masoch* (Éditions de Minuit, 1967). Krafft-Ebing: 'I feel justified in calling this sexual anomaly "Masochism", because the author *Sacher Masoch* frequently made this perversion, which up to his time was quite unknown to the scientific world as such, the substratum of his writings', *Psychopathia Sexualis*, trans. F. S. Klaf (London: Mayflower, 1967), p. 87. First published in 1886.

4. Deleuze, op. cit., p. 6.

5. Ibid.

6. Bertrand refers to Pétra as the 'Ange Exterminateur', an allusion to Buñuel's (typically anti-bourgeois) film of the same name, premièred in 1962. Bertrand also identifies himself as a enthusiast of the music of Alban Berg ('moi qui me repais d'Alban Berg', p. 74), a composer who is perhaps best known for his opera *Wozzeck* (1925), but who also composed a violin concerto dedicated 'to the memory of an angel' (composed in 1935 and first performed in 1936). The 'angel' in question was Manon Gropius, daughter of Mahler's widow, Alma Mahler, who married Walter Gropius, an architect. . . (a profession which comes in for considerable criticism in *Quand tu vas*). Berg, born in 1885, died shortly after composing his concerto.
7. Deleuze, op. cit., p. 69.
8. Freud, '"A Child is Being Beaten": A Contribution to the Study of Sexual Perversions' (London: Pelican Freud Library, 1979), vol. 10, 'On Psychopathology', p. 171. (Standard Edition, London, Hogarth Press, 1955, vol. 17.)
9. Ibid., p. 186.
10. Deleuze, op. cit., p. 66.
11. Ibid., p. 86.
12. Ibid., p. 89.
13. Ibid.
14. Ibid.
15. Ibid., p. 100.
16. Ibid., p. 97.
17. Ibid., p. 20.
18. I. Girard, interview with Annick Foucault, *L'Evénement du jeudi*, 19–25 mai 1994, pp. 110–11.
19. Deleuze, op. cit., pp. 29–33.
20. F. Nietzsche, *Thus Spoke Zarathustra*, p. 93. The title of *Quand tu vas*, like that of *Le Repos du guerrier*, comes from the section 'Of Old and Young Women'.
21. Foucault suggests that giving birth is one of the masochist's key phantasies: 'la douleur qui redescend, générant plaisir et bien-être, ressemble à la caresse après un coup de fouet! [. . .] l'homme maso rêve d'être enceint' (op. cit., p. 31).
22. Deleuze, op. cit., p. 16.
23. Foucault describes the Minitel (a terminal linking phone-users to a database) as a 'lieu des initiés', op. cit., p. 159. F. Martel points out that Minitel users could, as of 1984, access the s-m directory under the server 'Service Médical', *Le Rose et le noir*, p. 204.
24. Deleuze, op. cit., p. 39 and p. 133. A similar point is made by Victor Smirnoff: 'There can be no possible sadistic–masochistic meeting: the sadist only accepts to be the tormentor of an innocent and protesting victim; the masochist can only be the victim of a reluctant executioner *malgré lui*.' 'The Masochistic Contract', *International Journal of Psychoanalysis*, vol. 50, 1969, p. 668.
25. Foucault, op. cit., p. 160.
26. Deleuze, op. cit., p. 21. Deleuze adds: 'le contrat masochiste n'exprime pas seulement la nécessité du consentement de la victime, mais le don de persuasion' (76).
27. For an often fascinating (but at times rather far-fetched) analysis of *Quand tu vas* as an autobiographical text, see Barbro Nilsson's *Le Mot chien n'aboie pas*.

The first part of Nilsson's study focuses on *C'est bizarre l'écriture, Le Repos du guerrier,* and *Les Stances à Sophie,* and seeks to demonstrate that certain recurring words and symbols in Rochefort's texts acquire a specific 'Rochefortian' meaning. In Part 2, which focuses on *Quand tu vas,* Nilsson suggests that various characters and scenes reflect aspects of Rochefort herself and her writing career (for example, Bertrand in the kitchen at the close of the text is interpreted as a symbol of uninspired writing; the militant Gilles-Henri is presented as a caricatural view of Rochefort as seen by some critics). Nilsson does not comment on the 'chausettes' incident.

28. Radiocopie de Jacques Chancel avec Christiane Rochefort. Rochefort repeats the same phrase in an interview with Hurtin, *Magazine littéraire,* no. 111, avril 1976, p. 9.
29. Earlier in the text we learn that Malaure, who had previously gone by the name of Marie-Laure de Rothen, decided to marry Bertrand when she was pregnant with their daughter Simone, at least partly in order that the child not be called de Rothen (41). Nilsson draws attention to the fact that 'Marie-Laure de Rothen' is an anagram of 'horreur de la matinée', and from this, draws a comparison between Malaure and Céline in *Les Stances à Sophie* (Céline having expressed a horror of rising early). Nilsson goes on to compare Bertrand's unflattering description of Simone, who is gay, to the perception many critics had of Céline. See *Le Mot chien n'aboie pas,* pp. 184–8.
30. An interesting comparison can be drawn with Sartre's existential analysis of the masochistic project. According to Sartre, the masochist aims primarily to engage himself wholly in his 'being-as-object'; to deny his transcendence. For Sartre, however, this project can never succeed: the masochist's objectivity necessarily escapes him. Indeed, in attempting to apprehend his own objectivity he often apprehends that of the Other, which in spite of his desire to the contrary, frees his own subjectivity. 'Mais le masochisme est et doit être en lui-même un échec: pour me faire fasciner par mon moi-objet, en effet, il faudrait que je puisse réaliser l'appréhension intuitive de cet objet tel qu'il est *pour l'autre,* ce qui est par principe impossible. Ainsi le moi aliéné, loin que je puisse même commencer à me fasciner sur lui, demeure, par principe, insaisissable. Le masochiste à beau se traîner à genoux, se montrer dans des postures ridicules, se faire utiliser comme un simple instrument inanimé, c'est *pour l'autre* qu'il sera obscène ou simplement passif, pour l'autre qu'il *subira* ces postures; pour lui, il est à jamais condamné à *se les donner.* C'est dans et par sa transcendance qu'il se dispose comme un être à transcender; et plus il tentera de goûter son objectivité, plus il sera submergé par la conscience de sa subjectivité, jusqu'à l'angoisse. En particulier le masochiste qui paye une femme pour qu'elle le fouette, la traite en instrument et, de ce fait, se pose en transcendance par rapport à elle. Ainsi le masochiste finit par traîter l'autre en objet et par le transcender vers sa propre objectivité'. *L'Être et le néant* (Gallimard, 1943), p. 428.
31. Foucault, op. cit., p. 43. Foucault also states: 'Je considère la souffrance réelle dans la relation sadomachiste comme le résultat négatif de cette relation' (p. 38).
32. Pedneault, art. cit., p. 26.
33. Foucault, op. cit., p. 36.

34. *Printemps au parking*, p. 197. Martel refers to both the problems of institu-tionalization with respect to the male gay community, and to an s-m trend which emerged in the mid-1970s. See *Le Rose et le noir*, Chapter 4, 'La Dérive', and pp. 189–90.
35. For further discussion of militancy in *Quand tu vas*, see C. Robinson's *Scandal in the Ink*, pp. 219–21.
36. Foucault, op. cit., p. 64.
37. Deleuze, op. cit., p. 69.
38. The 'plaisanterie divine' alludes to Dante's *Inferno*. Nilsson (*Le Mot chien*, p. 107) suggests that Bertrand may take his name from Bertrand de Born, whom Dante meets in the Ninth Chasm, in which the 'sowers of Scandal and Schism' are to be found. De Born's head is severed from his body. See Canto XXVIII, lines 112–42. The opening phrase of *Quand tu vas*—'Aux deux tiers du chemin de la vie, à peu près'—echoes that of the *Inferno*: 'In the middle of the journey of our life' ('Nel mezzo del cammin di nostra vita'), Canto I, line 1. Bertrand's laughter is also reminiscent of Michel Tournier's analysis of what he calls 'l'humour blanc': 'Mais il y a un comique cosmique: celui qui accompagne l'émergence de l'absolu au milieu du tissu de relativités où nous vivons. [. . .] Le rire blanc dénonce l'aspect transitoire, relatif, d'avance condamné à disparaître de tout l'humain. [. . .] L'homme qui rit blanc vient d'entrevoir l'abîme entre les mailles desserrées des choses. Il sait tout à coup que rien n'a aucune importance. Il est la proie de l'angoisse mais se sent délivré par cela même de toute peur.' *Le Vent Paraclet* (Gallimard, 1977), pp. 198–9.

Notes to Chapter 9

1. Anna Salter, *Treating Child Sex Offenders and Victims* (London: Sage, 1988), p. 25. This chapter is largely based on my article, 'Assuming responsibility: Christiane Rochefort's Exploration of Child Sexual Abuse in *La Porte du fond*', *The Modern Language Review*, vol. 90, no. 2, 1995, pp. 333–44.
2. Judith Herman, *Father–Daughter Incest* (London: Harvard UP, 1981), pp. 36–49.
3. Vladimir Nabokov, *Lolita* (Harmondsworth: Penguin Books, 1980), p. 132.
4. Textual references allow us to reconstruct an age profile: the sexual abuse began when the child was eight (45); we learn that she remained silent about the abuse for fifteen years, thus until she was approximately twenty-three years old: 'et moi, d'avoir ouvert ma bouche après quinze années muettes' (163). An allusion to this first breaking of the silence and to what appears to be the present moment of the narrative act, suggests that the narrator who tells her tale is approximately thirty-five years old: 'moi, voici une bonne douzaine d'ans, à ma première sortie bafouillante' (162).
5. See M. Bernstein, 'Christiane Rochefort. On ne parle pas de ces choses-là', *Libération*, 1er septembre, 1988; R. Bud-Printems, 'Fleurs d'automne, fleurs de nombril', *Le Figaro Magazine*, 10 sept. 1988.
6. Salter, op. cit., p. 53.
7. Herman, op. cit., p. 49.
8. The section entitled 'La Leçon du chat' indicates fear as a possible reason for the mother's failure to act. The narrator records an anecdote dating from a

later period in her life when she allowed an ailing cat to come close to death: 'J'avais la trouille de tous les diables que je voulais même pas reconnaître. J'avais tellement peur qu'il meure que je le laissais crever! Alors le chat dans mes bras ronronnant, tout à coup, je vois ma mère. Peur' (p. 179).

9. *Les Enfants d'abord*, p. 183.
10. Ibid., p. 181.
11. Ibid., p. 35.
12. Jeffrey Masson, *The Assault on Truth* (London: Fontana, 1992). All references are to this edition, trans. by Claude Monod as *Le Réel escamoté* (Aubier-Montaigne, 1984).
13. Freud, *The Aetiology of Hysteria*, in the Standard Edition, 24 vols (London: Hogarth Press, 1953–74), III (1962) trans. J. Strachey, p. 203.
14. The tendency today is to employ the term 'trauma theory', thereby removing any possibility or suggestion that the child might be the 'seducer' as well as the 'seduced'.
15. See also Alice Miller's *Thou Shalt not be Aware* (London: Pluto Press, 1991), and Florence Rush's *The Best Kept Secret* (New York: McGraw-Hill, 1981), especially 'A Freudian Coverup', pp. 80–105. Masson, in fact, argues that Freud privately held faith with his original 'trauma theory', and he cites letters written by Freud to Fliess (12 Dec. 1897, and 22 Dec. 1897) to support his claim. (In 1978 Masson was granted permission by Anna Freud to publish all 284 of Freud's letters to Fliess; only 116 had previously been published). See Janet Malcolm, *In the Freud Archives* (London: Jonathan Cape, 1984), pp. 62–3 (this work is also cited by Rochefort as a source text).
16. As in *Les Petits Enfants du siècle*, the term 'papa' is employed only in contexts in which it takes on an ironic function: 'J'emploie aujourd'hui l'attendrissant vocable mais à l'époque je ne pouvais l'émettre, ça m'aurait écorché la gueule. Toute mon enfance je ne désignai le personnage que par "il" et "lui"' (p. 122).
17. Freud, *The Complete Letters of Sigmund Freud to Wilhelm Fliess*, trans. and ed. by J. M. Masson (London & Cambridge, MA: Belknap Press, Harvard UP, 1985), p. 264.
18. Freud, Standard Edition XVI (1963), p. 370.
19. Rochefort alludes in this section to another incident involving Jeffrey Masson: 'Ça me rappelle l'analyste Sam Ritvo, citant les paroles d'un de ses patients: "Auschwitz a fait de moi un homme"' (91). Janet Malcolm records Masson's disbelief in the face of Ritvo's approval of his patient's remark: 'So I said, "What do you do with something like Auschwitz? Surely you're not going to tell me that the reality of Auschwitz doesn't matter—that all that matters is how people experience it?"' (*In the Freud Archives*, pp. 54–5).
20. C. Waldby suggests that this is indeed the case: 'The reinterpretation of Oedipal and incestuous dynamics has been largely ignored by the orthodox psychiatric community. However, psychiatry has now begun to revise some of its notions concerning incest, most particularly the notion that it is a rare phenomenon. The overall effect of these developments on the literature has been a new focus on the medical presentation of incest to promote its recognition by psychiatrists and staff. *Child Sexual Abuse: Feminist Perspectives*, ed. E. Driver and A. Droisen, (London: Macmillan, 1989), p. 92.
21. Masson, op. cit., p. 133.

22. Herman, op. cit., p. 11.
23. Under the old Penal Code, the father in *La Porte*, if found guilty under section 331 ('attentats à la pudeur'), would face 5–10 years' imprisonment and a fine of between 12,000F and 120,000F. Under the new Code, brought in in March 1994, child sexual abuse comes under Art. 222–30 'agressions sexuelles' (defined as 'toute agression sexuelle commise avec violence, contrainte, menace ou surprise'). An act committed, as in this case, by a father against a minor under the age of 15 years would incur 10 years' imprisonment and a fine of 1,000,000F.
24. *Les Enfants d'abord*, p. 94.
25. Herman, whilst not rejecting Freudian theory wholesale, adopts a similar line in this context: 'Scrupulously honest and courageous in other respects, Freud falsified his incest cases. In *The Aetiology of Hysteria*, Freud implausibly identified governesses, nurses, maids and children of both sexes as the offenders. In *Studies on Hysteria*, he managed to name an uncle as the seducer in two cases. Many years later, Freud acknowledged that the "uncles" who had molested Rosalia and Katharina were in fact their fathers' (op. cit., p. 9).
26. Miller, op. cit., p. 222.
27. Ibid., pp. 223–8.
28. See the chapters entitled 'The Bible and the Talmud: An Infamous Tradition Begins', and 'The Christians', in *The Best Kept Secret*, pp. 16–48.
29. Ibid., p. 21.
30. Herman, op. cit., p. 61.
31. We may be reminded here of Renaud's relationship with Geneviève: he too sought to distinguish love from sex; he too was an oppressive figure, although, as we saw in Chapter 1, the power-play dynamic of that relationship was rather more complex.
32. It is worth noting that the father, too, is linked to *Archaos*: in his efforts to gain the narrator's confidence he too promotes the notion that sin should be disregarded in favour of pleasure (see above), and he too, significantly, treats the young child—or pretends to—as an equal: 'Il me parlait comme à une personne' (49). It emerges from this that those in power may have recourse to dangerous—because subtle—tactics.
33. They must also, of course, disregard the fact that Paul is married. Readers who fall in line with the narrator's point of view are, in fact, implicitly rejecting the legal implications of the relationship. Although the situation differs from that of *Les Petits Enfants* to the extent that the narrator of *La Porte* is older than Josyane (we can calculate that at the time of the relationship with Paul she is approximately 14 years old), she is nonetheless still a minor in the eyes of the law. Although the Penal Code does not deal directly with incest, the Code Civil (article 163) does prohibit marriage between uncle and niece. With respect to the Penal Code, Paul would be in same situation as Guido—i.e. liable under article 331 'attentats à la pudeur' to a penalty of three to five years' imprisonment and/or a fine of 6,000F to 60,000F. Under the new 1994 Penal Code, article 227–25 'atteinte sexuelle', he would incur a penalty of two years' imprisonment and a fine of 200,000F.
34. *Les Enfants d'abord*, p. 88.
35. Ibid., p. 104.

36. The father, ironically, calls in the police when the relationship with Paul is discovered, and the narrator is obliged to undergo a medical examination in order to determine whether or not penetrative sex has taken place (235). Had either the father or the uncle been found guilty of rape, they would have faced a prison sentence of ten to twenty years (section 332). (Under the new code, both would automatically be sentenced to twenty years' imprisonment, article 222–24.)

Notes to Conclusion

1. For a discussion of discourse and ideology, see S. Mills, *Discourse* (London & New York: Routledge, 1997), pp. 29–47.
2. Ibid., pp. 41–2.
3. Ibid., p. 21.
4. A. Ault, 'The Dilemma of Identity: Bi Women's Negotiations', in S. Seidman (ed.), *Queer Theory/Sociology* (Blackwell: Oxford & Cambridge, Mass., 1996), p. 322.
5. S. Epstein, 'A Queer Encounter: Sociology and the Study of Sexuality', in S. Seidman, op. cit., p. 154.
6. Seidman, op. cit., p. 20.
7. Ibid., p. 11.
8. S. Phelan, *Playing with Fire: Queer Politics, Queer Theories* (London & New York: Routledge, 1997), p. 234; J. Dollimore, 'Bisexuality', in A. Medhurst and S. Munt (eds), *Lesbian and Gay Studies* (London & Washington: Routledge, 1997), p. 251.
9. Phelan, op. cit., p. 108.
10. Mills, op. cit., p. 18.

Bibliography

Note on editions: readers should be aware that the Grasset and Livre de Poche editions of Rochefort's novels are not identical. In the majority of cases alterations to the text are minor; in some, for example *Archaos*, they are more substantial. Due to restrictions of space an extended study of these alterations has not been carried out here, although this is clearly an area for future research. I have referred in most cases to the Livre de Poche edition in my text. In the case of *Les Stances à Sophie,* and *Printemps au parking* I have used the Grasset edition for the simple reason that Livre de Poche editions are extremely hard to locate. Rochefort's two essays, *C'est bizarre l'écriture*, and *Les Enfants d'abord* are available only in the Grasset edition.

Details given are for the first edition, and then for the edition used, where this is different. All books are published in Paris unless stated otherwise.

A. Writings of Christiane Rochefort

1. Books and short stories

'Le Démon des pinceaux', *Les Œuvres libres* (A. Fayard, août 1953), pp. 173–224.
'Le Fauve et le rouge-gorge', *Les Œuvres libres* (A. Fayard, février 1955), pp. 121–78.
Cendres et or (Editions de Paris, 1956).
Le Repos du guerrier (Grasset, 1958; Livre de Poche, 1992).
Les Petits Enfants du siècle (Grasset, 1961; Livre de Poche, 1988).
Les Stances à Sophie (Grasset, 1963).
Une Rose pour Morrison (Grasset, 1966; Livre de Poche, 1983).
Printemps au parking (Grasset, 1969).
C'est bizarre l'écriture (Grasset, 1970).
Archaos, ou le jardin étincelant (Grasset, 1972; Livre de Poche, 1984).
Encore heureux qu'on va vers l'été (Grasset, 1975; Livre de Poche, 1986).
Les Enfants d'abord (Grasset, 1976).
Ma Vie revue et corrigée par l'auteur (Stock, 1978).
Quand tu vas chez les femmes (Grasset, 1982; Livre de Poche, 1984).
Le Monde est comme deux chevaux (Grasset, 1984).
La Porte du fond (Grasset, 1988; Livre de Poche, 1990).
Adieu Andromède (Grasset, 1997).
Conversations sans paroles (Grasset, 1997).

2. Translations by Rochefort

Lennon, John, *En flagrant délire,* translated with Rachel Mizrahi (Robert Laffont, 1965). *In His Own Write* (London: Jonathan Cape, 1964).

Kenan, Amos, *A la Gare,* illustrated by Pierre Alechinsky (Milan: G. Upiglio, 1964).

Kenan, Amos, *Le Cheval fini* (Grasset, 1966).

Kenan, Amos, *Holocauste II* (Flammarion, 1976).

Kenan, Amos, *La Route d'Ein Harod* (A. Michel, 1984).

Kenan, Amos, *Les Tireurs de langue* illustrated by Pierre Alechinsky (Turin: Fratelli Pozzo, 1962; Paris: G. le Prat, 1962; Paris: Rivière, 1974).

B. Critical works on Rochefort

1. Books or parts of books

Arsène, C., 'The Privilege of Consciousness' [interview], in *Homosexualities in French Literature,* ed. G. Stamboulian and E. Marks (Ithaca and London: Cornell UP, 1979), pp. 101–13.

Bartkowski, F., 'The Houses of Women: Christiane Rochefort's *Archaos, ou le jardin étincelant* and E. M. Broner's *A Weave of Women',* in *Feminist Utopias* (Lincoln and London: University of Nebraska Press, 1989), pp. 110–30.

Becker, L.F., 'Rebellion, Alternative Life-styles, and Visions of Utopia: Christiane Rochefort, Violette Leduc, Monique Wittig, and Hélène Cixous', in *Twentieth Century Women Novelists* (Boston: Twayne, 1989), pp. 136–49.

Bourdet, D., *Visages d'aujourd'hui* (Librairie Plon, 1960), pp. 34–40.

Chapelon, M., 'Qui a découvert *Le Repos du guerrier?',* in *Lire et Ecrire* (Grasset, 1960), pp. 195–7.

Colville, G., 'Christiane Rochefort' [interview] in *Women Writers Talking,* ed. J. Todd (New York & London: Holmes and Meier, 1983), pp. 209–28.

Constant, I., *Les Mots étincelants de Christiane Rochefort: langages d'utopie* (Amsterdam & Atlanta: Rodopi, 1996).

Cordero, A.D., 'Effects of Urbanisation in the Novels of Christiane Rochefort', in *Faith of a (Woman) Writer,* ed. A. Kessler-Harris and W. McBrien (Westport, Conn: Greenwood, 1988), pp. 83–93.

Giannoli, Paul, *Les Grandes Rencontres* (Presses de la cité, 1973), pp. 11–21.

Herz, M., 'Christiane Rochefort', in *French Women Writers: a Bio-Bibliographical Source Book,* ed. E. Sartori and D. Zimmerman, (New York and London: Greenwood Press, 1991), pp. 369–79.

Holmes, D., 'Eroticism and Femininity in the Novels of Christiane Rochefort', in *France, Image and Identity,* ed. J. Bridgford (Newcastle Polytechnic Publications, 1978).

Holmes, D., 'Realism, Fantasy and Feminist Meaning: the Fiction of Christiane Rochefort', in *Contemporary French Fiction by Women: Feminist Perspectives,* ed. M. Atack and P. Powrie (Manchester: Manchester UP, 1990), pp. 26–40.

Holmes, D., 'Angry Young Women: Sex and Conflict in Bestselling First Novels of the 1950s', in *Violence and Conflict in French Culture,* ed. R. Gunther and J. Windebank (Sheffield: Sheffield Academic Press, 1994).

Holmes, D., 'Feminism and Realism: Christiane Rochefort and Annie Ernaux', in *French Women's Writing 1848–1994* (London; Atlantic Highlands, NJ: Athlone: 1996).

Jardine, A. and Menke, A. (eds), [An Interview with Rochefort], trans. C. Noland, in *Shifting Scenes: Interviews on Women, Writing and Politics in Post-68 France* (New York: Columbia UP, 1991), pp. 174–91.

Kazin, A., 'No Sky for Renaud', in *Contemporaries* (London: Secker and Warburg, 1963), pp. 300–3.

Loffredo, S., *A Portrait of the Sexes: The Masculine and the Feminine in the Novels of Simone de Beauvoir, Marguerite Duras and Christiane Rochefort* (London and Michigan: Ann Arbor, 1979).

Marks, E., & Courtivron, I. de, *New French Feminisms* (Brighton, Sussex: The Harvester Press, 1985), pp. 183–6.

Nilsson, B., *Le Mot chien n'aboie pas* (Stockholm: Almqvist & Wiksell, 1990).

Ophir, A., *'Les Stances à Sophie'*, in *Regards féminins: condition féminine et création littéraire* (Denoël/Gonthier, 1976), pp. 89–151.

Ramburen, J.-L. de, 'Du Happening en chambre', in *Comment travaillent les écrivains* (Flammarion, 1978), pp. 138–42.

Robinson, C., *Scandal in the Ink* (New York: Cassell, 1995).

Ross, K., *Fast Cars, Clean Bodies* (London & Cambridge, Mass., 1996).

Thody, P., *Les Petits Enfants du siècle* [critical edition] (Harrap XXV Modern World Literature Series,1982).

Verthuy, M., 'Christiane Rochefort. De la conscience de classe à la conscience de caste', in *Féminité Subversion Ecriture*, textes réunis par S. Lamy and I. Pagès (Editions du remue-ménage, 1983), pp. 245–57.

2. Articles and reviews

Alter, J., *'Une Rose pour Morrison'*, *French Review*, 40, 1966–7, pp. 585–7.

Arraye, J., 'Lecture suivie et dirigée, Catherine R. *Les Petits Enfants du siècle'*, *L'Ecole des lettres*, 15 sept. 1977, pp. 25–33.

Aubier, D., 'Christiane Rochefort: *Le Repos du guerrier'*, *Esprit*, no. 27, 1–6, jan.–juin, 1959, pp. 372–5.

Barberet, G. T., *'La Porte du fond'*, *Bulletin de la Société des professeurs français en Amérique*, 1988–9, pp. 365–7.

Baüer, G., 'Une championne de musardise et du temps perdu', *Biblio* 39, 9, nov. 1965, pp. 2–4.

Bernstein, M., 'Christiane Rochefort. Les fleurs, les petits oiseaux' [*Le Monde est*], *Libération*, 18 oct. 1984, p. 38.

Bernstein, M., 'Christiane Rochefort. On ne parle pas de ces choses-là' [*La Porte*], *Libération*, 1er sept., 1988.

Bory, J.-L., *'Encore heureux qu'on va vers l'été'*, *Nouvel observateur* no. 557, 12 juillet 1975, p. 56.

Bory, J.-L., 'Des fleurs carnivores' [*Une Rose*], *Nouvel observateur* no. 77, 4–10 mai, 1966, pp. 33–4.

Bory, J.-L., 'Platon au zoo', *Nouvel observateur* no. 238, 3–9 juin 1969, p. 44.

Bouchard, G., 'Les utopies féministes francophones', *Revue francophone de Louisiane*, vol. 6, no. 1, 1992, pp. 39–62.

Bourdet, D., *'Le Repos du guerrier'*, *Revue de Paris*, mars 1959, pp. 134–8.

Brochier, J.-J., 'Capitale de la douleur' [*Quand tu vas*], *Magazine littéraire*, no. 184, mai 1982, p. 7.

Brochier, J.-J., 'La vérité n'est pas un jeu' [*La Porte*], *Magazine littéraire* no. 257, sept. 1988, p. 6.

261

Brunhoff, M.-C. de, 'Un humour rageur' [*Printemps*], *Quinzaine littéraire*, no. 75, 16–30 juin 1969, p. 7.

Bud-printems, R., 'Feuilles d'automne, fleurs de nombril' [*La Porte*], *Le Figaro magazine*, 10 sept 1988.

Caminade, P., '*La Porte du fond*', *Sud*, no. 80–1, 1988, pp. 360–1.

Caminade, P., '*Le Monde est comme deux chevaux*', *Sud*, no. 64–5, 1986, pp. 252–3.

Camproux, Ch., 'La langue et le style des écrivains', *Les Lettres françaises*, 2 avril 1959, p. 5.

Casanova, N., 'Christiane Rochefort: "L'être humain est le plus voyou des créatures de Dieu"', *Quotidien de Paris*, no. 1571, 11 déc. 1984, p. 19.

Chalon, J., 'Les casquettes de Christiane Rochefort', *Figaro littéraire*, no. 1045, 28 avril, 1966, p. 10.

Chalon, J., 'Médicis: Christiane Rochefort' [*La Porte*], *Le Figaro*, 22 nov. 1988.

Chancel, J., 'Radioscopie de Jacques Chantel avec Christiane Rochefort', Radio France, 1976 (60 minute interview).

Charensol, G., '*Le Repos du guerrier*', *Nouvelles littéraires*, 20 fév. 1964, p. 12.

Chraïbi, D., 'Christiane Rochefort: *Le Repos du guerrier*', *Confluent*, no. 29, mars 1959, p. 125.

Clouard, H., '*Printemps au parking*', *Revue des deux mondes*, 1er sept. 1969, pp. 577–9.

Cluny, C.-M., 'Entretien avec C. Rochefort', *Les Lettres françaises*, no. 1284, 21 mai 1969, pp. 3–4.

Cluny, C.-M., 'L'Art du kezkadi' [*Le Monde est*], *Le Quotidien de Paris*, no. 1571, 11 déc., 1984, p. 18.

Colombo, L., '*Archaos*: Christiane Rochefort', *Post-Scriptum*, no. 1, déc. 1972, p. 20.

Combescot, P., 'Pas de repos pour les masos!' [*Quand tu vas*], *Nouvelles littéraires*, no. 2837, 20–26 mai, 1982, p. 41.

Constant, P., 'Quand le pouvoir est sans limites', *Revue des deux mondes*, nov. 1988. pp. 184–7.

Courtivron, I. de, '*Le Repos du guerrier*: New Pespectives on Rochefort's Warrior', *Esprit Créateur*, vol. 19, no. 2, 1979, pp. 23–35.

Crochet, M., 'Entretien avec Christiane Rochefort', *French Review* vol. 54, no. 3, 1980–1, pp. 428–35.

Crochet, M., 'La Création littéraire dans *Une Rose pour Morrison*', *Modern Philology*, 83, no. 4, 1986, pp. 379–94.

D. A., 'Quand Rochefort l'ouvre' [*La Porte*], *Le Combat syndicaliste*, no. 87, fév. 1989.

Delais, J., 'Delais accuse, Rochefort se défend', *Figaro littéraire*, no. 1519, 28 juin 1975, pp. 15–16.

Demornex, J., 'Christiane Rochefort: Féminité? Virilité? Un schèma à liquider d'urgence', *Elle*, no. 1320, pp. 32–3.

Dijkstra, S., '*Encore heureux qu'on va vers l'été*', *French Review*, vol. 50, no. 1, 1976–7, p. 203.

Durand, D., 'Des patrons, minettes!' [*La Porte*], *Le Canard enchaîné*, 31 août, 1988.

Ezine, J.-L., 'Entretien sur *Encore heureux qu'on va vers l'été*,' *Nouvelles littéraires*, no. 2492, 30 juin, 1975, p. 3.

Forrester, V., 'Une savante naïveté' [*Archaos*], *Quinzaine littéraire*, no. 152, 16–30 nov. 1972, p. 9.

Franck, J., 'Christiane Rochefort: *Une Rose pour Morrison*', *Revue Général Belge*, no. 7, juill. 1966, pp. 103–4.

Freustié, J., 'Où est le mal?', *Nouvel observateur*, no. 415, 23 oct. 1972, pp. 64–5.

G. A. de, 'Fémina, Médicis & Cie' [*La Porte*], *Libération*, 22 nov., 1988, p. 33.

Galey, M., 'Le Journal de quand on écrit' [*C'est bizarre*], *L'Express*, no. 996, 10–16 août, 1970, pp. 54–5.

Galey, M., 'Christiane Rochefort: au tour de la famille . . .' [*Encore heureux*], *L'Express*, no. 1249, 16–22 juin 1975, pp. 31–2.

Galey, M., 'Rochefort de désarme pas' [*Le Monde est*], *L'Express*, 23–29 nov. 1984, pp. 172 & 175.

Gazier, 'Christiane Rochefort: ruptures en continuité', *Pages et Livres*, no. 8, oct. 1988, p. 6.

Germain, A., 'Christiane Rochefort: les femmes, c'est comme les nègres', *Nouvelles littéraires*, no. 1928, 13 août 1964, p. 3.

Goury, G.-H., 'La nostalgie du bonheur', *Magazine littéraire*, no. 111, avril 1976, pp. 14–16.

Goury, G.-H., 'Aujourd'hui, *Le Repos du guerrier*', *Magazine littéraire*, no. 111, avril 1976, pp. 16–17.

Greenberg, J., '*La Porte du fond*' *TLS*, no. 4478, 1988, p. 88.

Hartwig, R. '*La Porte du fond*', *French Review*, vol. 64, 1990–1, p. 390.

Helman de Urtubey, S., 'Christiane Rochefort et la jeunesse d'aujourd'hui', *Humanitas*, no. 15, 1968–9, pp. 47–55.

Herz, M., 'Le Groupe et l'amour dans l'œuvre de Rochefort', *Perspectives on Contemporary Literature*, III, no. 2, 1977, pp. 52–7.

Hirsch, M., Green, M. and Higgins, L., 'An Interview with Christiane Rochefort', *Esprit créateur*, vol. 19 no. 2, 1979, pp. 107–20.

Hirsch, M., Green, M. and Higgins, L., 'Rochefort and Godard. 2 or 3 Things about Prostitution', *French Review*, vol. 52, 1979, pp. 440–48.

Hurtin, J., 'Christiane Rochefort: l'écriture c'est la distance' [interview], *Magazine littéraire*, no. 111, avril 1976, pp. 9–11.

Hurtin, J., '*Les Enfants d'abord*', *Magazine littéraire*, no. 111, avril 1976, p. 17.

Hutton, M.-A., 'A la guerre comme à la guerre: A Reappraisal of Christiane Rochefort's *Le Repos du guerrier*', *Forum for Modern Language Studies*, vol. 31, no. 3, 1995, pp. 233–45.

Hutton, M.-A., 'Assuming Responsibility: Christiane Rochefort's Exploration of Child Sexual Abuse in *La Porte du fond*', *The Modern Language Review*, vol. 90, no. 2, 1995, pp. 333–44.

Jardin, C., 'L'Anticonformisme de Christiane Rochefort' [*Encore heureux*], *Figaro littéraire*, no. 1519, 28 juin 1975, [1] (15).

Jardine, A. & Menke, A., 'Exploding the Issue: "French" "Women" "Writers" and "The Canon"?', *Yale French Studies*, no. 75, 1988, pp. 255–7.

Josselin, J., 'Rochefort-sur-père' [*La Porte*], *Nouvel observateur*, no. 1245, 16–22 sept., 1988, p. 57.

Jossin, J., 'Christiane Rochefort et les enfants' [*Les Enfants d'abord*], *L'Express*, no. 1284, 16–22 fév. 1976, p. 34.

Kalda, A., 'Au ciel des tinageurs' [*Une Rose*], *L'Express*, no. 778, 16–22 mai 1966, pp. 131–2.

Kanters, R., 'Rochefort et les baladins du monde occidentale' [*Une Rose*], *Figaro littéraire*, no. 1046, mai 1966, p. 5.

Kanters, R., 'Garçons et filles d'hier et aujourd'hui' [*Printemps*], *Revue de Paris*, juillet-août 1969, p. 122.

Kanters, R., 'Nos grandes Zazies', *Figaro littéraire*, no. 1204, 16 juin, 1969, pp. 19–20.

Kanters, R., '"Il" regarde "je" écrire, disent-ils', *Figaro littéraire*, no. 1261, 16 juill. 1970, pp. 24–5.

Kanters, R., 'Pour les grands enfants du siècle' [*Archaos*], *Figaro littéraire*, no. 1387, 16 déc. 1972, p. 14.

Kanters, R., '*Printemps au parking*', *Revue de Paris*, no. 76, juillet–août, 1969, pp. 121–2.

Kibedi, V., 'Christiane Rochefort, *Les Petits Enfants du siècle*: quelques suggestions pour une lecture en classe', *Rapports* 54, 1984, pp. 157–9.

Kyria, P., 'Quand Christiane Rochefort réinvente *Candide*' [*Une Rose*], *Combat*, no. 6799, 30 avril 1966, p. 7.

Lalou, E., 'Le Petit Christophe de Christiane Rochefort' [*Printemps*], *L'Express*, 2–8 juin, 1969.

Lalou, E., 'L'envers du jeu de massacre' [*Archaos*], *L'Express*, 30 oct –5 nov., 1972, p. 130.

Landes, M.-G., 'Christiane Rochefort: le bonheur n'est pas mon idéal', *Arts*, no. 1009, juin 1965, p. 4.

Lauter, P., 'The Hero of Nothing' [*Le Repos*], *The Nation*, vol. 189, no. 11, Oct. 1959, pp. 216–17.

Le Clec'h, G., 'Entre le réalisme et l'utopie, la liberté' [*Archaos*], *Nouvelles littéraires*, no. 2353, 30 oct.–5 nov. 1972, p. 3.

Lescaut, S., 'Christiane Rochefort entre le beatle et l'hebreu', *Arts et Loisirs*, no. 27, 30 mars 1966, p. 11.

Loriot, N., 'Christiane Rochefort: toujours en guerre' [*Ma Vie revue*], *L'Express*, 16–22 déc., 1978, p. 59.

Mauriac, Cl., 'Christiane Rochefort: une femme et un écrivain parmi d'autres', *Le Figaro*, 22 oct. 1958.

Mauriac, Cl., '*Le Repos du guerrier* par R. Vadim d'après Christiane Rochefort', *Figaro littéraire*, 15 sept 1962, p. 16.

McDermott, H., 'Rochefort's *Ma Vie revue et corrigée par l'auteur*: autobiographie à la dérive', *French Literature Series*, 12, 1985, pp. 188–92.

McLeary, D., '*The Warrior's Rest*', *New York Times Book Review*, 20 Sept. 1959, p. 49.

McMahon, J., 'What Rest for the Weary' [*Le Repos*], *Yale French Studies*, no. 27, 1961, pp. 131–9.

Meillon, J., 'La déprime des petits enfants du siècle' [*Encore heureux*], *Quinzaine littéraire*, no. 216, 1–15 sept. 1975, p. 8.

Melchior-Bonnet, C., 'Sorti des presses' [*Une Rose*], *A la Page*, no. 26, août 1966, p. 1276.

Mora, E., 'Christiane Rochefort: le roman, ça doit être une improvisation totale', *Nouvelles littéraires*, no. 1629, 20 nov. 1958, p. 6.

Nourissier, F., 'Une Robe [*sic*] pour Morrison', *Nouvelles littéraires* no. 2020, 19 mai 1966, p. 2.

Nourissier, F., '*Printemps au parking*', *Nouvelles littéraires*, no. 2174, 22 mai 1969, p. 2.

Nourissier, F., 'Christiane Rochefort: l'art de le dire' [*La Porte*], *Point*, no. 846, 5–11 déc. 1988, p. 80.

Orel, O., '*La Porte du fond*', *Bérénice*, XIII, 1991, pp. 347–49.

Orel, O., '*La Porte du fond*', *Il Cristallo*, XXXV, 1, April 1993, pp. 149–51.

Orenstein, G. F., 'The Feminist Rebirth of the Divine Child: Eroticism and Trans-cendence in Christiane Rochefort's *Encore heureux qu'on va vers l'été*', *Journal of Women's Studies in Literature*, 1, 1979, pp. 61–73.

Ormesson, J. de, 'Zazie chez Candide' [*Archaos*], *Le Point*, no. 2, 2 oct. 1972, p. 107.

Owen, C., 'Christiane Rochefort's *Les Stances à Sophie*: From Prescription to Script', *Romance Studies*, vol. 19, Winter 1991, pp. 91–103.

Pedneault, H., [Interview], *La Vie en rose*, no. 25, avril 1985, pp. 22–7.

Penrod, L., 'Consuming Women Consumed: Images of Consumer Society in Simone de Beauvoir's *Les Belles Images* and Christiane Rochefort's *Les Stances à Sophie*', *Simone de Beauvoir Studies*, vol. 4, 1987, pp. 159–75.

Penrod, L., 'Humour e(s)t sagesse: *Les Stances à Sophie* de Christiane Rochefort', *Women in French Studies*, 1, July 1993, pp. 55–65.

Perrier, J.-C., 'Avez-vous été scandalisé par *Le Repos du guerrier*?', *Le Quotidien de Paris*, no. 1571, 11 déc., 1984.

Piatier, J., 'Black Rose' [*Une Rose*], *Atlas*, XII no. 2, Aug. 1966, pp. 58–60.

Piatier, J., 'Conte rose sur fond noir' [*Printemps*], *Le Monde*, no. 7582, 31 mai 1969, p. I.

Piatier, J., 'Christiane Rochefort aux prises avec les bizarreries de l'écriture' [*C'est bizarre*], *Le Monde*, no. 7910, 20 juin 1970, p. VIII.

Piatier, J., 'Débauche et insuffisance de l'imagination' [*Archaos*], *Le Monde*, no. 8648, 3 nov. 1972, pp. 15–16.

Piatier, J., 'Christiane Rochefort au meilleur de sa forme' [*Ma Vie revue*], *Le Monde*, no. 10566, 19 jan. 1979, p. 13.

Piatier, J., 'Virulente et tendre Rochefort' [*La Porte*], *Le Monde*, no. 13578, 23 sept. 1988, pp. 15 and 19.

Plessy, B., 'Christiane Rochefort: *Encore heureux qu'on va vers l'été*', *Bulletin des lettres*, no. 371, 15 oct. 1975, p. 295.

Poirot-Delpech, B., 'Utopies: *Encore heureux qu'on va vers l'été* de Christiane Rochefort; *L'Espoir Grave* d'Hélène Bleskine', *Le Monde*, no. 9461, 20 juin 1975, p. 13.

Quereuil, A., 'Le roman féminin aujoud'hui et l'amour', *Revue générale belge* 96, 4 avril 1960 pp. 89–107.

Rey, H.-F., 'Christiane Rochefort: *Le Monde est comme deux chevaux*', *Magazine littéraire*, no. 213, déc. 1984, pp. 76–7.

Rochefort, C., 'Au Secours', *Magazine littéraire*, no. 111, avril 1976, pp. 12–13.

Rochefort, C., 'Une Découverte de Christiane Rochefort' [on Valérie Valère, *Le Pavillon des enfants fous*], *Le Monde*, 23 déc. 1978.

Rochefort, C., 'Comment peut-on être *femme de lettres*', enquête d'A. Germain avec Françoise Mallet-Joris, Christiane Rochefort & Marguerite Duras, *Nouvelles littéraires*, 13 août 1964, p. 3.

Rochefort, C., 'Sept romancières jugent le livre de Sagan' [*Aimez-vous Brahms*], *La Nef*, 16, 31, Oct. 1959, pp. 63–7.

Rochefort, C., 'J'ai perdu mes utopies', *Magazine littéraire*, no. 139, juillet 1978, pp. 42–3.

Rochefort, C., 'Cher absolu—les adieux de CR à Henri-François Rey, mort le 22 juillet', *Le Monde*, 7 août, 1987.

Rochefort, C., 'De Belles Paroles', *Pages et Livres*, no. 10 déc. 1988– jan. 1989, p. 6.

Rochefort, C., 'Prophylaxie' [on M. Vivian, *Les Imposteuses*], *Magazine littéraire*, no. 167, déc. 1980.

Rochefort, C., 'Entre le droit et le gauche, c'est la bagarre . . . (Pas de connotations: il ne s'agit que de mes hémisphères', *Ecrire aujourd'hui*, ed. Annie Mignard (Autrement), no. 69, avril 1985.

Rochefort, C., [Postface to C. Himes's *Une Affaire de viol*], trans. by A. Mathieu, (Editions les yeux ouverts, 1963), pp. 169–72.

Rolin, G., 'Quand les bébés voient rouge. . .' [*Les Enfants d'abord*], *Le Monde*, 13 fév. 1976.

Rolin, G., 'Le dernier défi de Christiane Rochefort' [*Quand tu vas*], *Le Monde des livres*, no. 11598, 14 mai 1982, p. 21.

Rothenberg, J., '*Les Petits Enfants du siècle*: Rochefort's Angry Comedy', *Modern Languages*, vol. 69 no. 4, 1988, pp. 249–52.

Rouart, J.-M., 'Ombres et lumières du scandale' [*Le Monde est*], *Le Quotidien de Paris*, no. 1571, 11 déc. 1984, p. 17.

Roudiez, L., 'Christiane Rochefort: *Printemps au parking*', *French Review* vol. 43, no. 5, April 1970, p. 869.

Rouge, 'Quand Christiane Rochefort est mise à l'index', 23 juillet 1977.

Sasu, V., 'Tradition et modernité dans le roman autobiographique' (Christiane Rochefort's *Le Repos du guerrier* and Hélisenne de Crenne's *Les Angoysses douloureuses qui procèdent d'amors*', *Zagadnienia Rodzajow Literackich* XXIII, 1, 1980, pp. 33–43.

Savigneau, J., 'Le "désespoir actif" de Christiane Rochefort' [*Le Monde est*], *Le Monde*, 19 oct. 1984, p. 22.

Savigneau, J., 'Médicis: Christiane Rochefort pour *La Porte du fond*', *Le Monde*, no. 1330, 23 nov. 1988, p. 46.

Schmitt, M.P. and Viala, A., '*Les Petits enfants du siècle* de Rochefort. Compte rendu d'un exercice de lecture active en Première', *Le Français aujourd'hui*, no. 40, déc. 1977, pp. 31–42.

Schwartz, L.M., '*Encore heureux qu'on va vers l'été*', *International Fiction Review*, vol. 3, no. 2, 1976, pp.164–5.

Sherzer, D., 'Christiane Rochefort: *Archaos*', *French Review*, vol. 47, no. 4, 1974, pp. 837–8.

Spens, L. de, '*Printemps au parking*', *Nouvelle revue française*, no. 34, 1969, pp. 465–6.

Thiré, C., '*Les Petits Enfants du siècle*, ou la thématique du quotidien', *French Review*, vol. 67, no. 4, March 1994, pp. 580–90.

V. B., '*Les Enfants d'abord*', *Nouvel observateur*, 17 avril 1976, p. 20.

Venault, P., 'Le chemin de la connaissance, c'est la sexualité' [*Archaos*], *Magazine littéraire*, no. 30, juillet 1969, pp. 44–5.

Venault, P., 'Un Roman historique-utopiste-optimiste' [*Archaos*], *Magazine littéraire*, no. 69 oct. 1972, pp. 30–1.

Venault, P., 'L'Enfance et l'utopie' [*Encore heureux*], *Magazine littéraire*, no. 103–4, sept. 1975, pp. 77–8.

Verthuy, M., 'Christiane Rochefort. De la conscience de classe à la conscience de caste', *Atlantis*, 9, 1, Fall 1983, pp. 59–67.

Villelaur, A., 'Une histoire d'amour', *Lettres françaises*, no. 1286, 4 juin 1969, p. 6.

Villelaur, A., 'Portraits d'écrivains', *Lettres françaises*, no. 1336, 27 mai 1970, p. 10.

Wright, B., 'Down with School' [*Encore heureux*], *TLS*, no. 3838, 3 Oct. 1975, p. 1152.

Wright, B., 'Latterday Lamentations' [*Le Monde est*], *TLS*, no. 4272, 15 Feb. 1985, p. 160.

Wright, B., 'The Grip of the Great Strategist' [*La Porte*], *TLS*, no. 4478 Jan. 27–Feb. 2, 1989, p. 88.

C. Other works consulted

Ager, D., *Sociolinguistics and Contemporary French* (Cambridge & New York: Cambridge UP, 1990).

Annas, P., 'New Worlds, New Words: Androgyny in Feminist Science Fiction', *Science-Fiction Studies*, vol. 5, 1978, pp. 143–56.

Atwood, M., *The Handmaid's Tale* (London: Virago, 1987).

Aury, D. [Pauline Réage], *Histoire d'O* (Livre de Poche, 1989).

Bakhtin, M.M., *The Dialogic Imagination. Four Essays by M. M. Bakhtin*, ed. M. Holquist, trans. C. Emerson and M. Holquist (Austin: University of Texas Press, 1981).

Barr, M. (ed.), *Future Females: A Critical Anthology* (Ohio: Bowling Green University Popular Press, 1981).

Benjamin, J., *The Bonds of Love: Psychoanalysis, Feminism, and the Problem of Domination* (London: Virago Press Ltd 1990).

Blumenthal, R., 'Scholars Seek the Hidden Freud in Newly Emerging Letters', *The New York Times*, 18 August 1981, pp. C1–2.

Blumenthal, R., 'Did Freud's Isolation Lead Him to Reverse Theory on Neurosis?', *The New York Times*, 25 August 1981, pp. C1–2.

Cardinal, M. and Leclerc, A., *Autrement dit* (Livre de Poche, 1988).

Chancer, L., *Sadomasochism in Everday Life* (New Brunswick, New Jersey: Rutgers UP, 1992).

Chekhov, A., *Plays*, introduced and translated by E. Fen (Harmondsworth: Penguin Books, 1972).

Cohn, N., *The Pursuit of the Millenium* (London: Mercury Books, 1962).

Cooper, D., *The Death of the Family* (London: Allen Lane, Penguin Press, 1971).

Dante, *Inferno* (London: J. M. Dent & Sons Ltd., 1954).

Debord, G., *La Société du spectacle* (Buchet-Chastel, 1967).

Deforges, R., '"O m'a dit": entretiens avec Pauline Réage' (Pauvert, 1995).

Delale, A. and Ragache, G., *La France de 1968* (Seuil, 1978).

Delanoë, N., *La Faute à Voltaire* (Seuil, 1972).

Deleuze, G., *Présentation de Sacher Masoch* (Éditions de Minuit, 1967).

Driver, E. and Droisen, A., *Child Sexual Abuse: Feminist Perspectives* (Basingstoke: Macmillan, 1989).

Duchen, C., *Feminism in France* (London, Boston & Henley: Routledge & Kegan Paul, 1986)

Duras, M. and Gauthier, X., *Les Parleuses* (Minuit, 1974).

Dyer, C., 'Still a Victim', *The Guardian*, 12 Jan. 1993, p. 15.

Engels, F., *The Origin of the Family, Private Property and the State* (London: Penguin Classics, 1986).

Eskapa, R., *Bizarre Sex* (London: Grafton, 1989).

Fabbri, P., *Monteverdi*, trans. T. Carter (Cambridge: Cambridge UP, 1994).

Countering the Culture

Fernandez, D., *La Gloire du paria* (Grasset, 1987).

Fiske, J., *Understanding Popular Culture* (London & New York: Routledge, 1989).

Flaubert, G. *Madame Bovary* (Garnier-Flammarion, 1979).

Flower, J. (ed.), *France Today* (London: Hodder & Stoughton, 1993).

Forbes, J. and Kelly, M., *French Cultural Studies: An Introduction* (Oxford: Oxford University Press, 1995).

Foucault, A., *Françoise Maîtresse* (Gallimard, Série Digraphe, 1994).

Fraenger, W., *The Millenium of Hieronymous Bosch: Outlines of a New Interpretation*, trans. E. Wilkins & E. Kaiser (London: Faber & Faber, 1952).

Freud, ' "A Child is Being Beaten": A Contribution to the Study of Sexual Perversion' (London: Pelican Freud Library, 1979), Vol. 10, *On Psychopathology.*

Gaulle, Charles de, *Discours et Messages. Vers le terme*, tome IV, jan. 1962–déc. 1965 (Plon, 1970).

Gelman, D., with Hager, M., 'Finding the Hidden Freud', *Newsweek*, 30 Nov. 1981, pp. 64–73.

Gibson, W. S., *Hieronymous Bosch* (London: Thames & Hudson, 1973).

Girard, I., 'Les vrais secrets d'une fouetteuse' [interview with Annick Foucault], *l'Événement du jeudi*, no. 498, 19–25 mai 1994, pp. 110–11.

Grant, L., 'A Past Imperfect?', *The Guardian*, 24 May, 1993 pp. 10–11.

Gray, C., *The Incomplete Work of the Situationist International* (London: Free Fall Publications, 1974).

Green G. and Green C., *S-M: The Last Taboo* (New York: Ballantine Books, 1974).

Griffin, G., *Heavenly Love? Lesbian Images in Twentieth-century Women's Writing* (Manchester & New York: Manchester UP, 1993).

Guilleminault, G., *Le Roman vrai de la IIIe et IVe république*, 2e partie 1949–58 (Robert Laffont, 1991).

Halls, W. D., *Education, Culture and Politics in Modern France* (Oxford: Pergamon Press, 1976).

Herman, J., *Father–Daughter Incest* (Cambridge, Mass., Harvard UP, 1981).

Huxley, A., *Brave New World* (London: Flamingo, 1994).

Illich, I., *Deschooling Society* (Harmondsworth: Penguin Books, 1973).

Jerome, J., *Families of Eden: Communes and the New Anarchism* (London: Thames & Hudson, 1974).

Joffrin, L., *Mai 68. Histoire des Evénements* (Seuil, 1988).

Kahn, M., *Alienation in Perversions* (London: Karnac, 1989).

Krafft-Ebing, *Psychopathia Sexualis*, trans. F. Klaf (London: Mayflower, 1967).

Lacouture, J., *De Gaulle* (Seuil, 1969).

Larkin, M., *France since the Popular Front: Government and People 1936–1986* (Oxford: Clarendon Press, 1988).

Le Guin, U., *The Dispossessed* (New York: HarperPaperbacks, 1974).

Leclerc, A., *Parole de femme* (Grasset, 1974).

Leclerc, H., *Le Nouveau Code pénal* (introduction et commentaire) (Seuil, 1994).

Lefanu, S., *In the Chinks of the World Machine. Feminism and Science Fiction* (London: The Women's Press, 1988).

Levitas, R., *The Concept of Utopia* (London: Philip Allan, 1990).

Lewis, H. D., *The French Education System* (London & Sydney: Croom Helm, 1985).

Louys, P., *Les Chansons de Bilitis* (Albin Michel, 1894).

268

Bibliography

Malcolm, J., *In the Freud Archives* (London: Jonathan Cape, 1984).

Marcuse, H., *One-Dimensional Man* (London: Routledge & Kegan Paul Ltd., 1964).

Marcuse, H., *Eros and Civilisation* (London: Ark Paperbacks, 1987).

Marshall, P., *Demanding the Impossible: A History of Anarchism* (London: HarperCollins, 1992).

Martel, F., *Le Rose et le noir: les homosexuels en France depuis 1968* (Seuil, 1996).

Masson, J. *The Assault on Truth: Freud and Child Sex Abuse* (London: Fontana, 1992).

Medhurst, A. and Munt, S., *Lesbian and Gay Studies: A Critical Introduction* (London & Washington: Cassell, 1997).

Meller, A., 'On Feminist Utopias', *Women's Studies*, vol. 9, 1982, pp. 241–62.

Melville, K., *Communes in the Counter Culture* (New York: William Morrow & Co. Inc., 1972).

Miller, A., *Banished Knowledge* (London: Virago, 1991).

Miller, A., *Thou Shalt not be Aware. Society's Betrayal of the Child* (London: Pluto Press, 1991).

Miller, D., *Anarchism* (London & Melbourne: J. M. Dent & Sons Ltd., 1984).

Mills, S., *Discourse* (London & New York: Routledge, 1997).

Mitchell, P. and Anderson, S., (ed.) *Child Sexual Abuse: An Introductory Handbook* (Birmingham: PEPAR, 1988).

Mond, S. le, *Bondage and Humiliation* (London: Diamond Star Books, 1968).

More, T., *Utopia* (London: Penguin Classics, 1965).

Nietzsche, F., *Thus Spoke Zarathustra* (Harmondsworth: Penguin Classics, 1982).

Offord, M., *Varieties of Contemporary French* (London & Basingstoke: Macmillan, 1990).

Orwell, G., *1984* (London: Penguin Books, 1989).

Phelan, S. (ed.), *Playing with Fire: Queer Politics, Queer Theories* (London & New York: Routledge, 1997).

Plato, *The Symposium*, trans. W. Hamilton (Harmondsworth: Penguin Books, 1980).

Plato, *The Phaedrus*, trans. with introduction and notes by A. Nehamas & P. Woodruff (Indianapolis: Hackett, 1995).

Rigby, B., *Popular Culture in Modern France* (London: Routledge, 1991).

Roszak, T., *The Making of a Counter Culture* (London: Faber and Faber, 1970).

Salaman, N., *The Garden of Earthly Delights* (London: HarperCollins, Flamingo, 1994).

Salter, A., *Treating Child Sex Offenders and Victims* (London: Sage Publications Ltd, 1988).

Sartre, J.-P., *L'Être et le néant* (Gallimard, 1943).

Schad-Somers, S.P., *Sadomasochism* (New York: Human Sciences Press Inc, 1982).

Seidman, S. (ed.), *Queer Theory/Sociology* (Oxford & Cambridge, Mass.: Blackwell Publishers, 1996).

Smirnoff, V., 'The Masochistic Contract', *International Journal of Psychoanalysis*, vol. 50 1969, pp. 665–71.

Strinati, D., *An Introduction to Theories of Popular Culture* (London & New York: Routledge, 1995).

Tint, H., *France since 1968* (London: B. T. Batsford, 1970).

Tournier, M., *Le Vent Paraclet* (Gallimard, 1977).

Vaneigem, R., *Traité de savoir-vivre à l'usage des jeunes générations* (Gallimard, 1967).

Winchester, H., *Contemporary France* (Harlow, Essex: Longman Scientific and Technical, 1993).

Winock, M., *Chronique des années soixante* (Seuil, 1987).

Young, I., *The Stonewall Experiment* (London: Cassell, 1995).

Zohar, D., *The Quantum Self* (London: Flamingo, 1991).

INDEX

271